CONFRONTING THE "GOOD DEATH"

Confronting the "Good Death"

NAZI EUTHANASIA ON TRIAL, 1945–1953   Michael S. Bryant

University Press of Colorado

© 2005 by the University Press of Colorado

Published by the University Press of Colorado
5589 Arapahoe Avenue, Suite 206C
Boulder, Colorado 80303

 The University Press of Colorado is a proud member of
the Association of American University Presses.

The University Press of Colorado is a cooperative publishing enterprise supported, in part, by
Adams State College, Colorado State University, Fort Lewis College, Mesa State College,
Metropolitan State College of Denver, University of Colorado, University of Northern
Colorado, and Western State College of Colorado.

Library of Congress Cataloging-in-Publication Data

Bryant, Michael S., 1962–
  Confronting the "good death" : Nazi euthanasia on trial, 1945–1953 / Michael S. Bryant.
    p. cm.
  Includes bibliographical references and index.
  ISBN 0-87081-809-0 (alk. paper)
  1. People with disabilities—Nazi persecution. 2. Euthanasia—Germany—History—20th
century. 3. Trials (Genocide) I. Title.
  D804.5.H35B79 2005
  940.53'18'0874—dc22

                                                                                2005017419

Design by Daniel Pratt

14 13 12 11 10 09 08 07 06 05   10 9 8 7 6 5 4 3 2 1

Support for this publication was generously provided by the Eugene M. Kayden Fund at the
University of Colorado.

To my son Reed
For whom I wish a world free from the events described in this book.

CONTENTS

ACKNOWLEDGMENTS

This study is the child of a gestation period that stretches back into the late 1980s, when I encountered the bizarre phenomenon of Nazi euthanasia for the first time as an exchange student at Göttingen University. Ernst Klee's *Euthanasie im NS-Staat* was my guide through the apocalyptic landscape of Nazi violence against the mentally handicapped. After a five-year career as an attorney, I returned to this grim subject out of a conviction of its importance for all of us today, dedicating my doctoral studies to its representation in postwar trials.

Many people have been involved in one way or another with the project, both within the United States and abroad. I would like to thank my wife, Patty, for her support throughout the research and writing of this study. She provided not only encouragement and astute readings of the manuscript, but bore up under periods of separation that lasted for several months as I conducted research in foreign archives. Thanks go also to my mother, Elizabeth Bryant, who provided invaluable childcare for our infant son, Reed, that enabled me to finish the manuscript.

A special debt of gratitude is owed to my adviser, Dr. Alan Beyerchen, for his thoughtful comments on my chapters, as well as for planting the inspiration years ago to pursue my interests in Nazi euthanasia via a study of postwar criminal trials. Throughout my training as a graduate student, Dr. Beyerchen was a tireless supporter of my project. I would also like to express my appreciation for the superb feedback from my second and third readers, Professors Steve Conn and John Rothney.

I am grateful for the guidance and inspiration given me by Dr. Raul Hilberg, whose seminar in teaching Holocaust history at the college level was one of the formative moments in my scholarly career. Dr. Hilberg's receptive attitude toward the stumbling efforts of a junior historian has been an example to me of graceful collegiality. The same may be said of Dr. Erich Loewy, a renowned bioethicist from the University of California at Sacramento. Dr. Loewy supported my applications for grants to underwrite the research and writing of this project. He generously placed me in contact with his colleagues in Germany and Austria, whose considerable knowledge of Nazi euthanasia enriched my project enormously.

I would like to extend my heartfelt thanks to the staffs of the World War II Records Division at the National Archives in College Park, Maryland, and the Max Planck Institute for Foreign and International Criminal Law in Freiburg, Germany. Thanks should also be given to the staff of the Dokumentationsarchiv des Österreichischen Widerstands in Vienna, Austria.

I would like to express my deep appreciation for the warmth and tutelage of Dick de Mildt and C. F. Rüter of the Institute for Criminal Law in Amsterdam. Without their pioneering work in assembling the texts of the postwar German verdicts, the present study would assuredly have never come into existence. Thanks are also due to the assistance rendered by three dear friends, Eckhard Herych, David McEvoy, and Robert Kunath, for their insightful comments on my research.

I greatly appreciate the advice given me at the beginning of the project by Christopher Browning to focus on a specific *Tatkomplex* rather than the sprawling and unmanageable spectrum of Nazi criminality. Gerhard Weinberg encouraged my efforts and furnished me with excellent materials concerning the postwar prosecution of Nazi war crimes.

Finally, I would like to give my profound thanks to the two organizations that provided generous financial support of my research and writing: the National Science Foundation and the Woodrow Wilson Foundation (through the Charlotte W. Newcombe Doctoral Dissertation Fellowship). A specific debt of gratitude is owed to John Perhonis of the National Science Foundation's Ethics and Value Studies section for his helpful guidance and encouragement.

But I'll tell you here . . . it is the nature of villainy to absent itself, even as it stands before you. You reach for it and close on nothing. You smash your hand on the mirror. Who is this looking back at you? Perhaps you're aware by now of the elusiveness of my villains. This is a story of invisible men, dead men or men indeterminately alive . . . of men hidden, barricaded, in their own created realm. . . . You have not seen them, except in the shadows, or heard them speak, except in the voices of others. . . . They've been hiding in my language . . . powerful, absent men.

—E. L. DOCTOROW, *THE WATERWORKS*

Germany, 1940–1945

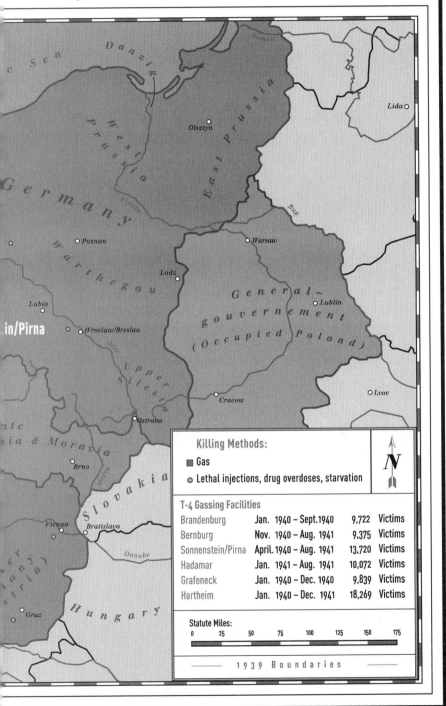

Killing Methods:

▪ Gas

◉ Lethal injections, drug overdoses, starvation

T-4 Gassing Facilities

Brandenburg	Jan. 1940 – Sept. 1940	9,722	Victims
Bernburg	Nov. 1940 – Aug. 1941	9,375	Victims
Sonnenstein/Pirna	April. 1940 – Aug. 1941	13,720	Victims
Hadamar	Jan. 1941 – Aug. 1941	10,072	Victims
Grafeneck	Jan. 1940 – Dec. 1940	9,839	Victims
Hartheim	Jan. 1940 – Dec. 1941	18,269	Victims

Statute Miles:
0   25   50   75   100   125   150   175

1939 Boundaries

We can only speculate about the thoughts that raced through the head of Dr. Alfred Leu in December 1953 as he awaited the verdict of the Cologne state court (*Landgericht*) presiding over his criminal case. Leu was charged with the murders of hundreds of adults and seventy children in 1941 during his tenure as a physician at the Sachsenberg mental hospital near Schwerin, Germany. The state's evidence against Leu was impressively incriminating. Numerous eyewitnesses had stepped forward to attest to their observation of murders committed in Leu's wards through lethal injections of veronal and luminal. Others testified about Leu's admission during the war that he was a confirmed advocate of euthananizing the mentally ill. His connections with the Berlin office entrusted with the mass killing of handicapped patients were well documented.

Whatever anxiety Leu experienced as the court prepared to announce its verdict could only have been accentuated by the recent history of West German prosecution of physicians for their participation in killing the mentally ill. Leu was assuredly aware of the 1946 case of Dr. Hilde Wernicke, convicted of murder by the Berlin state court for her role in passing on the names of selected patients to her nurses for extermination. Wernicke was executed for her crimes. Other euthanasia personnel in the late 1940s were, like Wernicke, convicted of murder and sentenced to death or lifelong prison terms. To make matters worse for Leu's equanimity, these earlier physicians were convicted even though they had not directly administered the coup de grace to their patients. By contrast, Leu had not only transmitted patient lists to his nurses for killing but had himself personally participated in the murders. Although the Constitution of the Federal Republic of Germany had abolished capital punishment in 1949, Leu faced the possibility of life in prison if convicted.

Leu's fears proved to be unfounded. The Cologne state court acquitted Leu of all charges on the ground that he had participated in the destruction of patients only to oppose it from within. His choice to follow his conscience rather than the law of homicide justified his actions, even if it did involve him in killing handicapped children who, in the court's words, were "completely below the zero line." With this legal benediction, Dr. Alfred Leu, the proven killer of patients at the Sachsenberg mental hospital, left the Cologne courthouse a free man.

How did German courts travel the light-year from convicting euthanasia doctors of murder to not only acquitting them, but celebrating their conscientious devotion to the healing craft? How can we account for so prodigious a change in judicial interpretations of murderous violence against the mentally handicapped during the war? Were West German courts merely applying the law in a neutral manner to the facts before them, or were they bending the law and finessing evidence in order to achieve a result that served an agenda rather than the ideals of substantive justice? To what degree were the extralegal forces that may have conditioned the outcomes of German euthanasia trials also at work in the U.S. prosecutions of euthanasia criminality? What kinds of general conclusions may be drawn from a comparative juxtaposition of the two groups of national trials immediately after the war? These important questions are the focus of this study.

The central argument is that, despite the sincere desires of many policymakers, jurists, and politicians to punish the crimes of euthanasia criminality, the matrix of power relationships in the immediate postwar era played havoc with the prosecution of euthanasia killers. For both Americans and West Germans,* concerns about preserving or recuperating sovereign power consistently bedeviled the neutral quest for justice. On the U.S. side, the tendency to view Nazi euthanasia (and genocide more generally) as the excrescence of Germany's

---

* Although the Federal Republic of Germany was not formally established until 1949, I will refer throughout this book to that portion of the country under U.S., British, and French occupation prior to 1949 as "West Germany."

war of aggression, a view originating in U.S. insistence that to prosecute crimes unrelated to waging aggressive war might detract from U.S. sovereignty, skewed the Americans' construction of euthanasia as early as 1945. Preoccupation with its own sovereignty inclined the United States to relate all forms of National Socialist criminality—including euthanasia—to Hitler's grand plan to subjugate the peoples of Europe. In the process, individual degrees of participation in the destruction of the mentally ill were dissolved in an overarching conspiracy that equated the smallest participant with the greatest on a theory of joint and several criminal liability. The effect was not only to obscure the origins of Nazi euthanasia by over-identifying it with military conquest but, in some cases, to invert the usual presumption of innocence in U.S. criminal trials.

The West Germans, too, were concerned with national power in the immediate postwar years. For them, however, the issue was not to preserve sovereign power, but to regain it after the unconditional surrender to the Allies in 1945 and the military occupation of their country. Growing disenchantment with denazification, a restive impatience with continued prosecution of accused war criminals, and mounting demands for a general amnesty for the perpetrators of Nazi crimes and for their reintegration into German society sapped the will of the West Germans to prosecute and punish euthanasia personnel. Particularly in the late 1940s, these extralegal forces increasingly affected the kind and quality of justice dispensed in West German euthanasia trials. The effect, as in the case of the Americans, was to reverse conventional burden of proof standards: where German criminal procedure tended to presume guilt with formal indictment, German courts in the waning years of the 1940s assumed the innocence of euthanasia defendants, despite voluminous evidence against them. The impact on the progress and outcome of euthanasia trials of this drive to preserve or recover sovereign power is the focus of this study.

The word *euthanasia*, the Greek roots of which translate as "good death," may be interpreted on at least two separate levels. On the first, euthanasia is the election by morally autonomous beings to end their lives in the face of excruciatingly painful and terminal illness. Recent manifestations of euthanasia in Western culture, such as the controversial practices of Dr. Jack Kevorkian and the adoption of a voluntary euthanasia law in the Netherlands, belong to this first level. Because deference to the choice of the individual underlies it, euthanasia of the first level may be called the "libertarian" theory of euthanasia.

On the second level, euthanasia emerges as a means to eliminate "useless" or "valueless" life from society for racial, economic, or aesthetic motives. Because its animating force is the alleged welfare of the collective over and above that of the individual, we may call this second level "eugenic" euthanasia.

Eugenic euthanasia is the extreme possibility of the pseudoscience of eugenics, an international sociopolitical movement between the late nineteenth century and 1945. Coined by its founder, Francis Galton, the term *eugenics* derives from the Greek, meaning "well born." In both theory and practice eugenics movements can be diverse, but they have in common the aim to improve the genetic timbre of the individual members of a social order through government intervention. The hardnosed variant of eugenics tended to oppose the role of environment in heredity, stressing instead the brute facticity of genetic fitness. Accordingly, it was pessimistic about improving human potential through social means, and thus tended to be politically conservative. The hardnosed eugenic approach favored a "negative" eugenics that sought to prevent genetic inferiors from reproducing by forbidding them to marry, imposing birth control on them, sterilizing them, or, in the most extreme case, killing them. In Great Britain and the United States, eugenics initiatives never went beyond sterilization. The eugenicists of the Third Reich, however, ran the gamut from forced sterilization to the centrally planned destruction of human beings branded as worthless by the Nazi regime.

Clearly, accomplices were needed at all levels of the German mental health-care system to bring the killing program to fruition. The plan to eliminate human beings considered strange and disturbing beckoned to one of the most nazified professions in Germany—German medicine. As compared with other professional groups, doctors were overrepresented in the Nazi Party: in 1933, 33 percent of German doctors were party members, constituting just under 25 percent of Nazi academic professionals, or one-fifteenth of the social elite within the Nazi Party. By 1937 (a year when the membership rolls of the Nazi Party were open to all Germans over the age of seventeen), almost 44 percent were party members, or one-third of Nazi academic professionals and one-tenth of the Nazi social elite. These figures far exceed statistics from other German professions: neither lawyers nor teachers with party membership ever rose above 25 percent, and other civil servants lagged considerably behind doctors. Significant percentages of physicians also belonged to the ideological bastions of Nazism, the SA (26 percent between 1935–1945) and the SS (9 percent between 1933–1939, and possibly more from 1939–1945). Again, we can better appreciate these figures when compared with other professions, such as teachers (among whom only 0.4 percent were SS members). As Canadian historian Michael Kater points out, 1.3 percent of all SS men were doctors by 1937—a figure indicating that physicians were overrepresented in the SS by a factor of seven relative to their percentage within the population. Kater further notes that only lawyers, with a ratio of twenty-five to one, were more overrepresented in the SS than doctors.[1]

Of the 90,000 doctors practicing in Germany during the era of the Third Reich, how many were involved in the crimes of the Nazi regime? In a lecture delivered at the Fifty-first German Doctors' Day in 1948, Fred Mielke, at the time a German medical student, estimated that between 300 and 400 doctors were implicated in Nazi criminality. Alexander Mitscherlich, Mielke's co-author in one of the first studies of medical crimes under Hitler,[2] subsequently revised this estimate, stating that Mielke's figure represented only the direct perpetrators who committed crimes with their own hands. Standing behind these doctors was an elaborate bureaucratic structure that had facilitated their wrongdoing. When we consider the vast program of institutionalized destruction, ranging from euthanasia killing facilities, transit centers, federal and local health ministries, research institutions, and the concentration/death camp system, Mitscherlich's more capacious approach seems closer to the mark.[3]

After the war, the Allies were faced with the task of sorting out personal responsibility for Nazi crimes and prosecuting the offenders in formal proceedings. In addition to the International Military Tribunal (IMT) conducted by the Big Four (the United States, Great Britain, France, and the USSR) and trials held by military commissions and military government courts, numerous national trials prosecuted Germans involved in Nazi criminality, including euthanasia killings. In twelve separate trials between 1946–1949, U.S. authorities indicted and tried 184 representatives of Nazi organizations deemed criminal by the IMT. Of these, 142 were convicted; sentences varied from eighteen months to death. Among the most important of the U.S. trials was the Medical Case held in Nuremberg between October 1946 and August 1947. It involved twenty-three defendants (primarily physicians) charged with heinous concentration camp experiments on human subjects and the mass killing of mental patients pursuant to the government's euthanasia program. Only four of the twenty-three defendants were charged with euthanasia killings: Karl Brandt, Viktor Brack, Waldemar Hoven, and Kurt Blome. All save Blome were convicted and executed.

As the IMT and national trials were moving forward, the Germans prosecuted their own Nazi criminals. The lion's share of investigations and trials of Nazi crimes took place in the five-year period following the end of the war. By late 1950 West German courts had convicted 5,228 Nazi defendants (roughly 81 percent of Nazi crimes successfully prosecuted from 1945–1992). If we examine the West German trials by category, we find that they embraced six distinct categories of crime: (1) political denunciations; (2) deportations of Jews and Gypsies; (3) euthanasia; (4) "last phase" killings; (5) killings of prisoners of war, concentration camp prisoners, eastern (European) workers (*Ostarbeiter*), and Jews; and (6) a miscellaneous category of homicide. Among these six categories, euthanasia cases amounted to just under 13 percent of Nazi crimes tried between 1945–1950 (37 out of 288 cases). Beginning in 1951, the numbers of convictions plummeted. In 1950 West German courts convicted 809 Nazi defendants, but that figure fell to 259 in 1951 and a paltry 21 by 1955.[4]

How can we account for the dramatic decline in Nazi criminal prosecution? The most immediate (if superficial) explanation for the decline is the web of legal limitations that inhibited prosecution in the postwar years. First, the structure of German criminal investigation in the postwar years impeded efficient location and prosecution of Nazi war criminals. German state prosecutors were required by law to investigate a crime only if it was committed within their jurisdiction or the perpetrator either resided or was arrested within it. Because the crimes of the Final Solution had been committed on foreign soil, they had no geographic link to West German jurisdiction, nor could the bare possibility that a perpetrator might reside within the prosecutor's jurisdiction create a prima facie reason for investigation. In theory, a prosecutor could know of the existence of a mass shooting in the Soviet Union by Germans, and even the identity of the killers, yet still be legally hamstrung from setting an inquiry in motion. The absence in Germany of a federal investigative body like the U.S. FBI contributed to the judiciary's paralysis.[*]

Second, the Allied Control Council (the occupational government formed by the Allies as a successor to the defunct Nazi state) deprived the German judiciary, at least technically, of jurisdiction over any crimes perpetrated by Germans on foreign nationals. This ban was rescinded in August 1951, but until that time it was a stumbling block to efforts by German prosecutors in the crucial five years after the war to investigate, arrest, and prosecute the suspected murderers of foreign Jews and others.

---

[*] The absence of a federal authority capable of coordinating nationwide investigations of Nazi war crimes suspects was to a degree alleviated by the establishment in December 1958 of the Central Office of the State Justice Administrations for the Clarification of National Socialist Crimes in Ludwigsburg. The office was charged with investigating Nazi war crimes, collecting records about them, and ascertaining the whereabouts of suspected perpetrators. Although the office was vested with no indictment authority, it forwarded its evidence to state prosecutors who could issue indictments based on the documentation. See Adalbert Rückerl, *The Investigation of Nazi Crimes 1945–1978: A Documentation* (Hamden, CT: Archon Books, 1980), 49; Erwin Schüle, "Die Zentrale der Landesjustizverwaltungen zur Aufklärung nationalsozialistischer Gewaltverbrechen in Ludwigsburg," *Juristenzeitung*, 1962, 241.

Third, efforts to prosecute Nazi offenders sometimes ran afoul of the statute of limitations, which barred prosecution of certain offenses after a specified period of time had elapsed. In May 1950 the first statute of limitations expired, immunizing from prosecution all offenses of a relatively minor criminal nature (i.e., crimes punishable with a sentence of up to five years). In 1954 an amnesty law decreed by the *Bundestag* immunized a second category of offense—manslaughter punishable with a prison sentence up to three years. The following year, the statute expired for all crimes subject to a maximum jail term of ten years. Five years later, offenses punishable with fifteen years or less (i.e., manslaughter, infliction of grievous bodily harm, deprivation of liberty resulting in death, and robbery) were beyond the reach of the judicial authorities. Thus, by 1960 only perpetrators of murder were susceptible to prosecution.[5]

The structure of West German criminal investigation, restrictions imposed by the Allied Control Council on German jurisdiction over Nazi crimes, and the statute of limitations are systemic factors that obstructed a thorough judicial accounting of National Socialist crimes by West German courts. They do not, however, fully explain the plunge in indictments after 1950, nor do they address the psychological, political, demographic, and cultural forces afoot in German postwar society that inhibited an open confrontation with Nazi criminality. Scholars have cited several explanations to account for the refusal, characteristic of broad segments of the population in the immediate postwar period, to look Germany's "brown" past fully in the face. First, reports on the IMT proceedings indiscriminately blended the defendants' military, political, and genocidal offenses, thereby effacing the differences between political or military crimes and the racially inspired crimes of the Third Reich. The result was to plant the idea in the minds of many Germans that the regime's murderous treatment of Jews, Soviet POWs, Gypsies, and the mentally ill were the unfortunate but common byproducts of total war. Political or war crimes were a recognizable species of offense, committed by both the victors and the vanquished in the heat of battle. On this view, the Nazis' crimes were acts carried out in the course of service to the Fatherland; in no sense could they be identified with the asocial depravity of "real" criminals.[6] From this set of dubious premises, some drew the conclusion that Allied trials of "war criminals" were little more than *Siegerjustiz* (victor's justice), punishing German defendants for crimes the Allies had also perpetrated.

Furthermore, many Germans regarded the Allied trials as violations of a traditional cornerstone of German criminal jurisprudence, the Roman law maxim *nullum crimen sine lege* (no crime may be charged without a preexisting law that defines it). Because neither the London Charter (the legal basis of the IMT) nor Control Council Law #10 (the legal basis for the subsequent trials and for German prosecution of Nazi defendants until September 1951) was in existence prior to 1945, some argued that the categories of offense spelled out by them were ex post facto laws. (German courts were not persuaded by this argument; they indicted, tried, and convicted defendants in the postwar years for infringing the German law of murder or for committing crimes against humanity in violation of Control Council Law #10—the latter often justified on natural law grounds.)

No effort to explore the West Germans' unfavorable attitudes toward Nazi war crimes trials after 1948 should overlook the perceived failures of the U.S. denazification program. Germans living in the U.S. zone were obliged in the immediate postwar years to complete a questionnaire on their prior political and social engagements. These forms were reviewed by denazification courts, which classified the subjects of the questionnaires into one of five categories: exonerated, follower only, lesser offender, offender, and major offender. The denazification bodies could impose penalties based upon this classification, ranging from fines to confinement in a labor camp for no more than ten years. They could also ban an individual from his profession for a period of time. Mere membership in certain Nazi organizations (like the SS or the SD) created a prima facie case against the subject of the questionnaire; once this affiliation was proven, the burden shifted to the subject to rebut the presumption of guilt.

Aiming to scour German society of the Nazi taint, the U.S. denazification program achieved notable successes. Sometimes, however, its implementation was farcical, as major criminals neglected to mention on the forms their involvement in mass killings in the east, thus escaping with trivial sentences, while easily documented but minor party memberships occasioned draconian punishment. The spectacle of mass murderers receiving "detergent certificates" (*Persilscheine*), cleansing them of egregious wrongdoing, discredited the process in the eyes of many. The bad odor surrounding the denazification proceedings may have clung by association to Allied and German trials of Nazi defendants, viewed by the public as an extension of denazification under a different name.[7]

Deep psychological and cultural forces also contributed to the German public's unwillingness to confront Nazi crimes. In their study *The Inability to Mourn*,[8] psychologists Alexander and Margarete Mitscherlich argued that postwar Germans suffered from an incapacity to "work through" the traumas of the era of the Third Reich, a process Sigmund Freud had called *Trauerarbeit*, or "the work of mourning." The vast amplitude of National Socialist criminality precluded the German people from coming to terms with a past that was still cancerously alive. The alternative—openly confronting the Nazis' crimes, in which so many Germans at all levels of society and vocation were implicated—

risked plunging the German people into a society-wide psychosis that would have jeopardized all efforts at postwar reconstruction and renewal.

A more recent account by Aleida Assmann likewise traces the failures of German confrontation with Nazi mass murder in the postwar era to psycho-cultural factors. Drawing on the anthropological distinction between "shame" and "guilt" cultures, she contends that Germany immediately after the war, like militaristic societies in general, was a shame culture that enforced the conformity of its members by exposing them to "the gaze" of formal and informal social control. A guilt culture, by contrast, expiated individual guilt through public confession, acknowledgment of responsibility, and internal conversion. In such a culture, guilt properly confessed and accepted became a "resource of individuation" for both the individual perpetrator and for society collectively. This process obviously includes criminal trials as a means of uncovering offenses, restoring order to the society discomposed by them, and facilitating the "conversion" of the perpetrator through punishment. Where, however, criminal guilt was repressed because of the shame evoked by it, particularly in a culture transitioning from a shame to a guilt paradigm (like postwar Germany), the willingness to acknowledge past criminality and recognition of the need to punish it with the devices of the criminal law are blocked. Although Germans would eventually shrug off their shame culture and confront the crimes of National Socialism after 1958, its paralyzing effects prior to that time induced a "massive defense against memory" among the German population. One casualty of this repression was continued judicial engagement with the trials of Nazi offenders.[9]

The cumulative effect of these circumstances was to engender strong opposition to continued prosecution and punishment of Nazi defendants beginning in the late 1940s. Although most Germans supported the trial of the major war criminals by the IMT in 1946 (insofar as it buttressed the mistaken but fervid German belief in the "exclusive guilt" [Exklusivschuld] of Hitler and his top-echelon henchmen for the regime's crimes), an equal number disapproved of the trials of German elites after the IMT had concluded. Fueled by the movement into western zones of millions of displaced Germans from the east, political opposition quickly arose against a sustained war crimes trial program. Obscure far-right parties formed, demanding an end to denazification and to prosecution of Nazi war crimes defendants. Leaders in both Catholic and Protestant churches like Bishop Wurm and the director of the chancellery of the German Protestant Church Hans Asmussen pressed Allied officials to end war crimes prosecutions. In 1949 a group of German jurists was established, composed of among others the foremost defense attorneys from the Nuremberg trials. Called the Heidelberg Circle, the group set about to achieve a final liquidation of the war crimes trials by influencing politicians and public alike. The ability of these and other critics to mold and channel the negative attitudes of West Germans toward war crimes trials was considerable: in 1946 70 percent of West German respondents approved of prosecuting the major war criminals, but by the end of the decade a comparable percentage disapproved of continued trials.[10]

Politicians like Konrad Adenauer were, of course, keenly aware of the topography of West German sentiment regarding further prosecution. As previous scholars have convincingly demonstrated, Adenauer pursued a "policy toward the past" that consisted of amnesty for many Nazi war criminals (the Christmas amnesty law of 1949 and a second amnesty law passed in 1954), their reintegration into German society through the Article 131 law (which required the civil service to allocate a prescribed percentage of jobs for former members of the Nazi government), and a process of what Norbert Frei has termed "normative demarcation," that is, affirming the democratic, pro-Western character of the Federal Republic by contrasting it with its alleged opposites— unreconstructed Nazis and Communists. The trifecta of amnesty, reintegration, and normative demarcation achieved simultaneous goals: it preempted the appeal of ultra far-right political parties, won adherents to the new German state, and placated the Western allies. The victory of Adenauer and the CDU in the 1953 elections was a sign of popular assent to this policy. Adenauer's accomplishments, however, could only be paid for in the coin of forgetting and repression—an attitude of willed amnesia that retarded the progress of war crimes trials.[11]

Adenauer's "policy toward the past" was thus cunningly designed to serve both domestic and foreign objectives. At home, it subverted nationalist politicians, stabilized the fledgling democracy, and won votes for the CDU. Abroad, it conveyed the image to the United States and its allies of a rehabilitated Germany, democratic, capitalist, confident, and, most important, securely in the Western camp. The late 1940s witnessed the rise of the Cold War as Europe fissioned into two armed camps. As political tensions between the Eastern bloc and Western allies threatened to turn into a shooting war, the Allies' need for West Germany as a bulwark against Communism in central Europe became poignant. A remarkable seachange had occurred in the space of a few years: the Soviets had displaced the Nazis as the clear and present danger to Western security interests. Adenauer was acutely aware of Germany's importance in the geopolitical chess match between the two superpowers. Only months after the outbreak of the Korean War—a time when hostility between east and west was at its peak—Adenauer sought to exploit this opportunity to recover German sovereignty from the Allies via the quashing of war crimes trials. He dispatched a memorandum to the Allied High Commission, demanding that the occupation statute be revised to enhance German sovereignty. If no revision (read: repeal) was made, he warned ominously that Germans might be unwilling to "sacrifice" themselves for freedom, and plans for a European defense community to protect the West from Soviet invasion would be stillborn. Frank Stern summarizes Adenauer's strategy and the degree to which it encapsulated the feelings of West Germans in 1950:

> Sovereignty via integration into the West and rearmament, which included rehabilitation of the Wehrmacht, were essential aspects of the developing national consciousness and key points of official government policy. In concrete terms, this ultimately meant negotiations: on canceling the debt of the German Reich, repealing of the Statute of Occupation and creation of a European defense community.

In short, the price Adenauer demanded for a German contribution to fighting the Soviets was recuperated national power achieved, at least in part, by discontinuing Nazi war crimes trials.[12]

A salient component of Adenauer's policy toward the past was the reintegration of former Nazis into the German civil service, including the judiciary. As denazification petered out, onetime Nazi judges and prosecutors, many of whom had served on the infamous "special courts" (*Sondergerichte*) and "People's Court" (*Volksgerichtshof*), returned to their positions in the German legal system during the Adenauer era. In the British zone of occupation, by the late 1940s between 80 and 90 percent of state court judges were former Nazi Party members. By 1949, 81 percent of all judges and prosecutors in Bavaria had belonged to the party—a percentage, asserts Nazi war crimes trial expert Willi Dressen, that corresponds to the proportion of Nazi jurists in the judiciary prior to 1945.[13] For such individuals, Adenauer's program of amnesty and integration nourished by an atmosphere of collective forgetting must have been especially attractive.

The present study limns a portrait of U.S. and West German euthanasia trials against this background of a society yearning for an end to constant evocations of Nazi atrocity, particularly as embodied in continued war crimes trials. Rather than reenact what other scholars have already done,[14] in this book I undertake close readings of transcripts and verdicts generated in the trials of euthanasia defendants. Accordingly, with the exception of periodic references to the context of the trials, this study does not focus specifically on the socioeconomic, political, and cultural forces that shaped the prosecution of Nazi defendants. Instead, through close textual readings of actual trial transcripts and verdicts, I seek to chart how social, geopolitical, and cultural forces shaped the actual verdicts of the trials. The focus is on the texts of the trials, in which are registered the skewing influence of extrajuridical forces in West Germany in the crucial eight-year period following the war. The extraordinary impact of contextual (or non-legal) factors on the trials of the Nazi euthanasia doctors will emerge as a palimpsest underlying the trial documents. Our examination of the court records will reveal that the influence of these non-legal factors was determinative of the verdicts. In locating the judgments squarely within their historical context, the study suggests that considerations of national sovereignty were an intrinsic and predestinating force in the postwar trials of the euthanasia doctors, a force so irresistible and pervasive as to alter the legal burdens of proof in both the U.S. and German cases.

Of course, tracing decisively the arcs of causality between a force and its effect (or, in this book, between an alleged bias and a final verdict) is impossible in historical investigation; too many causes interact in shifting permutations that directly or indirectly impinge on the ultimate result. E. H. Carr's hypothetical about the length of Cleopatra's nose and the founding of the principate is a facetious but telling illustration of this point.[15] To develop a narrower account of the progress of euthanasia trials after the war, the enormous range of potential causes would have to be ranked lexically: primary status assigned to some, secondary to others. In the final analysis, any such ranking of causes as they pertain to Nazi war crimes trials must by necessity be artificial. Did the structure of German criminal investigative agencies after the war contribute more to the decline of these trials than the unpopularity of the denazification program? Did the pain felt by Germans when reflecting on their collective guilt for the multitudinous criminality of the Nazi government have greater weight than the active lobbying efforts of far-right nationalist parties to draw a *Schlußstrich* to further trials? Did the checkered pasts of West German judges outweigh Adenauer's policy toward the past as factors in the movement toward leniency, acquittal, and amnesty, and were these factors more important than the geopolitics of the Cold War?

To ascribe priority to any one of these factors over the others would amount to an arbitrary valuation, because all of them affected the trend toward an abatement of Nazi war crimes trials, yet to none can be assigned a numerical value that would justify its super- or subordination to the others. In this respect, a Foucauldian methodology of looking for contingencies rather than causes in historical change is more appropriate. On this approach, the phenomenon to be explained—the subsidence of euthanasia trials into leniency and acquittal—was a result of a complex set of interrelated causes. The phenomenon, in other words, was contingent on political, institutional, cultural, demographic, and international developments in the postwar era. Subtract any one or more of them—say, the lack of an integrated criminal investigation system or the outbreak of the Cold War—and the result may have been considerably different. It is hard to imagine, for example, that Alfred Leu would have been acquitted if the Allies were less intent on establishing West Germany as a partner in the defense of Western Europe against Soviet attack and more concerned with punishing former executioners of the Nazi regime at large in the Federal Republic. Similarly, the existence of a federal criminal investigation agency might have alerted prosecutors' offices to the presence within their jurisdiction of Nazi war criminals, thus facilitating their arrest and prosecution. The point is that all of these factors played a role in undermining the spirit of Nuremberg; in their absence, the outcome may not have ensued and, if it did, may not have taken the form in which we currently understand it.

I would suggest that a Foucauldian emphasis on historical contingencies does not preclude generalizations about causality in history. This study seeks to knit together into a general concept many diverse causes underlying the decline of euthanasia prosecution: that is, the desire for national power. Without reference to the quest for sovereign power, neither the U.S. conspiracy approach to Nazi euthanasia nor Adenauer's quid pro quo of German support for a European Defense Community in exchange for ending war crimes trials is explicable. The Americans' desire for a democratic, armed, and anti-Soviet Germany opened the door to the German longing for restored sovereignty. If in fact the eclipse of justice in the cases of Nazi murderers is overdetermined in this account, that fact proves the complexity and multi-causality of postwar efforts to prosecute the offenders. A tidier explanation may convey an appearance of greater mastery, but it would do so at the price of imposing an artificial simplicity on a densely tangled historical situation.[16]

The first trial group we will analyze relates to the prosecution of euthanasia personnel by the United States between 1945 and 1947. The U.S. euthanasia trials are composed of two separate proceedings: the prosecution by military commission of the medical staff at the Hadamar killing center in Hesse-Nassau (where both foreign nationals and mentally ill Germans were killed) and the Medical Case (Case #1) against some of the high-ranking designers and implementers of the euthanasia program, tried before the U.S. National Military Tribunal at Nuremberg. The U.S. euthanasia trials were premised on violations of international law. In the Hadamar case, the defendants were charged with violating the Laws of Armed Conflict, a body of customs and rules set forth in various treaties, international agreements, and decisions of international and domestic courts and designed to temper the brutality with which modern war is waged. Offenses proscribed by the Laws of Armed Conflict are generally called war crimes. In the 1946 Medical Case, on the other hand, the four defendants indicted for their roles in the Nazi euthanasia program were charged with committing "crimes against humanity," a species of offense related to war crimes but conceptually distinct from them. Whereas war crimes were derived from the treaties, accords, and court opinions that made up the Laws of Armed Conflict, crimes against humanity were not defined in an international instrument until the London Charter (August 1945) that became the basis for the International Military Tribunal at Nuremberg. Article 6(c) of the charter defined crimes against humanity for the first time in international legal history. They consisted of "murder, extermination, enslavement, deportation, and other inhumane acts" against a civilian population, as well as "political, racial, or religious" persecution "whether or not in violation of domestic law of the country where perpetrated." Although the U.S. prosecution teams at the IMT and the National Military Tribunal (NMT) often treated war crimes and crimes against humanity synonymously, they were—and continue to be—separate and distinct crimes under international law.[17]

By contrast, the West German euthanasia trials were for the most part based upon alleged violations of the German law of homicide (sections 211 and 212 of the German Penal Code). Until August 31, 1951, the Germans could charge euthanasia defendants with committing either a crime against humanity as defined under the IMT Charter (and incorporated into Control Council Law #10) or a homicide under their own penal code.[*] Beginning in September 1951, Control Council Law #10 became null and void, and Nazi defendants could only be charged by West German courts with infringing German law. Until that time German prosecutors sometimes charged defendants with both offenses, but the prevailing practice was to indict them for violating domestic law. The Germans' aversion to ex post facto prosecution may explain their preference for trying their accused under their own laws of homicide.

The time frame of this study is the critical eight-year period following the end of the war, when all of the U.S. and most of the German trials were conducted. Chapter 1 provides the reader with the historical prelude to the trials. It sketches the history of the idea of "life unworthy of life" with reference to what we might justly call the crucible of eugenic euthanasia—the German experience of World War I and the traumas of the early 1920s. In this chapter I suggest that the fusion of eugenics with racial hygiene in Germany became a potent cocktail for many Germans in the Weimar years. I recount

---

[*] German courts in the west could charge defendants with crimes against humanity under Control Council Law #10 only in the British and French zones of occupation. The United States never formally authorized the German courts in its zone to try cases under the auspices of Law #10. See Brief an die Herren Dienstvorstände der Gerichte und Staatsanwaltschaften betr. Strafverfahren nach Kontrollratgesetz Nr. 10, Bad. Ministerium der Justiz, 6 December 1951, Staatsarchiv Freiburg, Bestand F 178/1, Nr. 1112.

how voices advocating negative eugenic solutions to the problem of "worthless" life, relegated to the fringe in the prewar years, had moved to the center by the 1930s. Further, Chapter 1 explores the evolution of euthanasia killing from 1933 to 1941 as a prelude to the expanded killing projects of the Third Reich by late 1941 and early 1942. Finally, the chapter takes up the question of the "radicalization" of Nazi mass killing as it spread from the disabled to Soviet POWs, the European Jews, and other groups in the summer and fall of 1941.

The remaining chapters excavate from the U.S. and West German trial records interpretations of the motives behind the mass killing of the disabled. Chapter 2 shows that U.S. prosecutors and judges regarded euthanasia as an auxiliary to the Nazis' efforts to wage aggressive war against their European neighbors. The U.S. conspiracy theory was driven by a predisposition to interpret Nazi crimes in terms of the regime's ambitions to conquer by military force the peoples of Europe. Without this link to the conduct of the war, U.S. policymakers feared the euthanasia program would be deemed a domestic program. In their eyes, interfering in the purely domestic policies of a sovereign state might set a dangerous precedent in international law. Consistent with their war-connected theory of euthanasia, U.S. authorities portrayed the killing of the mentally ill as a war measure to strengthen the German army by enriching it with booty (chiefly medical supplies and hospital space) plundered from "useless eaters." Because all the euthanasia defendants belonged to the same "conspiracy" to attack other European countries, it mattered little how large or small a function they discharged; they were equally liable for all acts carried out on behalf of the conspiracy.

Chapters 3, 4, and 5 contrast the U.S. approach with that of the Germans, who generally depicted their defendants as accomplices (*Gehilfe*) rather than perpetrators (*Täter*), a distinction that in German law hinges upon the degree of a defendant's self-interest in the crime. Portraying Nazi physicians, nurses, and health service bureaucrats as accomplices driven less by ideology than characterological shortcomings, German courts virtually assured lenient treatment of their defendants. The trend toward leniency and acquittal began in the late 1940s and grew in intensity as political and psychological factors (the Cold War, the mounting resentment by the German population of trials viewed as Victor's Justice, and other extralegal factors) increasingly affected the adjudication process.

A subsidiary but intriguing theme is taken up in Chapter 3: U.S. and West German conceptions of their jurisdiction over these crimes. The U.S. authorities premised their jurisdiction over euthanasia defendants on the traditional laws of armed conflict, including the Geneva and Hague conventions. Because Nazi euthanasia, on the U.S. view, was designed to promote the German war effort, it was legally and conceptually related to war crimes codified in international documents. By asserting a nexus between war crimes and crimes against humanity (as the euthanasia crimes were charged), the Americans could argue they were not meddling in the Nazis' internal state affairs but prosecuting matters recognized as breaches of international law by the world community. For U.S. authorities, concerns about ex post facto prosecution were less significant than upholding the principle of sovereignty, under which no country was permitted to intervene in the domestic affairs of another state.

The Germans, by contrast, were deeply concerned about the ex post facto question, not least because the ban on retroactive prosecution was fundamental to the continental legal tradition. They faced a vexing dilemma: how could they hold defendants accountable for crimes that were not regarded as illegal at the time they were committed? In both U.S. and West German trial records, the issue is repeatedly raised of the defendants' awareness of illegality at the time they participated in euthanasia crimes. The U.S. authorities were generally unfazed by this issue, inferring from their defendants' purposive conduct on behalf of the euthanasia program the requisite intent to commit the offense. The Germans initially countered the problem of lack of consciousness of illegality with resort to natural law: all sane human beings were able to perceive the injustice of a course of action in the light of the "law of nature." By the early 1950s, however, natural law as a liability-producing device was on the wane as courts began to express doubts about their defendants' awareness of wrongdoing.

Now that I have acquainted the reader with my argument and method, I would like to say what this book is *not* about. It is not a polemic against human rights trials nor a critique of those who advocate an enlarged international jurisdiction over notorious war criminals. Despite the case presented here that considerations of national power often beset the process of adjudication, it is my firm belief that the effort to hold international criminals liable for their atrocious assaults on humanity should and must be pursued. If the present study proves anything of value to the war crimes question in contemporary debate, it is that the wisest course yet devised for dealing with war criminals is the International Criminal Court (ICC), created by the Rome Statute in 1998. Arguably, a permanent body representing a broad cross section of the world's nations will be less susceptible to forces of politics, power, and international contingency that have plagued ad hoc tribunals since 1945. Insofar as we aspire to do justice at the international level, the ICC is our best hope. This book is merely a caveat for the champions of prosecuting war crimes offenders; like the retainer who whispered in the ear of the Roman conqueror that all glory is fleeting, it reminds us that all human justice is limited. The striving is still worth the endeavor.

LAW vs. HISTORY

It might be objected that the purpose of a criminal trial is not to present a historically truthful account of the episode at its center; hence, it is pointless to find fault with the historical inaccuracies and distortions of a criminal proceeding like the U.S. Doctors' Trial. Whatever the merits of this criticism as it pertains to conventional criminal trials, it fails to understand one of the primary motives behind the Nuremberg proceedings: to preserve the history of Nazi criminality for the education of future generations. In his Report to the President of June 6, 1945, Robert Jackson affirmed that the "groundwork" of the Allied case against the major war criminals had to be

> factually authentic and constitute a well-documented history of what we are convinced was a grand, concerted pattern to incite and commit the barbarities which have shocked the world. . . . Unless we write the record of this movement with clarity and precision, we cannot blame the future if in days of peace it finds incredible the accusatory generalities uttered during the war. We must establish incredible events by credible evidence.[18]

The Nuremberg trials, including the subsequent proceedings, were different from conventional criminal trials: in the minds of leading policymakers like Jackson, they were to serve an educative purpose for future generations by memorializing a history that might in palmier days seem beyond belief. Jackson and his colleagues were not oblivious to the historical significance of their work; on the contrary, in Jackson's own words, their aim was to use the trials as a stylus to write a "factually authentic . . . well-documented history" for the benefit of posterity.

Given the extraordinary nature of Nazi criminality, and in view of the trial planners' own conception of their purpose in holding the trials, it is hardly amiss to hold the U.S. judiciary's conception of Nazi crimes up to critical scrutiny. Much of the analysis in Chapter 2 will subject U.S. constructions of Nazi euthanasia to historical cross-examination—particularly the overarching theory that euthanasia was driven by the voracious resource demands of aggressive warfare.

A NOTE ON SOURCES

Like all works of history, this one employs primary and secondary sources to document the judicial encounter with Nazi euthanasia killing. These include the German court opinions collected in the 34-volume series, *Justiz und NS-Verbrechen* (*The Judiciary and Nazi Crimes*).[19] For the U.S. trials I have relied on trial transcripts, exhibits, and interrogation protocols located in the World War Two Records Division at the National Archives in College Park, Maryland. I have also drawn on essays about the euthanasia cases, German law, and related judicial themes written by German jurists in the immediate postwar period, published in diverse German legal periodicals.[20] Some of the primary source documents cited in this study are taken from two compendia, Ernst Klee's *Dokumente zur "Euthanasie"* and Michael Marrus's *The Nuremberg War Crimes Trial, 1945–46*.[21] Finally, my study makes liberal use of secondary sources by European and U.S. scholars. The reader will note my debt to Henry Friedlander and Ernst Klee in Chapter 1.[22] The structure of Chapters 3–5 on the German euthanasia trials was influenced to a considerable degree by Dick de Mildt's pioneering study on postwar Nazi trials by West German courts.[23]

The time period that brackets this study is roughly 1945–1953. (Reference is made to some euthanasia trials after 1953, but only to illuminate issues raised during the eight-year period after the war.) My reasons for focusing on this period are twofold. First, it was a formative time in the crystallization of West German judicial attitudes toward euthanasia criminality. Many of the primary legal theories and historical perceptions of Nazi euthanasia coalesced during this period. Second, a narrower focus enabled more sustained analysis of the leading cases in the euthanasia trials. A third reason could also be cited: the post-1953 cases did not affect my conclusions about the German euthanasia trials in the immediate postwar period. On these grounds, I felt justified in restricting my study to its current time frame.

One further point should be made concerning trial records. The reader will note that the U.S. proceedings are recorded in verbatim transcripts, a format unknown in German trials (although used in pre-trial interrogations of the accused). U.S. law does not require a detailed written verdict by the court "of first instance" (i.e., the court that first hears the case), in part because a verbatim transcript of the proceedings exists, and in part because the role of the judge in a criminal case is restricted to that of umpire because it is the jury that typically determines guilt or innocence. Appeals of guilty verdicts are reviewed by a court of appeals with reference to this trial transcript. German trials, by contrast, are dominated by the persons of the judges and lay assessors (*Schwurgericht*) working in tandem. Verbatim transcripts and jurors are alien to German criminal proceedings. Chiefly as a result of the judge's enhanced role as both investigator and trier of fact, a detailed written justification of the verdict by the court is required, setting forth the background of the case, findings of fact, applicable law, viability of defenses, verdict, factors in extenuation or aggravation, and sentence.[24] Although the verdict of the U.S. tribunal in the Doctors' Case contains some explanatory material, it is remarkably brief in comparison with the German decisions. Thus my discussion of the U.S. Medical Case in Chapter 2 is based on the transcript of the proceeding (nearly 11,000 pages), while my treatment of the German euthanasia trials in Chapters 3, 4, and 5 relate to the courts' sometimes elaborate written opinions.

Russians consider feebleminded people holy. Despite that, killing necessary.

—EXTRACT FROM THE DIARY OF
GENERAL FRANZ HALDER, 26 SEPTEMBER 1941[1]

Let the lamp affix its beam. The only emperor is the emperor of ice-cream.

—WALLACE STEVENS, "THE EMPEROR OF ICE-CREAM" (1923)

If you've got criminal tendencies . . . one of the places to make your mark is law enforcement.

—DON DELILLO, *LIBRA*

Chapter 1 | THE EMPEROR OF ICE-CREAM

NATIONALIST SOCIALIST EUTHANASIA, 1933–1945

In this chapter we examine at some length the Nazis' murderous assault on the mentally handicapped. Because the postwar prosecutions of euthanasia defendants heavily depend on the factual context of that assault, a clear understanding of the trials requires some familiarity with the history of the euthanasia program. The German government's war on the disabled progressed from discriminatory legislation requiring involuntary sterilization of "worthless" people to their planned destruction as the war began. In this chapter I analyze the organizational structure of the killing process, inasmuch as the bureaucratic configuration of the euthanasia program largely shaped how Nazi mass murder developed between 1939 and 1945.

After examining the roots of Nazi euthanasia in the interwar period, I focus on "phase one" of the euthanasia program, in which "incurable" patients were gassed in one of six killing facilities. Phase one ended in August 1941 on Hitler's orders, apparently as a result of growing popular protest against the euthanasia program. The alleged stop, however, did not terminate the killing program. A second phase of the euthanasia program promptly ensued, characterized by "wild euthanasia"—the centrally planned but locally administered killing of patients by means of fatal overdoses of narcotics. The second part of the chapter recounts this development in the history of Nazi euthanasia, as well as its connections with the "Final Solution," the Nazis' scheme to make occupied Europe *Judenfrei* (free of Jews) through the physical obliteration of European Jewry.

By fall 1941, what had begun as a program to eliminate "incurable" mental patients had ballooned into an official policy of state-sponsored murder. The targeted groups included Soviet POWs, "asocials," the Sinti and Roma, and European Jews. Without refined destruction techniques and killers trained in the euthanasia program, the attack on these other groups, when it came, would have been substantially different, or perhaps would not have occurred. The euthanasia program furnished an already murderous government with the skills, personnel, and materiel for expanded genocide. Equally important, the euthanasia program gave the Nazis a precedent for solving problems through mass killing. Beginning in late 1941, the "questions" that confronted the Third Reich—such as the "Gypsy question," the "Eastern Worker question," and the "Jewish question"—were answered through mass murder. The regime's experiences with euthanasia would make the unthinkable thinkable.

WORLD WAR I, THE WEIMAR YEARS, AND THE TRANSFORMATION OF GERMAN ATTITUDES TOWARD THE MENTALLY ILL

Scholars of Nazi criminality identify World War I as a major turning point in the history of the National Socialist assault on "unworthy life."[2] Before 1919, proposals to use state power to eliminate "undesirables" from a society perceived to be in the throes of degeneration were on the fringes of public discourse. The radicalizing effects of World War I, however, pushed these dissident voices from the fringe toward the center. From 1919 until Hitler came to power in 1933, increasing numbers of Germans—doctors, psychiatrists, health officials, politicians, policymakers, and university professors—were won over to the cause of violent solutions to the mental illness problem.

The privations of the German population during World War I (1914–1919) cast a long and fateful shadow over German attitudes toward the mentally ill in the interwar period. Without question, the Great War was a demographic disaster not just for the mentally ill in German institutions—who between 1914 and 1918 suffered a mortality rate of 30 percent because of neglect, hunger, and disease—but for all of Germany, which suffered a loss of 1.9 million men with another 3.6 million wounded or captured. The British blockade led to severe food shortages that brought the populace to—and beyond—the brink of starvation by 1918. Both soldiers and civilians became embittered, and the source of their anger was food: the rank and file within the navy and army resented a system of rationing that gave larger portions to officers, while German mothers lashed out at authorities for failing to provide adequate nourishment for their children.[3]

By 1920, the effects of military defeat, political upheaval, mass death, and famine had altered the moral landscape within German medicine. The new decade was ripe for ideas that openly called for the physical sacrifice of the mentally ill for the health of German society. In 1920, as Germany reeled from the double humiliation of military defeat and what was perceived as a Carthaginian peace treaty, a pamphlet entitled *The Permission to Destroy Life Unworthy of Life* was published. An eminent retired jurist from the University of Leipzig, Karl Binding (1841–1920), and a professor of psychiatry at the University of Freiburg, Alfred Hoche (1856–1944), were the co-authors of the tract. It was divided into two sections, one written by Binding, the other by Hoche. Binding started his section with a defense of the individual's right over his or her body—an overarching right that entailed the right to suicide. Although he conceded society's interest in preserving valuable members, the right of a terminally ill patient experiencing intense pain to have a physician end his or her life by artificial means overrode the social interest. Binding referred to this act of voluntary euthanasia as an "act of healing." Although he emphasized that euthanasia in such a case had to be consensual, the principle of autonomy was at war with his conception of "valueless" life. He asked: "Is there human life which has so far forfeited the character of something entitled to enjoy the protection of the law that its prolongation represents a perpetual loss of value, both for its bearer and for society as a whole?" The question was of course rhetorical. By posing it, he had segued from an issue involving a competent terminally ill patient in excruciating pain to the question of whether society may destroy individuals whose lives have no value, either for themselves or for society.[4]

Binding identified three groups who qualified for his proposed euthanasia measures: (1) terminally ill patients (including the mortally wounded) who expressed their wish for a premature death; (2) "incurable idiots," no matter whether their idiocy was congenital or acquired; and (3) people who had suffered grievous physical war injuries that rendered them unconscious but who would desire a foreshortening of their lives if they were able to express their wishes. These three groups represented a class of individuals Binding called *lebensunwertes Leben* ("life unworthy of life"), an ambiguous phrase that covered persons whose lives had been made unbearable because of physical pain *and* persons whom society regarded as so defective by virtue of their mental impairment that their lives had no value.[5]

Unlike terminally ill patients, who under Binding and Hoche's proposals could freely choose euthanasia to end prolonged suffering, the state could destroy

Die
Freigabe der Vernichtung lebensunwerten Lebens
Ihr Maß und ihre Form
Zweite Auflage
Von den Professoren
Dr. jur. et phil. Karl Binding und Dr. med. Alfred Hoche

A fateful document in the historical prologue to the Nazis' extermination of the mentally ill was a pamphlet authored by Karl Binding and Alfred Hoche, The Permission to Destroy Life Unworthy of Life, *published in 1920. An apologia for the planned, systematic killing of the mentally disabled, the pamphlet would be widely cited by both the T-4 killers and postwar German courts responsible for adjudicating their crimes. Courtesy U.S. Holocaust Memorial Museum Collection* the "inferiors" even if they would otherwise live without pain for years. Binding conjured visions of battlefields strewn with the flower of German youth, contrasting their sacrifice with the pointless maintenance of worthless "idiots": "If one thinks of a battlefield covered with thousands of dead youth . . . and contrasts this with our institutions for the feebleminded with their solicitude for their living patients—then one would be deeply shocked by the glaring disjunction between the sacrifice of the most valuable possession of humanity on one side and on the other the greatest care of beings who are not only worthless but even manifest negative value." Binding goes on to describe the "terribly difficult burden" that the "incurably" feebleminded imposed on both their families and society. Enormous amounts of money and medical personnel were lavished on them, while the basic needs of the healthy went unmet. In his section of the tract, Hoche concurred with Binding's points. He referred to the mentally retarded and feebleminded as "ballast" that could be jettisoned to right the ship of state, and echoed Binding's economistic argument for killing them: "It is a distressing idea," he laments, "that entire generations of nurses shall vegetate next to such empty human shells, many of whom will live to be seventy years or even older." Hoche was untroubled by violations of the Hippocratic Oath, which he dismissed as a superannuated document "of ancient times." Instead, he asserted the physician's duty to promote the interests of the collective, even at the cost of sacrificing the lives of "idiots."[6]

Binding ends his contribution with an outline of procedures to govern the proposed killing program. The patient, the doctor, or the patient's relatives could initiate a request for euthanasia, but only the state could authorize it. Binding provided for a panel of "experts" consisting of a jurist and two doctors responsible for evaluating each application. Their decision, Binding stipulated, had to rest on the most current scientific knowledge, the mode of killing had to be "absolutely painless," and the person administering the killing had to be an expert. Errors would doubtlessly occur, but Binding brushed them aside, because "humanity loses due to error so many members, that one more or less really does not make a difference."[7]

Binding and Hoche's work ignited a vigorous debate among lawyers, doctors, and theologians in Weimar Germany. A leading critic of their thesis was Ewald Meltzer, director of the Katharinenhof psychiatric hospital in Saxony. Meltzer's is one of the obscure but extraordinary voices in twentieth-century European history. His scalding retort to the euthanasia school suggests that proto-Nazi ideas of biological inferiority and mass murder were not entrenched in Germany prior to 1933. He presciently warned in 1925 of the slippery slope down which euthanasia could take Germany, and with comparable foresight pointed out that to assign such power over life and death to the state would invest it with tyrannical control over its citizens. Further, he asserted, the mentally handicapped slated for killing under the Binding/Hoche proposal had in fact retained human personalities and were capable of enjoying their lives.[8]

Troubled by the controversy over Binding and Hoche's pamphlet, Meltzer conducted a survey in 1920 to explore parental attitudes toward the euthanasia of their incurable mentally ill children. The central question of the survey read: "Would you agree to the painless curtailment of the life of your child if experts had established that it was suffering from incurable idiocy?"[9] Meltzer was astonished when, of the 162 parents who responded, 119 (73 percent) answered in the affirmative. These parents sought relief from the burden of a severely handicapped child, but they wished to be disburdened without their knowledge. Some even desired that the physicians "deceive" them by identifying false causes of death. Postwar doctors facing prosecution for their involvement in the National Socialist euthanasia program would later invoke the Meltzer survey to justify the cloak of secrecy and deceit thrown around the killing program.

Parental support for destroying "unworthy" life to the contrary, the German medical profession opposed it during the Weimar Republic. A change in attitudes toward the mentally ill, however, gradually crept over the German medical community in the 1920s. Perhaps the most momentous contribution to this change was a shift of the doctor's duty from the individual patient to the "body of the people." Late nineteenth-century eugenics had always subordinated the individual to the wellbeing of the collective, conceived as state, society, nation, or in Germany as *das Volk*. The prewar German eugenics movement, unlike its decentralized counterparts in the United States and Great Britain, was concentrated in a single group, the German Society for Race Hygiene. The society shared with U.S. and British eugenicists a belief in congenital "superiority" and "inferiority," setting for itself the aim of preserving Germany's "genetic heritage" from biological degeneracy. Prior to World War I, German eugenicists had de-emphasized the negative implications of their beliefs (i.e., sterilization of the unfit), realizing that little support existed for it in the population, and focused instead on promoting the nation's health by raising the birthrate of "superior" individuals. The privations of Germany's military collapse, however, radicalized German eugenics. Among physicians, the locus of care shifted from the individual to the community. Because German eugenicists tended to be physicians and academic psychiatrists working in state hospitals and university clinics, this meant that caregivers directly responsible for the mentally handicapped were abandoning the Hippocratic ethic of devotion to their patients' wellbeing. As early as 1915 Alfred Hoche, reflecting an attitude that would win increasing support in the 1920s and 1930s, proclaimed the end of individualism and the beginning of a new order in which the nation emerged as an organism with rights ascendant to those of the individual.[10]

The Germans did not have a monopoly on eugenic ideas of social improvement. The founders of eugenic thought—Thomas Huxley, Francis Galton, Herbert Spencer, and Karl Pearson—were British. Influenced by their thought, U.S. eugenicists like Charles Davenport and H. H. Goddard embraced a hereditarian view of social characteristics, constructing hierarchies that ranked individuals, groups, races, and nations in terms of their biological value. Yet, despite the presence of eugenic policy and practice in other Western countries, only in Germany did state-organized mass killing of the mentally handicapped come into being. As mentioned previously, one of the primary reasons for Germany's singularity was the brutalizing effects of World War I, which wrought a change in the German medical profession's attitude toward "life unworthy of life," causing ever larger numbers of doctors, psychiatrists, and health officials to embrace radical approaches to treating the mentally ill. Organic views of society as a biological organism in need of medical care gradually supplanted the Hippocratic devotion of the doctor to the individual patient. A tendency to problematize the care and treatment of "worthless life" manifested itself; in addressing this "problem," mainstream voices in the German medical and public health fields increasingly called for violent "solutions" by the state in the form of forced sterilization or outright killing of patients. A position advocated only by fringe elements prior to the war had become a part of mainstream public policy discourse by the 1920s.

THE NAZIS IN POWER: STERILIZATION AND THE BEGINNING OF "EUTHANASIA," 1933–1939

The most obvious and important reason why Germany became the cradle of medical mass murder is politics. A political party sympathetic to the most radical views of German eugenicists, the National Socialist German Workers Party (NSDAP), came to power in January 1933. The rise of the Nazis was at once the victory of the most radical far-right political movement in Germany and the defeat of those moderates who in earlier decades had consistently opposed eugenic and racial-hygienic proposals. By the time Hitler came to power, these voices of criticism had been silenced, effectively relegated to the fringe.

Although numerous German political parties endorsed, in varying degree, the idea of eugenic sterilization, none was as fervent in its support as the Nazi Party. In 1931 Hitler identified sterilization as "the most humane act for mankind," urging his listeners to overcome their misplaced pity and misgivings about it. His call for a sweeping program to sterilize a substantial number of the German population received plaudits from eugenicists like Fritz Lenz and Ernst Rüdin, who lauded Hitler for being the only politician to introduce "the importance of eugenics . . . to all intelligent Germans."[11] Prior to 1933, however, involuntary eugenic sterilization was an act of criminal assault under German law. With political power came the opportunity and means to change the status quo. Hitler published a sterilization law on July 26, 1933, that would become effective on January 1, 1934. It was modeled on an earlier Prussian proposal from 1932, with the critical difference that the Nazi variant did not require the consent of the affected individual. The law made it legally permissible to sterilize any person suffering from the following illnesses: "(1) congenital feeblemindedness; (2) schizophrenia; (3) manic-depressive psychosis; (4) hereditary epilepsy; (5) Huntington's chorea; (6) hereditary blindness; (7) hereditary deafness; (8) severe hereditary physical deformity; or (9) severe alcoholism on a discretionary basis." It went on to establish a legal procedure for sterilization. The mentally handicapped patients themselves, public health service doctors, and directors of hospitals, nursing homes, and prisons were all competent to apply for sterilization under the new guidelines. Hereditary health courts would receive and evaluate all applications. Each court was attached to a local court of general jurisdiction (*Amtsgericht*), and consisted of three members: an *Amtsrichter*, or judge; a doctor from the public health service; and a physician specializing in genetics. A system to handle cases on appeal was built into the regional appellate courts (*Oberlandesgerichte*); a similar triad of one judge and two doctors constituted these courts of appeal, the decisions of which were final and nonappealable.[12]

A positive finding by the courts in a given case permitted local health authorities throughout Germany to sterilize the person, whether or not consent was given. With the passage of the law, nonconsensual sterilization ceased to be a criminal assault and battery; in fact, now physicians and public health officials could invoke the police power to enforce compliance. In the years following the law's passage, these local and state doctors and administrators had tens of thousands of German men and women involuntarily sterilized. In 1934 the majority (52.9 percent) were the "feeble-minded," followed by those diagnosed with schizophrenia (25.4 percent) and epilepsy (14 percent). The criteria for a presumptive case of feeblemindedness were lying, argumentativeness, laziness, and receptiveness to influence. The overarching issue, however, was the question of the person's value to the *Volk*: if a case could be made for the person's social usefulness, sterilization might be stayed; if not, then the decision was made to proceed.[13] The inflationary potential for including ever-greater numbers of people in this largest of the sterilization categories is clear and prefigures the expansive direction the euthanasia program would take in coming years, as it swept up into its net mentally ill children, then mentally ill adults, and later Jews, Gypsies, shell-shocked residents of bombed-out cities, and "asocials."

The wave of legislation between 1933 and 1936, of which the sterilization law was a part, identified categories of "unworthy life" that would become the targets of National Socialist killing policy between 1939 and 1945. The Law for the Prevention of Offspring with Hereditary Diseases, published in July 1933, was followed by another four months later, the Law Against Dangerous Habitual Criminals and Regulation of Security and Reform (enacted on November 11, 1933). Section 42 of this law provided that *Asozialen* (asocials) could be detained in mental institutions if they were deemed by the courts to have committed their crimes in a state of diminished responsibility. It also permitted authorities to detain recidivists in public workhouses and detoxification centers and required castration for sexual offenders. Finally, the law forbade offenders from working in their professions.[14]

For both habitual criminals and the mentally ill, the basis of their "worthlessness" was considered genetic and unalterable. (In the Commentary to the sterilization law, the authors declared that "there can be no doubt that the predisposition for crime is also hereditary."[15]) For decades eugenicists and racial hygienists had associated mental disability with criminal activity. The Nazis' detention law made this alleged connection explicit by establishing a legal basis for imprisoning the "asocials" in mental hospitals. During the war, as we will see, many of these individuals were caught up in the euthanasia program or deported to concentration camps for extermination through work.

At his trial in front of the American NMT in 1947, Karl Brandt, Hitler's escort physician and later a leading euthanasia operative, testified that sometime in 1935 Hitler had informed Reich Health Leader Gerhard Wagner of his intention to implement euthanasia of the mentally disabled once war had begun. According to Brandt, Hitler believed the opposition to euthanasia from church circles would be less pronounced during war than in peacetime.[16] Despite voices demonstrably sympathetic to euthanasia within both the Catholic and Protestant churches, the National Socialists remained apprehensive in the late 1930s of ecclesiastical attitudes toward a formal euthanasia program. Albert Hartl, an ex-priest and from 1935 the Chief of Church Information for the government's security service, testified before a German court in 1970 that Reinhard Heydrich (later head of the Reich Security Main Office, to which Hitler entrusted execution of the Final Solution) instructed him in 1938 to report to Viktor Brack of the Führer's personal chancellery (*Kanzlei des Führers,* or KdF). Brack would inform him of a top-secret matter, concerning which he would receive further orders. When Hartl met with Brack, the latter related that a considerable number of petitions had arrived at the KdF requesting that "incurable patients be granted a mercy death." Brack stated, however, that Hitler had expressed reservations about euthanasia because of possible opposition from the Catholic and Protestant churches. As a trained theologian, Hartl was in an ideal position to evaluate the attitudes of the churches toward euthanasia. Accordingly he was commissioned to prepare a report on the subject.[17]

Hartl allegedly expressed to Brack his qualms about preparing such a study, because he did not feel competent to do so. Instead, he contacted moral theologian Dr. Josef Mayer, the author of the 1927 *Legal Sterilization of the Mentally Ill*. Mayer had already declared his openness to the possibility of eugenic sterilization; for this reason, Hartl believed he would be qualified to address the question of the Church's attitude toward it. Hartl met with Mayer in early 1939 and offered him the job of preparing a memorandum on the subject. Mayer accepted, and six months later Hartl received five copies of the completed 100-page memorandum. In his judicial testimony, Hartl recalled that Mayer's study was "neither 100 percent in favor of nor against euthanasia." Mayer's equivocal conclusion was based on the history of debate about the destruction of "unworthy life": because authorities for centuries had marshaled sound arguments pro and con, euthanasia was a "defensible" act. Copies of Mayer's study were forwarded to Viktor Brack in the KdF, who approached Hitler with Mayer's findings. In a subsequent meeting, Brack told Hartl that, in view of Mayer's opinion that the Church would not strenuously condemn euthanasia, Hitler had overcome his own reservations about it. The green light had been given, and the euthanasia program could now begin.[18]

CHILDREN'S EUTHANASIA, 1938–1941: THE KNAUER CASE AND THE BEGINNING OF THE CHILDREN'S OPERATION

According to Albert Hartl, the decision to proceed with killing mentally ill patients was made sometime during summer 1939, probably in July. As early as 1938, however, the Nazi government had participated in the destruction of mentally handicapped children. In that year, a severely handicapped child from a family called Knauer was admitted to the Children's Clinic at Leipzig University. The child's father requested that the director, Werner Catel, euthanize the child, an entreaty that Catel declined on legal grounds. The father then applied directly to Hitler through his private chancellery for permission to kill the child. Hitler was intrigued by the case and sent his escort physician, Karl Brandt, to see the child to determine whether he was as severely handicapped as the family claimed in their petition. Brandt traveled to Leipzig, confirmed the doctors' diagnosis, and authorized them to euthanize the child, which was done shortly thereafter. Hitler authorized Brandt and the chief of the KdF, Philipp Bouhler, to take the same actions in all future cases of a similar nature.

Adolf Hitler shaking hands with Philipp Bouhler, chief of the Führer's private chancellery, on October 1, 1938, one year before Hitler authorized him and Karl Brandt to implement the destruction of the mentally ill. Courtesy Bundesarchiv Koblenz

The Knauer case inaugurated the "Children's Operation," a program designed to kill mentally and physically handicapped children.[19]

As Hartl testified in 1970, the Knauer family's petition for euthanasia was only one of a multitude of similar requests for a "mercy death" received by the KdF. This organization, intimately associated with the person of Adolf Hitler, was destined to play a central role in the mass murder committed by the Nazis during the war. The KdF was not a state but a party agency, separate from the Nazi Party Chancellery located in the Munich party headquarters and from Hitler's Presidential Chancellery. It was also independent of the Reich Chancellery under Hans Heinrich Lammers. Hitler had established it as the "Chancellery of the Führer of the Nazi Party" in 1934 to handle correspondence from party members specifically addressed to him. The aim was to create the impression of Hitler's accessibility to the rank and file. Although much of the correspondence that flowed into the chancellery's offices was trivial, the volume grew to 250,000 letters by the late 1930s. The request of the Knauer parents that a mercy death be administered to their child was just a molecule in the ocean of correspondence that flooded into the chancellery in 1938.[20]

Hitler could have entrusted the children's euthanasia program to other offices within the Reich government or the party, such as the Reich Ministry of the Interior (within the Reich Chancellery), the Party Chancellery, or the SS. That he chose to give the commission to his own personal chancellery requires some explanation. Two factors may account for this election. First, the role of the KdF within the National Socialist system of government virtually guaranteed its participation in euthanasia when Hitler had finally resolved to implement it. In 1938 Hitler's chancellery consisted of five offices. Of the five, Main Office II, which typically handled "matters affecting the state and party," was responsible for dealing with applications to Hitler. The chief of Main Office II was Viktor Brack, the bureaucrat who had given Hartl his orders to feel out the Church's position regarding euthanasia. (We will encounter Brack again when we turn to the U.S. "Doctors' Trial," for he was a major figure not only in the Nazis' murder of the mentally disabled, but in the unfolding of the Holocaust in 1941 and 1942.) Within Main Office II, Office IIb (with Dr. Hans Hefelmann as chief) was charged with solving average Germans' problems with the state and party governmental organs, and to do so in an informal manner. The key word here is "informal": the very inconspicuousness of the KdF in the bureaucratic wilderness of the Nazi state, along with its intimate ties to Hitler, enabled the organization to fulfill Hitler's wishes without going through the customary bureaucratic channels. It could, in short, act directly, discreetly, and without hindrance to accomplish the tasks given it by the Führer. In view of its very raison d'être, we should not be surprised that the director of Office IIb, Hans Hefelmann, was placed in charge of the children's euthanasia program (although Viktor Brack was Bouhler's choice as general head of the killing program).

Second, the chancellery's closeness to Hitler recommended it as an executory agency of the euthanasia program. As Henry Friedlander has pointed out, to have entrusted the program to a government office (e.g., the Reich Ministry of the Interior) would have expanded the number of officials with knowledge of it. The larger the circle of people aware of euthanasia killing was, the greater the chance the public would discover what was happening. Although Hitler had some basis for believing the German public might accept "mercy killing," he still feared popular opposition and unrest. Further, commissioning a state agency with the program would have required a paper trail of official orders signed by Hitler—orders that Hitler was loath to put into writing. Similarly, had he given the task to a prominent Nazi Party office like the SS, the participation of conspicuous party members in the killing program might have compromised its secrecy. By charging his own chancellery with implementing euthanasia, on the other hand, Hitler could rest assured that a low-profile, compact, and relatively independent organization devoted exclusively to his own person would carry out the killing quietly and with discretion. Thus, the KdF was a natural vehicle for officially sanctioned but secret mass murder.[21]

The KdF was the leading organizer and administrator of Nazi euthanasia (including the children's operation), but it was not the only government office involved in the killing process. Department IV ("Public Health Service and Care of the *Volk*") of the Reich Ministry of the Interior became the sole non-party office to participate in the euthanasia program. Department IV oversaw the local health administrations of the individual German states (*Länder*) and supervised the state mental hospitals. From the earliest years of the Nazi regime, it was no stranger to state violence against the disabled: as part of its mandate to improve the public health, it had been an enforcer of the government's racial and eugenic laws. The chief of Department IV, Dr. Leonardo Conti, was an erstwhile physician of the "martyred" Horst Wessel and founder of the Nazi Doctor's Association in Berlin. Conti was a true apostle of the National Socialist world view: asked about the Nazi law published in 1938 barring Jewish doctors from treating Aryans, Conti replied, "It is only the elimination of the Jewish element which provides for the German doctor the living space due to him." One level below Conti in Department IV was Dr. Herbert Linden, who served as a section chief at the rank of ministerial councillor. As section chief, Linden superintended state hospitals, nursing homes, and the regime's marital and sterilization legislation. In addition, he had been a coauthor with Arthur Gütt on a commentary on the Nuremberg and sterilization laws. Thus jurisdictional competence, along with the eugenic interests of Department IV's directors, drew the Reich Ministry of the Interior ineluctably into collaboration with the euthanasia program.[22]

Shortly after the Knauer case had been addressed in 1938, Viktor Brack, Hans Hefelmann, and Herbert Linden met to discuss the commission that Hitler had given Brandt and Bouhler. They developed a plan of action, then expanded the planning group to include pro-euthanasia doctors—Karl Brandt, Werner Catel, Hans Heinze, Hellmuth Unger, and Ernst Wentzler. The reasons for including these five men are straightforward. Brandt had been involved in the Knauer case and had been given co-responsibility with Bouhler for euthanasia; Catel had been director of the Leipzig clinic where the Knauer baby was born. Heinze was a psychiatrist and neurologist in charge of the Brandenburg-Görden state hospital and had been recommended by Linden for inclusion in the planning group. Unger, an ophthalmologist, had written a novel called *Mission and Conscience* that advocated euthanasia. (The novel was later adapted as a screenplay for the propaganda film *I Accuse*, intended to generate support among the German people for "mercy killing.") Wentzler was a Berlin pediatrician recommended by Reich Health Leader Leonardo Conti.[23]

From its earliest stages, the program was shrouded in secrecy, labeled a "secret Reich matter." Subsequent initiates into the program, especially at the field level, were admonished that divulging details of the euthanasia campaign to unauthorized persons would result in the severest punishment, possibly even the death penalty. The most striking feature of the Nazis' dissimulation was the elaborate structure of camouflage organizations invented to hide the central role of Hitler's personal chancellery in the killing. The members of the group planning the children's euthanasia realized that an organization so closely connected to Hitler should not be the direct conveyor of orders to kill handicapped children—at least not on the surface. Accordingly, they concocted a sham organization with an impressively scientific name: the Reich Committee for the Scientific Registration of Severe Hereditary Ailments. This organization, it must be stressed, was purely fictitious; from its origins, its sole purpose was to mask the involvement of KdF members in systematic murder. In fact, the nominal heads of the committee were two high-ranking chancellery officials, Hans Hefelmann, chief of Office IIb of the KdF, and his deputy, Richard von Hegener. To thicken the fog of secrecy, Hefelmann and von Hegener used the pseudonym "Dr. Klein" in all committee correspondence relating to euthanasia. This practice of using false names was common among euthanasia officials and physicians during the war.[24]

The clandestine nature of the euthanasia program is one of its most arresting aspects. Why did the architects of euthanasia, from Hitler and his chancellery officials to the physicians and nurses in the killing centers, insist so strenuously on keeping the program secret? There is no unambiguous answer to this question. The most cogent theory is that Hitler and his associates feared public reaction were the program to be disclosed. We know that Hitler ultimately rejected his subordinates' pleas for a formal euthanasia law because of the damaging uses to which it could be put in foreign propaganda. Real or not, Hitler's concern for enemy propaganda may reflect the actual ground for the program's secrecy: a genuine apprehension that the German people might not accept the destruction of their mentally disabled relatives and countrymen. If this explanation of the program's secrecy is true, then it helps illuminate how the Führer conceived of the wrongfulness of killing disabled patients. Like his agents in the regime's killing projects, he was aware that the euthanasia program clashed with traditional German moral and legal culture. The extraordinary lengths the Nazis resorted to in order to conceal the euthanasia program is a significant index of their realization that the laws and mores of German society would condemn euthanasia, no matter how much the public was indoctrinated with the ideology of "life unworthy of life."

In addition to creating the bogus Reich Committee for the Scientific Registration of Severe Hereditary Ailments, the euthanasia planning group faced a fundamental logistical problem: how would the killing experts in the KdF know precisely who qualified for destruction and where were they to be found? The problem was solved with the introduction of a registration system, on the basis of which infant patients would be selected for killing. Registration forms would be sent to mental hospitals, nursing homes, and pediatrics clinics throughout Germany, where on-site medical staff would fill them out for each of their patients and return them to the committee. The forms arrived at a post office box in Berlin; from there, Hefelmann and von Hegener picked them up for distribution to a group of experts for review.[25] Sometime in summer 1939, this planning phase came to an end. In the meantime, Mayer had delivered his memorandum on the Church's conjectured acquiescence to euthanasia, allaying Hitler's fears of a religious backlash. Meditating on the impending war against Poland, Hitler may have felt it was time to initiate the killing program he had mentioned to Gerhard Wagner in 1935. The first systematic killings of handicapped children would occur in October 1939—scarcely one month after the war had started.

The Reich Ministry of the Interior stiffened the enforcement arm of the euthanasia planners on August 18, 1939, with a decree, the "Requirement to Report Deformed etc. Newborns." The decree, like virtually everything connected with the killing program, was designated a "secret Reich matter," a status that explained why it did not appear in the official ministry gazette. Its source was Department IV of the Interior Ministry. The decree enjoined all midwives and physicians to report to the competent local health office newborns and children under the age of three "suspected" of suffering from the following "congenital" illnesses:

(1) idiocy as well as mongolism (especially cases involving blindness and deafness);

(2) microcephaly;

(3) hydrocephaly of a severe and advanced degree;

(4) deformities of every kind, especially missing limbs, severely defective closure of the head and the vertebrae, etc.;

(5) paralysis, including Little's Illness (i.e., spastic diplegia).[26]

Attached to the decree was a reporting form to be filled out by the health-care provider. The form required, among other things, name, age, and sex of the child, description of the illness, impact of the illness on the child's ability to function in the hospital, estimated life expectancy, and prognosis for improvement. Once health-care providers had completed and forwarded these reports to local health officials, the reports were sent to the committee postbox in Berlin for review by the expert evaluators.

The preamble to the reporting decree offered no hint of the actual reasons behind the procedure. Instead, the language of the preamble lent a reassuring air of scientific legitimacy to it: "In order to clarify scientific questions about deformed newborns and mental retardation, the earliest possible registration of appropriate cases is necessary." Despite the uncanny secretiveness of the procedure and the curious use of a post office box to receive the completed forms, the reporting process was broadly accepted as an innocuous request for governmental data.[27]

Once the forms arrived in Berlin, Hefelmann and von Hegener of the KdF collected and sorted them. Although neither man had a medical background, each selected the forms deemed appropriate for review and passed them on to three experts in the KdF: Werner Catel, Hans Heinze, and Ernst Wentzler. We have already encountered this trio in our discussion of the euthanasia planning group; each was a committed advocate of killing the mentally disabled. The KdF attached its own form to every copy of the incoming reports. It bore the letterhead of the fictitious "Reich Committee" and contained little space for explanatory comments. A cryptic semiotic system determined the life or death of the child: a plus sign (+) meant that the child was to be destroyed, a minus sign (–) signified that the child's life would be spared. Final decision about uncertain cases was deferred with the word "observation." In the absence of carbon copies, the same forms along with the original reports were sent to each of the three experts for review and notation—meaning that each expert knew how the others had voted.[28]

When the experts arrived at a positive finding, the committee wrote to the local public health office with orders to prepare the selected child for transport to one of several "children's wards" established in state mental institutions and clinics throughout Germany. The sole purpose of these children's wards was to kill mentally and physically disabled children. The first was erected at Brandenburg-Görden near Berlin under the direction of the Hitler chancellery expert Hans Heinze. Subsequently, children's wards were erected in clinics throughout the German Reich. There were approximately thirty such wards, staffed with medical personnel recruited for killing by the KdF. Hefelmann and von Hegener of the KdF, Office IIb, and Herbert Linden of Department IV of the Reich Ministry of the Interior did the recruiting. Once a doctor agreed to participate in the euthanasia program, he or she became an associate of the committee.[29]

The children's ward at Brandenburg-Görden was the prototype for those that followed. Hermann Wesse, indicted by German authorities in 1947 for his involvement in child murder at the Rhineland mental hospital Waldniel, was mentored at Brandenburg-Görden before undertaking his killing assignments. Furthermore, the director of the institution, Hans Heinze, and his students used the occasion of the children's deaths to conduct medical research—a practice that would become characteristic of the euthanasia program in general (as well as the Holocaust) as it spun outward to embrace mentally ill adults.

At Brandenburg-Görden and the other children's wards, the KdF left it to their hand-selected physicians to devise efficient means of killing. Their preferred method was overdoses of medication. At Steinhof in Vienna, mentally disabled children were given excessive dosages of morphine-scopolamine; at Eglfing-Haar in Bavaria, they received lethal cocktails of luminal and veronal. The "medication" usually was administered in tablets or in liquid form to the children. Occasionally, it was injected directly into them. From the standpoint of preserving secrecy, there was much to commend these medications as killing agents. First, they were readily available in German mental hospitals as sedatives. Second, they were not poisons and became deadly only in overdoses. Third, they did not immediately kill the child; rather, they typically gave rise to complications like pneumonia, which then became the "official" cause of death after two or three days. The physician could then soberly ascribe the child's death to a conventional cause, rather than to poisoning. Although the KdF supplied the children's wards with sufficient amounts of morphine, veronal, and other sedatives, the chancellery's own supplier was Office V of the Reich Security Main Office, the Criminal Police Office (Kripo). From the time the children's wards were established until the end of the war, Kripo was the KdF's main provider of medications used to kill both mentally ill children and adults.[30]

Clearly, this program required that the children identified by the chancellery's medical experts for killing be transported to the children's wards. The chancellery did not itself arrange the children's transfer; rather, this was left to individual state health offices within local ministries of the interior. Thus, for example, Business Section X of the Württemberg Ministry of the Interior, which administered mental institutions in both Baden and Württemberg, orchestrated the transportation of ninety-three children from Württemberg institutions in late 1942 to the children's ward at Eichberg, where they were murdered. The order to put the children to death, however, always originated with the central authorities at the KdF, working through their front organization, the Reich Committee for the Scientific Registration of Severe Hereditary Ailments. The killing order arrived as an official document under the letterhead of the committee, bearing the signature of a chancellery bureaucrat.[31] The language of the order was couched in euphemisms: the word "treatment" (Behandlung) functioned as a code word for killing.

The incomplete historical record makes a death toll for the children's action impossible to ascertain with certainty. The Frankfurt prosecutor's indictment of Werner Heyde, Gerhard Bohne, and Hans Hefelmann in May 1962 estimated a figure of around 5,000.

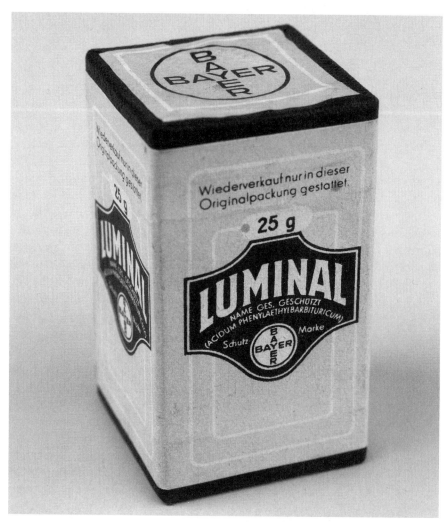

A canister of the sedative luminal, used in overdoses by T-4 medical personnel to cause the deaths of handicapped children during the children's euthanasia program. Luminal was sometimes mixed with veronal as a lethal cocktail and administered through injections or in tablet or liquid form. Courtesy Bayer-Archiv, Leverkusen

THE ADULT EUTHANASIA PROGRAM, PHASE ONE (1939–1941)

Children's euthanasia was a prologue to the more ambitious and destructive campaign to kill mentally ill adults. Sometime in July 1939, Hitler commissioned Karl Brandt and Philipp Bouhler to organize adult euthanasia. In collaboration with Herbert Linden of the Reich Ministry of the Interior's Department IV, they assembled a circle of ideologically reliable doctors to assist with planning and executing the program. The circle included, inter alia, the chaired professor of neurology and psychiatry, Max de Crinis; the director of the Clinic for Psychiatry and Neurology of Heidelberg University, Carl Schneider; Professor Berthold Kihn of Jena; and Werner Heyde, professor of psychiatry and neurology at the University of Würzburg. In late July and August 1939, a series of meetings occurred between these hand-selected individuals in Berlin. Bouhler explained to the participants that euthanizing mental patients in German asylums and nursing homes would create necessary hospital space for the impending war and free up medical staff to care for the wounded. He further indicated that Hitler had refrained from publishing a euthanasia law for foreign policy reasons but reassured the attendees that they would be immune from criminal prosecution for their actions in connection with the killing program. He then invited dissenters to withdraw from involvement if they so desired. None present opted out.[32]

After the initial recruitment meeting with Bouhler in summer 1939, the physicians returned to their institutions and sought out suitable personnel there for the work of mass killing. The names of these individuals were then relayed to the KdF in Berlin. In the meantime, having found accomplices for their murder project, Bouhler and Brack applied their ingenuity to choosing an appropriate means of killing. Desiring something that was quick, lethal, and painless, they consulted three prominent pharmacologists, who recommended the substance that would become the murder agent of choice in the first phase of Nazi euthanasia: carbon monoxide gas. A chemist in the Criminal Technical Institute (KTI) within the Reich Security Main Office, Dr. Albert Widmann, confirmed the pharmacologists' recommendation in a meeting with Brack. Brack commissioned Widmann and the KTI to obtain canisters of carbon monoxide and deliver them to the KdF. Widmann accepted this commission and thereafter received orders for the poison from the individual killing centers, which he filled in the name of the KTI at the I. G. Farben factories in Ludwigshafen. A chancellery official, Dr. August Becker, arranged for picking up and transporting the carbon monoxide canisters to the killing centers. All costs incidental to these orders were charged to the KTI.[33]

Concerns about the legality of the killing program nonetheless persisted. Under German law (StGB section 211), illicitly killing a human being was a capital offense in Germany even during the Nazi era. At a meeting convoked by Hitler sometime in September 1939 to discuss the euthanasia program, the chief of the Reich Chancellery and Hitler's closest legal advisor, Hans Heinrich Lammers, argued that the program should be established on a legal basis. If Lammers's testimony under U.S. Army interrogation is to be believed, Hitler commissioned Lammers with drafting a euthanasia law. The draft was prepared accordingly, but Hitler subsequently changed his mind on the grounds that an official law would "cause too great a sensation."[34] Throughout the duration of the killing program, many of the health-care providers and public health officials involved would express their fears of criminal liability without an authorizing statute. Acting on their concerns, the KdF asked Hitler for a written authorization for euthanasia. He assented, and the chancellery prepared for his signature an authorizing document, printed on Hitler's own stationery. He signed the authorization in October 1939, but backdated it to September 1, 1939, perhaps in an attempt to convey the symbolic linkage of the war with purifying the *Volkskörper*. Because so many postwar German defendants would appeal to this document as a legal basis for their actions, it merits quotation in full:

> Berlin, 1 September 1939
>   Reich Leader Bouhler and Dr. med. Brandt are charged with the responsibility of enlarging the competence of certain physicians, designated by name, so that patients who, on the basis of human judgment, are considered incurable can be granted mercy death after a critical evaluation of their state of health.
>
>   (signed) A. Hitler[35]

The legal status of this "euthanasia authorization" was hotly debated in the postwar euthanasia trials, when doctors implicated in the mass killing of disabled patients invoked it as a legal justification for their activities. Never was the decree accepted by a West German court as a valid law, as we will see in subsequent chapters.

Although Bouhler was in charge of the adult euthanasia program, he rarely participated in its daily operations. He chose, rather, to entrust the hands-on supervision of euthanasia to his deputy, the chief of Section II of the chancellery, Viktor Brack. Brack, whose educational background was not in medicine but in agriculture (he received a diploma in agriculture from the University of Munich in 1927), confronted the task of designing a killing program that, like the fictive Reich Committee in the children's euthanasia program, would conceal the central role of the KdF. From the beginning, it was understood that adult euthanasia would surpass in scope the relatively modest children's operation. It was therefore clear to Brack and his associates that their current offices on Voss Strasse in Berlin would be inadequate to accommodate the enlarged staff needed to administer the program. Central Office II of the KdF thus relocated to a confiscated Jewish house at number 4, Tiergartenstrasse, in Berlin-Charlottenburg. This address was eponymous for the central killing administration, which was thereafter referred to as "T-4"; the killing program itself was called "Operation T-4" (*Aktion T-4*).[36]

"T-4" (i.e., the KdF, Main Office II) subsumed numerous offices within its bureaucratic structure. These offices—particularly the T-4 Medical Office, which evaluated registration forms, selected patients for killing, and both appointed and trained the medical staffs detailed to the killing centers—were the sub-rosa puppet masters behind a series of front organizations invented by the KdF to disguise its direction of the program. Whereas in the children's euthanasia a single front organization, the Reich Committee, concealed the chancellery's involvement, four such entities were established for the adult program: (1) the Reich Cooperative for State Hospitals and Nursing Homes; (2) the Charitable Foundation for Institutional Care; (3) the Central Accounting Office for State Hospitals and Nursing Homes; and (4) the Charitable Foundation for the Transport of Patients, Inc. The Reich Cooperative for State Hospitals and Nursing Homes (RAG), a front for the T-4 Medical Office, conducted correspondence with private and governmental parties about the process of registering, evaluating, and selecting adult patients for euthanasia. The Charitable Foundation for Institutional Care was a front for the T-4 Central Office and dealt with all matters related to financing the program, including hiring and compensating employees of T-4. The Central Accounting Office for State Hospitals and Nursing Homes collected payments for patient care. Its practice of charging per diem expenses for patients even after they had been liquidated enabled T-4 to run consistently in the black, using the excess proceeds to finance its operations. The Charitable Foundation for the Transport of Patients, Inc., (*Gemeinnützige Kranken-Transport G.m.b.H.*, or Gekrat) camouflaged the T-4 Transport Office; it transferred patients selected for euthanasia to the killing centers. The Reich Cooperative and Gekrat were established in November 1939; the Charitable Foundation for Institutional Care and the Central Accounting Office were erected in April 1940, coinciding with the Main Office II's move into the Tiergartenstrasse villa.[37]

As in the *Kinderaktion,* so with adult euthanasia a decree by the Reich Ministry of the Interior facilitated the registration process. On September 21, 1939, the Reich Ministry of the Interior issued a decree to state governmental offices called "The Registration of State Hospitals and Nursing Homes." It required that local authorities supply the names of all mental hospitals within their region to the Reich Ministry by October 15, 1939, in which "mental patients, epileptics, and the feebleminded" were institutionalized. All institutions, public, private, religious, and charitable, were included, as were old-age homes. The Ministry of the Interior informed the respondent state authorities that the information was needed because the ministry wished to send questionnaires directly to such institutions throughout Germany; local governments were to ensure timely completion and submission of the questionnaires. Once the lists of institutions had been returned, the Reich Ministry sent the questionnaires to them, either directly or through the local state offices. The documents consisted of a single-page questionnaire (called the *Meldebogen 2*) that canvassed data about size, staffing, and patient population of the institution. More ominously, it inquired about the number of patients with a criminal background, the number of Jewish patients, and the proximity of the institution to transportation arteries. In addition to *Meldebogen 2*, the document package included a set of one-page reporting forms (*Meldebogen 1*) to be filled out by a doctor on individual patients. The form asked for the name, birth date, nationality, race, period of institutionalization, the names of relatives and frequency of their visits, the name and address of the guardian and the payor, and whether the patient had been institutionalized for criminal insanity. Finally, the doctor was invited to offer a diagnosis in a cramped section on the form and to evaluate the patient's ability to perform work.[38]

Attached to these *Meldebogen* forms was a one-page instruction sheet that identified the kinds of patients to be registered. These included patients who had been institutionalized for five years or longer; patients suffering from schizophrenia, epilepsy, senile illnesses, therapy-resistant paralysis and other syphilitic diseases, feeblemindedness, encephalitis, Huntington's disease and other terminal neurological diseases—so long as these patients were incapable of any work in the institution other than pure mechanical work (such as weeding); patients institutionalized for criminal insanity; or patients who were neither German citizens nor of German or related blood. For patients falling into the last category, the instruction sheet required the reporting doctors to describe the citizenship and race of the patient. In a footnote, the sheet provided examples: "German, or related blood (German-blooded), Jewish, Jewish hybrid (*Mischling*) of the first or second degree, Negro, Negro hybrid, Gypsy, Gypsy hybrid, etc."[39]

Over the course of the euthanasia program, patients within each of the categories specified above would be annihilated. The single most important criterion for selection, however, was capacity for work. Already in September 1939, registration form 1 (*Meldebogen 1*) and the accompanying instruction sheet stressed the importance of labor productivity beyond mere "routine" work as a factor in identifying patients to be reported. The prewar literature on "life unworthy of life"—especially that strain of it inspired by Binding and Hoche's work—had made the utilitarian argument the linchpin of the pro-euthanasia viewpoint, referring to the mentally disabled as "ballast lives" and "useless eaters." In this sense, then, the Nazi assault on the mentally disabled can be interpreted as the terminus of post–World War I attitudes about the "uselessness" and costliness of such patients.

As it did with the children's program, the KdF established a system of medical experts to review the incoming registration forms submitted from German mental hospitals. The system of expert review in the adult example, however, was more intricate than the children's program. The Medical Office of Hitler's Chancellery, Section II, in its guise as the Reich Cooperative for

State Hospitals and Nursing Homes (RAG), established a two-tiered structure of expert review. The first tier consisted of medical experts to whom the registration forms were first sent for evaluation. Their assessments were then proofed by a second tier of experts to guard against error. Extant documentation indicates that approximately forty doctors, among them nine professors of medicine, served at one time or another as medical experts for T-4. Of this number, the overwhelming majority were first-tier experts. As the program unfolded, only three doctors—Werner Heyde, Paul Nitsche (Heyde's successor), and Herbert Linden—would function as second-tier experts.[40]

When the registration forms arrived at the Reich Ministry, Herbert Linden sent them to the T-4 Medical Office (the RAG), where they were collated and catalogued. Five photocopies were made of the original forms; one copy was sent to each of three first-tier medical experts for evaluation. After a period of time the photocopies were returned to the Medical Office, marked with one of three characters: a plus sign (+) in red meant that the patient was to be killed; a minus sign (–) in blue signified that the patient should be spared; and a question mark indicated a borderline case. A majority of the three first-level evaluators determined whether a patient lived or died; unanimity was not required. Once the three photocopies with their annotations were collected, they were sent with the original form and the other photocopy to the second-tier experts, typically Werner Heyde and Paul Nitsche. These men, in no way bound by the opinions of the first-tier experts, marked the additional photocopy with either a plus sign (death) or a minus sign (life). The second tier experts were the ultimate arbiters of life and death for the registered patients, determining literally with the stroke of a pen who would be allowed to live and who would be destroyed. If the form bore a plus sign, the RAG sent it to the T-4 Transport Office, which drafted lists of patients designated for killing.[41]

The RAG contacted the institutions that accommodated the selected patients several days prior to transport. The institutions, called by the T-4 killing specialists "surrendering institutions" and by the postwar German courts "original institutions," were instructed to send all medical records and personnel reports along with the patients, as well as all the patients' personal possessions (such as money and jewelry), which were to be logged on special forms. Prior to pickup day, Gekrat sent a list to the surrendering institution of patients to be transported. Perhaps as a result of the doctors' intentional practice of underestimating their patients' capacity for work, perhaps because of the haste with which the forms were reviewed by the T-4 experts, Gekrat's lists often contained the names of patients who did productive work in the institutions. In such cases, institutional directors tried to persuade the Gekrat representatives to exempt these patients from transport. Because a sum-certain quota of transportees had to be filled, Gekrat typically agreed to exemptions only if other patients could be substituted. The patients appearing on the final Gekrat list were picked up in large gray busses. Occasionally, some patients among those transferred sensed what was happening, and heartrending scenes of crying, pleading, and protest broke out as they were forced into the busses.[42]

Once the patients had left the surrendering institution, it notified the next of kin that the patient had been transferred to another facility on orders of the Reich defense commissar and that this facility would eventually contact them about their relative. Within a brief span of time, the killing center wrote to them that the patient had arrived, but it forbade them from visiting their relative with the assurance that they would be apprised of any change in his or her condition. When the patient was killed, the euthanasia center authorities informed the family of the death, ascribing it to natural causes and reporting that the risk of epidemic disease had forced the institution to cremate the body. An urn containing the ashes was available for shipment to them.[43]

It should be emphasized here that these patients were killed without their or their families' or guardians' consent. And they were not transferred with the notification and agreement of themselves, their families, or their guardians. The killers did not inform local magistrates who had institutionalized the patients; welfare and insurance organizations that financed their medical care were likewise kept in the dark.[44] The functioning of the murder apparatus was so mysterious that even the staffs of the surrendering institutions—at least at the beginning—often had no inkling of what lay in store for their patients. The postwar courts would seize on the byzantine aspect of the euthanasia program as evidence that the T-4 killers were fully conscious of the wrongfulness of their actions.

The stealth of the Nazis' euthanasia program had an immediate—and tragic—sequel. Doctors in local mental hospitals who completed the registration forms on their patients often did so without knowledge of the registration's purpose. In fact, in a rueful misapprehension of the central government's goals, many physicians deliberately underestimated their patients' ability to do work, fearing that patients capable of work would be sent away from the institution to perform war-related labor. As a result, these patients became ensnared in the nets of the T-4 killing program.[45]

The idea of establishing killing centers developed out of discussions between representatives of KdF, the Reich Ministry of the Interior, and the chemist Albert Widmann of the Criminal Technical Institute of the Reich Security

Main Office (RSHA). Under interrogation by German authorities in 1960, Widmann claimed that Leonardo Conti, the Reich Health Leader and head of the Department of Health in the Ministry of the Interior, had rejected injections as a killing agent in favor of poisonous gas. As we have seen, in the aftermath of these discussions, Widmann met with Viktor Brack to work out the mechanics of how patients would be gassed. Widmann's suggestion that carbon monoxide gas be released through the air ducts of the patients' hospital rooms was dismissed on practical grounds. The notion of the killing center emerged as a more expedient alternative.[46]

Brack and Karl Brandt had a short-lived difference of opinion about the most efficacious way to kill the patients. From his discussions with Widmann, Brack was convinced of carbon monoxide's utility. Brandt, however, initially opposed this idea, arguing that because the euthanasia program involved "medical measures," a correspondingly "medical means" must be adopted; he favored injections. (Brandt eventually overcame his scruples and agreed on carbon monoxide.) The decision to test the effectiveness of carbon monoxide gas on human guinea pigs grew out of this disagreement between Brack and Brandt. The experiment took place sometime in early winter 1939–1940 at Brandenburg an der Havel, a former jailhouse in the city of Brandenburg conveniently linked to Berlin by rail. In this vacant prison workers from the SS Main Construction Office installed something that would become an infamous symbol of Nazi genocide—a gas chamber disguised as a shower room. The KTI's own Dr. Widmann conducted the first gassing. A postwar eyewitness described the spectacle that unfolded:

> around 18 to 20 people were led into this "shower room" by nursing staff. These men had to undress in the antechamber, so that they were completely naked. The doors were closed behind them. These people went into the room quietly and with no signs of agitation. Dr. Widmann operated the gassing equipment. Through the viewing window I could see that after a few minutes the patients keeled over or lay down on the benches. There weren't any kind of scenes or tumults. After another 5 minutes the room was aired out. SS people designated for the task removed the dead from the room on specially-constructed stretchers and brought them to the cremation ovens. If I say specially-constructed stretchers, I mean stretchers constructed just for this purpose. These could be set directly in front of the cremation ovens and by means of a device the corpses could be mechanically conveyed into the ovens without the need for the carrier to touch the corpse. These ovens and stretchers were built in Brack's office.

During this same period at Brandenburg, approximately six mentally disabled patients were given lethal injections of morphine and scopolamine by Brandt and Conti. The purpose of the injections was to compare their effectiveness with that of carbon monoxide. According to Werner Heyde, our primary source for this episode, the results cast doubt on the injection method: "The patients," Heyde remembered, "died quite slowly, and it is possible . . . that the injections had to be repeated." According to August Becker, Brack was "satisfied" with the carbon monoxide experiment. Even Brandt was won over to carbon monoxide. "In this way," Becker summed up, "the beginning [of gassings] in Brandenburg was deemed a success."[47]

Brandenburg became the first of six institutions specifically designed to kill "unworthy life" with carbon monoxide gas. Shortly after Brandenburg became operative, Grafeneck in Württemberg opened its doors in January 1940. In order to deal with the volume of victims, T-4 opened two other killing centers at Hartheim near Linz (May 1940) and Sonnenstein in Pirna near Dresden (June 1940). The final two euthanasia centers, Bernburg on the Saale River and Hadamar just north of Wiesbaden in Hessen, were designed as successor institutions to Brandenburg and Grafeneck. In each of these killing centers, a suitable room was chosen for conversion into a gas chamber disguised as a shower room. The design in all material respects followed the model of Brandenburg. Moreover, jurisdiction over killing was divided among each of the institutions. Brandenburg killed mental patients from Berlin; the Prussian provinces of Brandenburg, Saxony, and Schleswig Holstein; and the states of Brunswick, Mecklenburg, Anhalt, and Hamburg. (As Brandenburg's successor, Bernburg would cover this region after 1941.) Grafeneck disposed of south German patients from Bavaria, Württemberg, and Baden; its own successor, Hadamar, took over these regions plus the state of Hessen and the Prussian province of Hanover. Hartheim killed patients from Austrian mental institutions, as well as some from southern Germany and Saxony. Finally, Sonnenstein gassed patients from Saxony, Thuringia, Silesia, and southern Germany.[48]

The appearance of normality surrounding the procedure lulled the patients into the mistaken belief that they were being transferred to a hospital no different from other institutions already familiar to them. Gekrat buses transported the patients to the killing center; in some cases, they arrived by rail and were then picked up by "death buses" and driven to the institution. Upon arrival, patients were met by staff members who conducted them to a changing room, where they were instructed to remove their clothes. The testimony of a Hadamar nurse from the German Hadamar trial illustrates the procedure that usually prevailed in all the killing centers:

> On the ground floor, the victims came into a reception area divided at the time into two rooms, the first of which served as a waiting area. Here some beds were provided for non-ambulatory patients. The second room of the

reception area was the changing room, in which I was involved. There first the men and then the women were disrobed. From here, the patients were led through a hallway into the doctor's room, where they were again given a brief medical exam and were given a number with reference to their medical papers. These numbers were written on their backs with a colored marker. From the doctor's room they came into an adjacent room, the purpose of which I do not know. From this room they were led into a photography room next door, in which they had to wait until all the members of the transport had been gathered. They were then brought together down a staircase into the gas chamber lined with glazed tiles, which outwardly resembled a shower.[49]

Another eyewitness, a "stoker" who cremated the victims' corpses at the Sonnenstein killing center, testified before an examining judge in 1966 that at least some of the patients he observed "still had a certain mental ability," as evidenced by the fact that they carried washcloths and soap with them into the gas chamber. When the patients had all entered the gas chamber, the gassing technicians ensured that the door and ventilation shafts were tightly sealed. Only then did the physician open the valve of the gas tank and fill the chamber with carbon monoxide. Within five minutes, all the patients were unconscious; within ten, they were dead. Staff members waited a couple of hours before airing out the chamber with fans. Once this had been done, attending physicians pronounced the victims dead and the corpses were carried out (or, in some instances, dragged out) by the stokers to a nearby room, where the bodies were arranged in piles. The bodies were done one final indignity before cremation: they were plundered by staff members. Patients with gold teeth had been marked prior to gassing with a cross on their back or chest. A staff member identified the corpses with gold teeth by these markings and wrenched the teeth out of their mouths with pliers. They were deposited with a secretary in the institution's main office, and eventually forwarded to the T-4 authorities in Berlin. Some corpses became the objects of autopsies, designed both to train younger physicians (who received academic credit from the autopsies) and to harvest brains for study in German research institutes.[50]

The stokers cremated the bodies of the murdered patients in ovens, working in shifts through the night to reduce the corpses to ashes. The ashes were literally swept into a pile and indiscriminately deposited in urns. Each urn bore the name of a patient killed in the gas chamber, but it did not necessarily contain that patient's ashes. The names of the patients were then entered in the death book maintained at every killing center. Obviously, the T-4 killers could not report that a large number of patients (some transports contained as many as 150) had all died simultaneously of natural causes. False causes and

Camouflaging mass murder: the Hadamar gas chamber disguised as a shower room. The architects of the Final Solution would imitate this practice—first introduced during the T-4 program—of deceiving murder victims by conveying to them a false appearance of normality. Courtesy Archiv des Landeswohlfahrtsverbandes Hessen, Kassel

dates of death had to be concocted. At the beginning of the euthanasia program, the T-4 Medical Office disseminated lists of "causes of death" to its participating doctors that could be cited by them in furtherance of the charade. One such list contained sixty-one different illnesses, along with brief descriptions of the etiology, course, therapy, and complications of each disease. Stroke, pneumonia, heart attack, tuberculosis, and circulatory collapse were among the causes of death most frequently given. The killing center doctor recorded the fraudulent cause of death on the death certificate, certifying it with a false name, and this fiction was reproduced in official correspondence and in "consolation letters" sent to the patient's family or guardian. Because the patient had been gassed before the killing center's notification of his or her safe arrival had been sent to the relatives, it was likewise necessary to falsify the date of death. The administrative offices of the killing centers sent the letter of consolation to the family or guardian approximately ten days after the patient's death. The letter was boiler plate, informing the family of the patient's death and the "cause" and "date" of his or her demise, and offering a reassurance that the patient had been "delivered" from suffering. It also indicated that, in order to "hinder the outbreak and spread of communicable diseases," the local police authorities had required the cremation of the patient's body and the "disinfection" of the patient's belongings. Urns containing the ashes would be sent to the family if they responded within fourteen days and presented proof that they had made arrangements for proper interment.[51]

From the historical record it is clear that T-4 operatives, both in the KdF and in the killing centers, were concerned that the patients' relatives would discover what had really happened to their family members. This fear helps account for the extraordinary lengths T-4 personnel resorted to in an effort to conceal the mass murder from the victims' families. In each killing center, maps of Germany with colored pins demonstrated how many patients from different geographic areas had thus far been killed. If too many pins accumulated in a given region, the dates and places of death had to be changed in order to avert the suspicion that too many patients from the same area had died simultaneously in the same locale. A Grafeneck staff member told the Münsingen *Amtsgericht* in 1947 that in spring 1940 the Berlin T-4 authorities had ordered Brandenburg and Hartheim to exchange patient records, so that a different place of death could be recorded for some of the patients.[52]

Worries about public protest nonetheless continued. Scholars of National Socialist euthanasia have differed over whether such fears contributed to the decision to close Brandenburg and Grafeneck in late 1940. For Henry Friedlander, gradually spreading knowledge among the civilian population of the killing program was a proximate cause of Brandenburg's and Grafeneck's closures. Ernst Klee, on the other hand, discounts the role of public pressure, arguing that Brandenburg and Grafeneck were closed because they had served their purpose of decimating "unworthy life" in their regions. Whatever the actual reasons, the first two killing centers in the assault on the lives of mentally disabled patients were closed by December 1940, only to be replaced by Bernburg and Hadamar. The killing went on without pause.[53]

Concern for public opinion among Nazi leaders may also account for the creation in fall 1940 of transit centers. On an increasing basis, patients designated for killing were transferred from surrendering institutions to these transit centers, where they stayed for two to three weeks before final transfer to a killing institution. Euthanasia defendants like Karl Brandt and Viktor Brack devised the ruse that the transit centers had a quality control function, ensuring that no mistakes had been made in the selection process. In fact, the transit centers were designed to confound any efforts to trace a given transport to its ultimate destination. The more labyrinthine the program, the more difficult it was to follow T-4's sleight of hand—or so it seemed to T-4 directors. Nonetheless, some of the transit centers did on occasion seek to withhold patients capable of work from transfer to the killing centers. When they did so, they were admonished by the Berlin authorities that such exemptions were "impeding" the "operation." The director of the Hadamar euthanasia institution alluded to a rebuke from Berlin in reminding the director of the Wiesloch transit center to "distance himself from every exemption."[54]

By August 1941, the death toll of mentally disabled patients murdered in T-4's killing centers had reached 70,273. These figures are culled not from official T-4 records, many of which were destroyed before the end of the war, but from figures compiled by a T-4 statistician discovered at the Hartheim institution after the war. The figures document the number of those killed at each of the six killing centers for each calendar month beginning in January 1940 and ending in August 1941. As Henry Friedlander points out, however, German prosecutors after the war believed these figures underestimated the number of the dead. Based on evidence they had collected, they argued the T-4 statistician had, among other errors, miscounted the patients euthanized at Hartheim and Sonnenstein. They arrived at a conservative estimate of 80,000 patients killed until the official "end" of the operation in August 1941.[55]

The reason why Hitler ended the first phase of adult euthanasia in August 1941 is a subject of controversy among historians. For years, pressure from the Catholic church was credited for persuading Hitler to terminate phase one of the killing program. The bombshell was a sermon delivered on August 3, 1941, by Count Clemens August von Galen, the bishop of Münster. Galen, who had learned in July 1940 of the euthanasia program, went public with this information in a sermon delivered in August 1941. In the sermon, Galen referred to the high mortality rate among the mentally ill in German institutions that "did not occur randomly, but rather was intentionally produced." Despite the declaration of the German Bishops on July 7, 1941, condemning the killing of an "innocent person except in wartime or in justified self-defense," the murder of mental patients had continued and now threatened the province of Westphalia. Galen condemned the killings as violations of statutory law and the Fifth Commandment, "Thou Shalt not Kill." Galen's sermon was read from pulpits throughout his diocese and soon became a topic of discussion both within and outside Germany. (British pilots dropped thousands of copies of the sermon on German cities.) The Nazi elite was furious. Walter Tiessler, a propaganda director, suggested to Bormann that Galen be hanged. The proposal was rejected on the grounds that executing Galen would only turn him into a martyr and stir up even more popular unrest.[56]

According to Ernst Klee and Henry Friedlander, the opposition of the churches and the public protest occasioned by it induced Hitler to cancel the official euthanasia program on August 24, 1941. The German historian of Nazi genocide, Götz Aly, does not reject the impact of church protest and public discontent on Hitler's decision, but points out that other motives may have been equally important. For Aly, the end of phase one may be the result of the simple fact that the program had reached (and even exceeded) its initial target of killing 70,000 patients. Galen's sermon also happened to coincide with the release of a propaganda film, *Ich klage an*, produced by the KdF to render the public more sympathetic to euthanasia; the stoppage in late August may have been ordered to give the film a chance to influence public opinion.[57]

Although the evidence permits more than one interpretation of the motives, it is undisputed that the killing program underwent a sea change after August 1941. Thereafter, in terms of organization, method, and scope, the National Socialist attack on "life unworthy of life" attained new and unprecedented levels of virulence. The language of resource scarcity was used to legitimate killing increasingly driven by racial and political motives. As we will see, the official "stop" of the euthanasia program did not diminish the killing but witnessed its expansion to other "valueless" groups after August 1941—including European Jews.

PHASE TWO OF EUTHANASIA AND THE EXPANDED KILLING PROJECTS OF NATIONAL SOCIALISM, 1941–1945

On August 24, 1941, in the face of mounting pressure from the Church and public unrest, Adolf Hitler ordered an official cessation to the euthanasia program. Notwithstanding this order, however, the murder of mentally disabled patients continued in T-4 killing centers with one critical difference: whereas the pre–August 1941 T-4 killings were restricted to psychiatric patients, the radius of killing after the August stoppage was expanded to new categories of "unworthy life," defined less in medical than in social, racial, and political terms. The centrifugal tendency of Nazi genocide between late 1941 and the end of the war is the central feature of this second phase of euthanasia.

At the end of November 1941, Viktor Brack met with T-4 representatives from all euthanasia centers. During the meeting he informed them that the operation would continue despite its official termination. The evidence available to us indicates that only the means of killing—gas chambers—changed as a result of the stop order. Beginning in late 1941, instead of gassing patients T-4 doctors murdered handicapped adults with the method used to eliminate disabled children: overdoses of medication. Others starved patients to death by slowly depriving them of food, a program referred to as *Hungerkost*.[58]

The waning months of 1941 are a climacteric in the history of National Socialist mass murder. During this period, a succession of events took place that changed fundamentally the Nazi assault on "life unworthy of life." In this extraordinary time official euthanasia ended and a new phase of "wild" euthanasia (i.e., decentralized killing loosely overseen by the Berlin authorities) began, using not only psychiatric criteria but novel categories like "public menace," "criminality," "anti-sociality," "psychopathy," and "racial inferiority" to identify individuals for destruction by the T-4 physicians. Sometime in this period Hitler issued what is generally believed to have been an oral order to exterminate the European Jews. The death camps of the Final Solution would not become operational until late 1941 or early 1942; yet, the fate awaiting Europe's Jews was already presaged in the murder of concentration camp Jews in the T-4 killing centers—the notorious Operation 14f13. In the remainder of this chapter I would like to discuss each of these events—"wild" euthanasia, the application of euthanasia to other groups, and Operation 14f13—as they relate to the original plan to eliminate mentally disabled Germans. What we will find is that the foundational premise of Nazi euthanasia—that "useless" or "valueless" life should be eradicated through state-organized violence—was extended in late 1941 from the mentally ill to justify the murder of other socially marginal groups.

"Wild" Euthanasia, September 1941–April 1945

Even after the official euthanasia "stop," the Reich Ministry continued to distribute questionnaires to German mental institutions biannually. In his role as Reich Commissioner for Mental Hospitals, Herbert Linden submitted the forms to the medical experts of the KdF for evaluation. Killing proceeded on the basis of these expert assessments, but the gas chambers of the killing centers were largely dismantled; henceforth, patients selected for euthanasia were given lethal overdoses or injections of narcotics, or simply starved to death. Furthermore, while original killing centers like Hadamar and Bernburg were still euthanizing patients after the stop order, the locus of killing shifted to the transit centers—many of which were simultaneously murdering disabled children in their children's wards. Facilities such as Eichberg, Kalmenhof, and Eglfing-Haar began to kill adult patients on-site. The Meseritz-Obrawalde mental hospital in Pomerania and Tiegenhof in the Wartheland became major centers for destroying the mentally handicapped. These institutions represent only a fraction of the facilities involved in killing the disabled during the period of wild euthanasia that ensued after August 24, 1941. A considerable number of hospitals murdered their patients when transportation to defunct killing centers became impossible.[59]

Under cross-examination at the Nuremberg Doctors' Trial, Karl Brandt tried to portray the T-4 euthanasia program as ending in late August 1941. Whatever killing of mental patients occurred after this date, Brandt claimed, had nothing to do with the "humane" program he and Bouhler had been commissioned to establish.[60] *Pace* Brandt, the reality was that the T-4 offices continued to register and evaluate patients for killing even after the official stop; it never fully relinquished control over euthanasia to local institutions. Just as they had before August 24, the T-4 authorities in Berlin directed the transport of patients to destinations where they were killed, provided these facilities with narcotics to poison them, and made available its experienced personnel to perform the killings. Nonetheless, T-4's control of euthanasia was not as top-down as it had been during phase one, when the T-4 Central Office had orchestrated a program of selection, transportation, and immediate killing on arrival at one of the six killing centers. Phase two transpired in numerous institutions, the diversity of which posed obstacles of command and control to the Berlin offices.[61]

The period of wild euthanasia also saw intense aerial bombardment of German cities and production centers by the Allies. Beginning in February 1942, the Royal Air Force embarked on a devastating campaign to demoralize German citizens and workers by destroying their cities. In some instances (e.g., the attack on the German town of Lübeck in March 1942), cities that were especially flammable were chosen for bombing. Allied sorties on Germany culminated in summer 1943 in Operation Gomorrah, a joint U.S.-British assault on Hamburg designed to reduce it to ashes. The numerous wooden buildings in Hamburg conduced to rapid combustion, and within a short time the city was an inferno. When Operation Gomorrah had ended, 45,000 civilians had been incinerated; 13 square miles of the city were a charred ruin.[62]

One result of Allied bombing was a grave crisis in hospital space to accommodate the wounded. Already in 1941, possibly in response to the demolition of a hospital at Emden by British pilots, Hitler had charged Karl Brandt, his escort physician, "to designate evacuation hospitals for other cities that were in danger." Under U.S. Army interrogation after the war, Brandt claimed that his new duties, modest at first, were significantly enlarged in 1942 and 1943—most likely because of damage caused by Allied bombing. On July 28, 1942, Hitler appointed Brandt Commissioner for the Health Care System. Brandt described his duties to his army interrogator:

> The basic task of a general [Commissioner] meant the adjustment of the needs of the civilians for materials and physicians to the Wehrmacht sanitary needs and also space for hospital cases. This basic task could not be carried through after 1942 because on every one of these sides there was a greater need than materials available. This is why the adjustment always meant taking something away from somebody who had nothing anyway.[63]

Brandt's work as Commissioner for the Health Care System (which had really begun in late 1941) developed into an official program code-named Operation Brandt. Under its auspices, mentally disabled patients were evacuated from psychiatric hospitals and clinics. The reason offered for their removal was to protect them from air raids. The chief of the T-4 Central Office, Dietrich Allers, dispatched evacuation orders to local mental hospitals throughout the Reich, stating that Brandt as general commissioner was ordering the transfer of patients from psychiatric hospitals in areas "particularly endangered" by Allied bombing.[64]

With Operation Brandt, National Socialist euthanasia branched outward from allegedly incurable mental patients (the "terminal cases") to embrace a variety of victim groups. As the war ground on, creating new problems for the German government within the Reich, the Nazis employed mass killing as an instrument of population policy. In the aftermath of the Hamburg incendiary bombings in late July 1943, for example, Hamburg women deranged by the trauma of the firestorm were transported to Hadamar, where, it is believed, they were all murdered. When a concerned parent sought information about his shell-shocked daughter at the Eppendorf Hospital, he was told that she and others had "been transferred to less dangerous areas, in order to make room for victims of the Hamburg raids." In addition to traumatized civilians, members of old-age homes became ensnared in the coils of Operation Brandt after the July bombing of Hamburg. They were transported to Neuruppin Mental Hospital and to Meseritz-Obrawalde for killing.[65]

Other Victims of Euthanasia:
The "Asocials" and Eastern European Forced Laborers

Increasingly in the Third Reich, as the euphoria of the German army's initial conquests evaporated amid military reversals and sustained Allied bombing of German cities, genocidal violence was employed to "solve" political, social, and economic problems facing the Nazi government. Many of the problems were related to population policy questions, particularly the need for army and civilian hospitals. After officials involved in Operation Brandt expanded euthanasia to include not only "incurable" mental patients but shell-shocked civilians as well, two additional groups became victims of the National Socialist killing project: the "asocials" and sick eastern European laborers.

In 1945 the Nazi government drafted a law regarding "aliens to the community" but never enacted it. According to its terms, those prone to unruliness, drunkenness, and laziness were "aliens to the community." Beggars, thieves, grifters, and criminals also fell into this category. On June 20, 1942, the Information Service of the Racial Political Office of the Nazi Party issued a call to the Gau of Vienna to suppress its asocials, because they "represent an element of political unrest of the first order." In the eyes of the Information Service, a person was an asocial if he or she violated the criminal law, suffered from unemployment although able-bodied, lived parasitically off state or private welfare proceeds, had no settled residence, was a compulsive alcoholic, or lived off the earnings from "immoral activities" (e.g., pimping or prostitution). The instruction sheet setting forth this capacious definition of asociality then affirmed the biological inferiority of "those incapable of community," underscoring the futility of "ameliorative" measures to address this problem. From such premises Nazi functionaries like Dr. H. W. Kranz, Gau Office Director of the Nazi Party's Racial Office, Gau Hessen-Nassau, drew the conclusion that only "special treatment"—that is, killing—could cure the problem of asociality.[66]

Such attitudes permeated the upper echelons of the Nazi Party. On July 2, 1943, the Justice Ministry issued an order to send "criminally insane" patients to the concentration camps. Section 42 of the "Law Against Dangerous Habitual Criminals and Regulation of Security and Reform," enacted on November 11, 1933, had supplied a basis for detaining asocials in psychiatric institutions if they were deemed by the courts to suffer from mental illness. Invoking Section 42 of this law on August 8, 1943, Herbert Linden of the Interior Ministry apprised directors of affected institutions that all patients institutionalized under the Detention Law were to be surrendered to police authorities. Quite apart from "cleansing the institutions of undesired and destabilizing elements," Linden wrote, the removal of the criminally insane would free up much-needed beds for German citizens. Again, the ideological impulse to blot out "value-less" life from the people's community intersected with the population policy need for medical resources. Once in police custody, the criminally insane were transferred to the Mauthausen concentration camp and Auschwitz. There they were subjected to hard labor; at Mauthausen, after the last ounce of stamina had been wrung from them, they were sent to the Hartheim killing center and gassed.[67]

Along with the criminally insane, sick eastern European workers living in the Reich were caught up in the lethal nets of wild euthanasia. Beginning in late 1941, as hopes for a meteoric victory over the Soviets faded and the prospects of a long-term war of attrition took shape, the need for labor to sustain the wartime economy became acute. In response, Hitler deployed So-viet and Polish POWs and civilian workers throughout the Reich as forced laborers. Harsh living conditions and maltreatment, however, gave rise to epidemic disease among the Ostarbeiter. By 1944 substantial numbers of them were unable to work because of tuberculosis. With the Red Army closing in and fearing the spread of the contagion, German health authorities began sending these unfortunate people to facilities for killing. The problem of epi-demic disease was an issue of population policy; destruction of the disease-bearing agents was the regime's solution. Between July 29, 1944, and March 18, 1945, 465 Ostarbeiter were given lethal injections at Hadamar; others were gassed at Hartheim. On September 6, 1944, the Interior Ministry gave an official imprimatur to these killings by decreeing that all eastern laborers incapable of work because of mental illness were to be sent to designated hos-pitals. This decree reflected the Nazis' tendency to blur distinctions between separate concepts; the Ostarbeiter targeted by the Interior Ministry were not mentally but physically ill. The regime had already equated asociality with mental illness; now, tubercular eastern workers were also identified with the mentally disabled. The logic of the Nazis' hierarchy of human value was play-ing itself out in the form of a murderous syllogism: because the mentally ill were "unworthy of life," they were to be killed; and because "asocials" and tubercular eastern workers were "mentally ill," they should be accorded the same "treatment."[68]

The September decree identified eleven state hospitals that would serve as "collection points" for sick Ostarbeiter. They included notorious killing centers like Tiegenhof, Kaufbeuren, Maur-Öhling, and Hadamar. The T-4 Central Of-fice under Dietrich Allers provided the transportation and financing for this new chapter in National Socialist euthanasia. By February 17, 1945, however, war conditions were such that the September decree was revised: henceforth, the patients were to be remanded to local mental hospitals responsible for areas in which the sick Ostarbeiter were located.

Euthanasia and the Murder of the European Jews

Respected scholars of Nazi genocide regard the T-4 euthanasia program as a prelude to the murder of the European Jews, conceptually, organizationally, and logistically related to that infamous event. "Euthanasia," Raul Hilberg writes, "was a conceptual as well as technological and administrative prefiguration of the 'Final Solution' in the death camps." Ernst Klee, describing the way in which Jews, Soviet POWs, Gypsies, and others were murdered at Chelmno (the first death camp on Polish soil), refers to the killing process there as "a copy of the euthanasia measures." Along the same lines, Henry Friedlander affirms an intimate link between the T-4 killings and the Final Solution.[69]

Even before the beginning of the Holocaust, T-4 members were killing Jewish concentration camp prisoners based solely on their racial background. The murders occurred as part of an operation conceived and administered by the SS to reduce the escalating population of Germany's concentration camps. As they did in their assault on the disabled, asocials, and sick eastern workers, the Nazis solved a problem of population policy through mass murder. Aware of T-4's efficient work in the euthanasia program, Himmler had contacted in early 1941 the chief of the KdF, Philipp Bouhler, about the possibility of using T-4's "personnel and facilities" to deal with camp populations. The issue of their colloquy was a new killing program that began in April 1941, the *Sonderbehandlung* (Special Treatment) 14f13. The term *Sonderbehandlung*, as we already know, is verbal camouflage for killing, a euphemism widely used by the SS and police forces. The label "14f13" referred to a file number employed by the Inspectorate of the Concentration Camps, designating the annihilation of camp prisoners in T-4 killing centers. Victims of 14f13 were prisoners in concentration camps administered by the Inspectorate. SS camp doctors selected the prospective victims based on an "official" criterion of incurable physical illness that rendered the individual incapable of work. Unofficially, these SS physicians received oral instructions to use racial and eugenic guidelines in making their selections. At Buchenwald, SS doctors were ordered to select the disabled, Jews, and prisoners with criminal records. The major criterion in every case, however, was fitness for work (although this standard, like all criteria that supposedly governed National Socialist euthanasia, was arbitrarily enforced).[70]

Once the victims had been chosen, T-4 physicians arrived in the camps to proof the SS selections. These visits are reminiscent of similar trips made by T-4 employees to German mental hospitals to ensure that euthanasia was properly carried out. At least twelve T-4 doctors appeared in concentration camps as participants in Operation 14f13. Each of these individuals had extensive experience with T-4 as euthanasia medical experts. Seated at tables, the T-4 doctors reviewed the prisoners selected by the SS as they were paraded before them. The SS had previously filled out questionnaires on every selectee, containing the prisoner's name, birth date and place, last residence, citizenship, religion, race, and date of arrest. As a prisoner walked past the table, the T-4 physician decided whether to uphold the SS determination to include the selectee in the operation. A plus sign (+) entered at the bottom of the form signified inclusion in 14f13. This haphazard method of processing did not admit time for a thorough medical exam. At Buchenwald, in fact, two T-4 doctors reviewed 873 prisoners in five days. As Friedrich Mennecke confided to his wife about one such examination, the T-4 personnel did little more than rubber stamp the SS's selections. Nonetheless, they were obliged to give a "diagnosis" of the prisoner's condition.

No such diagnosis was required with Jewish prisoners selected for liquidation in 14f13. Instead, justifications for inclusion were culled from personal records, especially arrest records; this data was then entered on the prisoner's questionnaire. Mennecke, for example, recorded as "medical diagnoses" such characterizations from Jewish prisoners' personal records as "anti-German agitator," "lazy and indolent," "anti-German behavior," "vile Germanophobe," and "attitude hostile to the State."[71]

Prisoners selected under 14f13 were subsequently transported to the euthanasia centers Bernburg, Hartheim, and Sonnenstein, which were all actively involved in killing the 14f13 prisoners. Prior to the stoppage ordered by Hitler on August 24, 1941, these institutions gassed both the mentally handicapped and 14f13 selectees; after August 24, the handicapped were murdered by overdoses of medication, whereas the 14f13 selectees continued to die in the gas chambers. Five hundred seventy-five prisoners were murdered at Sonnenstein alone. By the time Himmler ordered the end of 14f13 in 1943 (on the grounds that too many prisoners capable of work were being liquidated), the operation had claimed the lives of between 10,000 and 20,000 prisoners.[72]

Operation 14f13 was not the only nexus between Nazi euthanasia and the Holocaust. In a letter regarding "the solution to the Jewish Question" from Ernst Wetzel, an expert in the Reich Ministry for the Occupied Territories, dated October 25, 1941, to Heinrich Lohse, the Reich Commissar for the Ostland, Wetzel reported that "Oberdienstleiter Brack of the Führer's Chancellery has indicated his readiness to assist in producing the required accommodations as well as the gassing equipment." According to Wetzel, the "equipment" was not at that time available in the eastern territories and thus had to be manufactured. Wetzel reported Brack's apprehensions of the "many great difficulties" that would be occasioned if the equipment was produced within the Reich. To forestall such problems, Brack considered it "most expedient" to

Left: Dr. Friedrich Mennecke, director of the Eichberg Mental Hospital and T-4 medical expert. In the latter role, Mennecke traveled to various concentration camps to evaluate prisoners—many of them Jewish—for inclusion in the euthanasia program. In December 1946, a German court convicted him of murder under German law and sentenced him to death—a punishment he avoided by dying in his prison cell in January 1947. Courtesy HHSTAW Abt. 3008, Friedrich Mennecke. Right: Friedrich Mennecke in happier times. Courtesy HHSTAW Abt. 3008, Friedrich Mennecke

send his chemist, Dr. Helmut Kallmeyer, to Riga, "who would take care of everything there." Because the "procedure under consideration" was "not without danger," certain "protective measures" would have to be observed. Accordingly, Wetzel asked Lohse to have his Higher SS and Police Leader contact Brack about sending to the east both Dr. Kallmeyer "and other auxiliary resources."[73]

This document was the smoking gun at the Doctors' Trial that implicated Viktor Brack in the earliest planning stages of the Final Solution. In the letter, Wetzel asserts that Adolf Eichmann was "in agreement with this procedure"; Eichmann had informed Wetzel that "camps for Jews were to be erected in Riga and Minsk, into which Jews from the 'old Reich territory' would also eventually come." Jews were even then being evacuated from the Reich, Wetzel confided, and sent to the Litzmannstadt (Lodz) ghetto and "to other camps"; later, these German Jews would be transferred to the east as slave laborers, "so far as they were capable of work." Concerning those Jews deemed incapable of work, however, "there should be no second thoughts about removing them with the Brackian devices." The thrust of this last sentence is clear: Jewish deportees to Riga and Minsk capable of work would be used as slaves, while those unfit for hard labor would be gassed. Recently discovered German documents from Moscow reveal that the SS had ordered a monstrous crematorium for Mogilev (in eastern Byelorussia, the site of carbon monoxide gassing experiments) that would incinerate in excess of 2,000 corpses per day. These documents suggest, as Götz Aly has noted,[74] that the Nazis may have been planning to erect a major extermination center for European Jews in Mogilev— a thesis that gains in persuasive power when read together with Wetzel's gassing letter. In fact, as a result of military reversals on the eastern front and the obvious difficulties they posed to transports, the Jewish camps envisioned in Wetzel's letter never materialized; instead, they were erected in former Poland.

The "Brackian devices" Wetzel referred to in his letter were gas vans. Beginning in late December 1939 and January 1940, SS special units had murdered the mentally disabled from Wartheland hospitals with these vans. In September 1941, after experiments with gas vans were conducted by KTI employee Albert Widmann in Mogilev, Himmler had ordered the KTI to engineer an "improved" gas van that would recycle the vehicle's own motor exhaust into a sealed compartment. The new van was tested at the Sachsenhausen concentration camp in late fall 1941; thereafter, the vans were manufactured and sent in early 1942 to assist the *Einsatzgruppen* in their war on the eastern European population. Even before their formal introduction to the USSR in early 1942, these vans were being used to murder Jews and other groups at the Nazis' first death camp, Chelmno (Kulmhof in German).

Established by the SS in October and November 1941 near Chelmno, a village in the Polish countryside, the Chelmno death camp's purpose was to kill and cremate human beings. By December 1941, camp personnel were using gas vans to kill Gypsies, malarial patients, Soviet POWs, the mentally disabled, and even a group of Austrian World War I officers. By far the largest number of victims murdered at Chelmno, however, were the Jews (particularly Jews from the Lodz ghetto). In its technique and style of execution, the modus operandi was almost identical to the T-4 euthanasia killings. On arrival, victims were told to remove their clothes for a shower. Supervised by SS members wearing the white coats and stethoscopes of doctors, victims were herded down a flight of steps and along a camouflaged ramp into a waiting gas van. When the full complement of victims had been loaded into the van's interior, the doors were closed and a hose connected to the floor of the van was joined to the exhaust pipe. In theory the victims were supposed to fall asleep painlessly and die from asphyxiation within ten minutes, but the reality was other. Their shrieks could be heard from the van interior as they pounded frantically on the locked doors and walls of the van. The death throes of the victims could last for hours until they finally expired.

When the screams abated, the gas van departed the camp premises and drove to a wooded area, where Jewish prisoners were forced to unload the corpses. Victims who had miraculously survived the ordeal were shot on the spot. Body cavities were searched for objects of value, including gold teeth, which were torn from the corpses' mouths with a pair of pliers. After the dead had been looted, they were thrown unceremoniously into a mass grave. In this manner, at least 152,000 victims were murdered at Chelmno between 1941 and 1944.[75]

While Chelmno was beginning the first systematic gassings of Jews and others at a fixed location, Himmler gave the Higher SS Police Leader in Lublin, Odilo Globocnik, an order to initiate the mass murder of the Jews of central and southern Poland. Globocnik thereupon erected three killing centers in the Lublin area of the General Government. The three killing centers—Belzec, Sobibor, and Treblinka—became operational in late winter and early spring 1942: Belzec from March 1942 to December 1943, Sobibor from April 1942 to October 1943, and Treblinka from July 1942 to autumn 1943. In contrast with Chelmno, which murdered its victims in mobile gas vans, these extermination centers employed a technique that had earlier proven successful in the T-4 killing centers—immobile gas chambers disguised as showers.[76]

In addition to these three sites, Himmler designated two others to help expedite the new killing program. They were Auschwitz in Upper Silesia and the POW camp at Majdanek, a Lublin suburb. The extermination arm of Auschwitz, known as "Auschwitz II," was at Birkenau, where more than a million people were gassed with a pesticide used throughout the concentration camp system as a fumigation agent, hydrogen cyanide (better known under its trade name, Zyklon B). The first experiment with Zyklon B gassing was carried out on September 3, 1941, at Auschwitz; by 1942, the SS had converted two farmhouses in Birkenau into gas chambers, which were used to gas Jews and others until four gas chambers were installed there in early 1943. The idea of employing a stationary gas chamber was inspired by the example of the T-4 killing centers.[77]

Gassing unsuspecting Jews in gas chambers disguised as shower rooms was not the only continuity with Nazi euthanasia. At least ninety-two T-4 operatives were assigned to the Operation Reinhard (the extermination of Polish Jewry) death camps. These individuals had been crematorium stokers, drivers, transport escorts and office personnel with T-4. All wore the field gray uniforms of the Waffen-SS, receiving a rank no lower than *Unterscharführer* (a non-commissioned officer rank within the SS); they were paid by the T-4 Accounting Office in Berlin. T-4's managerial staff was central to the efficient administration of killing centers in the General Government. Christian Wirth, an active participant in the killing of mentally ill patients at Grafeneck, Hadamar, Hartheim, and Brandenburg, established the death camp at Chelmno; thereafter, he was assigned to supervise with Odilo Globocnik the killing of two million Jews at the Belzec, Sobibor, and Treblinka camps. Franz Stangl was the Police Superintendent of Hartheim before taking up duties as commandant of the Sobibor death camp in May 1942. During one interview in the 1960s, he commented that the Sobibor gas chamber "looked exactly like the gas chamber at Schloss Hartheim." His successor at Sobibor was Wirth's replacement as office director at Hartheim, Franz Reichleitner. The first camp commandant at Treblinka was Dr. Irmfried Eberl, director of the killing centers at Brandenburg and Bernburg.[78]

In their work within Operation Reinhard, the T-4 killers must have surpassed their masters' expectations. In two years of operation (1941–1942 and again in 1944), Chelmno murdered 152,000 people; in one year (1942), the Belzec camp killed 600,000. The Sobibor and Treblinka camps also required a single year (1942–1943) to murder 250,000 and 900,000 people, respectively. By the time Operation Reinhard came to an end in November 1943, it had taken almost 2 million lives. Of the nearly 2 million people sent to Chelmno, Belzec, Sobibor, and Treblinka, only eighty-seven survived. Although Auschwitz has become the symbol par excellence of Nazi depravity, lethality among the four Polish death camps was actually much higher. Gerald Reitlinger has estimated that approximately 700,000 of the 851,200 Jews deported to Auschwitz were gassed at Birkenau (a mortality rate just over 82 percent); mortality rates at the four Polish killing centers, by contrast, were almost 100 percent. For efficiency in murder, the Nazis could not have made a better choice than the euthanasia killers.[79]

After the fall of Germany in spring 1945, the forces of military occupation confronted the prodigious destruction wrought by the Nazi government. In the dingy confines of German mental hospitals, in the charnel houses of the concentration and death camps, the advancing armies uncovered the corpse-strewn highway to the Nazis' biological utopia. The awful tale of Hitler's assault on the human race was told in the physical bodies of both the dead and the living. It could be read from the mounds of emaciated corpses that had once been healthy human beings, or from the gaunt, disease-wracked frames of the survivors. Many of the men responsible, like Hitler, had already eluded justice through suicide. Others, like Himmler, Bouhler, Leonardo Conti, and

Dr. Irmfried Eberl, SS doctor, director of the Brandenburg and Bernburg killing centers, and first commandant of the Treblinka death camp. Indicted for his manifold crimes after the war, he committed suicide in his Ulm jail cell while awaiting trial in February 1948. Courtesy Ghetto Fighters' House, Kibbutz Lohamei Hagetaot, photographer unknown

Herbert Linden, would take their lives in the months following the end of the war. It fell to the Allies to decide the fates of the surviving perpetrators. As we will see, in approaching euthanasia criminality the U.S. conception was not driven purely by the factual record, revulsion from the grisly handiwork of Nazi genocide, or the imperatives of international law, but was substantially shaped by a concern for its own sovereignty. We take up the U.S. judicial encounter with the euthanasia killers in the next chapter.

Until a more complete code of the laws of war has been issued, the High Contracting Parties deem it expedient to declare that . . . the inhabitants and the belligerents remain under the protection and the rule of the principles of the law of nations, as they result from the usages established among civilized peoples, from the laws of humanity, and the dictates of public conscience.

—PREAMBLE TO THE 1907 HAGUE CONVENTION
(THE "MARTEN'S CLAUSE")

Chapter 2 | CONSTRUCTING MASS MURDER

THE UNITED STATES EUTHANASIA TRIALS, 1945–1947

In the years prior to World War II, the United States had long resisted international criminal tribunals as threats to its own national sovereignty. The U.S. government had opposed forming an international tribunal after World War I to prosecute violations of the "laws of humanity," particularly in connection with the Turkish government's alleged destruction of its Armenian population. At the time, the U.S. government supported its opposition with reference to the "vague" nature of ill-defined crimes against humanity, so far as they involved outrages committed on civilians rather than military members. When we examine the U.S. position in the context of the subsequent rejection of U.S. participation in the League of Nations, however, it would seem that U.S. refusal to endorse an international tribunal had more to do with fears of diminished sovereignty than with legal niceties like the prohibition of retroactive criminal law. This notwithstanding, the United States emerged in 1945 as the most ardent champion of postwar trials to punish the crimes of the Third Reich. The process by which this inversion came about requires explanation. As we will see, the U.S. Army's abrasive encounter with Nazi criminality, the extreme nature of that criminality, and the lobbying efforts of numerous central and eastern European émigrés during the war all contributed to making the United States the foremost adherent of postwar trials. In the course of our discussion, we will also see how the early commitment of U.S. war crimes trial planners to a theory of conspiracy as the glue holding together its case against Nazi defendants came to dominate the U.S. approach to the regime's criminality in both the International Tribunal and the Doctors' Trial proceedings. Ultimately, U.S. insistence on the centrality of conspiracy to its legal interpretation of Nazi criminality is a recrudescence of U.S. fears that its own sovereignty might be diminished.

We next explore how concerns with preserving U.S. power affected judicial constructions of euthanasia criminality. In order to penetrate to this issue, we will focus on two proceedings in U.S. courts: the Hadamar trial before a military commission (in October 1945) and the Medical Case against doctors and high-ranking policymakers involved in the euthanasia program, which took place from December 1946 to August 1947. From early on, the U.S. government viewed euthanasia as the direct result of the Nazis' efforts to launch aggressive wars to bring all of Europe under German hegemony. On the U.S. theory, euthanasia was a way to free up medical resources for use by the German army in its conquest of Europe. By connecting the destruction of "life unworthy of life" with the conduct of a criminal war, U.S. authorities were able to justify the prosecution and punishment of acts that the United States feared might otherwise be considered part of the Third Reich's domestic policy. In short, the war connection enabled the United States to uphold the principle of sovereignty, and to do so as it passed judgment on a euthanasia program that, in its original design, targeted only German nationals. Linking euthanasia with waging aggressive war is the most salient feature of the U.S. approach to euthanasia criminality and indicates the determinative impact of extra-legal factors—namely, U.S. leaders' preoccupation with national power—on the U.S. euthanasia trials.

EUTHANASIA CRIMINALITY AND THE LAW OF CONSPIRACY

Although the Geneva conventions laid the foundation for international recognition of duties and prohibitions incumbent on combatant nations, before 1945 no international accord defined "crimes against humanity" as a distinct category of offense, the commission of which would expose an offender nation to criminal liability. The embryo of crimes against humanity actually goes back to a landmark fin-de-siècle document: the preamble to the First Hague Convention of 1899 on the Laws and Customs of War (enlarged in the Fourth Hague Convention of 1907) and the annexed Regulations Respecting the Laws and Customs of War on Land. The preamble to the 1899 and 1907 versions refs explicitly to "laws of humanity" that afforded protection to "populations and belligerents" not specifically covered by the language of the conventions. Thus, although the Hague conventions of 1899 and 1907 dealt primarily with "war crimes," their jurisdiction over such acts derived from a larger, more capacious source called "laws of humanity." According to the framers of the Hague conventions, the term "laws of humanity" would extend to "unforeseen cases" not anticipated in its enumerated instances of wrongdoing. The vital paragraph of the preamble, reproduced as an epigraph to this chapter, contains the Martens clause. The thrust of the Martens clause is that "general principles" may be used as a gap-filler to cover acts formally outside the scope of the conventions. Article 22 of the Hague regulations presupposes these "general principles" in its assertion that "the right of belligerents to adopt means of injuring the enemy is not unlimited."[1]

Not until the London Charter of 1945, which served as the basis for the International Military Tribunal at Nuremberg, were crimes against humanity prosecuted as violations of international law. Even so, U.S. jurists, politicians, and policymakers never entirely overcame their tendency to identify crimes against humanity with war crimes. One of the primary arguments of this book is that the desire to defend U.S. sovereignty from external interference, not the abstract, undiluted pursuit of justice, conditioned U.S. interpretation of Nazi criminality, causing U.S. policymakers and courts in the immediate postwar years to elide the distinction between crimes against humanity and war crimes.

The Overture to Nuremberg:
The Moscow Declaration and the Morgenthau Plan

In spring and summer 1942, the first reports of the Nazi annihilation of European Jews began to trickle out of occupied Europe. These were not ephemeral rumors but soundly documented accounts from firsthand witnesses. The Inter-Allied Conference on War Crimes, a group of fugitives from Nazi Germany who lobbied for legal punishment of Nazi perpetrators, implored the Allies to act. Moved by their plea, Winston Churchill warned in a speech delivered in the House of Commons on September 8, 1942, that "those who are guilty of the Nazi crimes will have to stand up before tribunals in every land where their atrocities have been committed in order that an indelible warning may be given to future ages." Franklin Roosevelt echoed this commination in his statement that the United States would ensure, once the war ended, that war criminals were delivered up to the United Nations for trial. At the same time, the Soviet Union declaimed against "the barbaric violation by the German Government of the elementary rules of international law." Soviet Foreign Minister Molotov spoke of a "special international tribunal" that would try German leaders after the war.[2]

The brio of their public statements masked the Anglo-American leaders' fears of acting hastily in the matter. Their concerns were several: assigning too much clout to governments-in-exile; provoking reprisals on Allied POWs in German hands; and a growing disquietude at the prospect of cooperating with the Russians on war crimes trials. In October 1943 U.S., British, and Soviet foreign ministers met in Moscow to formulate a concerted policy on war crimes trials. The immediate result of this meeting was the Moscow Declaration, a joint resolution announcing the Allies' intention to return Nazi war criminals to the countries where they had perpetrated their crimes for prosecution by national tribunals. The Moscow Declaration went on to exempt "the major war criminals whose offences have no particular geographical location" from these national trials. Instead, the major war criminals would "be punished by a joint decision of the Governments of the Allies." The phrase "joint decision" was vague; its wording left open the possibility—although the Moscow Declaration made no explicit mention of it—of an international tribunal convened to adjudicate the crimes of the major war criminals.[3]

From all accounts, the Allies were deeply affected by mounting evidence of crimes without historical parallel. Shock yielded to outrage, and outrage to a spirit of vengeance that gripped the Allied leadership on all sides. At the Yalta Summit in April 1945, Churchill had suggested to Stalin that a list of the "grand criminals" be compiled, and these criminals were to be arrested and shot after establishing their identity. Churchill had grounds for thinking his proposal would strike a responsive chord in Stalin: during their meeting at Teheran in November 1943, Stalin had proposed that after the war the Allies should decapitate the German army by executing 50,000 of its officers and technicians.[4] The British and Soviets were not alone in wishing to deal punitively with Nazi war criminals. Roosevelt's secretary of the treasury, Henry Morgenthau Jr., was an assimilated Jewish American profoundly angered by reports concerning the mass destruction of European Jews. In 1944 he urged FDR to deindustrialize Germany after the war—a plan that would destroy Germany's capacity to wage war in the future. He outlined a postwar reckoning with Nazi war criminals, striking a balance between the Moscow Declaration and the British proposal for summary executions. Morgenthau recommended that military commissions be established to prosecute second-tier war criminals. If the governments of countries in which criminal acts were committed requested extradition of a defendant, these military commissions would relinquish jurisdiction to the requesting government. But first-tier war criminals, dubbed by Morgenthau the "arch-criminals," would not be given their day in court. Because their "obvious guilt has generally been recognized by the United

Nations," the formalities of a trial could be dispensed with in their cases. Morgenthau recommended that they be arrested, identified, and shot by a U.N. firing squad.[5]

Morgenthau's plan found a doughty opponent in Secretary of War Henry Stimson. He objected that Morgenthau's "pastoralization" of Germany would raise the specter of starvation for millions of Germans, sowing the seeds for a future war. Instead, Stimson proposed that major war criminals be prosecuted before an international tribunal assembled for that purpose. It would be an authentic trial, not a kangaroo court in which guilt was a foregone conclusion; a war crimes defendant would enjoy U.S.-style legal rights, "namely, notification to the accused of the charge, the right to be heard and, within reasonable limits, to call witnesses in his defense." According to Stimson, defendants would be charged with violating the "laws of the Rules of War." He pointedly discounted the notion of prosecuting anything other than war crimes, implying by analogy that a military commission had no more jurisdiction over a crime unconnected to the conduct of war than a foreign court would have to prosecute defendants involved in lynchings in the American South.[6] Stimson's argument by analogy ruled out the possibility of trying Nazi defendants for crimes against humanity.

Members within FDR's administration also were outspokenly opposed to Morgenthau's plan. FDR vacillated, affording Stimson and like-minded Pentagon officials the opportunity to formulate a concrete alternative to the Morgenthau scheme. A New York lawyer, Colonel Murray C. Bernays of the Pentagon's Special Projects Branch, was tasked with developing this alternative plan. He prepared a six-page memorandum ("Trial of European War Criminals") setting forth the details of a comprehensive postwar prosecution of Nazi war criminals. Historian Bradley Smith has characterized Bernays's memorandum as "the most important single source for the ideas that shaped the subsequent prosecutions at Nuremberg." Foremost among Bernays's influential ideas was the strategy of making the Anglo-American theory of conspiracy the cornerstone of war crimes prosecution.[7]

The power of conspiracy as a theory of criminal liability is manifold, but its chief attraction for Bernays was its extension of liability to all members of the conspiracy for the crimes of any individual member, where such crimes were the foreseeable results of the conspiracy and furthered its goal. The law of conspiracy, Bernays realized, would solve one of the vexing problems of Nazi war crimes prosecution that had haunted the British—that is, the logistical difficulty involved in prosecuting the enormous number of defendants in individual trials. He proposed trying the Nazi Party and assorted government organizations (the Gestapo, the SA, and the SS) *corporately* for violations of the laws of war before an international tribunal. Although individual defendants would be prosecuted on the merits of their cases, each accused would represent an organization charged with participation in the criminal conspiracy; thus, once the accused was convicted and punished by the court, his confederates within the organization would *as co-conspirators* be subject to arrest, a summary trial, and sentencing by the Allies. In this way, the need to try unmanageable numbers of defendants individually would be obviated. There are glaring due process problems in this scheme, but Bernays was less concerned with giving Nazi defendants U.S. constitutional guarantees than was Stimson. Nor were Bernays's superiors in the War Department disturbed by these considerations any more than they were troubled by building a prosecution plan around the Anglo-American doctrine of conspiracy, a charge that had never before surfaced in international law. For the pragmatic minds in the War Department, Bernays's approach served two crucial functions: it responded to public calls for an articulate policy to deal with Nazi atrocities and challenged the Morgenthau plan at its root.[8]

As it moved upward through the hierarchy of the War Department, Bernays's memorandum won adherents, among them Henry Stimson. In January 1945 Stimson, Edward Stettinius Jr. (the new secretary of state), and Francis Biddle (the U.S. Attorney General and later the U.S. judge at Nuremberg) developed a war crimes trial program along the lines suggested by Bernays. Central to the plan was the charge of conspiracy. It also followed Bernays in recommending that both Nazi leaders and organizations like the SA, SS, and Gestapo be charged with war crimes *and* with conspiracy to carry them out. Once the major war criminals and the organizations they represented had been tried and convicted before an international court, it would remain to arrest and prosecute smaller cogs in the Nazi criminal conspiracy. These lesser defendants would be prosecuted in "subsequent trials," in which "the only necessary proof of guilt of any particular defendant would be . . . membership in one of these organizations."[9]

FDR's successor, Harry Truman, wasted little time in adopting the Stimson plan as official U.S. policy. In May 1945 Truman appointed Supreme Court Justice Robert H. Jackson "chief of counsel for the prosecution of Axis criminality." After his appointment, Jackson had effective control of war crimes planning. His task in the ensuing months was to persuade other nations to endorse the U.S. plan. At roughly the same time as Jackson became chief of counsel, the United States presented a sketch of its plan to representatives from other countries assembled in San Francisco for the United Nation's founding conference. On May 3, Stettinius and Judge Sam Rosenman, whom FDR had appointed as his personal representative on Nazi war crimes, met with envoys from Great Britain and the USSR. The United States dilated on its proposed plan for trying Nazi war criminals before an international tribunal consisting of a representative judge from each of the four Control Council powers (Great Britain, the United States, France, and the USSR). Each of the four powers would also designate a representative (as Truman had already done with Jackson) to serve on a committee to gather evidence for the trials. In addition to the "top Nazis," war criminals to be extradited to the countries where they had perpetrated their crimes, and criminals "whose crimes were not geographically located," the United States identified a final group of defendants whose prosecution would be more problematic—those involved in crimes in which all the witnesses were dead or evidence was not extant. To solve this problem, Rosenman proposed to "place on trial the Nazi organizations themselves rather than the individuals and . . . convict them and all their members of engaging in a criminal conspiracy to control the world, to persecute minorities, to break treaties, to invade other nations and to commit crimes." After an organization had been "convicted," every member shown to have joined it freely "would ipso facto be guilty of a war crime."[10]

The British, Soviet, and French delegates assented to the U.S. plan. In the wake of the San Francisco conference, legal representatives from Great Britain, the United States, France, and the USSR met in London to prepare an accord regarding the trials of German war criminals, containing a charter that, in its detailed enunciation of the charges against the major offenders, would subsequently become the governing instrument of the tribunal, as well as the touchstone of both the prosecution and the defense. Article 6(c) of the charter, dealing with "crimes against humanity," would later serve as the primary charge against the euthanasia specialists in the U.S. Doctors' Trial. The U.S. approach to Nazi criminality in the charter stayed remarkably faithful to Murray Bernays's original conspiracy plan. Conspiracy, in fact, was the axle around which the wheel of the three primary charges—crimes against peace, war crimes, and crimes against humanity—revolved, as reflected in the charter's statement that "leaders, organizers, instigators, and accomplices participating in the formulation or execution of a Common Plan or Conspiracy to commit any of the foregoing crimes are responsible for all acts performed by any persons in execution of such plan." In brief, this meant that defendants would not only be charged with the substantive charge but also with conspiracy to commit the illegal act. Articles 9 and 10 extended the U.S. conspiracy theory even further by authorizing the tribunal to criminalize German organizations, thus enabling any signatory nation of the London Charter to prosecute former members of such organizations solely on the basis of their membership. In this manner, state authorities in subsequent national trials would need only submit proof that the IMT had declared the organization in question criminal; once this was done, a defendant indicted for membership in it could not challenge the court's findings on the issue.[11]

The centrality of Bernays's conspiracy theory to the U.S. conception of Nazi criminality is also evident in Jackson's Report to President Truman of June 6, 1945. In his report, Jackson set forth with lapidary clarity the U.S. intention to prosecute only those crimes committed in furtherance of a "master plan" to wage aggressive war against other nations:

> Our case against the major defendants is concerned with the Nazi master plan, not with individual barbarities and perversions which occurred independently of any central plan. The groundwork of our case must be factually authentic and constitute a well-documented history of what we are convinced was a grand, concerted pattern to incite and commit the aggressions and barbarities which have shocked the world.[12]

This paragraph—particularly the language in the first sentence, excluding the prosecution by the Allies of "individual barbarities and perversions which occurred independently of any central plan"—makes clear the U.S. refusal to proceed against crimes arising from motives unrelated to the larger plan to attack Germany's European neighbors. For Jackson and his compatriots, the IMT would only try and punish those Nazi defendants whose crimes promoted Hitler's imperialistic war of domination.

Based on Jackson's report, one would think that crimes against humanity as a separate count would find cold comfort in the U.S. conspiracy-based approach, inasmuch as they are not technically war crimes. In fact, this was not the case. The U.S. decision to push for including crimes against humanity in the indictment against the major war criminals was influenced by anti-fascist German, Austrian, and Czechoslovakian refugees (many of them Jewish) from Nazi Germany, who, fearful that the Nazis' brutalization and mass murder of German nationals and stateless persons would not be redressed in a postwar trial, implored the Allies to render justice for these outrages. The U.S. delegate to the U.N. War Crimes Commission in 1944, Herbert Pell, championed their cause, arguing that "crimes committed against stateless persons or against any persons because of their race or religion" must be punished after the war. The U.S. representatives in London carried this commitment to crimes against humanity with them into their negotiations with the other Allies. In their drafts of crimes potentially chargeable against the Nazis, the United States cited "wars of aggression," violations of the "laws and customs of war," and, in support of a count based on crimes against humanity, "atrocities and persecutions," whether or not German law at the time had recognized their legality. These same drafts used language that would eventually filter into Article 6(c) of the charter, particularly the phrase "persecutions on racial or religious grounds."[13]

Crimes Against Humanity and the Ex Post Facto Question

The U.S. interests in prosecuting crimes against humanity received sympathetic responses from the other Allies. Like Jackson and the U.S. team in London, the British had been implored by Jewish groups to prosecute racially and religiously motivated crimes perpetrated by the Nazis. The French and Soviet representatives, whose civilian populations had experienced firsthand the barbarism of National Socialist racial policy, readily agreed to include a reference to such crimes in the charter. In 1943 Professor Hersh Lauterpacht, an eminent international legal scholar, had called upon the Allies to prosecute Nazi war criminals for their murderous treatment of European Jews that did not formally qualify as war crimes. He used the phrase "crimes against humanity" to describe such crimes.[14] Influenced by Lauterpacht, Robert Jackson adopted the phrase to denote crimes of racial or religious persecution. The term "crimes against humanity" thereafter was incorporated into a final draft of the London Charter, which later served as the legal basis for Article 6 of the Nuremberg charter and the Allies' indictment. The text of Article 6 of the IMT Charter defined "crimes against humanity" as follows:

> . . . murder, extermination, enslavement, deportation, and other inhumane acts committed against any civilian population, before or during the war, or persecutions on political, racial, or religious grounds in execution of or in connection with any crime within the jurisdiction of the Tribunal, whether or not in violation of domestic law of the country where perpetrated.[15]

There is more to the charter's definition of crimes against humanity than meets the eye. According to scholars like Bradley Smith, Lawrence Douglas, and M. Cherif Bassiouni, one of the Allies' paramount concerns at the London Conference was to avoid the appearance that the Allies' trials of German war criminals were instances of ex post facto law—that is, holding a defendant legally accountable for an action that, at the time it was performed, was not specifically proscribed by law. Prior to the outbreak of war in 1939, there was no statute that forbade genocide or racial persecution; hence, prosecuting Nazi defendants for crimes against humanity as an independent theory of criminal liability would be an application of ex post facto law. For this reason, Smith, Douglas, and Bassiouni contend, the drafters made crimes against humanity an "auxiliary category" of the two other charges in the charter, "crimes against peace" and "war crimes." The relevant inkblot in the charter's definition of "crimes against humanity" is the comma after the phrase "before or during the war." The original draft had inserted a semicolon after this phrase. The Berlin Protocol of October 6, 1945, changed the semicolon to a comma in the final version. This alteration effectively bound crimes against humanity to any act under the tribunal's jurisdiction—that is, to war crimes and crimes against peace. The change meant that crimes against humanity could be prosecuted only where they were proven to further the Nazis' conspiracy to wage aggressive war on its neighbors or commit war crimes.[16]

Although Smith, Douglas, and Bassiouni's argument about the Allies' concern for the principles of legality may be sound enough with respect to France and the USSR, I believe it has less merit as applied to the United States and Great Britain. The Anglo-Americans had more scruples about principles of sovereignty than the principles of legality, and it was these concerns that caused them to insist on mooring crimes against humanity to war crimes and crimes against peace. In his address to tribunal members on this issue, the British prosecutor, Hartley Shawcross, made clear the British concern not to infringe purely domestic matters in Germany in prosecuting crimes against humanity:

> The considerations which apply here are . . . different to those affecting the other classes of offense, the crime against peace or the ordinary war crime. You have to be satisfied not only that what was done was a crime against humanity but also that it was not purely a domestic matter but that directly or indirectly it was associated with crimes against other nations or other nationals, in that, for instance, it was undertaken in order to strengthen the Nazi Party in carrying out its policy of domination by aggression, or to remove elements such as political opponents, the aged, the Jews, the existence of which would have hindered the carrying out of the total war policy.[17]

That the principles of legality, in contrast to the principle of sovereignty, were of relatively minor importance to U.S. and British authorities is proven in other Anglo-American primary source documents. In an article published in German in 1947 defending the national trials of Nazi war criminals under Control Council Law #10, English jurist and University of London professor R. H. Graveson admitted that charging crimes against humanity under Law #10 was an example of retroactive legislation, that is, an ex post facto law. He pointed out, however, that retroactivity was only one interest to be protected in criminal law, and by no means the only one. A more compelling interest within the scope of Nazi criminal prosecution was the need to punish abhorrent and monstrously unjust acts. This need overrode the ban on retroactive prosecution, as the IMT itself had recognized. For Graveson, as for the IMT, the principles of legality were subordinate to the demands of justice.[18]

U.S. Chief of Counsel Robert Jackson was adamant about the overriding imperative to sanction Nazi war criminals. In his Report to the President in June 1945, Jackson posed the rhetorical question of how the Allies should treat Nazi perpetrators:

What shall we do with them? We could, of course, set them at large without a hearing. But it has cost unmeasured thousands of American lives to beat and bind these men. To free them without a trial would mock the dead and make cynics of the living.

Jackson's report foreshadows language he would use a few months later in his opening address at Nuremberg: "The wrongs which we seek to condemn and punish have been so calculated, so malignant, and so devastating, that civilization cannot tolerate their being ignored, because it cannot tolerate their being repeated."[19] Given the moral ardor of Jackson's words, it is hard to imagine how the formalistic principles of legality could have guided his decision to make crimes against humanity dependent on recognized principles of international law (war crimes and crimes against peace).

We have already observed the reticence of some U.S. policymakers to violate the perceived sovereignty of the Nazi government. Secretary of War Henry Stimson denied the jurisdictional authority of an international court to try any offense unrelated to the conduct of war. In his memo to Roosevelt, Stimson appeared to believe that wielding jurisdiction over crimes independent of war would open the door to international violations of territorial sovereignty. Nor is Stimson's position unrepresentative of ideas about the inviolability of sovereignty in U.S. history—and the fear that foreign powers will trench upon it. Much of the curious nineteenth-century bigotry in the United States toward Catholics and Freemasons was rooted in irrational but real concerns that the Papacy, or some other foreign agency, would insinuate itself into U.S. political life and sabotage the Republic. Woodrow Wilson's failure to gain Congressional approval for the League of Nations after World War I was largely because of apprehensions that an international body with superordinate jurisdiction would compromise U.S. sovereignty. Arguably, U.S. opposition to an international war crimes tribunal after World War I was premised on the sovereignty principle. When seen in historical context, the attitudes of U.S. policymakers toward crimes against humanity as an independently actionable species of criminality seem more intelligible. We cannot but marvel, given this context, that the United States emerged as the primary advocate of international trials following World War II.

Furthermore, by focusing on crimes related to the war, Jackson could better redeem the U.S. all-encompassing theory of Nazi criminality: a conspiracy among virtually all sectors of German society (the Nazi Party, the German government, the military, and business) to wage aggressive war against other countries. On the U.S. view, crimes against humanity, including the murder of the mentally ill and European Jews, were byways along the highway of imperialistic war. They were not, on this view, the animating force behind Nazi criminality, but incidental byproducts of the Germans' implacable urge to wage war to expand Germany's borders at the cost of its European neighbors. This conception of Nazi criminality was embodied in the London Agreement and the IMT Charter; it dominated the U.S. approach to Nazi criminality, both during the IMT proceedings and the U.S. Doctors' Trial.

The hinge joining the IMT Charter and Control Council Law #10 (the legal instrument that served as the basis for the 1947 Doctors' Trial) was a document issued by the U.S. Joint Chiefs of Staff, "JCS 1023/10." JCS 1023/10 was a directive approved by the U.S. Joint Chiefs of Staff on July 15, 1945, setting forth what its authors hoped would be the model for war crimes policy throughout occupied Germany. It was heavily influenced by Jackson's Report to the President of June 1945, reproducing almost word for word his definition of the crimes chargeable against Nazi defendants. Like the IMT Charter, JCS 1023/10 envisioned prosecuting both principals and accessories, as well as "members of groups or organizations connected with the commission of such crimes." These included Nazi Party and SS officers, members of the General Staff, and the legal staffs of the Nazi "Peoples' Courts," who were to be detained by theater commanders and tried if evidence warranted trial. Theater commanders, however, were instructed to delay trial of higher-ranking officials until it was decided whether they would be prosecuted before an international tribunal. Jackson's Office of the U.S. Chief of Counsel at Nuremberg was chosen as the administrative office, charged with implementing the terms of the directive. In late November 1945, the legal adviser to the Office of the Military Government U.S. (OMGUS) approached Telford Taylor (at the time involved in prosecuting members of the German General Staff before the IMT) about heading the project.[20]

Crimes Against Humanity and Control Council Law #10

The Control Council, which served as the Allied occupation government of Germany, meanwhile prepared a draft of its own law on Nazi war crimes prosecution. Modeled on JCS 1023/10, the draft was enacted as Control Council Law #10 on December 20, 1945. The framers of Law #10 defined its purpose as threefold: first, to implement the terms of the Moscow Declaration (specifically, those portions of the declaration that envisioned the return of minor war criminals to the countries where their crimes were committed and a separate proceeding to deal with the major war criminals); second, to implement the London Agreement and Charter; and finally, "to establish a uniform legal basis in Germany for the prosecution of war criminals and other similar offenders, other than those dealt with by the IMT." Further, Law #10 outlined the scope of crimes for which Nazi defendants could be held criminally liable.

In defining such crimes, the drafters of Law #10 drew explicitly on the charges sketched in Jackson's Report to the President (and embodied in JCS 1023/10), as well as those propounded in the London agreement. These included "crimes against peace," "war crimes," and "crimes against humanity"—all virtually the same as the charges in the London Charter and JCS 1023/10. Consistent with these two antecedent documents, Law #10 also provided the charge of membership in organizations deemed criminal by the IMT.[21]

To assert that Law #10's definition of crimes against humanity was substantially the same as that described in the charter and JCS 1023/10 is not to say they were identical. In fact, the wordsmiths who fashioned Law #10's version of crimes against humanity introduced a crucial amendment—or, rather, a crucial omission—in its version. Consider again the charter's Article 6 version defining crimes against humanity:

> . . . murder, extermination, enslavement, deportation, and other inhumane acts committed against any civilian population, *before or during the war*, or persecutions on political, racial, or religious grounds *in execution of or in connection with any crime within the jurisdiction of the Tribunal*, whether or not in violation of domestic law of the country where perpetrated.[22] (emphasis added)

Law #10's definition, on the other hand, defines crimes against humanity as "atrocities and offences, including but not limited to murder, extermination, enslavement, deportation, imprisonment, torture, rape, or other inhumane acts committed against any civilian population, or persecutions on political, racial or religious grounds whether or not in violation of the domestic laws of the country where perpetrated." The critical omissions from Law #10's version are the two phrases in the charter's definition above, "before or during the war" and "in execution of or in connection with any crime within the jurisdiction of the Tribunal." With these elisions, the drafters of Law #10 dissolved the link between crimes against humanity and war crimes, transforming the former into its own self-contained, independently chargeable offense.[23]

The odor of ex post facto law would cling to the prosecution of the major war criminals in front of the IMT. Defenders of these trials, however, could always rebut charges of retroactivity by pointing to specific written documents that expressed an international condemnation of war crimes before Hitler came to power in 1933; in some cases, as with the Kellogg-Briand Pact (1928), Germany had been among the signatories. By connecting crimes against humanity to war crimes, defenders of the IMT trials could at least make a plausible case that prosecuting crimes against humanity was in keeping with prior law, and thus did not violate the principles of legality. This argument became less convincing once the link with war crimes was annulled. The U.S. jurists presiding over the subsequent trials under Law #10 deflected the ex post facto objections of defense counsel with various justifications. In the Justice Case (Case 4), which prosecuted sixteen defendants charged with perverting the judicial process (particularly its involvement in "racial defilement" cases), the judges first pointed out that ex post facto law is not an absolute bar to prosecution in international law, then added that in any event the defendants must have known their actions were wrongful. In the *Einsatzgruppen* and *Krupp* cases (Cases 9 and 10),[24] the judges defended their jurisdiction on the grounds that international law had criminalized the defendants' conduct well before they had perpetrated their crimes. These justifications were often made by way of ex cathedra statements with little analysis or sustained argumentation.

To a certain extent, we are jumping ahead of ourselves in discussing the subsequent trials under Law #10. The first of these proceedings, the Doctors' Trial, would bring U.S. judicial authorities face to face with the Nazis' campaign of annihilation against "life unworthy of life." Even before the Doctors' Trial, however, U.S. military officials presided in judgment over German medical personnel charged with murdering hundreds of Russian and Polish workers at the Hadamar killing center. As we will see, the U.S. Hadamar trial in fall 1945 already presages the U.S. tendency to conceive of Nazi criminality as an outgrowth of imperialistic war. This tendency was nourished and reinforced by extra-legal concerns to protect the principle of sovereignty. U.S. policymakers, in short, feared that allowing crimes perpetrated by governments on their own people to be prosecuted in international criminal courts would open the door to future trials of U.S. officials. Such a possibility represented an erosion of sovereignty that U.S. policymakers would not tolerate.

THE U.S. HADAMAR TRIAL, OCTOBER 1945

Americans first glimpsed the Nazi euthanasia program through the fogged lens of sensationalized accounts in hometown newspapers. The unvarnished truth of what happened at the Hadamar euthanasia center in Hessen-Nassau, however, was more chilling than any of the embroidered newspaper stories. The sensational features of these news accounts were unnecessary to portray Hadamar in a notorious light; the reality was grotesque enough. Yet, the distortions in the newspaper stories are emblematic of the fumbling early efforts by the United States to understand the National Socialist destruction of "life unworthy of life." Although that understanding improved with time, it never wholly overcame the tendency to squeeze Nazi euthanasia into misleading a priori categories and questionable interpretive frameworks. This tendency was intrinsic to the correspondence and memoranda generated in the planning stages of the Nuremberg International Military Tribunal. It manifested itself in an U.S.

The Hadamar killing center in Hessen-Nassau, the subject of the 1945 U.S. Army trial by military commission and the 1947 trial by a German court. Courtesy Archiv des Landeswohlfahrtsverbandes Hessen, Kassel

criminal proceeding in the case of *U.S. v. Alfons Klein et al.*, the U.S. Hadamar trial held October 8–15, 1945.

Hadamar was a town of 6,000 people in the German state of Hessen-Nassau, twenty-seven miles south of the city of Wiesbaden. From 1939 until 1940, the institution at Hadamar served both as a mental hospital and a hospital for German soldiers and POWs. In late 1940, it was selected as a replacement killing center for the euthanasia institution at Grafeneck, which, along with Brandenburg, was closed in December 1940. Over the next nine months, until it temporarily closed in August 1941, the T-4 medical staff at Hadamar gassed at least 10,000 mentally disabled German nationals. In his interrogation by the U.S. Army in 1945, the director of Hadamar, Alfons Klein, claimed that euthanasia at Hadamar ceased from August 1941 until August 1942, at which time the killing of mental patients resumed, this time by means of narcotics overdoses. During this second phase, children's wards were established at Hadamar to murder two distinct groups of children: mentally disabled German youngsters and *Mischlingkinder*, or half-Jewish children (many of whom were healthy before they were killed). Also during the second phase, Hadamar personnel killed concentration camp prisoners as part of the "14f13" operation. It is unclear whether another group of victims, the asocials, was murdered at Hadamar; although a witness at the German Hadamar trial in 1947 testified about plans to exterminate the inmates of workhouses there (i.e., beggars, the homeless, and prostitutes), the evidence—much of it destroyed in the waning months of the war—is not definitive on the issue. The final victim group killed at Hadamar, hundreds of Polish and Russian forced laborers ill with tuberculosis, was the subject of the U.S. Hadamar trial by army personnel in October 1945.[25]

U.S. jurisdiction over the Hadamar defendants was premised on JCS 1023/10, which assigned authority for war crimes trials to military theater commanders. Under its terms, responsibility for conducting the trials was reserved to the Office of the Military Government for Germany (OMGUS) and the Deputy Judge Advocate for War Crimes, European Command. On August 25, 1945, U.S. generals were authorized to indict and prosecute German defendants suspected of war crimes. The trials would be conducted before one of two bodies: either a "specially appointed" military court or a military commission formed by the commander of an army in the field. A significant component in the legal foundation of the military commissions was not statutory;[26] rather, it was the "common law of war," which did not specify the kind of trial to be given a war criminal—only that the procedure be a fair one. In trials before military commissions, the commission itself was free to fashion rules of procedure ad hoc, although, to facilitate the proceeding, the forms of General Courts-Martial (such as the use of charge sheets) could be adopted. Significantly, the rules of evidence observed in General Courts-martial were not binding on military commissions. Rules of evidence were to be applied only to expedite the trial and to prevent irrelevancies "lacking probative value." The principle governing admissibility was whether the proffered evidence "has probative value to a reasonable man" as determined by the president of the commission.[27]

The U.S. Army's early intramural correspondence about the Hadamar killing center set the tone for the U.S. Hadamar trial. In a memorandum from HQ V Corps, Office of the Inspector General, dated April 6, 1945, Col. John W. McCaslin described Hadamar as part of the "mercy killing program" established in Germany "in accordance with the existing laws of Germany, which permitted mercy killings and which became effective in 1939." McCaslin was no doubt referring to the Hitler decree of September 1, 1939 (actually signed on October 1 and backdated to September 1), a document that empowered Philipp Bouhler of the KdF and Karl Brandt to authorize doctors to "grant a mercy death" to "incurable" patients. According to McCaslin, the Nazis employed Hadamar to murder political enemies and foreign laborers. He then declares that under international law the army was "only concerned with the murder of these foreign forced laborers, and the fact must be established that the forced laborers were in good health at the time of extermination, otherwise no war atrocity has been committed under the existing laws of the German government."[28]

The claimed legality of the euthanasia program under German law appears in other army correspondence from spring and summer 1945. In a War Crimes Branch Summary Worksheet, an anonymous army officer portrays the killings at Hadamar as "systematic murder in which 20,000 political prisoners, Jews, and slave laborers are estimated to have been put to death by unidentified SS men on orders from Berlin at a concentration camp at Hadamar, Germany under a 1939 statute." Revisionist historians would have a field day with the inaccuracies in this statement: Hadamar was not a concentration camp, but a mental institution devoted to ridding Germany of "unworthy life"; little if any evidence exists that "political prisoners" were killed there; the killers were not, for the most part, SS men but employees of the KdF and, later, rank-and-file staff members of the institution; and, finally, the Hitler decree was not a statute, but an unpublished decree—no law, as we have seen, was ever published formally legalizing euthanasia in Germany. These mistakes recur in an office memo to Lt. Col. Leon Jaworski (appointed decades later as the special prosecutor in the Watergate scandal) from a Major Burton, dated May 31, 1945, who depicted the Hadamar killings as "the wholesale massacre and murder of thousands of political prisoners, Jews, and slave laborers at Hadamar concentration camp, Germany, by Gestapo and SS men." The factual errors in these documents suggest that U.S. military authorities regarded the euthanasia killings through the optic of their prior traumatic encounters with Nazi brutality—particularly the discovery of concentration camps in Germany by the U.S. Army and of the death camps by the Red Army in Poland, as well as the Malmédy massacre on December 17, 1944. The inextricable association of these events with the SS may account for the army's predisposition to (mis)interpret other instances of National Socialist violence in light of it.[29]

Most significantly for our purposes, these documents reveal the degree to which the army had assumed a legal basis in German law for the euthanasia program. Their presumption of legality meant that army officials would only consider prosecuting defendants who had killed mentally healthy victims at Hadamar. To prosecute these same defendants for killing the mentally disabled would breach the principle of sovereignty, according to which foreign powers are not legally permitted to intervene in the domestic affairs of another country. A July 1945 memorandum to a Lt. Col. Mize amply demonstrates the U.S. overriding concern with state sovereignty. Affirming that the Hadamar staff had carried out the killings pursuant to a 1939 German law, the memo's author denies that the army had any business prosecuting the accused for killing mentally ill German patients, "because there appears to be no substantial evidence that those Germans who were killed were not, in fact, incurably insane." On the other hand, the author continues, "there is an abundance of evidence that many of the Russians and Poles were neither insane nor incurably ill from any other disease. . . . [I]t matters little whether the law itself, which permitted the killings under certain circumstances, would be a good defense if those circumstances were complied with because they were not, in fact, complied with insofar . . . as the Russians and Poles were concerned."[30]

It is clear from these excerpts that U.S. Army officials were concerned above all else with defending state power. Technically, the Americans *could* have prosecuted the Hadamar defendants for killing mentally ill Russian and Polish workers; their mental capacity had no bearing on their protection by the Geneva and Hague conventions. In the pre-trial army correspondence, however, the option of trying the Hadamar staff for murdering the mentally ill of any nationality was ruled out from the beginning. As Colonel McCaslin asserted, only if the United States could prove the murdered eastern workers were healthy at the time of their death could they obtain a conviction under international law. If, on the contrary, the workers were incurably insane, then they were covered by German law—or so the United States presumed. For the U.S. Army officials, to prosecute the defendants for performing an act legal under German law at the time of its commission would be an impermissible incursion into the domestic affairs of the Third Reich.

The aversion of U.S. military officials to prosecuting acts considered legal under then existing German law structured the army JAG lawyers' approach to the Hadamar killings during the trial. The commitment of U.S. officials to focus only on the murders of mentally healthy eastern workers clearly emerges in the prosecution's opening statement before the military commission, in which the prosecution describes Hadamar as a mental hospital that cared for the mentally disabled until summer 1944, when it was converted into a killing center for Poles and Russians.[31] This depiction ignores the thousands of German adults, disabled children, and half-Jewish youngsters murdered at Hadamar long before then. The prosecution not only neglected to mention this prior history but strove throughout the trial to counter the defense's attempts to locate the murders of the eastern workers within the context of the euthanasia program. Inasmuch as this contextualization was the defendants' best chance of escaping the hangman's noose, the struggle over the degree to which it should be foregrounded became the central theme of the trial.

From the outset, the basic theory of the defense was straightforward: the defendants may have been involved in killing through lethal injections the tubercular eastern workers, but they had believed at the time their actions were sanctioned by a 1939 German law and thus were unaware their actions were wrongful. Of course, to raise this defense required the presentation of evidence concerning the alleged law and the program of mass killing developed under its aegis. Attempts by defense counsel to do just that led to the trial's most important legal clashes. During the presentation of its case in chief, the prosecution called a former nurse at Hadamar, Minna Zachow, to recount how Polish and Russian forced laborers were given lethal injections there during summer 1944. On cross-examination, defense counsel asked the witness to estimate how many German mental patients were killed at Hadamar between August 8, 1942 (i.e., the date when killings resumed after the "pause"), and March 3, 1945. This line of questioning drew an objection from the prosecutor, who argued:

> [T]he charge doesn't cover any Germans at all. We could be here a month trying that. Counsel's clients are not on trial for any German nationals they may have killed. This is confined entirely to the Russian and the Polish.[32]

Defense counsel responded that "there was no distinction made between the Russians and Poles and . . . thousands of Germans were killed at the same hospital by the prosecution's witnesses and they thought it perfectly proper." The prosecution retorted that defense counsel's exploration of the euthanasia program as it affected German mentally disabled patients at Hadamar was irrelevant, because the defendants were not charged with murdering German nationals. Defense counsel defended the relevance of the questioning on the grounds that "it goes to the heart of the defense, i.e. the action against the Poles and Russians was part of the larger program of euthanasia authorized by the 'law of the land.'" Although admitting the commission had no jurisdiction over the murders of mentally disabled German victims, the defense insisted that their deaths were relevant "in order that we get a complete history and picture of this institution at Hadamar. . . . [The court] must consider the picture as it was at Hadamar and become acquainted with the state of mind of the accused and all other personnel at the institution."[33]

Defense counsel had logic, law, and the military rules of evidence on its side in this argument. The widely recognized defense of "mistake of law" was relevant to the Hadamar proceedings, because it could have negated the defendants' intent to commit murder, an element necessary to finding the defendants guilty of the offense.[*] Further, when a defendant has received incorrect advice about a law or administrative ruling from a person charged with administering it, the defendant may raise reliance on such advice as a valid defense.[34] Given the prosecution's admission that a law on euthanasia was in existence, according to which mentally ill Germans were put to death at Hadamar for

---

[*] A mistake of law occurs when a defendant reasonably relies on the legitimacy of a law, judicial decision, or administrative ruling later declared to be invalid.

years prior to the murders of the eastern European forced workers, evidence of the degree to which defendants reasonably relied on the euthanasia "statute" was relevant and material to the "determination of the action" under the rules of military evidence. As we will see when we take up the German euthanasia trials in Chapter 3, characterizing the secret Hitler order as a law is dubious; yet, the U.S. government's strange willingness to assume the legality of the Hitler order certainly opened the door to examining the impact of that order—and the program conceived pursuant to it—on the defendants' state of mind.

The military commission hearing the case sustained the prosecution's objection on the grounds of relevance. Defense counsel did not quietly accept the commission's ruling but sought at several junctures in the trial to reopen the issue of whether the defendants believed their actions were legal based on the existence of the Hitler "statute." Each time the defense revisited the issue, the military commission rebuffed its efforts, holding this line of questioning irrelevant to the case at bar.[35] Only when the defense presented its case in chief did the commission grant some leeway to raise the issue of mistake of law.

In its direct examination of Alfons Klein (director of Hadamar from 1939 to 1945) and Adolf Wahlmann (assigned to Hadamar as chief doctor in August 1942), defense counsel elicited information about the institution's function within the T-4 euthanasia program. Replying to the question whether Hadamar personnel were aware of the Hitler decree that "permitted the killing of . . . incurable and mentally diseased patients," Klein testified that they were informed in 1940 of the euthanasia "law," and were instructed that "the Reich Government decided upon this law, that all incurable, mentally diseased should die." On redirect exam, he related that a Gauleiter Sprenger had told him the Polish and Russian workers would fall under the same euthanasia "law"; for this reason, he claimed, "I didn't doubt to any extent that it was not correct." In a sworn statement, Adolf Wahlmann claimed that both Klein and State Councillor Fritz Bernotat, who was in charge of all mental hospitals and nursing homes in Hessen-Naussau, had assured him the eastern workers brought to Hadamar in summer 1944 were covered by the Hitler euthanasia order. Other defendants charged with the murders alluded to the connection between the "mercy deaths" of mentally ill German patients under the Hitler decree and the killing of sick eastern workers.[36]

The prosecution's discomfiture regarding this testimony is evident in the trial transcript. On Klein's redirect examination, his defense counsel invited him to talk about the refusal of the German legal authorities to intervene in the killing process at Hadamar, despite their awareness of its existence. The prosecution balked at this line of questioning. Although the matter was rel-

Dr. Adolf Wahlmann, chief doctor at the Hadamar mental hospital beginning in August 1942. Convicted by a U.S. military commission in 1945 for his role in the murders of sick eastern workers, he was found guilty of murder by a German court in March 1947 for euthanizing German patients at Hadamar. Courtesy HHStAW Abt. 3008, Adolf Wahlmann

evant to the defendants' perception of the illegality of their conduct, the military commission sustained the objection. The prosecution had less success in objecting to the testimony of Dr. Hans Quanbusch, the former public prosecutor of Wiesbaden, called as a witness for the defense. He testified that all the prosecutors and presidents of the German appellate courts throughout the Reich were summoned to a meeting in the Berlin state court, during which a photostatic copy of Hitler's 1939 euthanasia decree was shown to the participants. Quanbusch described the decree as an administrative order rather than a law. Nonetheless, the chief prosecutors were instructed to inform their subordinates that "under no circumstances were they to do anything about charges that were being filed." In the event a relative of a patient killed in the euthanasia operation insisted on filing criminal charges against a mental hospital, the case was to be sent to the Ministry of Justice "as a secret state matter" (*geheime Reichssache*). Quanbusch concluded that "through this [quashing of legal action] the physicians were protected from any suing, and it was impossible for the prosecutor to start any proceedings." The prosecution moved to have Quanbusch's testimony excluded from consideration by the commission in its findings of fact on the grounds of relevance, arguing that the testimony dealt with the euthanasia of German mental patients—which was not properly before the court—and not with eastern workers. The commission overruled the objection, perhaps because defense counsel claimed it was offering Quanbusch's testimony as evidence of the duress under which defendants had acted.[37]

The government's efforts to restrict the case to mentally healthy Polish and Russian forced workers were consistent with the views expressed in the pre-trial legal memoranda we have previously examined. As in the memoranda, so in the Hadamar trial the U.S. commitment to the principle of sovereignty skewed its conception of Nazi euthanasia criminality, leading to a number of misrepresentations. First, by excluding the mentally ill from the picture, the prosecution entirely discounted Hadamar's connection with the euthanasia program directed at "unworthy life," in the service of which Hadamar played a pivotal role. There is little in its portrayal of Hadamar to suggest the progression of cumulative violence as it spiraled outward from "incurable" mental patients to include Jews, half-Jewish children, disabled children, and eastern workers. In the illusory image of Hadamar invented by the prosecution, the institution "cared" for the mentally ill until the moment when the tubercular eastern workers arrived in 1944.

The commission's second misrepresentation concerned the erroneous assumption that the Hitler decree of September 1939 was a valid law affording a legal basis for the euthanasia of mentally disabled Germans. The first newspaper accounts about Hadamar in April 1945, presumably based on information provided by army public relations, referred to the decree as a "German law" or "statute." Intramural army communiqués leading up to the trial in October 1945 at no time questioned the legality of the Hitler order. The U.S. prosecution team's theory of the case during the trial demonstrated uncritical acceptance of this belief, steering the prosecution away from any conception of Hadamar that might involve prosecuting Germans acting under color of German law. In this fashion, the United States virtually provided a ready-made defense to the lawyers representing the defendants. By connecting the killing of the eastern workers to an alleged euthanasia "law," defense counsel could persuasively argue that Klein and his codefendants lacked the knowledge that what they were doing was illegal. That local law enforcement authorities were aware of the killings but did nothing to prevent them or to hold the perpetrators legally accountable for them only strengthened the defense counsel's argument.

A third misrepresentation concerned the U.S. application of the Anglo-American doctrine of conspiracy to the Hadamar killings, a doctrine that portrayed euthanasia criminality as an offshoot of Nazi warmaking and the Hadamar defendants as jointly and equally liable for the crimes. We have seen the degree to which the law of conspiracy dominated the thinking of U.S. policymakers within the government in the years preceding the Nuremberg trials. On this theory, the Nazis' plan to wage an aggressive imperialistic war was a criminal conspiracy from which all of the regime's criminality flowed. In its closing argument before the military commission, the prosecution laid out its theory of conspiracy, wherein all distinctions between principal and accomplice, based on their varying contributions to the criminal conspiracy, are completely annulled:

> In the cases that are carefully schemed and plotted, you will find that there may be some 10 or 15 who participated in various stages in the matter laying the preparations and the foundation for the . . . commission of the act of murder itself. Every single one of those who participated in any degree toward the accomplishment of that result is as much guilty of murder as the man who actually pulled the trigger. That is why under our federal law all distinctions between accessories before the fact and accessories after the fact have been completely eliminated. Any who participate in the commission of any crime whether formerly called as an accessory or what are now co-principals and have been so for several years.[38]

The prosecution cited U.S. Code Title 18, section 550: "Whoever directly commits any act constituting an offense defined in any law or aids, abets, counsels, commands, induces, or procures its commission is a principal." It then applied this notion to the Hadamar killings:

Now, talking about the facts of this case, why with each of them being a principal, considered a co-principal, one is equally as guilty as the other. . . . When you do business on a wholesale production basis that they did at the Hadamar murder factory it means that you have several people doing different things of that illegal operation in order to produce results and you cannot draw a distinction between the man that may have initially conceived the idea of killing them and those that participated in the commission of those offenses.[39]

When, in the course of its closing argument, the prosecution referred to the abolition of distinctions between principals and accomplices, it was describing the U.S. law of conspiracy as it existed in the mid-1940s. According to conspiracy law, where two or more individuals conspire to commit a crime, each is liable for offenses committed by his or her confederates in furtherance of the conspiracy. Conspiracy essentially did away with the common law distinctions between principals and accomplices/accessories.

The intial impetus behind the U.S. decision to apply the law of conspiracy to the prosecution of Nazi criminality was functional in nature: by obtaining judicial declarations that certain German organizations were criminal conspiracies, U.S. war crimes planners hoped to avoid the intractable problem of trying the tens of thousands of potential defendants on the merits of each case. There are, however, obvious drawbacks to conspiracy, chief among them its tendency to obscure the distinctive contribution of each conspirator to the crime. In the Hadamar trial, the prosecution successfully argued for the conviction and punishment of the defendants as principals—even though they were all subsidiary actors in the Nazi scheme to destroy "life unworthy of life."

Surveying the actual contributions of each defendant to the Hadamar murders highlights the shortcomings in the prosecution's understanding of the crime. Seven defendants were indicted at the Hadamar trial: Alfons Klein, the director; Adolf Wahlmann, the chief doctor; Heinrich Ruoff, the head male nurse; Karl Willig, the ward male nurse; Irmgard Huber, the head female nurse; Philip Blum, the institution's cemetery attendant; and Adolph Merkel, the registrar and bookkeeper. Despite the defendants' self-exculpatory representations during their army interrogations and at trial, the evidence presented allows us to recreate the killing of the eastern workers with a reasonable degree of certainty. Sometime in summer 1944, Klein met with State Councillor Bernotat, who informed Klein he had received a letter from the Gau Employment Office concerning the large numbers of tubercular eastern workers in Nazi labor camps. According to Klein's testimony at trial, the letter stated that these workers were incurably ill and inquired "whether any building or institution could be used to shelter these sick people." Bernotat then allegedly asked Klein whether the sick workers could be accommodated at Hadamar. We have reason to doubt Klein's innocuous portrayal of Bernotat's request; it seems highly unlikely that at this critical moment in the war, having already murdered millions of Jews, Poles, and Russians in Eastern Europe, the Nazis would have transferred "incurable" eastern workers to a killing center for the purpose of sheltering them. Our skepticism is bolstered by events that ensued after this meeting. Two weeks later, Bernotat visited Hadamar and supposedly informed Klein there was a change of plans: the "incurable" eastern workers were now to be killed at Hadamar. Bernotat, Klein alleged, had been told by Gauleiter Sprenger that all the workers were incurable and thus "it wouldn't pay to transport them any more." Wahlmann, on the other hand, declared that the workers were earmarked for killing in order to free up hospital space for war-related casualties. Klein claimed that Wahlmann was present at this meeting with Bernotat, an assertion Wahlmann denied. Wahlmann does admit that Klein informed him during the summer that Hadamar would receive transports of eastern workers suffering from incurable tuberculosis. These individuals were to be given "mercy killing," using the same techniques refined in the euthanasia of mentally ill Germans.[40]

The first transport of seventy-five sick eastern workers arrived at Hadamar in July or August 1944. Contrary to the statements of Klein and Wahlmann, postmortem exams of the corpses revealed that few were terminally or gravely ill before their deaths.[41] They were housed on the first floor of the institution in two modest rooms that had been cleared of their occupants by Nurse Huber prior to their arrival. Subsequent transports consisted of between one to ten eastern laborers and continued from late summer 1944 until March 1945. Once Huber had settled them in their beds, the eastern workers were attended by Ruoff and Willig. Before the workers' arrival both men had been briefed by Klein and Wahlmann on the need to kill them. Wahlmann prepared the overdoses of narcotics (chiefly veronal, trional, and chloral tablets and morphine/scopolamine injections) and handed them to Ruoff and Willig. The two nurses administered the "medication" to the eastern workers, who died shortly thereafter. The corpses were taken by Philip Blum (Klein's cousin) to the Hadamar cemetery for burial. Adolph Merkle recorded their names and phony causes of death in the hospital patient registry, which was later conveyed to the Office of Statistics (*Standesamt*) for the town of Hadamar. After the first transport, morning conferences involving Wahlmann, Huber, and Ruoff (or sometimes Willig) were regularly held to sign falsified death certificates and prepare lists of patients to be killed.[42]

Clearly, each of the defendants in this scheme discharged a specific function: Klein relayed the order from Bernotat and Sprenger, Wahlmann organized and set in motion the means of producing death through narcotics overdoses, Huber prepared space for and situated the victims, Ruoff and Willig administered the deadly cocktails, Merkle covered up the crime with false entries on patient lists, and Blum disposed of the bodies. Their roles in the plan to exterminate the ill eastern workers—reprehensible though they are—were subordinate to the higher authorities in Wiesbaden (Bernotat and Sprenger). Klein, Wahlmann, and the others did not contrive the plan themselves; they loyally carried out the wishes of those who *had* personally designed the plan. To treat them all as principals or co-perpetrators under a totalizing theory of conspiracy distorts their ancillary position in a much larger, much more nefarious program to annihilate individuals branded by the Nazis as "surplus" people.

The divergence between the truth of Nazi euthanasia at Hadamar and the U.S. construction of euthanasia at trial receives further confirmation when we examine the testimony of Wahlmann and Karl Willig. During his pre-trial interrogation by the U.S. Army, Wahlmann made a remarkable admission: the eastern workers were killed at Hadamar to clear hospital space for "the wounded," presumably German soldiers and civilians injured in air raids. "My primary consideration was, that through this mercy killing, beds would be made available for the wounded, friend and foe alike." Wahlmann opined that putting to death incurable mentally ill Germans, Russians, and Poles was justified, because "they are a handicap to us . . . when they take up room in our institutions."[43]

The case of Hadamar ward nurse Karl Willig lends credibility to Wahlmann's statement. From 1938 to July 1941, Willig worked at the Herborn asylum, where in mid-1941 he assisted in evacuating Herborn's mental patients, presumably to make possible the conversion of the facility into a hospital. After a brief stay at Hadamar, he was assigned to the mental hospital in Lübeck; here, in his own words, he "cleaned out the hospital of sick people," again for the purpose of transforming the institution into a hospital for the German army. From Lübeck he traveled to Neustadt, "clean[ing] out hospitals all the time," until, at the close of 1941, he returned to Hadamar, serving first as a telephone operator and later as a ward nurse under Heinrich Ruoff. Insofar as we know, in these earlier clearings of patients in mental hospitals Willig did not pursue the violent solution of killing as a way to free up hospital space. Instead, the evacuated patients were relocated to other institutions in Germany. Not until he reached Hadamar in late 1941 was he introduced to mass murder as a radical means to the end of creating hospital space for "valuable" Germans:

> They always told me before that they put them away with gas. When I came up there [to Hadamar] they told me that the hospital had to be cleaned out for use for soldiers and that there was no use in those people [the mentally ill] living. I was only a little man and had to do what people told me to do.[44]

Willig's confession rings true to what we know of the euthanasia program in late 1941 and early 1942. This was the period that witnessed the onset of the Allied bombing offensive against German cities, as well as alarming reversals on the Eastern Front. Operation Brandt, as described in Chapter 1, was developed to evacuate mental hospitals for use by bombed-out civilians and Wehrmacht soldiers. The mentally disabled evacuees (including shell-shocked Hamburg women in July 1943) were sent to places like Hadamar, Meseritz-Obrawalde, and Eichberg to be starved to death or killed with overdoses of medication. In this brutalizing atmosphere Willig cut his teeth. By the time the tubercular eastern workers arrived in Hadamar in summer 1944, he was an experienced and efficient killer.

The U.S. prosecutors presented a different theory of the Hadamar defendants' motives in their closing argument before the military commission: the motive of careerism, or "personal preferment." On this interpretation, Wahlmann, Klein, and Huber were gamblers wagering that Germany would win the war and that they would be rewarded for their work by a triumphant National Socialist state: "They were seeking personal preferment, and there is no doubt in the mind of anyone here but they would have received personal preferment had Germany won the war." A crass, self-regarding careerism was the force behind their descent into mass killing, the prosecution argued. It also scoffed at the defendants' claims that they were unaware their actions were anything but legal. If this had been the case, defendants would not have been at pains to falsify the death records in an attempt to conceal the killings from the public. Further, Huber and Wahlmann spoke openly to each other of the harsh retribution they could expect if the United States won the war. The commission hearing the case agreed with the prosecution's version of the Hadamar killings; on October 15, 1945, after a one-week trial, it found all the defendants guilty of murder in violation of the Geneva conventions and the Laws of War. It sentenced Klein, Ruoff, and Willig to death and the remaining defendants to hard labor for terms varying from life to twenty-five years.[45]

What emerges from the Hadamar trial when we focus on the prosecution's case in chief and the verdicts of the commission is the following image of euthanasia at Hadamar: the defendants were involved as perpetrators in a conspiracy to kill Polish and Russian workers suffering from tuberculosis with full knowledge that these murders were not sanctioned by the German euthanasia law of 1939 and for the purpose of furthering their careers in a postwar National Socialist Germany. By disconnecting the murders from the larger context of the Nazi campaign against "life unworthy of life," including the mass extermination of Jews, Gypsies, asocials, Soviet POWs, and the mentally disabled, the U.S. prosecutors presented a historically truncated version of the mass murder at Hadamar. U.S. concerns with protecting its own sovereignty, even as U.S. officials assumed a legal basis for euthanasia in German law, predisposed their case toward error. Karl Willig, speaking in tears before the military commission that would sentence him to death, complained: "It is a hard fate, that we the smallest ones who never had anything to say and only had to obey have to be here accused of such a charge." When Willig uttered these words in October 1945, there was certainly truth in them. The primary designers of Nazi euthanasia had yet to be tried; many would never be held accountable for their actions in a legal proceeding. By the time of the Medical Case one year later, however, two of the leading figures in the program to murder "valueless life" stood accused of crimes against humanity in the dock at Nuremberg. The U.S. Doctors' Trial would depart from the inadequate understanding of Nazi criminality that characterized the army's prosecution at Hadamar. At the same time, it would be encumbered with its own problematic conceptions of National Socialist euthanasia—conceptions that, like those of the U.S. Commission at Hadamar, were shaped by considerations of national power.

THE U.S. DOCTORS' TRIAL, NOVEMBER 1946–AUGUST 1947

Scarcely a month after judgment was pronounced on the Hadamar defendants, the International Military Tribunal convened to try the "major war criminals" under the terms of the London Charter. Consistent with the earlier recommendations of Stimson and Jackson, the U.S. authorities at Nuremberg equated Nazi criminality with a tentacular conspiracy to wage aggressive war. Their approach was summed up by Jackson during the London conference:

> [O]ur view is that this isn't merely a case of showing that these Nazi
> Hitlerite people failed to be gentlemen in war; it is a matter of their
> having designed an illegal attack on the international peace . . . and the
> other atrocities were all preparatory to it or done in execution of it.[46]

On this theory of Nazism, the Final Solution and the euthanasia program were mere byproducts of the Nazis' military conquests throughout Europe. Telford Taylor perceived the danger of this reductionist understanding of Nazi criminality. In his memoirs he wrote that "the conspiracy case . . . bid fair to swallow the greater part of the entire case."[47] Yet, Taylor and his associates remained loyal to the conspiracy theory of Nazi criminality. In his address before the IMT, Jackson's assistant prosecutor, Sidney Alderman, identified as the "heart of the case" the "planning, preparation, initiation, and waging of illegal and aggressive war." Alderman continued:

> All the dramatic story of what went on in Germany in the early phases of
> the conspiracy—the ideologies used, the techniques of terror used, . . . and

even the concentration camps and the Crimes against Humanity, the persecutions, tortures, and murders committed—all these things would have little juridical international significance except for the fact that they were the preparation for the commission of aggressions against peaceful neighboring peoples. Even the aspects of the case involving War Crimes . . . are aspects which are merely the inevitable, proximate result of the wars of aggression launched and waged by these conspirators.[48]

Alderman conceded that the defendants were involved in this conspiracy in varying degrees. However, the law of conspiracy rendered them all jointly and severally liable for the acts of each participant in the plot to wage aggressive war: "All the parties to a Common Plan or Conspiracy are the agents of each other and each is responsible as principal for the acts of all the others as his agents."[49]

At the London conference, the Soviets and the French had regarded the conspiracy charge in Article 6 of the charter with consternation. The Anglo-American theory of conspiracy was foreign to the tradition of continental law in which France, the USSR, and Germany were steeped. Although continental jurisprudence had laws to prosecute group criminality, the charge of criminal combination was absorbed into the substantive offense at trial; there was no separate conspiracy charge once a defendant's guilt for a crime was established. Interestingly, the historical adviser to the British Foreign Office, E. L. Woodward, shared the French and Soviets' misgivings about conspiracy, arguing that no such scheme to wage aggressive war existed. Like the French and Soviets, too, he believed the prosecution's case—and historical truth—would best be served by focusing on war crimes and crimes against humanity. The prosecutors at Nuremberg dismissed these concerns, committing themselves instead to the monolithic theory of a Nazi conspiracy to wage aggressive war, the central hub around which the spokes of war crimes and crimes against humanity revolved.[50]

Prosecuting German doctors in a separate proceeding for medical crimes was an idea that evolved gradually as the trial of the major war criminals unfolded. At first, the United States had no intention to prosecute Nazi doctors. Control Council Law #10, enacted in December 1945, had furnished the basis for "zonal trials" (national trials conducted by each of the four occupying powers in its own zone, as opposed to the joint four-power prosecution of the major war criminals at Nuremberg). Until January 1946 Telford Taylor, appointed to succeed Robert Jackson as U.S. Chief of Counsel for War Crimes, was embroiled in the Allied prosecution of the Wehrmacht High Command and hence could not focus on organizing the subsequent trials under Law #10. Beginning in mid-January, he turned his attention to the successor trials, envisioning another international tribunal to try German industrialists and financiers and a U.S. trial of "other major criminals" in the U.S. zone of occupation. In a memorandum to Jackson dated January 1, 1946, Taylor reported that France, Great Britain, and the USSR also desired one more IMT to try the industrialists and financiers. In this memo, he sketched the proposed shape of future trials, which included, in addition to a second IMT and trials by U.S. courts in the U.S. zone, trials of "local criminals" by military courts-martial, trials of other "major war criminals" in the courts of "allied powers" or in countries formerly occupied by the Nazis, and denazification proceedings to deal with "organizational cases." Taylor makes no mention at this stage of plans to prosecute German doctors for medical crimes.[51]

Although plans to hold a second IMT went forward during the first half of 1946, the U.S. and British authorities soon reconsidered their support of this plan. In a memo to Taylor dated February 5, 1946, Jackson expressed his concerns that a second IMT would lack political support in the United States. He also presciently warned that the Russians would insist on holding a second IMT in the Russian zone of occupation, with a Soviet judge presiding over the trial. Taylor and his staff continued to entertain the possibility of a four-power tribunal, especially for the purpose of trying the German chemical conglomerate, I. G. Farben. By summer 1946, however, they had developed their own misgivings about a second IMT. Taylor had apprehensions about "continental and Soviet law principles unfamiliar to the American public," as well as the negative impact in the United States of a Soviet judge presiding over a second IMT. In June U.S. authorities adopted a "zonal courts policy," and by August 1946 Taylor had informed the War Department of his plan for a U.S. medical case based on criminal experiments performed on concentration camp inmates.[52]

The stimulus to prosecute German doctors for medical crimes in a subsequent trial arose during IMT proceedings against Reichsmarschall Hermann Göring, in which evidence came to light about the participation of German *Luftwaffe* doctors in heinous medical experiments on concentration camp prisoners. The complicity of the German medical profession in Nazi criminality was further revealed at the IMT by SS-Standartenführer Wolfram Sievers, former General Secretary of the Ahnenerbe Society and director of its Institute for Military Scientific Research. In his army interrogation, Sievers alerted the Allied investigators to the existence of a "Jewish skeleton collection" at the University of Strasbourg, created from the harvested bones of Jewish concentration camp prisoners murdered for this purpose. As early as May 1946, when the issue of a second IMT was still unresolved, Taylor's office had assigned to an investigative group under James McHaney the task of gathering evidence about the leaders of the SS and of the German health and medical service. The plethora of evidence on medical crimes gathered by McHaney's group and the IMT prosecution team, as well as the presence of potential medical defendants in U.S. and British custody, influenced Taylor in August 1946 to begin the U.S. subsequent proceedings with its case against the German doctors. In a letter to Secretary of War Howard Petersen in late September 1946, Taylor opined that the medical case would be "a rather easy one to try and to decide, and therefore I think a good one to start with."[53]

The U.S. Doctors' Trial was designed primarily around the barbarous medical experiments performed in German concentration camps during the war. Participation in National Socialist euthanasia, charged against only four of the twenty-three defendants as a crime against humanity in violation of Control Council Law #10, was an incidental subplot in the trial. Taylor and his team chose to prosecute twenty German doctors and three non-doctors involved in medical crimes. Their criterion of choice in all twelve subsequent trials was to find "those highly placed individuals who bore the greatest responsibility for formulating and ordering the execution of the criminal policies which directly led to and instigated the aggressive wars and mass atrocities . . . committed under the authority of the Third Reich."[54] Regrettably, a considerable number of potential defendants were unavailable for trial. Many had either been killed or, like Dr. Ernst Robert Grawitz, the highest-ranking SS and police doctor, had committed suicide; the whereabouts of others, such as Dr. Erich Hippke, the chief of the combat medical system of the Luftwaffe, was unknown.

Already in July 1946, U.S. war crimes investigators were aware that the British had assembled substantial evidence against the Hohenlychen Group, German doctors involved in lethal and disabling human experiments at the SS sanatorium of Hohenlychen. These included Karl Gebhardt, Fritz Fischer, Karl Brunner, Hertha Oberheuser, Percy Treite, Rolf Rosenthal, and Karl Brandt. Taylor's deputy, James McHaney, initiated negotiations with the British to have these individuals delivered to U.S. authorities with an eye toward prosecuting them for criminal medical experiments on concentration camp prisoners. Around the same time as the U.S. investigators became aware of the Hohenlychen Group, the U.S. neurologist Leo Alexander, tasked with researching the complicity of German neuropsychiatrists in medical crimes, submitted reports on hypothermia experiments and the sterilization and killing of the mentally disabled. The prosecution at the IMT offered these reports in evidence against the major war criminals. Identified in Alexander's reports as perpetrators of crimes against humanity were fifteen of the twenty-three defendants eventually prosecuted in the Medical Case. Thus, several months before the commencement of the trial in November 1946, the issue of Nazi medical experiments had come to dominate the thinking of the U.S. prosecution team in its approach to a future trial of German physicians once the IMT had concluded.[55]

One name that stood out conspicuously in both the Hohenlychen Group and Alexander's reports was the Reich Commissioner for Health and Sanitation and Hitler's personal physician, Dr. Karl Brandt. Brandt had been under investigation by both the British and U.S. authorities since early June 1946 for his role in medical crimes at the Dachau concentration camp. The highest-ranking defendant among those indicted at the Doctors' Trial, Brandt was an especially inviting target. His personal relationship with Hitler, his irrefutably leading role with Philipp Bouhler in the euthanasia program, and his ties to both the Hohenlychen Group and to medical atrocities performed at Dachau rendered Brandt a veritable poster child of Nazi medical criminality. By early September 1946, the U.S. prosecution team had added Brandt to a list that also included other members of the Hohenlychen Group, Rudolf Brandt (the personal administrative officer to Himmler), and the top bureaucrats in the KdF, Viktor Brack and Philipp Bouhler. By September 9, two cuts had been made that set the number of medical defendants at twenty-three.[56] The defendants were arraigned before the U.S. National Military Tribunal on November 21, 1946.

The indictment against the defendants charged them with four counts: (1) conspiring to commit war crimes and crimes against humanity ("common design or conspiracy"); (2) war crimes; (3) crimes against humanity; and (4) membership in a criminal organization. The second count (war crimes) subsumed criminal medical experimentation. Paragraph 9 of Count Two charged four of the defendants—Karl Brandt, Kurt Blome, Viktor Brack, and Waldemar Hoven—with complicity in euthanasia. The indictment describes it as a program to murder "hundreds of thousands of human beings, including nationals of German-occupied countries," as well as "the aged, insane, incurably ill, . . . deformed children, and other persons, by gas, lethal injections, and diverse other means in nursing homes, hospitals, and asylums." The indictment goes on to offer a laconic theory of why these people were killed: "Such persons were regarded as 'useless eaters' and a burden to the German war machine." The closing sentence of paragraph 9 affirms a link between National Socialist euthanasia and the Holocaust: "German doctors involved in the 'euthanasia' program were also sent to Eastern occupied countries to assist in the mass extermination of Jews." In paragraph 8, Count Two charged Rudolf Brandt and Kurt Blome with "the murder and mistreatment of tens of thousands of Polish nationals" who "were alleged to be infected with incurable tuberculosis." The authors of the indictment briefly theorized on the reasons for the killings: "On the ground of insuring the health and welfare of Germans in Poland, many tubercular Poles were ruthlessly exterminated while others were isolated in death camps with inadequate medical facilities." To an extent, Count Three (crimes against humanity) was redundant with Count Two. It enumerated the same charges of euthanasia against Karl Brandt, Blome, Hoven, and Brack and the murder of tubercular Poles in the Warthegau against Rudolf Brandt and Blome. (Count Three also charged Rudolf Brandt and Wolfram Sievers with involvement in the plot to murder Jews in order to supply a skeleton collection for the University of Strasbourg.)[57]

In the remainder of this chapter, we will focus on the U.S. prosecution team's conception of euthanasia as reflected in the cases of Karl Brandt and Viktor Brack. Blome and Hoven were relatively minor figures in Nazi euthanasia and thus did not command the attention of the United States to the extent that Brack and Brandt did. In its closing argument before the court, the prosecution described Brandt as the "first link" in the euthanasia chain, Philipp Bouhler as the second link, and Brack as the third. By the time of the Doctors' Trial, Bouhler was beyond the reach of U.S. justice, having committed suicide with his wife at Zell-am-See in May 1945. Hence, the two preeminent figures in Nazi euthanasia available for trial—at least in the estimate of the prosecutors—were Brandt and Brack.

The Questionable Humanitarian: Dr. Karl Brandt

By his own account, Karl Brandt enjoyed a peaceful and uneventful upbringing until the outbreak of World War I in 1914. He was born on January 8, 1904, at Mühlhausen, Alsace (at the time part of German territory). Brandt's father was a policeman; his mother hailed from a "medical family" (his maternal grandfather and uncle were both doctors, and a second uncle was a pharamacist). The Brandts were expelled from Alsace in 1919, sealing Karl's membership in a class of Germans peculiarly susceptible to the allure of Nazism—ethnic Germans from "lost territories" and "threatened borders."[58] A turbulent period ensued for the Brandt family, marked by Brandt's transfer to different schools and his father's detention in a French prison until 1921. In 1924 he arrived at the University of Jena to begin his medical studies.[59]

After completing his studies, Brandt served as a surgeon before working in the Surgical University Clinic in Berlin in 1934, where he became chief doctor in 1936. While his career burgeoned, Brandt climbed the ranks of the Nazi Party, which he had joined in January 1932. In 1933 he became a member of the SA. In June 1934 Brandt joined the SS, receiving a rank of *Untersturmführer*. Around the same time, he became Adolf Hitler's "escort physician" (*Begleitarzt*), a job that required him to accompany Hitler during his travels away from Berlin. In 1938, Hitler sent Brandt to examine the Knauer child in Leipzig. After confirming the attending physicians' diagnosis and giving the green light for its killing, Brandt received a commission from Hitler to dispose of all similar cases in the future in the same manner—a commission he held

Karl Brandt, escort physician to Adolf Hitler and from July 1942 Commissioner for the Health Care System in the German Reich. He and Philipp Bouhler were authorized to create the organizational framework for the children's euthanasia program, which, under the direction of the KdF, was administered through various children's wards installed in German mental hospitals. Along with Bouhler, he became a leading figure in adult euthanasia, agreeing to the use of poisonous gas as the most efficient means of causing patients' deaths. As Commissioner for the Health Care System, Brandt ordered the evacuation of mental patients from psychiatric hospitals to euthanasia centers, where they were murdered. Convicted of war crimes and crimes against humanity by the U.S. NMT, he was hanged at Landsberg prison on June 2, 1948. Courtesy the U.S. Holocaust Memorial Museum Collection

jointly with the chief of the KdF, Philipp Bouhler. Bouhler authorized his deputy, Viktor Brack (chief of Main Office II), to work with Hans Hefelmann (director of Office IIb) and Herbert Linden (minister within Department IV of the Interior Ministry and later the Reich Commissioner for Mental Hospitals) in establishing a planning group of pro-euthanasia physicians. This group, which included Brandt, developed the children's euthanasia program. His early involvement in National Socialist violence against the disabled earmarked him as a trustworthy accomplice when Hitler extended the program to handicapped adults.

Brandt participated with Viktor Brack in the carbon monoxide gassing experiments at Brandenburg in late 1939. Together they approved the carbon monoxide method of producing death—a method that would serve as the paradigm for the five other euthanasia centers in Germany. In late 1941 Brandt became Commissioner for the Health Care System. As commissioner he ordered the evacuation of mental patients from German psychiatric hospitals, allegedly in order to free up hospital space for wounded soldiers and civilians. The evacuees were transferred to other sites like Meseritz-Obrawalde, Hadamar, Eichberg, and Kaufbeuren, where they were often murdered through starvation or overdoses of narcotics. Both in his interrogations by the OCCWC (Office of the Chief of Counsel for War Crimes) and in his testimony before the NMT, Brandt portrayed euthanasia as motivated by high-minded ideals. He claimed his role in the killing of the mentally disabled ended with the first phase of euthanasia; after the official stop in August 1941, Brandt averred he had nothing further to do with it. He portrayed the first phase of euthanasia as a benign program targeting "terminal cases" that were refractory to therapy. Their deaths were a "deliverance" from protracted pain and suffering. Under interrogation he related that he saw in euthanasia "the law of nature and . . . the law of reason." In Brandt's eyes, this "law of nature" called into question the Hippocratic oath. During direct examination, he emphasized that "purely humane considerations" actuated Hitler's decision to euthanize "incurably ill persons." About his own actions within the killing program, Brandt was adamantly unrepentant.[60]

The U.S. prosecuting team's theory of Nazi euthanasia is discernible in its interrogations of Brandt and remained consistent throughout the trial. Not surprisingly, the U.S. view of euthanasia clashed with Brandt's portrayal of it as a humanitarian measure. However, even Brandt admitted that the second (or wild) phase of euthanasia was not primarily guided by humane considerations. In his interrogations in November and December 1946, Brandt took pains to distinguish the first "humane" phase of euthanasia from the second "wild" phase. He cited as an example two instances of euthanasia locally initiated by Gauleiter in Saxony and Pomerania that had come to his attention.

Brandt claimed he had informed Bouhler, Martin Bormann, and Hitler about these episodes; Hitler's reaction was to demand immediate cessation of the killing. Brandt believed that these examples of wild euthanasia were driven by the need to reduce the "overpopulation" of mental patients in the two regions. In other words, he advanced an economistic interpretation of the second phase of killing: mental patients were put to death to conserve scarce resources. The economistic interpretation of Nazi euthanasia has an echo in Taylor's opening statement before the tribunal, in which he identified as a motive for euthanasia the desire to rid Germany of those who had become "useless to the German war machine." Ultimately, the tribunal in the Medical Case would endorse the prosecution's economistic interpretation, identifying as one of the program's "prime motives" the aim "to eliminate 'useless eaters' from the scene, in order to conserve food, hospital facilities, doctors and nurses for the more important use of the German armed forces."[61]

As with the military trial of the Hadamar staff, the NMT's insistence that euthanasia was linked to Nazi imperialism enabled the United States to convict Brandt without compromising the principle of sovereignty in international affairs. In both proceedings, euthanasia killing was portrayed as an offense against international law—not as a systematic program to purify German society of "unworthy life." In both proceedings, too, preoccupations with retaining national power strictly determined the U.S. construction of Nazi euthanasia. When the focus of the Doctors' Trial shifted to Viktor Brack, the prosecutors had an easier time connecting the destruction of the mentally ill with Nazi war crimes, because Brack faced not only the charge of euthanasia, but of setting in motion the most notorious international crime in history: the destruction of the European Jews.

The Cynical Saboteur: Viktor Brack

The oldest of three children, Viktor Brack was born in 1904 in Haaren. Before World War I, he spent some of his childhood with his mother, a Russian ethnic German, visiting her relatives in Russia. After the war, Brack related that his family was informed by his mother's brother, who emigrated from Russia to Germany in 1920, that Brack's grandmother had been murdered by the Bolsheviks. His mother's sister had also reportedly died there of typhus brought on by starvation. These revelations, Brack alleged, extinguished in him any further desire to revisit the vast, sprawling country of his mother's family.[62]

After finishing his *Abitur* (college preparatory study) in 1923, Brack studied agriculture for a time until the loss of his parents' property and the poor agricultural conditions in the Rhineland Palatinate caused him to switch his major to economics. He graduated in 1928 from a Munich technical school with a major in economics and thereafter worked in different roles: as an assistant to his father farming a small plot of land the family had acquired, as a racer with BMW in Munich, and as a chauffeur of the future head of the SS, Heinrich Himmler, a personal friend of his father. In 1932 Brack was employed as the personal adviser to Reichsleiter Philipp Bouhler, at the time the Economics Director of the Nazi Party. When Bouhler established the KdF in 1934 and became its chief, Brack became his staff director. In 1936, Bouhler appointed Brack the head liaison officer with the Department of Health, despite his lack of medical training. Thereafter, Brack became Bouhler's deputy and the chief of Section II of the KdF. It was in this office that Brack became a major figure in organizing the euthanasia program in 1939 and the Final Solution in late 1941.[63]

Unlike the army prosecutors in the Hadamar case, in the months preceding the Doctors' Trial Taylor's prosecution team was interested in the links between the euthanasia program and the larger Nazi assault on groups deemed "unworthy of life." This interest is evident in Brack's pre-trial interrogations, in which his interlocutors confronted Brack with their theory that the euthanasia program, rather than ending, as Brack contended, in 1941, was extended to the extermination program by the end of 1943. According to the interrogators, Nazi euthanasia was little more than a "general test" (Generalprobe) for the expanded killing program in the last four years of the war. Brack adamantly denied a link between the two events, claiming that Hitler was not thinking of the Final Solution when he ordered euthanasia to proceed.

The issue of the motives behind the euthanasia program became the primary ground of contestation between Brack and his interrogators. The struggle centered on how to characterize the euthanasia program at its inception. The interrogators began with a definition of "true" euthanasia: "Euthanasia is, according to the jurisprudence of all states governed by the rule of law, as well as according to German law, the act of assisting a patient transition from an immediately occurring and extremely painful death to a less painful one. That is, in the last stage, the administration of a dose of morphine." Brack countered with the language of the Hitler order, which specified that only "incurable" cases were to be given a "mercy death." Brack's interrogators replied that the actual euthanasia program launched by the Hitler order in 1939 had nothing to do with real euthanasia: "If we assume the fiction that the Hitler order gave a certain legitimacy to this killing, do you not know that the scope of the Hitler order was grossly exceeded in the form of the execution? That not only those people who were, according to the Hitler order, ripe for euthanasia, but also others were killed?" The "other" victims referred to were "useless eaters," whose consumption of hospital beds and medical resources impeded Germany's conduct of aggressive war.[64]

Viktor Brack, Bouhler's deputy and chief of Main Office II in the KdF. In December 1939 Brack was charged by Bouhler with interviewing and employing personnel to staff the killing centers of the T-4 program. In 1941 he became involved in the "Final Solution," assisting in the construction of the death camps and, most notably, the gas chambers, as well as assigning euthanasia personnel to Odilo Globocnik to aid in the liquidation of Polish Jewry. He was convicted of war crimes and crimes against humanity by the U.S. NMT and executed in Landsberg prison on June 2, 1948. Courtesy the National Archives Records Administration, College Park, Maryland

The interrogators' conception of euthanasia was not uniform but contained at least two separate views of the Nazis' assault on "unworthy life." The first was economistic/utilitarian. On this theory, the mentally ill were killed to free up hospital space and health-care personnel for the German army as it waged aggressive war on Germany's neighbors. The second was the "general test" theory, according to which euthanasia served a probative role in testing both equipment and personnel for a future, more inclusive killing of other groups of people. When confronted with each of these theories, Brack vehemently denied them, countering that euthanasia meant solely "helping a person who is suffering." The interrogator conceded to Brack that "we could argue about euthanasia," but maintained that the Nazi variant was not true euthanasia. Rather, the interrogator told Brack he was "entirely convinced that the actual cause was the preparation for the eastern people. Furthermore, the Jews were not directly attacked, but [euthanasia] was only a preliminary step. The beginning was made with the mentally ill, and that is the danger."[65]

Brack's interrogator was a proponent of the general test theory of euthanasia. He opined that Brack had been selected to guide the euthanasia program because he was "a little soft," and needed "to be toughened up." With explicit reference to Himmler's Posen speech of 1943, in which Himmler commended his SS-Gruppenführer for carrying out the "extermination of the Jewish people," a disagreeable but necessary task that "made us tough," the interrogator suggested to a protesting Brack that the euthanasia program was "an experiment in toughness," designed to callous "soft" SS men like Brack for the massive extermination of eastern European peoples.[66] This general test understanding of euthanasia presupposes ideological indoctrination of the perpetrators in order to transform them into hardened killers of the Reich's enemies. On this account, euthanasia was less a means of transferring scarce medical resources from the mentally ill to the German army than a longterm preparation for the mass annihilation of Jews, Gypsies, Poles, Soviets, and other "worthless" groups, facilitated by immersing the perpetrators in the Nazi thought world and coarsening their moral sensibilities through acts of programmatic violence against the mentally ill.

The general test/ideological interpretation became a polestar of U.S. prosecution of Nazi euthanasia throughout the trial. In his opening statement, Telford Taylor previewed the prosecution's view that Nazi euthanasia sprang from "a perverted moral outlook in which cruelty to subjugated races and peoples was praiseworthy," instilled in the perpetrators in Nazi medical training centers like the Führer School of German Physicians. For the U.S. prosecution team, the defendants were not motivated by "hot blood" or by the desire for "personal enrichment," but by the National Socialist hierarchy of biological value. The United States pursued this theory of euthanasia in their cross-examination of Brack, who took the stand to address the two most damning charges against him: his involvement in the plot to murder European Jews and his proposal to sterilize a remnant of the surviving Jewish population with X-rays. By comparison with these charges, his role in the early stages of planning the euthanasia program paled into relative insignificance.

Brack and his attorney wasted little time in addressing each of the issues on direct examination. Their strategy could not be a policy of denying everything, because the documentary evidence against Brack was overwhelmingly incriminating. Instead, Brack and his lawyer concocted a defense that later defendants in the German euthanasia trials would advance with far greater success. Under German law, it is referred to as the "collision of duties" defense (*Pflichtenkollision*) and consists of the argument that the defendant committed the crime only in order to avoid greater harm. Ernst Kaltenbrunner, Heydrich's successor as head of the Reich Security Main Office, had raised this defense at the IMT in Nuremberg, where he claimed he had done everything in his power to work at cross-purposes with the Final Solution, a "system I could only seek ways of mitigating, but whose intellectual and legal foundations I could do nothing to change."[67] Whether Brack had Kaltenbrunner's defense in mind as a model is unclear. He did, however, stake his life on this "sabotage" theory of criminal wrongdoing.

According to Brack, it had become clear to him by the end of the 1930s that "a struggle was underway here against an entire segment of the people

[German Jews] and I did not consider this struggle to be a good one." Brack claimed he had marveled at the prospect of "depriving" humanity of the works of Jews like Mendelssohn and Heine. In view of the cultural richness of Jewish life, Brack felt it necessary "to repudiate such a policy of hate, and that is what happened." When he subsequently learned of the Final Solution, he resolved to make "the effort if possible to help," to "do anything I could to prevent [the destruction of the Jews]." Brack's claim that he was forced to give the glad hand to all around him as he secretly devised his sabotage of the Final Solution foreshadowed defenses in later euthanasia proceedings:

> If I had raised the least objection to [the Final Solution] openly I would have aroused great suspicion of myself and would have aroused an all together [sic] and false reaction in Himmler. Therefore, I had to make the best of a bad matter and had to pretend that I agreed with Himmler. Therefore, I pretended to be willing to clarify the question of mass sterilization through X-ray methods.[68]

The "question of mass sterilization through X-ray methods" that Brack refers to was a matter broached in a letter from Brack to Himmler, dated June 23, 1942, regarding "using European Jews as laborers." The text of this letter reads in part:

> Among 10 million Jews in Europe are . . . at least 2 to 3 million men and women who are fit enough for work. Considering the extraordinary difficulties the labor problem presents us with, I hold the view that these 2 or 3 million should be specially selected and preserved. This can be done, if at the same time they are rendered incapable of propagating. About a year ago I reported to you that agents of mine have completed the experiments necessary for this purpose.[69]

On direct exam, Brack was faced with neutralizing the incriminating power of this document. He tried to do so with the argument that "the real purpose of that letter [was] . . . not to exterminate the Jews, but to preserve them." The letter's reference to sterilizing the Jewish remnant was a sham calculated to buy time for at least some of the Jews until the war ended. His "strategy" was to induce Himmler to grant a moratorium on exterminating the Jews long enough to conduct X-ray experiments on Jewish guinea pigs and to evaluate the results. Himmler did, in fact, accede for a brief time to Brack's recommendation. On Himmler's order, Bouhler commissioned two euthanasia doctors to commence sterilization experiments with X-rays, a program later abandoned as impracticable. Brack told the U.S. court he was "convinced that by performing these experiments, hundreds of thousands . . . of Jews were saved."[70]

In addition to his sterilization plan, Brack claimed he sought to derail the Final Solution by persuading Hitler to use the Jews as a source of labor rather than kill them. Again, his alleged aim was to temporize until the war had ended. Implicit in Brack's defense is the view that the murder of the Jews was caused by the war: remove the war, and the Jews survive. Ironically, Brack's assumption in this regard parallels that of U.S. prosecutors, who maintained throughout the trial that the Nazis' destruction of "life unworthy of life" was the result of their waging aggressive war—a theory of Nazi criminality common to both the IMT and the U.S. NMT. Inevitably, to regard the crimes of National Socialism as the reflexes of a nation at war reduces their abhorrent quality by identifying them with excesses characteristic of war conditions. At the same time, it diminishes the centrality of these crimes to the Nazi movement, insofar as it suggests they would never have happened but for the occurrence of the war.

Ultimately, Brack's efforts to invoke a sabotage defense could not overcome the mountain of documentary evidence amassed against him. That evidence proved that Brack had assigned euthanasia personnel from T-4 to the virulent anti-Semite and SS Police Leader for the Lublin district, Odilo Globocnik, entrusted by Himmler with carrying out the liquidation of Polish Jewry. The T-4 staff Brack assigned to Globocnik helped organize and administer the Final Solution in Poland. As if this were not sufficiently damning, the prosecution also offered into evidence one of the most notorious documents in the history of the Final Solution, the "gassing letter" from the Reich Ministry for the Occupied Territories to the Reich Commissar for the Ostland, dated October 25, 1941. In the letter, Brack is mentioned as volunteering to supply both "accommodations as well as the gassing equipment" for use in killing Jews incapable of work. The hardier Jews would be used as slave labor; those unable to work would be disposed of using the "Brackian devices." These devices, as we have seen, were gas vans, deployed since late 1939 to murder mentally ill patients in the Wartheland. In the face of such evidence, Brack's portrayal of himself as a well-intentioned saboteur of the Final Solution shriveled like leaves in a bonfire.

This did not, of course, deter Brack from striking the pose of a humanitarian. In his discussion of the first phase of euthanasia, he rejected the prosecution's theory that the assault on the mentally ill was a pretext for politically and racially motivated killing. "When euthanasia was introduced, we welcomed it," Brack testified, "because it was based on the ethical principle of sympathy and had humane considerations in its favor, of the same sort that the opponents of euthanasia claim for their own ideas." He admitted "imperfections" in the way it was performed, but he added "that does not change the decency of the original idea, as Bouhler and Brandt and I myself understood it." How, then, did euthanasia degenerate into a comprehensive program of mass murder? Brack's counsel blamed Himmler for perverting the program by "distorting" it for "reasons of hatred and bigotry, and used it for the murder of the Jews."[71] Like Brandt, Brack resisted the prosecution's theory that euthanasia at its inception was inspired by economistic, political, or racial motives.

The U.S. tribunal hearing the case was not persuaded by Brandt and Brack's argument. It endorsed the prosecution's depiction of National Socialist euthanasia as a program "to eliminate 'useless eaters' from the scene, in order to conserve food, hospital facilities, doctors and nurses for the more important use of the German armed forces." At first, the court held, it was confined to "incurable" mental patients, but gradually "the program was extended to Jews, and then to concentration camp inmates." The dilation of Nazi euthanasia into wholesale mass murder transpired during the second, or wild, phase of the program.[72]

On this basis, the court found Brandt, Brack, and Hoven guilty of war crimes and crimes against humanity under Control Council Law #10. (Blome, who raised a sabotage defense of his own for his alleged role in the murder of tubercular Poles, was acquitted.) They were sentenced to death by hanging. After fruitlessly pursuing their appeals, including a writ of habeas corpus filed with the U.S. Supreme Court, the three defendants were hanged at Landsberg prison on June 2, 1948.

The U.S. approach to the crimes of the euthanasia specialists was remarkably consistent from the early views of Bernays, Stimson, and Jackson through the theories and arguments of U.S. prosecutors at the Doctors' Trial. The armature around which charges of war crimes and crimes against humanity were molded was Nazi Germany's launching of aggressive war. Even though the drafters of Control Council Law #10 had abolished the link between war crimes and crimes against humanity, U.S. prosecutors at the Doctors' Trial continued to assume that euthanasia-related crimes were the excrescence of Hitler's imperialistic war—an assumption that punctuates their indictment, opening statement, cross-examinations, and closing argument. The tribunal implicitly endorsed this conception of the prosecution by amalgamating Count Two (war crimes) and Count Three (crimes against humanity) and treating them as a single count. Henceforth, euthanasia crimes were equated in the court's mind with war crimes—that is, as crimes secondary to and contingent upon the waging of aggressive war. This tenacious commitment to viewing Nazi criminality in the funhouse mirror of German war policy is traceable to U.S. concern for the principle of sovereignty in international law. Nazi euthanasia *had* to be connected somehow to the war; if it were not, the Allies would be setting a dangerous precedent for intervening in the domestic affairs of a sovereign nation.

The problem with this understanding is one of causality. Hitler had confided to Adolf Wagner in 1935 his intention to inaugurate euthanasia if and when war broke out. Clearly, Hitler had the scheme to annihilate "unworthy life" in mind well before the actual start of the war in September 1939. Furthermore, although we have no compelling evidence that Hitler had planned to murder European Jewry before 1941, violent persecution of German Jews was by no means uncommon in pre-war Germany. As Herbert Jäger insightfully observed, Nazi genocide was not the product of the war; rather, "the war was the instrument for implementing genocide." What Jäger said about the destruction of the Jews during the war may be applied equally to other groups targeted by the Nazis:

> The life of the Jews in Germany was for a long time repressed by the totalitarian regime and undermined through growing defamation and degradation, before we can even speak of genocide in the verbal and actual sense: the mass killing represented only the organization and carrying out of that which was systematically prepared in the state system, and was already perfected in the spirit, when the bonds of human solidarity were ruptured and the illusory picture of the Jew as a parasitic Untermensch injurious to the Volk was established. If a minority is first equated with vermin, then the step to the intention to "eradicate" it is no longer so great. Human dignity and life were taken from the victims long before the gas chambers were opened to them: a process of development over many years only needed to be pushed ahead to its final consequence.[73]

For Jäger, identifying Nazi genocide with war crimes has the effect of misrepresenting genocide as something qualitatively different from—and less odious than—ordinary criminality. It emerges as the byproduct of ordinary men in extraordinary times, as periods of war always are. General William Tecumseh Sherman's famous phrase that "war is all hell" captures a common belief that acts deemed to be atrocities during peacetime become the common coin of the realm during times of war. Yet, the hell unleashed by war is different from the inferno of Nazi criminality.

In the postwar era prominent German intellectuals have realized the importance of distinguishing between these two orders of hell. The German existialist philosopher Karl Jaspers emphasized the conceptual divide between war crimes and Nazi crimes: a "completely different principle," he argued, distinguished the two kinds of criminality. Similarly, Hannah Arendt insisted on the singularity of crimes against humanity, warning that they should not be conflated with war crimes.[74] Combining them in a single criminological hotchpot can nonetheless be tempting, not least because the language of National Socialism (such as the rhetoric of resource scarcity marshaled in support of euthanasia) seduces us into drawing questionable inferences about the motives behind these crimes.

The Hadamar and Doctors' Trials reveal the extent to which U.S. commitment to preserve its own sovereignty from perceived encroachments by international judicial bodies had come to dominate U.S. approaches to Nazi criminality. On the U.S. view, euthanasia served as a means for transferring scarce resources from "unproductive" patients to the German armed forces. Neither the ends of justice nor the historical record compelled such an interpretation; rather, U.S. distrust of foreign bodies with superordinate jurisdiction predisposed U.S. authorities to connect euthanasia with the conduct of the war. Concerns with restricting U.S. prosecution only to crimes linked with Germany's war of aggression determined how the Nazis' assault on the mentally ill would be portrayed. In the U.S. Hadamar trial, the formidable power of this insistence inverted the customary burden of proof: in alleging that the murders of consumptive eastern workers were undertaken for the purpose of freeing up resources for the war effort, the U.S. military commission spurned the principle of individual responsibility. The result was *to presume guilt in advance (even in defiance) of the evidentiary record*—an inversion of the traditional presumption of innocence in Anglo-American law.

U.S. reticence to open the door to foreign interference with U.S. sovereignty is by no means a new theme in the country's history: the opposition of the U.S. delegation at Versailles in 1919 to international trials for crimes against humanity, as well as the refusal of the Senate to ratify the League of Nations and, more recently, the 1949 U.N. Genocide Convention (finally ratified by Congress in 1986), are all telling proofs of such reluctance. By the mid-1940s, this long-lived concern with preserving national power received a fresh stimulus as Europe fissioned into two armed camps. In the tension-fraught arena of the Cold War, the United States would not brook restrictions on its ability to project its considerable power across the globe. Simultaneously, the West Germans were involved in a bid for national power of their own. In the German case, however, the goal was not to sustain their sovereignty, but to regain it after the catastrophic defeat of the war. Although the aims of the United States and West Germany differed, each shared a common preoccupation with national power. In each case, too, considerations of sovereignty structured the judicial approach to and assessment of National Socialist crimes, including euthanasia. In the following chapters, we will see how the quest for power, understood as a restoration of political self-determination, led the Germans in the postwar era to exonerate the killers of the mentally ill.

There is a tendency of plots to move toward death.
—DON DELILLO, *LIBRA*

Chapter 3 | FIRST RECKONINGS

THE GERMAN EUTHANASIA TRIALS, 1946–1947

The early West German euthanasia trials share with their U.S. counterparts a retributive attitude toward the homicidal violence inflicted on the mentally disabled during the war. Between 1946 and 1947, West German courts convicted euthanasia killers of murder and sentenced them to death. Although attitudes toward individual participants in the euthanasia program would change after 1947, little quarter was given to defendants prosecuted in the immediate postwar period.

In this chapter we will examine the West German euthanasia trials in the two-year period after World War II. We will find that German courts punished doctors (and sometimes nurses) as perpetrators of murder under the German Penal Code, section 211 and sentenced them to either death or imprisonment. The initial rigor of these trials, however, would be short-lived. By 1948, as relations between the East and the West spiraled into the Cold War, German courts began to relent in their assessment of euthanasia defendants. The trend started with characterizations of euthanasia doctors as accomplices rather than perpetrators and reduced sentences based on their subjective state of mind when the crimes were committed.

By the late 1940s and early 1950s, this trend culminated in acquittals of proven killers. It is the main argument of this study that the trend line from punishing euthanasia killers to extenuating their crimes and, finally, acquitting them was driven by a nationwide yearning to recoup German sovereignty after years of military occupation—a process that uncannily resembled the interaction of power and criminal law in the U.S. approach to Nazi criminality, yet produced different results. In the case of the United States, concern with preserving the inviolability of sovereignty induced U.S. officials to consider all actors within the euthanasia program equally liable, despite the nature and degree of their actual contributions to the crime. For the Germans, the longing for restoration of national sovereignty would, over time, lead them to presume the innocence of euthanasia defendants, a presumption facilitated by evolving theories of criminal liability as applied to bureaucratic role performance within a criminal state (the Nazi government). We will explore these protean theories—and their adoption by German courts to exonerate euthanasia killers—in subsequent chapters.

We begin with a discussion of two legal postulates that structured the West German prosecution and punishment of euthanasia criminality in the postwar era. The first, the "subjective" theory of perpetration, grew out of the so-called Bathtub Case of 1940. The second postulate concerns the right of German courts to exercise jurisdiction over defendants charged with acts that, at the time of their commission, were not deemed to be criminal by the Nazi government. For a brief time German law had recourse to natural law theory as a means for affirming the right of German courts to punish such acts, despite the fundamental prohibition of ex post facto laws in continental jurisprudence. Our conversance with these two legal postulates sheds light on how German legal authorities conceived of Nazi criminality after the war, and how significantly these conceptions were beginning to change by the late 1940s as German aspirations for national sovereignty became irrepressible.

PRINCIPLES OF CRIMINAL RESPONSIBILITY IN GERMAN EUTHANASIA TRIALS: THE SUBJECTIVE THEORY OF PERPETRATION AND THE REVIVAL OF NATURAL LAW

The rigor of the first German euthanasia trials is remarkable when the context of West German popular attitudes toward the crimes of the Third Reich is taken into account. Although 70 percent of the population supported the trials of the major war criminals in 1946, German attitudes toward the successor trials (of which the euthanasia prosecutions were a part) were highly critical. Trying and punishing a criminal subculture that had rained misery on Germans and foreigners alike was acceptable to most of the population. To move beyond the top Nazis to indict lawyers, doctors, businessmen, industrialists, and military officers, however, was an entirely different matter. To prosecute these representatives of the best in German society, to arraign them as the murderers of innocent millions, was an intolerable affront to a precariously maintained national pride. In 1946, 70 percent favored the trials, but an equal number by 1950 opposed them as "victors' justice."

The first German courts called upon to adjudicate euthanasia-related killings did not share such sentiments. Article III of Allied Control Council Law #4 (promulgated in October 1945) on the "Reorganization of the German Judicial System" granted German courts jurisdiction over civil and criminal matters except for "criminal offenses committed by Nazis or any other persons against citizens of Allied nations and their property, as well as attempts directed towards the reestablishment of the Nazi regime, and the activity of the Nazi organizations." In this excepted category of crimes, Allied tribunals would enjoy exclusive jurisdiction. The terms of Law #4 were superseded in December 1945 by Control Council Law #10, which permitted German courts to exercise jurisdiction over "crimes committed by persons of German citizenship or nationality against other persons of German citizenship or nationality, or stateless persons." The practical import of this law was to restrict German courts—until Law #10 was repealed in the British and French zones on August 31, 1951—to cases involving denunciations ("grudge informers"), killings related to the terminal stages of the war ("end phase crimes"), deportations of Jews and Gypsies, concentration camp crimes on German soil, and euthanasia cases. Law #10, in effect, excluded German courts from placing under the judicial microscope the most notorious atrocity of the Nazi government—the million-fold murder of Jews in the eastern territories.[1]

What was an impediment to prosecuting the crimes of the Final Solution was a windfall to euthanasia trials. Because most euthanasia crimes were committed by Germans on German citizens, they fell squarely within the bounds of jurisdiction as defined by Law #10. In prosecuting these and other Nazi offenses, the German courts could apply either Law #10's definitions of war crimes and crimes against humanity or the German law of murder (section 211 of the German Penal Code). Although some latitude was given German prosecutors about how they could style an indictment, it was not unusual in euthanasia-related cases for defendants to be charged with both crimes against humanity under Law #10 *and* a variant of homicide (murder, aiding and abetting murder, or manslaughter) under the German criminal code. Where the two sources of law were in conflict, Law #10 would be supreme—at least in theory. The provisions of Law #10 were more favorable toward the prosecution than was the law of homicide under the German Penal Code. Unlike the code, Law #10, grounded in the Anglo-American law of conspiracy, did not recognize a distinction between perpetrators and accomplices: all participants in the crime were jointly liable as perpetrators for any acts carried out in furtherance of it. Under the German law of homicide, by contrast, a killer could be convicted as a murderer (i.e., a perpetrator) only if he fulfilled all the statutory elements of the offense, controlled the circumstances of its commission, or subjectively identified with the murder while assisting the main perpetrator to commit the crime—that is, if he embraced the murder "as his own." Another significant difference between Law #10 and the German law of murder was the former's relative disregard of subjective factors in its deliberations on a defendant's guilt. Under Law #10, issues that would tie German courts in knots, like a defendant's consciousness of wrongdoing, developmental background, or interior state of mind at the time of the offense, were immaterial. All that mattered was that the defendant intentionally committed or assisted in committing an act proscribed by the terms of Law #10, namely murder, extermination, enslavement, deportation, or political, racial, or religious persecution, all directed against "any civilian population." If the defendant was found to have committed any of these acts, regardless of the degree of his participation, then he was guilty as a perpetrator of a crime against humanity.[2]

German criminal law, on the other hand, was far more interested in the subjectivity of its defendants. Much of German criminal law is a variation on the Kantian idea that virtue (or its lack) has to do not with actions in the world but with intentions in the mind of the actor. Influenced by the Kantian tradition, German criminal law evinces a far greater concern for the subjectivity of the offender than does Anglo-American law. It is not that the Anglo-Americans are disinterested in subjective factors like intent. Rather, they tend to "read" the external act as an index of the actor's state of mind. As one U.S. court put it in 1918, "the law presumes that a man intends that which he does, and it is from the statements made and the acts done that this intent is to be determined."[3] German law, by contrast, spares no pains to excavate an actor's subjective intent from the facts of a criminal case. Where the Anglo-Americans infer intent from objective acts in the world, the Germans peer into the dim hyperspace of the human mind in search of a phantom, the actor's will. In this connection, a landmark decision of the German Supreme Court known as the Bathtub Case demonstrates the primacy of subjective analysis in modern German criminal law, especially in the postwar period.

The Bathtub Case came on appeal from the state court to the German Supreme Court six months after the outbreak of the war and involved a woman who had drowned her sister's illegitimate newborn in a bathtub. Her motive was to remove from her sister the stigma of having a bastard child. The lower court found the woman guilty as a perpetrator of murder under section 211 of the German Criminal Code. On appeal, the Supreme Court reversed this decision on the theory that the woman, although she had killed the baby with her own hands, had no "personal interest" in the final result of the crime. The real perpetrator in the murder was her sister; she had incited the defendant to the murder and had a personal interest in its occurrence. The woman was merely a "tool" of her sister, and thus qualified as an accomplice, rather than a direct perpetrator. The Bathtub Case was the cradle of the "subjective theory of perpetration" in German criminal law, a theory that made a judicial finding of murder contingent on the personal interest of the actor. In this fashion, defendants who kill others with their own hands, like the hapless woman in the Bathtub Case, could evade conviction as murderers if the court was satisfied they had acted on behalf of someone else's interest. As Jörg Friedrich has observed, the subjective theory was tailor-made for postwar Nazi defendants. Although they had the blood of thousands of innocent human beings on their hands, many argued successfully that they were mere tools of the arch-perpetrators, Adolf Hitler and his minions.[4]

In the years following the Bathtub Case, German courts did not always adopt the Supreme Court's subjective theory of perpetration. When we turn to euthanasia cases tried in 1946 and 1947, we notice the relatively high incidence of rank-and-file defendants found guilty as perpetrators. After 1947, however, German courts increasingly applied the subjective standard to convict euthanasia personnel of complicity—even those directly involved in mass murder—rather than perpetration. Only those defendants who killed from a personal interest were identified as perpetrators—that is, killers in whom the impulse to crime originated.

The second legal postulate that structured German approaches to euthanasia criminality after the war was natural law theory. Revival of natural law in the postwar euthanasia trials is intimately connected with the problem of in personam jurisdiction, a much thornier issue than it might at first appear. Although Hitler had vetoed enactment of a formal euthanasia law out of regard for foreign propaganda, he had issued a secret order under his signature authorizing Bouhler and Brandt to set the killing program into motion. Many euthanasia personnel were aware of the order; to some, copies were exhibited. Moreover, in an April 1941 meeting of German state prosecutors and judges in Berlin, Viktor Brack effectively immunized euthanasia operatives from arrest, indictment, or prosecution. Given the permissive atmosphere in which Nazi euthanasia evolved, postwar defendants could plausibly argue they had acted in conformity with the orders of the sovereign authority in Germany at the time, and thus could not be charged with acting illegally. Further, they could with some credibility maintain they had lacked any awareness that their conduct was wrongful and should thus be acquitted for a mistake of law (*Verbotsirrtum*).

If, as so many euthanasia defendants argued, their actions were countenanced by Hitler as the highest state authority in Germany during the war, then their postwar indictment for participation in euthanasia would violate a fundamental norm of German law, the ban on ex post facto (or retroactive) prosecution. This was a cornerstone of modern German criminal law, a principle codified in the German Penal Code of 1871, the Weimar Constitution of 1919, and the Basic Law (German Constitution) of 1949. The need to prosecute Germans involved in the mass murder of hundreds of thousands of mentally ill patients was compelling; yet, to violate the tenets of the *Rechtstaat* (a state governed by the rule of law) and criminalize actions that were not illegal at the time of their commission risked an arbitrariness that savored of National Socialist caprice. The Allies had encountered a similar dilemma at Nuremberg, one solved by joining uncodified crimes against humanity to the more securely established Laws of Armed Conflict. Where, as in the subsequent proceedings, the link between crimes against humanity and war crimes was dissolved, prosecution tended to invite charges of victors' justice from the German public. As we have seen, however, the common law lawyers and judges were less troubled by ex post facto considerations than were their continental counterparts: for the pragmatic U.S. and British authorities, to allow Nazi war criminals to escape indictment for their million-fold murders would be a far greater injustice than to prosecute them retroactively. The International Military Tribunal reflected the Anglo-American position in its assessment of one defendant: "[S]o far from it being unjust to punish him, it would be unjust if his wrongs were allowed to go unpunished."

Because of the centrality of the "principles of legality" in continental law (i.e., the ban on retroactive criminal laws), German judicial authorities had more scruples about breaching the prohibition of ex post facto laws. The strategy they developed to solve the problem differed in kind from the Anglo-Americans. Rather than brush aside ex post facto objections by invoking the overriding need to punish wanton criminality, the Germans revived a tradition of legal thought that had fallen into desuetude in German courts for 150 years—the theory of natural law. It is not an exaggeration to say that the application of natural law theory was the most significant factor in German jurisdiction over euthanasia-related crimes in the immediate postwar years. With reference to it, the courts could prosecute Nazi medical crimes, and do so consistent with the prohibition of retroactive prosecution (the principle of *nulla crimen sine lege*).

If natural law theory was the most important force in legal jurisdiction over euthanasia criminality, then the leading figure in reviving natural law was Gustav Radbruch. For much of his distinguished legal career, Radbruch was a steadfast positivist who urged German jurists to enforce all laws unconditionally, including unjust ones, offering them the cold comfort that they at least were promoting legal stability (*Rechtssicherheit*). Radbruch's prewar orientation is clear in his 1932 assertion of the positivist view of law: "We condemn the minister who delivers a sermon contrary to his conviction, but we honor the judge who does not allow himself to be deterred from his devotion to the law by his conflicting feeling of justice." That the writer of so consummate a statement of legal positivism could do a complete about-face thirteen years afterward is astonishing. In an article appearing on September 12, 1945, in the Rhein-Neckar newspaper, Radbruch revealed his conversion from legal positivism:

> There are basic legal principles that are stronger than every existing law. . . .
> These basic principles are called the law of nature or reason. If laws
> consciously violate the ends of justice . . . then these laws lack validity,
> then the people owe them no obedience, then jurists must summon the
> courage to deny them the character of law.

In the thirteen years between his 1932 and 1945 statements, much had transpired to effect this change: the triumph by legal means of a vicious dictatorship, the defeat of Germany in a catastrophic world war started by that dictatorship, and the murder of millions during the war, carried out by the same dictatorship. The twelve-year imperium of the Third Reich was an unmitigated disaster for Germany and all of Europe. Radbruch blamed German legal positivism for helping open the door to the jackbooted vandals of the Nazi state.[5]

Radbruch's message in the postwar years was all the more relevant because it addressed the crisis into which the Nazi experience had plunged German law—the crisis of uncertainty about the nature of what precisely bound judges in their interpretation of laws. Radbruch's public conversion resolved this unsureness—at least in the minds of many German lawyers and judges—in favor of "supralegal law." After his first anti-positivistic salvo in September 1945, Radbruch published his well-known defense of natural law theory, "Legal Illegality and Supralegal Law," in the *Süddeutsche Juristische Zeitung* (SJZ) in August 1946. Radbruch began his essay with the statement that the National Socialists secured the obedience of the military and the judiciary to its criminal purposes with two principles: "A command is a command" and "law is law." The first of these tautologies, he observed, was always qualified by the Military Code of Criminal Justice, section 47 of which forbade obedience to orders serving a "criminal purpose." The principle of "law is law," by contrast, admitted of no such limitations. "It was the expression of positivistic legal thinking, which ruled German jurists for many decades almost without challenge," Radbruch wrote. "Legal illegality was therefore as self-contradictory as supralegal law. Praxis was repeatedly confronted by both problems."[6]

The two "problems" Radbruch referred to were the "self-contradictory" maxim of positivism that "law is law" (the idea that the validity of a given law has nothing to do with substantive justice) and the natural law idea that an unjust law forfeits its legality. Both positions were problematic; yet, judges had to commit themselves perforce to one of the two theories. Radbruch found it meaningful that courts had already sided with natural law in their verdicts concerning the status of National Socialist law. One of the earliest cases was a 1946 verdict of the Wiesbaden district court in a civil matter. The case involved the heirs of Jews whose property had been confiscated according to Nazi laws during the war, before they were deported to Poland and killed there. The defendants had purchased the confiscated property at private auction. After the war, the heirs sued the defendants to return the property to them as the rightful owners. The defendants raised what in Anglo-American law is known as a "bona fide purchaser" defense, arguing they had innocently acquired the property at auction and thus were the rightful owners. In its verdict in favor of the plaintiff-heirs, the district court held that the Nazi laws declaring Jewish property subject to confiscation by the state "were in violation of the natural law, and were already null and void at the time of their decree."[7]

Radbruch also described a verdict by a Russian occupation court in an eastern German criminal case involving "denunciation" to the Nazi authorities. In this "grudge informer" case, the defendant had notified the police that his neighbor had called Hitler a "mass murderer" responsible for starting the war. The denunciatee was subsequently arrested, convicted of "preparations for treason," and executed. The *Schwurgericht* (lay assessors) convicted the denouncer of aiding and abetting murder despite his argument that he had acted in accordance with the law at the time, which required Germans to report cases of "high treason" to the local authorities. The court rejected this defense, evidently persuaded by the prosecutor's argument that Nazi laws targeting unjust ends were nullified ab initio. Later in the same essay, Radbruch cited with approval the words of the state prosecutor of Saxony, affirming that no judge could justify his enforcement of a law that was "not only unjust, but criminal," inasmuch as such laws contradicted the "inescapable, authoritative law, which denies validity to the criminal orders of an inhuman tyranny." These and other examples, Radbruch concluded, proved that "the struggle against positivism" raged throughout the German court system. And the courts were well-advised to maintain the struggle, because, in Radbruch's oft-quoted phrase, positivism had rendered German jurists "defenseless" against the "arbitrary and criminal content" of Nazi laws.[8]

What was the content of Radbruch's natural law, the "supralegal law" that both measured and determined the validity of positive law? The vagueness of his natural law invited different interpretations. According to Manfred Walther,

Radbruch's natural law harked back to the *Vernunftsrecht* (law of reason) of the Enlightenment, rather than to Catholic (Neo-Thomistic) natural law. Walther bases his assessment on Radbruch's statement from 1934: "Human rights, *Rechtstaat*, separation of powers, popular sovereignty, freedom and equality, the ideas of 1789, have again emerged from the flood of skepticism, in which they appeared to have drowned." Walther's identification of Radbruch's natural law with the secular French Revolution, however, does not take account of the impact of the war on Radbruch's thought, nor does it reckon with some of his postwar writings that evidence a more religiously oriented theory of natural law. In "The Renewal of Law" (1946), he referred to the "thousand year old common wisdom of antiquity, the Christian Middle Ages, and the period of the Enlightenment," all of which asserted the existence of "a law of nature, a law of God, a law of reason." Fritz Bauer, a former student of Radbruch and the motive force behind the postwar Remer and Auschwitz trials, traced Radbruch's natural law to both humanistic and religious principles of human dignity in Western cultural history. The jurist and legal historian Eberhard Schmidt pointed out in a 1952 lecture that Radbruch never endowed his natural law with substantive content, nor spelled out how exactly the natural law was to be discerned. In the wake of Radbruch's 1947 essay, attempts were made to flesh out the "Radbruch formula," but even these efforts could not overcome the conceptual fuzziness that clouds all attempts to establish a universal and unchanging principle of right.[9]

However interpreted, Radbruch's clarion call to revive natural law theory found an audience among German jurists in the years following its publication. Prior to the Nazi era, the *Reichsgericht* (forerunner to the postwar Supreme Court) subscribed to a positivistic theory of law, as typified in the famous dictum: "The lawmaker is independent and bound to no other limitations than those which he has himself drawn from the Constitution or other laws." The effects of the war and Radbruch's highly publicized critique of positivism wrought a thorough reorientation in the thinking of the *Reichsgericht*'s postwar successor, the *Bundesgerichtshof* (Federal Supreme Court). The *Bundesgerichtshof* in fact was the first legal forum to invoke Radbruch's formula. In a 1946 civil case the court stated, in language taken almost verbatim from Radbruch's "Legal Illegality" article: "If the principle of equality in the promulgation of positive law is violated, the law forfeits any quality of law and is generally not law." Nor was such language unusual in the court's opinions published after the war. Appeals to a "preexisting and accepted order of values and principles of duty governing human society," "an inviolable and supralegal domain of human freedom and right derived from the 'moral autonomy' of the person," and "an order of family life" that is "given by God" are scattered throughout the postwar jurisprudence of the high court.[10]

Radbruch's influence was not confined to the highest judicial authorities in West Germany. Anti-positivistic statements also appeared in the decisions of district, state, and appellate courts. "The judge serves the law and has to apply it unless its application is forbidden by the general moral law," held the appellate court (*Obergerichtshof*) of Cologne in 1949. The appellate court of Bamberg in 1950 adjured judges to nullify "laws contrary to natural law." In a strange case, the district court of Wuppertal in 1946 rejected the legally minimal penalty meted out to a defendant, reasoning that "the laws may no longer be interpreted as something rigid and completely unchangeable by subordinating all feelings of justice," because "the judge's absolute consciousness of duty regarding justice and morality and the citizen to be judged by him [is] higher than the positive law." Also in 1946, the district court of Wiesbaden held that laws "contradicting the natural law [are] at the time of their decree null and void." According to the district court, such laws were those that violated principles "so intimately connected with the nature of the human being in its essence that their infringement would destroy the mental-moral nature of the human being."[11]

Before his death in 1949, Gustav Radbruch had occasion to comment on the verdicts of the state and appellate courts of Frankfurt in the Eichberg case (Mennecke, Schmidt, et al.). At trial, the defendants had defended their participation in euthanasia with appeal to the Hitler order of September 1, 1939, arguing that as a valid and formally binding law it had afforded a legal basis for their actions. They further claimed that even if the order was not valid law they had nonetheless believed at the time in its validity, and therefore were not criminally liable because of a mistake of law. In opposition to this view, the prosecutor had urged that the order was not a law because it lacked the formal elements of legal validity: it had neither been published nor countersigned by the proper ministerial authority. The state court rejected the defendants' arguments, holding that whether the order was a law or not it was illegal. The court in other words refused to accept the prosecutor's view that the Hitler order be denied legal validity on the basis of its formal inadequacies. Instead, the court declared that the state was not the ultimate source of law; it was bound by the "moral law." Insofar as the Hitler order violated fundamental norms of justice, it forfeited any claim to legal validity, even if it was considered a law at the time of its decree. The manifest immorality of the Hitler order was so clear that it could not have been lost on the defendants. The Frankfurt appellate court upheld the state court's determination, noting that the defendants must have been aware the euthanasia program violated "evident natural law principles." In his commentary on the case, Radbruch applauded the courts' endorsement of natural law. The verdicts demonstrated that "even tyranny has its limits, and may not just proclaim any arbitrary act a law." He concluded with the prediction that the Eichberg verdict would be of "considerable importance for future euthanasia cases."[12]

Radbruch's words were indeed prophetic for many of the cases subsequent to the Eichberg trial. In the trials we examine in this and subsequent chapters, euthanasia defendants were usually charged with murder under section 211 of the German Penal Code. The true basis for the courts' jurisdiction, however, was the defendants' egregious violation of the "law of nature," which was superior to all positive laws inconsistent with it. The verdict in the German Hadamar trial is representative. Although acknowledging the importance of positivism to "legal unity and security," the state court of Frankfurt held that positivistic interpretations were curtailed wherever individual laws clashed with the eternal and unchanging law of nature. When a law violated the natural law, it lost all of its compulsory power and ceased to be valid law. The court identified one of the principles of natural law as the "sanctity of human life," with which the state could interfere only as the result of a valid legal judgment (such as a death sentence) or in times of war. Because the Hitler order—whether or not it was a law—vitiated this principle of natural law, it was null and void at the moment the Führer reduced it to writing. Hence, the defendants' actions pursuant to this so-called law were in reality "objectively illegal." Furthermore, held the court, their actions were *subjectively* illegal: no matter how much they may have believed in the existence of a valid euthanasia law, "the wrongful nature of the so-called euthanasia program was apparent even to the simplest and most psychologically immature people"—apparent by virtue of the natural law. The reasoning of the Frankfurt court in the Hadamar case—denying the state ultimate authority as a source of valid law, nullifying the Hitler order for its unjust content, and upholding the defendants' awareness of illegality with reference to the law of nature—is typical of many verdicts issued by German courts between 1946 and 1948.[13]

Natural law gave the German judiciary a normative basis on which it could condemn Nazi euthanasia, its top-level architects, and its field-level implementers without violating the principles of legality (ban on retroactive punishment). In trial after trial, euthanasia defendants portrayed the killing of the disabled as a program inspired by humanitarian concerns, with the aim of "releasing" incurably ill patients from their misery. In refuting this characterization and branding Nazi euthanasia as murder, German courts in the immediate postwar era insisted these killings were not motivated by compassion but by "reprehensible" and "crassly utilitarian" rationales that violated the most sacred principles of civilized peoples. By placing their talents and energies at the disposal of this criminal project, rank-and-file doctors and nurses had become parties to it. The unmistakable message was that the "small wheels" in the machinery of destruction were not the dupes of Hitler and his minions but culpable agents responsible for what they did.

Natural law theory also empowered postwar German courts to overcome a potentially exculpatory defense by euthanasia personnel—namely, that the outward trappings of legality surrounding the euthanasia program had led them to believe in its lawfulness. Under traditional German law, this "mistake of law," if proven, would result in acquittal. By invoking a law of nature accessible to all rational people, German judges neutralized these mistake-of-law defenses: the unjustified killing of disabled patients was a patent violation of the sanctity of life, a core value of the natural law, of which the defendants *had* to have been aware in virtue of their very existence as rational beings.

Interpreting natural law so as to deny mistake-of-law defenses continued until the early 1950s when the "exertion of conscience" cases phased out natural law theory. Henceforth, German courts would not assume that the law of nature was accessible to all rational beings; instead, they would examine whether individual defendants had "exerted" their consciences sufficiently to understand the natural law. The self-evident quality of natural law was thereby de-emphasized in favor of a subjective, case-by-case exploration of a defendant's capacity to comprehend the wrongfulness of euthanasia killing.[14]

With this context in mind, we can now turn to the German euthanasia trials themselves, beginning with those defendants who lacked the grace or good luck of a later trial. For in the early German trials, neither pleas of ignorance of wrongdoing nor subjective good intentions mattered. Euthanasia defendants stood before their accusers as perpetrators, and the flail of justice struck swiftly and without mercy.

THE PERILS OF BEING FIRST: THE WERNICKE AND WIECZOREK CASE

Less than a year after Germany's surrender, Dr. Hilde Wernicke and Nurse Helene Wieczorek stood before the state court in Berlin charged with murder in violation of section 211 of the German criminal code. They were former members of the medical staff at the mental hospital Obrawalde near the Pomeranian town of Meseritz. The Berlin court's findings of fact indicated that in 1943 Walter Grabowski, the new director of the Obrawalde mental hospital, informed Wernicke and Wieczorek of Hitler's order to kill all incurably ill mental patients. He then initiated them into Obrawalde's role in the killing program. At first, Wernicke withheld her agreement to participate, but eventually she overcame her scruples with the justification that incurable patients incapable of an adequate life should be eliminated. Wieczorek had fewer scruples, readily agreeing to participate. Grabowski swore both of them to secrecy under penalty of death. Thereafter, transports of patients arrived at Obrawalde along with lists of those designated for killing. Wernicke's job was to examine these lists and confirm the diagnosis of incurable mental illness. She relayed the names of patients deemed truly incurable to nurse Amanda Ratajczak. Over the next year, she studied on average four to six patient histories per day, giving special attention to patients who suffered from both incurable mental illness and physical impairment. Patients capable of work were spared. From spring 1943 to 1944, Wernicke communicated the names of approximately 600 patients to nurses Ratajczak, E., and Wieczorek (who succeeded Ratajczak when she became ill in summer 1944) for killing. Like her co-nurses Ratajczak and E., Wieczorek injected lethal dosages of morphine and scopolamine into each patient. She performed this grisly work until September 1944. On January 29, 1945, Obrawalde's role in the euthanasia program came to an end when the staff fled the institution to escape the advancing Red Army.[15]

The various judicial panels who heard the case within the state court of Berlin in March 1946 found the defendants guilty of murder as perpetrators. The German law of murder (codified in section 211 of the German Penal Code) is complex and highly nuanced. For this reason, readers steeped in Anglo-American legal culture may at first find German legal conceptions of murder perplexing. Prior to 1941, murder under German law was straightforward. The code's definition of murder in 1912 emphasized premeditation as the essential element of the offense: "Whoever intentionally kills a person, if he carried out the killing with premeditation, is guilty of murder for that killing."[16] In 1941 the German Ministry of Justice overhauled section 211, redefining murder as a killing prompted by any one of several motives:

A murderer is any one who kills another person out of joy in killing [*Mordlust*], satisfaction of the sexual drive, covetousness or other base motives, maliciously or cruelly or by means endangering the community or for the purpose of making possible or concealing the commission of another crime.[17]

Writing about this revision of section 211 in September 1941, Roland Freisler, State Secretary in the Prussian Ministry of Justice and president of the Berlin People's Court, hailed it as a "renewal" that better reflected the "natural feelings of the people." For Freisler, the older version of section 211 failed adequately to address the interests of "substantive justice" because its emphasis on premeditation did not permit a "moral assessment" of the perpetrator. Freisler quoted with approval the annotations supporting the revision:

The complete destruction of a member of the community directly affects the community itself. Further, in morally evaluating assaults on the life of another, the state of mind that produces the crime is decisive. . . . Murder is distinguished from manslaughter by a particularly base state of mind, which has application to especially reprehensible motives or in related, especially base means [of acting].[18]

Henceforth, German legal analysis to determine who was a murderer "must regard [the defendant's] entire personality." Although the text of the revised section 211 was not infused with Nazi terminology or concepts, it was justified with resort to National Socialist principles—specifically, the will to give legal effect to the "natural feelings of the *Volk*." The new version of section 211 survived postwar efforts to denazify German law and continues unchanged until the present day.[19]

At the trial of Wernicke and Wieczorek, the defendants were tried on the basis of the new version of section 211. Dismissing Wernicke's argument that her actions had been inspired by the humane motive of delivering incurable patients from their suffering, the court found that both defendants had acted from base motives. Moreover, they had also acted "maliciously"; that is, they had exploited the guilelessness and defenselessness of their victims after winning over their trust—an act that "runs counter to every human feeling on the grossest level." The defendants' subordinate status in the grand scheme of euthanasia did not help them as it would defendants in later years. On the issue of perpetration versus complicity, the court invoked the subjective standard of the Bathtub Case, finding that each of the defendants had identified with the killing "as her own act." Neither had declined or opposed Grabowski's offer; rather, they had inwardly assented both to the project itself and to its reprehensible philosophy of destroying "valueless" life. The state court's *Schwurgericht* held open the door to the legal permissibility of euthanasia but insisted that the defendants' actions were not motivated by compassion.

Nor did the state court authorities find the defendants' superior orders defense persuasive. On appeal from the *Schwurgericht*, the appellate court denied that Hitler's 1939 order was a law, because it was never published in the *Reich Legal Journal*, as was required for all newly promulgated laws. Furthermore, the appellate court held, even if the Hitler order had been a valid order, the German Civil Servant Law obligated every official to refuse orders that violated criminal law. The defendants not only did not refuse the order, but "inwardly approved" of it. For this reason, they were guilty as perpetrators under the new version of section 211.[20] Because German law prior to 1949 required the death penalty in all murder cases (absent extenuating circumstances), Wernicke and Wieczorek were sentenced to death on March 25, 1946. When their punishment was carried out, they became the first—and last—euthanasia defendants tried in West German courts to suffer this fate.

VANITY, AMBITION, AND LOVE: THE EICHBERG CASE

Nine months after the Berlin state court handed down its verdicts in the Wernicke and Wieczorek case, the state court of Frankfurt presided over the trial of medical personnel from the Eichberg mental hospital. In 1940 the KdF had designated Eichberg a transit center and collection point in the government's campaign against the mentally disabled. In this dual role, Eichberg received transports of mentally handicapped patients that were later dispatched to one of the six killing centers for "treatment." It also became a venue for murdering both disabled adults and children.

The most notable defendant at the Eichberg trial in December 1946 was Dr. Friedrich Mennecke, an infamous figure in the annals of Nazi euthanasia. Mennecke's swaggering wartime letters to his wife, interspersing banal comments on his meals with casual references to the annihilation of mental patients, reveal a man deeply involved in mass atrocity without a trace of self-accusation. In 1938 Mennecke became the director of the Eichberg mental hospital, which he briefly left when war broke out to assume duties as an army doctor on the Western front. In January 1940, the KdF released him from his military duties to participate in the nascent euthanasia program. Accordingly, he returned to Eichberg and resumed his directorship. In February 1940 he attended a meeting of psychiatrists at the Columbus House in Berlin, where Viktor Brack informed him and his colleagues of Hitler's decision to set the euthanasia program in motion. Brack reassured the attending doctors that the program was legal, a point he drove home by circulating a copy of Hitler's euthanasia order. Categories of patients exempt from the program were also discussed; these included patients injured in combat and elderly patients suffering from age-related dementia. To justify the operation, Brack marshaled the familiar economistic argument: mental patients unable to contribute to the people's community, but who nonetheless absorbed scarce resources, had to be eliminated, particularly during a time of war when so many of the nation's most valuable citizens sacrificed their lives on behalf of the fatherland.[21]

Like his colleagues in attendance, Mennecke readily agreed to participate in the program. After the February meeting with Brack, he returned to Eichberg and completed the registration forms on his patients, occasionally ordering his staff doctors to do the same without acquainting them with the reasons for it. In the ensuing months, Mennecke also became an itinerant registrar for the euthanasia program, visiting other institutions to complete forms on their resident patients. At various satellite mental hospitals that Mennecke visited during winter 1941, he was estimated to have filled out 200 forms; at his own institution of Eichberg, the number reached 1,000. In addition—and more ominously—he traveled in November and December 1941 to the concentration

Dr. Friedrich Mennecke with his wife, Eva. The director of the Eichberg mental hospital and a T-4 medical expert, Mennecke's prolific correspondence with his wife became an important source of evidence against him at his criminal trial before a Frankfurt state court in December 1946. Courtesy Bundesarchiv Koblenz

camps at Sachsenhausen, Ravensbrück, Buchenwald, Dachau, Gross-Rosen, Auschwitz, and Flossenbürg as a participant in the Nazis' 14f13 program. At these camps, Mennecke was believed to have filled out forms on approximately 1,000 inmates. The state court of Frankfurt declared that "there can be no question that some of the inmates from the camp system whom Mennecke designated for killing were gassed in the euthanasia centers." Among the concentration camp prisoners caught up in Mennecke's registration drive were large numbers of Jewish men and women. In making his assessment, Mennecke had reviewed photos of the prisoners from the camp files. On the backs of the photos he had written epithets gleaned from the records, such as "race defiler" (*Rassenschänder*), "malicious agitator and German enemy" (*Hetzer und Deutschenfeind*), "rumored Communist," "Jewish prostitute." Although conclusive evidence was unavailable, the state court believed that at least some of these Jewish prisoners were later murdered in the euthanasia centers on the basis of Mennecke's forms.[22]

Mennecke's service to Nazi euthanasia did not end with these activities. He also served as a *Gutachter* (medical expert), reviewing regular shipments of completed forms sent to him in packets from Berlin. In the lower left corner of each form, he wrote one of three characterizations: "Yes," "No," or "Questionable." His determinations were not based on medical exams but solely on the forms' contents. Wielding this divine power over the life and death of people he had never seen, Mennecke reviewed nearly 7,000 forms as a T-4 expert. Of this number, he designated around 2,500 for destruction. Furthermore, during his tenure as the director of Eichberg, 2,262 patients were transferred from the facility to the killing center at Hadamar, where almost all of them were gassed between January and August 1941. Mennecke gave the lists of transferees to his underlings, ordering them to prepare the affected patients for transport. At trial, the court heard eyewitness testimony that the transferees were not all severely ill mental patients; some were only mildly disabled patients capable of work. Not all of them, in other words, were the "burnt out ruins" (*ausgebrannte Ruinen*) that Mennecke claimed in his defense. Finally, the court was satisfied that Mennecke had participated in the murder of adult patients at Eichberg between summer 1941 and December 1942. His assertion that he knew nothing of the killings was refuted by his detailed letters to his wife.[23]

Mennecke's defense at his trial in December 1946 was that he had become involved in euthanasia only against his will and had done everything in his power to secure a reassignment to the front in 1942. Again, Mennecke's letters proved his undoing. In the eyes of the state court, they revealed his passionate engagement with the euthanasia program, a program that gave Mennecke the opportunity to interact with the "superstars" of mass killing. In one letter, he boasted to his wife of the praise that Dr. Werner Heyde (an *Obergutachter* in section II of the KdF and head of the T-4 Medical Department) had showered on him for his work on behalf of the program. It gratified his ego to be associated with the "famous Berlin organization," noting that he and his staff were fully cooperating with it. After his transfer to the field from Eichberg, he sought to maintain his active role as a *Gutachter*: in a 1944 letter to the Reich Committee (responsible for administering the children's euthanasia program), he advertised his willingness to continue his lethal work, indicating that he would accept the directorship of a children's ward in Plagwitz (lower Silesia) were it offered to him.[24]

Given this incriminating documentation, the court had no doubt that Mennecke had contributed to the killings at Eichberg willingly and enthusiastically. The court noted that the children's ward at Eichberg was established under Mennecke's regime as director, and that he had conducted correspondence with the Reich Committee in Berlin, whose "treatment" authorizations he forwarded to the ward's director, Dr. Walter Schmidt. Mennecke did not blanch at the implications of his orders: according to Schmidt's testimony, and as Mennecke himself confessed, he told Schmidt to proceed with "treatment" so long as the authorization had been given by the Reich Committee—an order that extended equally to adult patients and to children. Applying the subjective standard of the Bathtub Case, the court found that Mennecke had inwardly identified with the killings, which he had "willed as his own," and was accordingly guilty as a "co-perpetrator" of murder—this despite the absence of proof that he had directly performed the killings himself. In its discussion of Mennecke's motives under section 211, the court observed that he was not an ideological killer; rather, Mennecke was driven by a "boundless ambition" and an "illimitable need for validation." It "flattered his vanity" to interact as an equal with eminent professors and political figures, and he spared no effort to ingratiate himself with them. The 200 Reichsmarks he received every month in compensation for his work in the euthanasia program was an added inducement. In brief Mennecke was, in the estimate of the court, willing to sacrifice everything—"law, morals, professional ethics, honor and decency"— to attain his goal of professional advancement. Mennecke's unprincipled careerism was the goad to his participation in mass killing. Such motives the court deemed "base and reprehensible," thus satisfying the "base motive" element of murder under the new version of section 211.[25]

Because of his work as an itinerant expert, Mennecke could not assume direction over the children's ward installed at Eichberg in early 1941 for the purpose of killing disabled children. Instead, he assigned the directorship to his deputy, Dr. Walter Schmidt, who returned from the field to take up his duties in summer 1941. For his role in the Eichberg killings, Schmidt stood with Mennecke in the dock as a codefendant. The state court was convinced that Mennecke had briefed Schmidt on the euthanasia program and that it would have been impossible to conceal transfers of patients from Eichberg without his knowledge. Schmidt assumed control of the children's ward as the institution's chief doctor. He soon received a visit from Richard von Hegener, deputy director of the Reich Committee, and Professor Paul Nitsche, one of three chief medical experts and from December 1941 medical director of T-4. The Berliners informed Schmidt that mentally handicapped children in his ward were to be destroyed (the German word was behandelt, or "treated"). There was some evidence presented at trial that Schmidt unsuccessfully tried to extricate himself from his new commission when he learned of it—a fact that would weigh significantly in the court's assessment of his role in the killing program.[26]

From summer 1941 until the end of Eichberg as a euthanasia facility, children afflicted with severe physical and mental handicaps were transferred to its children's ward. On arrival they were subjected to medical observation; their physical and mental conditions, as well as their "educability," were noted on forms subsequently sent to the Reich Committee. Based on their review of these forms, committee employees ordered additional observation or issued an authorization to the Eichberg authorities to have the child "treated." In at least thirty documented cases, Schmidt himself administered lethal dosages of morphine and luminal to the children designated for "treatment." In another thirty to forty cases, he had one of his staff nurses, Heléne Schürg, dispose of handicapped children with lethal injections (or, in a few instances, with deadly doses of luminal tablets). It was significant to the state court that no evidence implicated Schmidt in self-initiated killing, as the indictment against him had alleged. All of his criminal actions, in other words, were carried out within the scope of orders from Berlin.[27]

The state court did not dwell exclusively on the destructive aspects of Schmidt's career at Eichberg but also cited in its verdict examples of his probity as a doctor. It noted that he had sought to cure his patients with the newest medical methods, including insulin shock therapy. Witnesses attested to his professionalism and dedication to his patients, many of whom experienced such an improvement in their condition as a result of Schmidt's interventions that they could be released from the hospital. Anticipating later (and more successful) defenses, Schmidt claimed these successes were his way of opposing euthanasia: by rehabilitating patients who might otherwise have been euthanized, he hoped to demonstrate the extreme nature of the government's killing program.[28]

For the court, Schmidt's actions on behalf of the euthanasia program were qualitatively different from Mennecke's. Unlike Mennecke's motives for participation, Schmidt's were not self-referential. He was not impelled by base factors like vanity, ambition, and acquisitiveness, all of which figured prominently in Mennecke's conduct. Instead, the court pointed to the possibility that Schmidt—perhaps because of his upbringing—suffered from a "falsely understood subaltern loyalty to obey," which prevented him from refusing to collaborate with the euthanasia program. Ultimately, in the court's estimate he was a different moral animal from Mennecke, one to whom "a certain professional ethos" had to be granted. The state court was clearly impressed with the evidence presented about Schmidt's "extraordinary efforts" to effect a cure in his patients. For this reason, it held that Schmidt—despite his proven involvement in the murder of his patients—had not acted from base motives as these were defined under section 211. The court did find, however, that Schmidt had acted "maliciously" by "secretly, treacherously, and falsely" transferring patients to killing centers like Hadamar, after forbidding their relatives to visit them and withholding information from the families of their whereabouts. Schmidt, in concert with his nursing staff, fostered trust in the patients and their families that they would be given medical treatment, a trust that was soon abused by lethal injections and gas chambers. The malicious nature of Schmidt's participation in the killing resulted in a finding of guilt as a co-perpetrator of murder under section 211.[29]

Alongside Mennecke and Schmidt in the dock were members of the Eichberg nursing staff. The most conspicuous among them was Eichberg's chief nurse, Heléne Schürg. She served as chief nurse at Eichberg from 1937 until her dismissal by U.S. authorities in July 1945. At trial, it was proven that she had killed between thirty and forty disabled children with lethal doses of morphine and luminal, given either intravenously or in tablets. Schürg did not dispute her role in the killings but raised a superior orders defense, arguing that she had acted under orders from higher governmental powers. She also argued—and I have yet to find an analogous defense in other euthanasia cases— that her amorous infatuation with Schmidt had transformed her into an almost robotic tool of the chief doctor. The state court rejected the superior orders defense, but found her lovelorn argument credible on the issue of whether she was a perpetrator or an accomplice. The court found "she had so divested herself of her own will that she placed all her fortitude at Schmidt's disposal, seeking to translate his will into reality and doing precisely that." Such prostration of her own will to act effectively nullified the "will to perpetration" necessary to qualify as a perpetrator. She was thus guilty as an accomplice to the murders perpetrated by Schmidt. (That is, she was guilty of aiding and abetting murder.)[30]

Schürg was not the only nurse convicted of complicity in murder by the Frankfurt court. Her colleague Andreas Senft had been a nurse at Eichberg since 1906. As a station nurse in the men's ward, he confessed to deliberately killing patients with injections of morphine and luminal. His defense that his forty years at Eichberg had conditioned him to obey doctors' orders and to support them in all circumstances was rejected as an exculpatory ground by the court, which found him, like Schürg, guilty of aiding and abetting murder.[31]

Until the promulgation of the German Basic Law in 1949, all defendants convicted as perpetrators of murder in German courts were given a mandatory death sentence, unless extraordinary factors were present to commute the sentence to life imprisonment. In the Eichberg case, the court found no reason to spare Mennecke from capital punishment. (The sentence was never carried out; he committed suicide in his cell at the Butzbach prison near Frankfurt on January 28, 1947.) Schmidt, however, was another story. The gap between Schmidt's subjective state of mind and his objective acts qualified him as an exceptional case in the reckoning of the court, warranting life imprisonment rather than the death penalty. A similar focus on subjectivity characterized the court's assessments of Schürg and Senft. Schürg's "strong relationship of dependence" on Schmidt was counted in her favor, as were her efforts to extricate herself from the program; she received a prison sentence of eight years. As for Senft, the court found that his long-standing habit of deference had rendered him "psychologically unprepared" to deal with his role in the euthanasia program. He received a four-year prison term.[32]

The significance of the Eichberg case in the history of German euthanasia trials can be interpreted on two levels. First, it typifies the willingness of German courts in the immediate postwar years to convict euthanasia killers as perpetrators under the German law of murder. In this respect, Eichberg is of a piece with the Meseritz-Obrawalde and Hadamar trials, representing with them a vein of cases that did not gladly suffer intentional mass killing—or the defendants responsible for it. Second, the Eichberg case adumbrates some new tendencies and directions that later courts would pursue with far more alacrity than the Frankfurt court did. These new approaches are especially evident in the court's treatment of Schmidt, Schürg, and Senft. Although it finally convicted Schmidt of murder, the court did so only after a searching examination of his subjective state of mind at the time he participated in the killings. Its analysis framed Schmidt's acts within the context of his "one-sided and false education" about his duty to obey authority. The court did not take the next logical step and deny Schmidt's ability as a moral agent to withhold his consent to and collaboration with an unjust exercise of the sovereign's will, based on his defective socialization. Yet, the raw material for such a step is implicit in the court's reasoning. In addition, the court's receptiveness to Schmidt's argument that he only participated in euthanasia in order to curb its effects (e.g., by curing patients through various shock therapies) is a precursor to later "collision of duties" defenses, in which euthanasia killers would contend, with increasing degrees of success, that they collaborated in the program only to sabotage it from within. Although the state court of Frankfurt did not accept this defense here as an exculpatory or justifying ground for Schmidt's actions, the basis for such a conclusion is discernible in the court's rationale.

The Frankfurt court took a similar approach in its assessment of the two nurses, Schürg and Senft. Their psychological temperament—Schürg's lovelorn reliance on Schmidt, Senft's forty-year habit of automatic deference to authority—could have, and probably would have, qualified them for acquittal in a later era based on the theory that they lacked the necessary awareness of illegality on which criminal liability hinges. In 1946 German courts were not yet ready to give their defendants' psychological makeup such exonerative effect. The memory of Nazi atrocities was still vividly etched in the minds of most Germans. Further, the Cold War had not yet reached its full stride, as it would in the late 1940s. The need to punish the killers of the National Socialist state still outweighed the need for a rehabilitated German nation as a democratic-capitalist buffer between the West and the Soviet sphere of influence in

The German Hadamar Trial. Second row, left to right: chief nurse Irmgard Huber, Dr. Adolf Wahlmann, Dr. Bodo Gorgass. Courtesy the Landeswohlfahrtsverband Hessen

eastern Europe. This geopolitical situation would change between 1946 and 1948. When the worm did eventually turn and the West began to perceive the Soviet Union as an immediate menace to international security, deserving of higher priority than the prosecution of Nazi war criminals, the effect was to douse the fire of German prosecution with cold water. One result would be the wholesale acquittal or sentence mitigation of euthanasia defendants.

HUMAN WEAKNESS AND THE INERTIA OF THE WILL: THE GERMAN HADAMAR CASE

Dr. Adolf Wahlmann, former chief doctor at the Hadamar mental hospital, may have had a sickening feeling of deja vu as he sat in the defendants' gallery in March 1947. A photograph from the trial shows Wahlmann sitting rigidly, his mouth frozen in a dispirited frown, his brows anxiously knitted, his chin thrust forward in an attempt at tremulous self-mastery. Wahlmann had already been convicted of war crimes at the U.S. Hadamar trial in October 1945. His prior conviction, however, related only to Wahlmann's role in the scheme to murder consumptive eastern workers during the war's waning stages. Sentenced to life imprisonment, the seventy-two-year-old Wahlmann now stood accused of murdering German patients at Hadamar between 1942 and 1945. A finding of guilt could have meant the death penalty for him.

When the war broke out in September 1939, Wahlmann was living in retirement in Heidelberg. Because of the shortage of doctors in Germany, he was brought out of retirement and appointed chief doctor at the Weilmünster mental hospital in June 1940. In August 1942 State Councillor Fritz Bernotat, who presided over the system of mental institutions and nursing homes in Hessen-Nassau, appointed him chief doctor at Hadamar. By this time, Hadamar had long since been transformed into an extermination center for the mentally ill, replacing the Grafeneck institution when it was closed in December 1940. Even before Wahlmann's arrival, at Hadamar 10,000 mentally disabled patients had been killed through gassing as part of the first phase of the Nazis' euthanasia program. A lull in the killing ensued from August 1941 until Wahlmann became chief doctor in August 1942. In late August or early September 1942, the first transport of phase two arrived in Hadamar, consisting of patients designated for killing from the cloister facility Hofen. Wahlmann had been briefed in advance on the killing program and Hadamar's role within it. He devised a system of morning conferences with his nurses, in the course of which they reported to him the names of patients deemed fit for euthanasia.

Wahlmann and his nurses examined the patient's records and illness history, then discussed whether killing was indicated based on their review. The final decision resided with Wahlmann. If he gave the green light, two nurses wrote the name of the patient on a sheet of paper, noting the amount of narcotics Wahlmann had specified to effect the patient's death (e.g., the number of tablets of luminal, trional, or similar drugs). The paper was given to the station nurses, who used it as an authorization for killing the patients so chosen. During the night, these patients were given substantial overdoses, usually in the form of narcotics tablets. If the tablets did not result in death, an injection of morphine was administered the following morning, which invariably ended the patient's life. Afterward, Wahlmann made a brief inspection of the corpse and fabricated false causes and times of death for the patient's death certificate. The Frankfurt state court estimated that at least 900 mentally ill patients had been killed in this fashion.[33]

At trial, the Frankfurt court found that Wahlmann's actions fulfilled section 211's definition of murder, insofar as he had acted "maliciously" by abusing the trust that existed between patient and doctor. His patients and their relatives looked to him to do everything in his power to either cure their illness or mitigate its effect. Instead, he exploited their trust by distributing overdoses of medication designed to cause their deaths. To this injury was added the insult of fraudulent causes of death, aimed at deceiving the victims' next of kin about the actual fate of the patients. Although the court found

Wahlmann guilty of murder as a perpetrator under section 211, it denied that he had acted from "base motives." On the issue of what precisely motivated Wahlmann to collaborate in the mass killings, the court cryptically attributed his involvement to "human weaknesses and inadequacy, and a certain inertia of the will."[34]

In the black-and-white photograph of the Hadamar trial, an unassuming, bespectacled man sits to the right of Wahlmann. He is tensely expectant, uncannily resembling in his dark suit and tie with his recessive chin and graying temples a mild-mannered accountant. This is Dr. Hans-Bodo Gorgass, convicted by the Frankfurt court of the murder of 2,000 patients during his five months as a T-4 doctor at Hadamar. Like many of his T-4 colleagues, Gorgass served on the front as a military doctor until given the "uk" (*unabkömmlinge,* or "indispensable") designation by Hitler's chancellery. Released from his military duties in 1941, he was ordered to report to Berlin, where he was received in the KdF by Viktor Brack. Brack told him that a law existed, according to which incurable mentally ill patients were to be granted a "mercy death" by specially appointed physicians. Although the law could not be published because of unspecified reasons of secrecy, Brack assured Gorgass that his work as a T-4 euthanasia doctor was perfectly legal. Brack then announced he would receive a crash course in killing at the Hartheim mental hospital near Linz. Without expressing concerns about the commission given him, Gorgass immediately departed for Hartheim.[35]

On arrival Gorgass met with the institution's director, Dr. Rudolf Lonauer. Lonauer briefed Gorgass on the circle of those involved in the euthanasia program, disclosing that the mentally handicapped were disposed of in gas chambers located in six separate facilities within the Reich. At his trial, Gorgass told the Frankfurt court that these revelations deeply shocked him. He claimed, however, that Lonauer assured him only severely ill patients refractory to therapy would be affected. This assurance, along with Lonauer's mention of the names of well-known physicians involved in the operation, pacified Gorgass's conscience. Over the next several weeks, Gorgass served an apprenticeship in killing at Hartheim under the tutelage of Lonauer. After his stint at Hartheim, Gorgass graduated to the killing center of Sonnenstein near Pirna, where he observed the asphyxiation of patients with carbon monoxide gas. From Sonnenstein he arrived at Hadamar in mid-June 1941 to begin his service. There he was introduced to his work by Alfons Klein's predecessor as director of the institution, Dr. Friedrich Berner. Gorgass claimed at trial that Berner told him he had a copy of the euthanasia law in his possession but for security reasons was not able to show it to Gorgass. Berner then placed Gorgass under oath and swore him to secrecy about the euthanasia program with a handshake.[36]

The killing process at Hadamar unfolded as follows: patients arriving at Hadamar in transports were measured, weighed, photographed, and disrobed before being led into an "examination room," where Gorgass inspected their patient histories and photocopies of their registration forms, upon which the *Gutachter* had inscribed his initials. The purpose of this final examination was to ensure that the patients' symptoms were fully noted on the photocopies and to guarantee that no war-wounded patients or foreigners had been inadvertently included. Afterward, hospital personnel brought them into the gas chamber—a room thirty cubic meters in area, disguised as a shower room. Once the entire transport (consisting of between sixty and one hundred patients) was locked in this room, Gorgass went into a passage behind the gas chamber, where he turned on a valve that poured carbon monoxide gas into the chamber. As he did so, he observed the effect of the gas through a peephole. After ten minutes Gorgass turned off the gas valve. Another one to two hours passed before the chamber was ventilated and the corpses removed for cremation. Gorgass's role in the killing process ended at this point, only to resume with each new transport, which arrived on average twice per week. With two exceptions—one involving a war veteran, the other a pregnant woman (subsequently killed with a lethal injection by the chief nurse)—Gorgass effected the deaths of all patients brought to him in the examination room. His role continued from June 1941 until the end of the first phase of euthanasia in August 1941.[37]

Like many of his colleagues in the euthanasia program, Gorgass claimed the patients he gassed were in advanced stages of mental illness and physical decrepitude. The Frankfurt court found this assertion questionable, because, in its words, "a not inconsiderable number of those killed [at Hadamar] were neither physically nor mentally ill. There were many who were still capable of light work, who could carry on a limited conversation, who experienced emotional impressions (like joy, or emotions tied to good or ill treatment), and who could even correspond with their relatives." One witness, a Dr. N., testified that many of those killed could have been treated with therapeutic measures that might have improved their condition. Eyewitness testimony heard at trial cited specific examples. Another witness, a medical doctor, described one of the victims as a small girl "who could not work at all, but was harmless, always happy, and greeted him every morning like a father." His efforts to gain her exemption from transport failed, and she was sent to Hadamar for gassing. Another victim, a farmhand from Fulda, was not only capable of work but cognitively aware enough to recognize a former acquaintance of his in the Hadamar disrobing room. In its verdict the court listed several other examples, including a Jewish assessor committed to Eichberg in accordance with section 42b for distributing communist leaflets. The man was later transferred to Hadamar to be killed.[38]

Dr. Hans-Bodo Gorgass, convicted by a German court in March 1947 for murdering 2,000 patients at Hadamar in summer 1941. Before his arrival at Hadamar, Gorgass was trained in techniques of mass murder at the killing centers of Hartheim (Linz) and Sonnenstein (near Pirna). Gorgass operated the valves in the Hadamar gas chamber that dispatched German patients with carbon monoxide gas. Like Adolf Wahlmann, Gorgass was convicted of murder under German law and sentenced to death. Both men's death sentences were commuted with the formal repeal of capital punishment in West Germany in 1949. Courtesy HHStAW Abt. 3008, Hans-Bodo Gorgass

In assessing the nature of Gorgass's actions in furtherance of the euthanasia program, the Frankfurt state court applied the criteria of section 211, beginning with "base motives." According to the court, no such motives were perceptible in Gorgass's conduct. "It has not been proven," held the court, "that greed, the need for validation, striving after material advantage, or other despicable motives have caused Gorgass to collaborate in the implementation of the program." Rather, the court believed Gorgass may have been dazzled by the eminent figures within the KdF who had approached him, "a small doctor," with "a secret Reich matter." Being awed into cooperating with a plot to commit mass murder did not "bear the stamp of moral reprehensibility"; it was instead the result of "a certain human weakness." Despite this finding, the court found Gorgass guilty of murder under section 211 because his actions were "malicious"; that is, he had acted "secretly, viciously, and fraudulently." Like his codefendant Wahlmann, Gorgass lulled transportees into a false sense of security by winning their trust, then coarsely abused this trust by killing them in gas chambers camouflaged as showering facilities. Gorgass was convicted with Wahlmann of murder ("malicious" killing) under section 211.[39]

Only Gorgass and Wahlmann were convicted as perpetrators of murder in the Hadamar case. Although neither was deemed to have acted out of base motives, the court denied extenuating grounds in sentencing the two doctors. Gorgass argued for mitigation under paragraph 3 of section 211, an argument rejected by the court based on his "extremely unethical conduct during the euthanasia operation." According to the court, had Gorgass "carried within himself high ethical values and a strong professional ethos," it would have been obvious to him that the mass killing at Hadamar was illegitimate "from a medical as well as a human-ethical standpoint." Presumably, only some form of disengagement from the program would have sufficed as "ethical" conduct. Likewise, the court based its rejection of Wahlmann's claims of extenuation on the "especially high measure of irresponsibility" and "strong renunciation of the medical professional ethos" his actions displayed. Absent mitigating factors, both men were sentenced to death.[40]

Besides Gorgass and Wahlmann, other members of the Hadamar administration faced judgment at the hands of the Frankfurt court. The nursing staff (including the luckless Irmgard Huber, convicted of war crimes in the U.S. Hadamar Trial) and the technical and office staff were all indicted. The logic of the Bathtub Case guided the court in categorizing the nurses as accomplices rather than perpetrators:

> They were all inwardly too dependent and possessed of a powerful inertia
> of the will in order to grasp situations of such gravity in a sufficient
> manner. Above all, however, they saw their medical role models, whom

they were accustomed to respect and esteem, [acting] weakly and without will, and found in them neither support nor a role model.[41]

Moreover, the Frankfurt court considered the nurses' ability to conform their actions to the law compromised by subjective factors, such as a "primitive nature" and (in one case) "pregnancy" that "restricted her power to resist." A habit of punctilious churchgoing also weighed in their favor. On this rationale, the nurses were convicted of aiding and abetting murder and given jail terms between three and eight years. The office staff, among them secretaries who had logged both the arrival of patients and property (including gold teeth) confiscated from them, were all acquitted on the ground that their criminal intent could not be sufficiently proven.[42]

On appeal from the state court, the appellate court of Frankfurt criticized the lower court's determination that the nurses were all accomplices rather than perpetrators. The appellate court held that the lower court had exaggerated the subjective theory of perpetration. This theory could only be applied in cases where the defendants "did not themselves commit the killing, but have collaborated in some way in the killings that were committed." In such cases, stated the court, "the question must be answered whether they were perpetrators or participants, . . . i.e., [whether they] identified themselves inwardly with [the killing] and approved of it." Where a defendant has fulfilled all the elements of the offense himself, however, that defendant is a perpetrator. "Whoever kills another person with his own hands, whoever administers the deadly shot, or mixes poison in another's food, is a murderer, even if he does it in the interests of another, i.e. 'for' him." However, because the defendants, and not the government, had lodged the appeal, the case could not as a matter of law be remanded to the lower court. The latter's characterization of the nurses as accomplices remained unchanged.[43]

The Hadamar case bears comparison with the Eichberg trial: in both, T-4 doctors were convicted as perpetrators of murder under section 211's definition of "malicious" killing; in both, nurses were characterized under the subjective theory as accomplices to murder, rather than as perpetrators. Although jurists in the two trials were willing to convict physicians of murder as perpetrators, we can discern in both a tendency to regard the motives of the doctor defendants as something other than "base": Schmidt was actuated by a "falsely understood subaltern loyalty to obey," Wahlmann by "human weaknesses and inadequacy, and a certain inertia of the will," Gorgass by "a certain human weakness" that awed him into collaborating with mass murder. Only Mennecke, in his overweening self-importance, was declared to have acted "basely." Both cases are notable, too, for their refusal to convict as perpetrators nurses who with their own hands had murdered thousands of disabled patients. By the end of the Hadamar trial in mid-1947, we are moving steadily toward an era in the prosecution of Nazi euthanasia in which the rationale governing the portrayal of nursing staff as accomplices will be extended to T-4 doctors.

THE BENEFITS OF A "WEAK AND UNSTABLE PERSONALITY": THE KALMENHOF CASE

In the history of National Socialist euthanasia prosecution, the trial of T-4 doctors Mathilde Weber and Hermann Wesse wears a Janus face. One face stares backward toward the earlier prosecutions of the Meseritz-Obrawalde and Eichberg medical staffs. The other looks toward new vistas in the evolution of German euthanasia trials. Although the first trial of the Kalmenhof doctors would end in early 1947 with the convictions of both Weber and Wesse as murderers, two years would pass before the Frankfurt court, on remand from the appellate court, would change its mind and find a T-4 doctor guilty not as a perpetrator, but as an accomplice.

The Kalmenhof mental hospital was founded in the mid-1920s as one of several charitable public institutions, "born," in the ironic words of the Frankfurt state court, "in the spirit of humanity and a practicing love of one's neighbor." The association to which Kalmenhof belonged undertook to nurture "feebleminded" (*schwachsinnig*) but educable children by means of instruction and work therapy, with the goal of making of them "useful people." When Hitler came to power in 1933, the Nazis wasted no time in subverting these constructive aspirations. They replaced Kalmenhof's director and appointed Nazi zealot Fritz Bernotat chairman of the association. This was a dire omen for Kalmenhof's patients; in 1936, at a conference of directors of mental hospitals in the castle of Dehrn, Bernotat was reported to have told the assembled directors, "If I were a doctor, I would kill these patients."[44]

When the killing program began, Kalmenhof was transformed into both a transit center, to which patients from other institutions were sent en route to Hadamar, and a miniature killing center in its own right, where individual murders were committed through lethal doses of narcotics. At the time Kalmenhof assumed these roles in 1940, Dr. Mathilde Weber was its managing physician. In January 1941, the Reich Cooperative for State Hospitals and Nursing Homes (a front organization for Hitler's chancellery) sent to Kalmenhof lists of patients to be prepared for transport on a predetermined day by the busses of Gekrat. These selections had been made by T-4 experts based on registration forms completed and returned to Berlin by the Kalmenhof staff in 1940. Of the 600 to 700 patients at Kalmenhof, 232 were transferred to Hadamar, where they were gassed between January 17 and April 29, 1941. Patients were also transferred to Kalmenhof from other institutions for a short time before transport to Hadamar. In 1942 a children's ward for the destruction of mentally disabled children was installed in Kalmenhof. Weber served as its managing doctor until May 10, 1944, when she was replaced by Hermann Wesse.[45]

During her tenure as managing doctor of the ward, transports of children arrived at Kalmenhof from Hamburg, Bonn, and the Ruhr. They were accommodated on the building's third floor, which was reserved for the "Reich Committee children." By this time, a portion of the hospital had been commandeered by the German army, causing acute shortages in hospital space. In the children's ward, conditions were such that several children were assigned to a single bed. After a brief stay in Kalmenhof, nearly all of the transferee children died. The killings were done by a floor nurse, Maria Müller, by means of luminal tablets mixed in deadly doses in the children's food. At trial, Weber claimed she never personally administered lethal injections or overdoses of medication to these children. She further argued she had no clear knowledge that killings were taking place, because she neither lived in the hospital nor lingered there beyond the morning hours. With respect to Müller's actions, Weber disclaimed knowledge of her work. When her suspicion grew that Müller might have a hand in the patients' deaths, she alleged that she warned the nurse repeatedly.[46]

The state court did not find her defense cogent. Her assertions notwithstanding, the court was convinced that Weber not only suspected Müller of killing mentally disabled children in the ward, but had actual knowledge of these killings. Further, the court believed Weber had condoned the killings and even promoted them by listing spurious causes of death on the death certificates. Weber herself admitted that "in the course of time" she understood that the children were to be destroyed under authorization by the Reich Committee in Berlin. With each newly arrived transport of children, Weber received a list with the children's names and a "treatment authorization"—a Nazi euphemism signifying that the children were to be killed. At trial, she testified that she had placed the list with the authorization in an open drawer in the desk in her office but did not forward it to Müller. The court established that hospital personnel had a passkey to Weber's office, with which they could have easily obtained access to it; thus, even if no direct evidence showed that Weber had given the list to Müller, the nurse could have inspected it with little trouble.[47]

Nor was the Frankfurt court impressed with Weber's defense that she, unlike her successor, Hermann Wesse, was not a "Reich Committee doctor." The court conceded this point but countered that Bernotat had instructed her to deal with the children in the ward as follows: "You don't have to do much, since there isn't any more treatment involved; it would be best if they disappear quickly." Weber admitted she understood at the time that "disappear" meant "be killed." Her claims of noninvolvement were further rebutted by mortality rates at Kalmenhof during her presence there as director of the ward. According to records in the Idstein registry office, prior to the installation of the children's ward at Kalmenhof, on average one to two children died per month; afterward, the death rate shot up to fifty-five per month. During one six-week period, seventy children—most of them patients transported to Kalmenhof from Hamburg on August 8, 1943—perished in the ward. On individual days in September 1943, as many as six children died there. The court was clearly impressed by the decline in mortality in the ward from September 26, 1943, to November 7, 1943, a period during which Weber and Müller took leaves of absence for health reasons. Weber was temporarily replaced by Dr. H., during whose brief tenure as director of the ward not a single child died. When Weber and Müller resumed their work in the ward on November 7, the mortality rate soared: from November 8 to November 11, the deaths of six children were recorded. For the Frankfurt court, this fact proved that most of the deaths in the ward were not due to natural causes but to poisonous doses of medication. It further showed a dramatic linkage between the children's deaths and the presence of Weber and Müller.[48]

The data on mortality were critical in refuting Weber's claim that the deaths of children in the ward were attributable to natural causes. The court rejected this defense, along with her representation that the children transported to Kalmenhof were in such a deplorable condition of health, aggravated by the strains of transportation and inadequate nutrition, that they died shortly after arrival. Three witnesses at trial testified to the children's stable condition: they described many of the children as conveying "no impression of idiocy" and, in some cases, playing like normal children. One witness stated that some of the children "were all able to run," and for this reason she had the "impression" they were not "terminal cases."[49]

Also weighing against Weber's assertions of innocence were her documented contacts with Professor Carl Schneider, a T-4 expert and chaired professor at the University of Heidelberg, where he was involved in research on brains plundered from euthanized patients. During summer 1942, Weber participated in a four-week course with Schneider, presumably on the subject of euthanasia. Weber portrayed the trip as purely recreational in nature—a portrayal the court discounted. In view of the shortage of doctors in 1942, the court speculated that Weber was sent to Heidelberg for initiation into the mechanics and goals of the euthanasia program. Her link with a leading figure in Nazi euthanasia, as well as her documented receipt of bonuses from the Reich Committee in compensation for her unspecified collaboration with its "purposes," put paid to her defense of innocent entanglement in the program.[50]

Weber's final line of defense foreshadowed the representations of other euthanasia doctors prosecuted in the years after her conviction. This was the "sabotage" argument, which she related to the court as a choice among three alternatives:

> (1) either to collaborate in the [euthanasia] project; (2) to seek a reason to extricate myself from the institution, where I also had my illness to consider; (3) to place myself in a position in which my life would be secure and the greatest good of the children could be at the same time preserved.[51]

Weber strove to convince the court that she had chosen the third alternative as a means of sabotaging the euthanasia program where she could. The court did not accept her story. Instead, it found that Weber had opted for the first alternative of collaborating in the operation despite her revulsion against it. The Frankfurt court agreed that she tried to disengage herself from the activities in the children's ward; however, time and again she allowed herself to be mollified by Bernotat's reassurances, so that she was never able to divorce herself from the program. The court held she could have accomplished this separation with little prejudice or difficulty to herself. In response to Weber's claim that she did in fact eventually sever her connection with the children's ward, the court replied that she did not leave Kalmenhof for ethical or legal reasons but, as she had written in a letter from 1944 to the authorities in Wiesbaden, because of her failing health.[52]

The two primary charges against Weber related to the transfer of adult patients from Kalmenhof to Hadamar and the destruction of disabled children in the Kalmenhof children's ward. The court acquitted Weber of the first charge on the ground that no evidence existed to prove she was aware of the purpose behind the registration forms when they were first circulated to the medical staff at Kalmenhof in 1940. Further, when she did finally learn of their function, it was unproven that any killings were carried out on the basis of the forms she had knowingly completed. With respect to the second charge (killings in the children's ward), Weber fared considerably worse. Although it was never proved Weber murdered anyone with her own hands, the court insisted on the importance of her contribution to the murders. Without a physician to falsify causes of death, the program could never have been kept secret. Nurse Maria Müller, the syringe-wielding killer in the ward, relied on Weber to conceal her murderous actions with misleading death certificates. Although Weber's contribution to the crime occurred after the killings were performed—lending an appearance of accessory after the fact to her role in the program—the court held that this contribution was "causal" to the occurrence of the murders. Without it, the success of the program could not have been ensured.[53]

Determining that Weber was co-responsible for the murders committed in the children's ward, the court had no difficulty in finding that she was a perpetrator, not an accomplice. In one of the last euthanasia cases to apply the principle of the Bathtub Case to the detriment of a defendant, the court held that Weber had embraced the killing operation as her own. In support of this finding, it pointed to an occasion in which Weber had accused two of her nurses of violating their oath of silence, threatening to denounce them to higher governmental authorities. She did this gratuitously, without external compulsion, in a manner of acting that proved "how very much she had made the 'operation' her own."[54]

For Mathilde Weber's successor, Dr. Hermann Wesse, Kalmenhof was one in a string of assignments that involved him in the mass killing projects of the Third Reich. By the time of his arrival in Kalmenhof, Wesse was an experienced hand in the medical destruction of human life. In 1942 he had worked briefly in the children's ward at Brandenburg-Görden under a leading architect of the euthanasia program and a T-4 expert, Dr. Hans Heinze, before reassignment to a clinic for juvenile psychiatry in Bonn. Here he was instructed in the techniques of euthanizing disabled children in accordance with the standards of the KdF. In October 1942 Wesse was an assistant doctor in the children's ward at the Waldniel mental hospital until its closure in mid-1943. From there he did a three-month stint at the children's clinic of the University of Leipzig under another T-4 potentate, Dr. Werner Catel. At Leipzig, Wesse acquired his doctor's diploma in "congenital and acquired feeble-mindedness." Thereafter he worked in the Uchtspringe mental hospital's children's ward. His time at Uchtspringe was cut short when in December 1943 he was drafted into the army. In April 1944, Berlin declared him "indispensable" and sent him to Kalmenhof as Mathilde Weber's replacement.

Prior to his assignment at Kalmenhof, Wesse reported to Berlin for orientation from Richard von Hegener of the KdF. Von Hegener informed him that as director of the Kalmenhof children's ward, he was to submit to the Reich Committee reports about the patients containing their medical history and "physical, neurological, psychiatric, intellectual, and characterological" assessments. Three medical experts in Hitler's chancellery would examine the reports and prepare expert assessments independently of each other. If all three agreed that the patient should be "put to sleep," Wesse would receive a killing order. Afterward, he was obliged to contact the Reich Committee about the outcome. At trial, Wesse claimed von Hegener had threatened him for noncompliance with these orders, allegedly warning him, "If you refuse, you will face dire consequences," then smiling and adding, "You don't think about spending your life in a concentration camp." After meeting with Fritz Bernotat and the acting director of Kalmenhof, his codefendant G., Wesse began his death-dealing work in the children's ward in May 1944.[55]

At trial, Wesse portrayed himself as a mere cog in an infernal machine. "I was there as a simple soldier," he told the court. "I could only say 'yes' and 'yes indeed,' and was accustomed to obeying orders." The evidentiary record contradicted Wesse's claim that he was just an obedient footman in the grand scheme of mass killing. Shortly after his arrival in Kalmenhof, Wesse wrote a letter to von Hegener, in which he virtually requested that potential euthanasia victims be sent to him. Wesse's request that he be sent disabled children for killing is enormously incriminating, inasmuch as it originated entirely from him. No pressure was applied, no compulsion exerted, no order issued to make such a request—it emanated solely from Wesse. His act was a gratuitous exceeding of what was required of him, much like Weber's castigation of her staff nurses for breaching the oath of secrecy.[56]

While serving as director of the Kalmenhof children's ward, Wesse prepared reports on the children based on their patient histories, medical exams, and intelligence tests. He forwarded between 100 and 150 such reports to the Reich Committee. When he had received a killing authorization from Berlin, he gave it to Nurse Müller for execution, who killed the patients by mixing luminal into their evening meals. The court found that Wesse furnished twenty-five such authorizations to Müller, affecting a wide range of children in the ward: "feebleminded" school-age and adolescent children, as well as "characterologically deviant" children (i.e., juvenile delinquents). In two cases Wesse himself administered lethal overdoses of morphine that caused the patients' deaths. The patients involved, Margarete Schmidt and Ruth Pappenheimer, were no more "hopeless" cases than some of Weber's patients. Margarete Schmidt was a twenty-three-year-old epileptic who worked as a servant girl in the hospital. The court described her as having a "good capacity for work:" she attended to much of the housework in the Kalmenhof facility, which, with some supervision, she could accomplish without difficulty. In January 1945 Wesse, who had earlier sent a report to Berlin on Schmidt detailing her physical and mental condition, received a killing authorization for her. For this reason, Wesse elected to kill Schmidt himself with an injection of luminal, a drug he chose because as an epileptic Schmidt was accustomed to taking luminal tablets. The injection did not effect her death, causing Müller to administer an additional injection, this time of morphine, from which Schmidt expired a short time later. The death records in the Idstein Registry Office listed her cause of death as "epilepsy, increasing dementia, status epilepticus, brain swelling." Why Wesse and Müller murdered Schmidt was a matter for speculation by the court. It conjectured that Schmidt's work as a housemaid likely exposed her to the crimes perpetrated there by Wesse and Müller. Wesse may have consciously slanted the report to her prejudice in an effort to authorize her killing and thereby "dispose of a burdensome witness" (*eine lastige Mitwisserin*).[57]

If the circumstances surrounding Schmidt's death were suspicious, those attending Ruth Pappenheimer's demise were sinister. Pappenheimer was an eighteen-year-old half-Jewish girl, described by the court as "mentally normal" but characterized by Wesse as "asocial." She was committed to Kalmenhof in fall 1944 after an adolescence of minor juvenile delinquency, including various sexual peccadilloes (among them, sexual relations with a variety of soldiers) and the theft of some bottles of wine and a wool scarf from her employer. For reasons not clarified in the court's opinion, State Councillor Bernotat in Wiesbaden took an especially malefic interest in doing away with her. According to Wesse, Bernotat had demanded that he prepare a report about Pappenheimer for the Berlin authorities. After the report was completed and sent to the Reich Committee offices, Bernotat supposedly badgered Wesse with questions about whether the killing authorization had been given, complaining that Berlin worked too slowly. Eventually the authorization arrived, and Wesse administered a lethal injection of morphine to Pappenheimer, a mentally and physically healthy young girl. The Frankfurt court was convinced that she was murdered only because she was Jewish.

The court's deliberation on whether Wesse was a perpetrator or an accomplice was brief and succinct. In twenty-five proven cases, he had collaborated in the murder of Kalmenhof patients; in at least two of them, he himself had caused the patients' deaths. Applying the standard of the Bathtub Case, the court found that Wesse "desired the killings as his own." For this reason, he was a co-perpetrator in the children's ward murders.[58]

What, according to the court, were Weber's and Wesse's motives for action? Neither was impelled by ideology, it held. Rather, they murdered for career-related reasons: Weber wanted to "preserve her cushy independent job," Wesse his "indispensability" status that exempted him from frontline military service. The court regarded both of these motives as "base" under section 211. As far as sentencing was concerned, the court weighed extenuating against aggravating factors for both Wesse and Weber and found no compelling reason to grant them a mitigated punishment. On January 30, 1947, they were sentenced to death.[59]

This pronouncement, however, did not end Mathilde Weber's judicial odyssey. Nearly fifteen months after her conviction by the Frankfurt state court, the appellate court of Frankfurt reversed the lower court's finding that Weber was guilty as a perpetrator. According to the appellate court, the lower court did not sufficiently clarify "why an action occurring after the completion of the crime [i.e., falsifying death certificates] can be considered co-perpetration," instead of aiding and abetting. The appellate court did not exclude the possibility that Weber was indeed a perpetrator. If, for example, her "guarantee of help" encouraged Müller's "will to perpetration," then such action would constitute perpetration, even though it was done after the crime was performed. This showing the lower court never made, according to the appellate court. For this reason, the case was remanded for reconsideration by the Frankfurt state court.[60]

When the case arrived in the lower court for retrial, Weber received a much more charitable reception than she had on her first go-around. By the time the court delivered its new verdict in February 1949, much had changed in the history of German euthanasia trials. Weber's prosecutions, in fact, are divided between two separate eras: the period of retribution (the first trial) and the era of growing leniency toward National Socialist euthanasia operatives (the case on remand). Between her first trial in early 1947 and the retrial in February 1949, the geopolitical landscape had changed considerably in Europe. The Truman Doctrine had been announced in February 1947, declaring U.S. intentions to "contain" Soviet communism wherever it appeared. The Truman Doctrine made clear U.S. commitment to maintaining a strong military presence in regions perceived to be threatened by Soviet invasion. For West Germany, this meant unabated U.S. troop strength on German soil as a counterweight to the Russian army. Irresistibly, as the decade of the 1940s wound down, the realization that Germany would be divided into two separate countries stole over the German people. The Council of Foreign Ministers, established at the Potsdam Conference in July 1945 to develop a uniform policy for Germany, repeatedly failed to produce a consensus on the German question. Between April 1946 and December 1947, the council met five times with nothing to show for its efforts except mutual denunciation and idle speechmaking. On June 23, 1948, the futile work of the council was interrupted when the Soviets instituted a blockade of West Berlin in response to West Germany's currency reform. The blockade isolated 2.5 million Germans living in West Berlin from the western allies and cut off the flow of food and electricity into the western half of the city. When the Russians lifted the blockade after 324 days, the Council of Foreign Ministers reconvened in Paris on May 23, 1949, the same day as the new Basic Law of the Federal Republic went into effect. By this point, however, the prospect that German division would become permanent had congealed into a certainty: Germany was now split between a West and an East Germany with a partitioned Berlin situated in the middle. The waning years of the 1940s marked the beginning of the Cold War, the incunabula of the bipolar world that would dominate and envenom international politics for the next half-century. The Cold War was in full force when Mathilde Weber's second trial began in March 1949.[61]

The Frankfurt court on retrial interpreted the subjective theory of perpetration to Weber's advantage. According to the court, the facts did not support a finding of perpetration: Weber never volunteered her services to the Reich Committee but was already involved as a doctor in Kalmenhof when the children's operation started; nor was she a Nazi Party member, from which the court inferred a presumption that she did not subscribe to euthanasia for ideological reasons. The court was persuaded by her defense that "she found her work in Kalmenhof unpleasant and quickly formed the desire to extricate herself from it." Where in the first trial the court had rejected Weber's argument that her distaste for the killing program had led to her removal from Kalmenhof in May 1944 (on the proven ground that she had departed for health reasons, not out of conscientious objection), the court now accepted Weber's claim that her "inward rejection" of euthanasia caused her dismissal. For all of these reasons, it found that Weber had not desired euthanasia "as her own" and was thus guilty only of aiding and abetting murder, that is, of being an accomplice. On the issue of punishment, the court affirmed extenuating grounds in Weber's case, based on her relative youth and immaturity at the time of her service at Kalmenhof, which affected her ability "to deal with the demands made upon her." Moreover, her educational background had not prepared her for agonizing ethical choices. "She had only the common school and career education behind her when she began her work in Kalmenhof in 1939," the court held. The court characterized her as "fundamentally a weak and unstable person," whose "guilt consists in the fact that she closed her eyes to what was happening around her and let the nurse subordinate to her do as she liked." Hence one could not lump her in with all the other euthanasia doctors; she was a distinct "exception." This indulgent line of reasoning led the court to sentence Weber to a jail term of three-and-a-half years.[62]

As trifling as her sentence was in comparison with the enormity of her crimes, Weber never served more than a month of her punishment. After her second trial she was released from custody and her sentence suspended because of poor health. Not until October 1954 was she deemed healthy enough to do her time. In November 1954 she was again released, apparently for time served prior to her second trial. *By 1960 she had resumed her career as a practicing doctor.* Hermann Wesse, also indicted and tried for his role in euthanizing patients at the Waldniel mental hospital, benefited from the abolition of the death penalty in Germany in 1949. Nonetheless, he was one of the few euthanasia doctors to spend considerable time in jail for his collaboration in the euthanasia program: after twenty years, he was released from prison in September 1966 for health reasons.

Mathilde Weber benefited from the trend toward leniency discernible in German euthanasia trials after 1947. Had her appeal come before the Frankfurt appellate authorities in 1946 or 1947, we might question whether she would have enjoyed such a favorable outcome. One historical factor that may account for this seachange in judicial attitudes was the growing antagonism between eastern and western Europe. The tension between the United States and the Soviet Union in the late 1940s was a godsend for Weber in her second trial. A politically and morally rehabilitated Germany was needed to anchor the Western alliance against the Soviet bloc. The imperatives of international politics intersected with a West German society eager to lay its scandalous past to rest and avid to recoup its sovereignty after a brief period of eclipse. Within this society, the West German judiciary—itself tainted by its prior contacts with Nazism—became an auxiliary to the nation's willed amnesia. The tools of German criminal law like the distinction between perpetration and complicity and the statutory definition of murder were used to further this act of collective forgetting. Although the most visible symbol of the yearning to forget appeared in late 1949 with the *Bundestag*'s amnesty of certain types of Nazi crimes, trials like Weber's had already proclaimed West Germany's determination to close the book on National Socialist criminality.

In the early phase of the German trials, however, the courts convicted defendants as perpetrators of murder under German law. The wrongdoers' motives, in the estimate of the courts, were various: they included ideological affinity with Nazi doctrine (Wernicke, Wieczorek), vanity and self-seeking ambition (Mennecke), a distorted sense of obedience (Schmidt), human weakness and an "inertia" of the will (Wahlmann and Gorgass), careerism (Wesse), and a weak, unstable personality (Weber). Among these euthanasia killers, only Wieczorek, Wernicke, Mennecke, Weber, and Wesse were deemed to have acted with "base motives" (i.e., in a morally reprehensible manner). Only Wernicke and Wieczorek paid for their participation in Nazi euthanasia with their lives. With the exception of Wieczorek, all nurses were convicted as accomplices to murder, based on motives ranging from love (Schürg) to thoughtlessness (Senft). These determinations were predicated on a subjective analysis of each defendant's moral and intellectual capacity to comprehend the wrongful nature of the killing operation. Of these early trials, only in the Kalmenhof case did a West German court categorize a T-4 doctor as an accomplice rather than a perpetrator. As we will see in Chapters 4 and 5, reducing euthanasia doctors' roles in the Nazi killing program from perpetration to complicity—and, in several cases, even acquitting them for "proven innocence"—would become inflationary in West German courts after 1947.

In the end, the destroyer triumphs—Lucifer upon the ruins
of the world.
—NORBERT ELIAS, ON HITLER'S DESTRUCTION
OF THE WEIMAR REPUBLIC

Chapter 4 | LUCIFER ON THE RUINS OF THE WORLD

THE GERMAN EUTHANASIA TRIALS, 1948–1950

In 1948 Brigadier General Telford Taylor, the U.S. Chief of Counsel
for War Crimes, noticed a change in the climate of opinion regarding the prosecution of Nazi crimes. It was already perceptible in
U.S. successor trials under Control Council Law #10, of which the
Medical Case was a part. "It was apparent to anyone connected with
the entire series of trials under Law #10 that the sentences became
progressively lighter as time went on," Taylor wrote. "Defendants
such as Darré, Dietrich, und Stuckart in the 'Ministries case' (Case
#11), who, although convicted under two or more counts of the
indictment of serious crimes, received very light sentences in April
1949, would surely have been much more severely punished in 1946
or 1947." Taylor attributed this trend toward greater leniency to "waning interest on the part of the general public" in war crimes trials
and heightened focus on "international events," by which he clearly
meant the Cold War.[1]

The impact of Cold War politics on the trials of Nazi war criminals cannot be overstated. With increasing stridency in the immediate
postwar era, West German politicians and policymakers connected
the liquidation of war crimes trials with the restoration of national

power. To a great extent, continued prosecution of Nazi criminals was framed by the larger issue of German rearmament, particularly after the outbreak of the Korean War in June 1950. Interpreted in the West as a gambit to export communism by force of arms, North Korea's invasion of South Korea dramatized the need to incorporate the Federal Republic into a western defense system in central Europe. In the ensuing year after the invasion, the West Germans prepared the draft of a security treaty with the allies, clearly intended to recover some measure of national power for West Germany. Discussions between representatives of the West German government and the Allied High Commission, held in the spring and summer of 1951, had raised the issue of overhauling the current system of pardoning as an element of a general security treaty. Monitoring the progress of the negotiations, the members of the Heidelberg Circle demanded a radical change to the pardon system: the right to pardon and to carry out sentences in the cases of convicted war criminals imprisoned in Germany should be transferred from the Allies to the German government. Adenauer's justice minister, Thomas Dehler, shared the aspirations of the Heidelberg Circle as they pertained to solving the war criminal problem. He signed a fifteen-point catalog prepared by the central bureau in fall 1951, setting forth demands that no death penalties be meted out in war crimes cases, sentences less than twenty years be commuted, new investigations be discontinued, and ongoing trials be terminated if the prosecution did not expect a sentence greater than twenty years.[2]

The extreme nature of such demands was in part fueled by the public's tendency to conflate atrocities unrelated to the war with "war crimes." Although many Nazi defendants were charged with murder and crimes against humanity rather than war crimes (only 88 of the 603 prisoners held by the Allies in spring 1952 were German soldiers), energetic campaigns to amnesty Germans in Allied custody leveled the distinction between war crimes (resented as victor's justice) and the racially inspired mass murder of the Nazi government. Even Konrad Adenauer was not immune to this fallacy. Rejecting calls for a general amnesty, Adenauer pointed out that a more limited amnesty was appropriate, because "among the convicted there was a certain percentage to whom the word 'war criminal' perfectly applies, and whose punishment must be maintained." For Adenauer, the "real" criminals—the lower-class sadists within the concentration and death camp system—should be prosecuted, and the rest left in peace.[3]

The pressures exerted by the West Germans to end the era of war crimes trials achieved two notable successes. First, they induced the Allies to release nearly 75 percent of their German war criminals between 1950 and 1952. No amnesty would be necessary: most of the remaining prisoners were released in the years after 1952. The British and French closed their prisons for war criminals in 1957, and the United States released the last of the "Landsbergers" in 1958. Second, pressures to liquidate continued trials of Nazi defendants found their mark in West German court rooms, where convictions of war crimes suspects plummeted by 68 percent between 1950 and 1951, and by 98 percent between 1950 and 1955. The euthanasia trials of the late 1940s and early 1950s, steeped in this spirit of leniency for Nazi killers, reflect in miniature this historic moment.

A series of cases beginning in 1948 inaugurated the new Cold War era of leniency in euthanasia-related prosecutions. A distinguishing feature of these cases was the legal doctrine of "collision of duties," by means of which euthanasia doctors not only evaded the charge of murder, but left German courtrooms as moral heroes dedicated to undermining euthanasia by participating in it. In this chapter, we explore how this transformation of medical killers into heroes served the purposes of German yearnings for rejuvenated national power—a power believed to be inconsistent with an ongoing judicial confrontation with the Nazi past.

DESTROYING LIVES IN ORDER TO SAVE LIVES: THE COLLISION OF DUTIES CASES

That an act of homicide may be justified or excused on a theory of necessity (*Notstand*) was an idea that arrived late in the history of German criminal law. The German Criminal Code of 1871 contained no mention of it as a justifying or exculpatory ground, nor did case law acknowledge it. Up until the third decade of the twentieth century, therefore, German law did not recognize as legal an action committed in violation of the law for the purpose of avoiding a greater harm—including a physician's efforts to save the life of a mother by aborting her fetus. Under German law prior to 1927, such a physician could face homicide charges. In 1927, however, the German Supreme Court made law by endorsing a new theory of justification in a criminal abortion case. The defendant, a German physician, had ordered an abortion for a woman believed to be a suicide risk if forced to carry her illegitimate child to term. His actions were objectively illegal; the law forbade the killing of a fetus unconditionally, admitting of no special circumstances (like the health of the mother) that might justify or excuse the killing. The German Supreme Court, however, expounded a new theory of "extra-statutory necessity" (*Übergesetzlicher Notstand*), holding that a doctor who commits an abortion is not guilty of criminal homicide if the doctor acted only after carefully weighing the legal interests (*Rechtsgüter*, literally "legal goods") involved and deciding that the mother's interest outweighed that of her fetus. In short, the court held that acting to prevent a greater harm or to preserve a higher legal interest did not make the actor criminally liable, even if the conduct fulfilled all the elements of the statutory offense.[4]

A variant of the extra-statutory necessity doctrine was the "collision of duties" defense. According to this form of the defense, an actor is to be acquitted of a crime if he was forced to commit it in order to avert a "greater injustice." The collision of duties would emerge in the late 1940s as the first successful defense in German courts against charges of murder for euthanasia crimes, beginning with the case of Drs. Karl Todt and Adolf Thiel of the Scheuern mental institution.

The "Merciless Quandary" and the Limits of the Law: The Scheuern Case

The mental hospital Scheuern in the province of Hessen-Nassau was, like the Kalmenhof institution, established on the lofty principle of Christian charity toward the mentally handicapped. Also like Kalmenhof, Scheuern was drawn into the euthanasia program early in the war. The institution had cared for epileptic and "feebleminded" patients since its creation by the Inner Mission of the German Evangelical Church in 1850. It remained true to its mission until 1937, when the provincial authorities replaced Scheuern's executive board with Nazified members of the local government. The president of the new board was State Councillor Fritz Bernotat, a ubiquitous presence in the ambitious killing project launched in Hessen-Nassau. His accession to president of Scheuern's executive board was an unmitigated disaster for its patients. Bernotat pressured the director of Scheuern, Dr. Karl Todt (a doctor of pedagogy, not medicine), into joining the Nazi Party, despite his tepid attitude toward Nazi ideology.[5]

Todt's medical assistant, Dr. Adolf Thiel, took up his duties at Scheuern in 1938. Although he had joined the Nazi Party well before 1933, the state court of Koblenz characterized him as a lukewarm supporter of Nazism. In summer 1940, both Todt and Thiel were at Scheuern; the two men had been exempted from military service, Todt because of his age, Thiel because of his medical unfitness. That summer, Todt received from Berlin the first batch of registration forms to be completed on his patients. Innocent of their purpose, Todt completed the forms on 500 to 600 patients and returned them to the Berlin authorities. In March 1941 the first transports of patients identified for killing were sent from Scheuern to unknown destinations. In the aftermath of these transports, Todt and Thiel received notices announcing the deaths of the transferred patients. At this point they realized their patients had been killed pursuant to the Nazis' euthanasia program.

March 1941 was also the month when provincial authorities decided to convert Scheuern into a transit center (*Zwischenanstalt*) at the service of T-4.

Scheuern henceforth received shipments of patients from other institutions designated for ultimate transfer to Hadamar. The purpose of the transit centers was twofold: to create an additional screen to obscure the fates of transferred patients by sending them to intermediate stations before final transport to a killing institution; and to afford more opportunity for exempting patients who did not meet the guidelines for killing, for example, war veterans, cases of age-related senility, or patients capable of work. Transit centers were established throughout Germany, but the province of Hessen-Nassau had a disproportionately high share. In addition to Scheuern, the provincial transit centers included Weilmünster, Herborn, Kalmenhof, and Eichberg—all favorably close to the killing center of Hadamar, which they supplied with victims.[6]

Between March 1941 and September 1944, Scheuern served as a transit center for approximately 1,640 patients. At trial the state court of Koblenz had no difficulty finding both Todt and Thiel guilty of complicity in the murders of around 1,000 of them. By aiding the transport of patients from Scheuern to Hadamar and continuing to fill out the KdF's registration forms after discovering their purpose, the pair had fulfilled the elements of the offense of aiding and abetting murder. Further, their actions were "objectively" illegal in the sense that no traditional justifying grounds like self-defense or emergency existed to legitimate their conduct. The novelty of the Scheuern case, however, occurred when the court refused to find the defendants personally culpable for their involvement in euthanasia killings. The court premised its acquittal of the accused on a defense that had been unsuccessfully raised by other defendants in earlier cases: the "collision of duties" defense.

According to the Koblenz court, Todt and Thiel were ensnared in a "merciless quandary" not of their own making: either to abstain from illegality by resigning their posts, as a result of which their patients would be abandoned to ideological zealots from Berlin who would ensure their complete destruction; or to collaborate in the euthanasia program, assisting with the destruction of patients already doomed to die in order to save whoever they could.[7] The court accepted Todt and Thiel's claim that they had chosen the second course of action—remaining at their posts in the Scheuern facility, at great risk to themselves, for the purpose of sabotaging the euthanasia program. The sabotage consisted of discharging patients who might otherwise have been transported, exaggerating patients' capacity for work and its importance to the institution, and concealing severely ill patients from the roving T-4 commission that occasionally visited Scheuern. In this manner, the court determined, the defendants saved 250 patients from transport at the cost of collaborating in the transfer of 1,000 patients, all of whom were subsequently murdered. A 20 percent rate of success was a significant accomplishment, the court held, given the "horribly constraining circumstances" the defendants faced. Moreover, if the defendants had resigned in protest, they would have been replaced by "some sort of SS man, an obedient minion, or one of the young doctors reared in the Hitler youth, who would have proceeded with the necessary ruthlessness." As a result, the court believed, more patients would have died.[8]

Remaining at one's post to save as many lives as one could, even at the price of assisting in the destruction of those whose fates were already sealed, did not justify the defendants' actions, the court held. Rather, the patent conflict of duties they faced excused their actions. In other words, their collaboration in euthanasia was objectively illegal, but they bore no criminal guilt for it. For this reason the defendants had to be acquitted. In arriving at this determination, the Koblenz court exhibited a degree of hesitancy and circumspection—we might even say humility—lacking in verdicts that were soon to follow. We see this attitude in the court's quotation of the German criminal law jurist von Weber on the subject of the collision of duties: "The solution of such a conflict can only be found in an absolute sense in the conscience; the individual must negotiate his conscience with his God. The legal order offers no standard for its solution." Von Weber concluded that he who has grappled with such a conflict "after earnest examination of his conscience" should not be held criminally liable for his actions. Von Weber's theological discourse, recalling Martin Luther's idea of the individual alone before God, must have struck a chord in the state court, which adopted von Weber's view of the matter in acquitting the defendants. Although they were excused from criminal wrongdoing, the court refused to speculate on the quality of their inward conscience: "Whether the defendants are able inwardly to feel themselves free of any guilt is a matter for their personal conscience."[9]

The argument that one has participated in criminal behavior in order to curb its worst excesses did not surface for the first time in the Scheuern case. Ernst Kaltenbrunner had raised a similar defense at the IMT in Nuremberg, as had Viktor Brack during his testimony at the U.S. Doctors' Trial. Neither had met with success. The Scheuern case was the first acquittal of euthanasia defendants on the basis of a "conflict of duties." Other courts would accept this defense in the aftermath of Todt's and Thiel's acquittals, albeit with more cocksureness than the Koblenz court had evinced. The latter had recognized that the Scheuern trial was, in the vernacular of U.S. law, a "case of first impression" (i.e., a case without precedents to guide its resolution). This may help explain the tentative quality of the opinion. The court's verdict in Scheuern was a bellwether of a new age in euthanasia prosecution, perfectly suited to a newly reconstituted West Germany seeking to cast off even the minimal reservations the Koblenz court had entertained.

The Rhine Province Case

The Scheuern case, as we have seen, was the first West German trial to acquit euthanasia defendants. Not until the Rhine province trial, however, would a German court characterize the actions of its defendants as not only legally justified, but as morally praiseworthy. The leading defendants in the trial were all charged with murder under section 211 of the German Penal Code and crimes against humanity under Control Council Law #10 for their roles in the Nazis' euthanasia program. They included Dr. Walter Creutz, the former state councillor and department chief for the Rhine province's system of mental institutions headquartered in Düsseldorf; Drs. We. and R., former departmental doctors in the mental hospital of Galkhausen; Drs. Kurt Pohlisch and Friedrich Panse, professors of psychiatry and neurology at the University of Bonn; and Dr. Hermann Wesse, former assistant doctor in the children's ward at the Waldniel mental hospital from October 1942 until July 1943. They had reason to be encouraged by the outcome of the Scheuern trial: its rationale would be applied to acquit all of these doctors (except Hermann Wesse), thus perpetuating the trend toward acquittals of euthanasia defendants.

When the war started in 1939, Dr. Walter Creutz was serving as a medical officer in the German army until given indispensability status and reassigned as departmental chief in the Rhine provincial administration. On his return to the Rhineland, he discovered that the rumors he had heard of measures against the mentally ill ordered by the highest levels of the Nazi government were true. The court found that Creutz consulted with friends of his within both the Protestant and Catholic institutional systems, particularly the director of the Inner Mission, Pastor O., and the Prelate Schulte-Pelkum. Pastor O. informed him that the institutions of the Inner Mission had declined filling out the questionnaires distributed to all public and private mental hospitals by the Reich Ministry of the Interior. Regrettably, other public and private institutions in Württemberg in 1940 had not followed the Inner Mission's example but, believing the forms were part of a statistical survey to determine the labor capability of their patients, had filled them out, taking special care to underestimate their patients' ability to work so as to avoid their conscription into the German war economy. In this manner, they unwittingly wrote the death warrants for the patients reported in the forms.[10]

The Düsseldorf state court was persuaded that Creutz was stung by these revelations and thereafter sought to organize a plan of resistance to the euthanasia program among the mental hospitals and nursing homes of the Rhineland. Toward the end of 1940 or beginning of 1941, he composed a memorandum to convince the governor, Heinrich Haake, to oppose implementation of the killing program in the Rhineland. The memo was allegedly tuned to the pro-Nazi biases of Haake and hence emphasized the unrest among the population and the erosion of public trust in health-care institutions that such a program would invariably cause. Creutz's ruse was for a time successful; impressed with the logic of the memo, Haake declared his intention to reject implementing euthanasia in the Rhineland. Haake even stiffened his resolve when Berlin announced that a "commission" would be sent to Haake's offices in February 1941 to "discuss this question." Haake invited Creutz to present his dissenting view to the commission. When the delegation from the KdF arrived on February 12, it was composed of some of the euthanasia program's leading figures. To this august group of killers Creutz made his pitch. When he had finished, Werner Heyde, a member of the delegation, responded with a single gesture: he removed a copy of Hitler's euthanasia order of September 1, 1939, and presented it to Haake.[11]

The Hitler decree had the desired effect. Haake immediately backpedaled, exclaiming that, in view of the expressed will of the Führer, he withdrew all his objections to adopting the euthanasia program in the Rhineland. The Berlin Commission then demanded that transit centers be erected in the Galkhausen and Andernach facilities. These two institutions were chosen because patients could be readily transported from them to Hadamar by the busses of Gekrat. Haake later called the directors of Galkhausen and Andernach and instructed them on the commission's decision to transform their institutions into transit centers. Creutz in the meantime found himself in a dilemma: whether to resign his position in protest, or to remain at his post to minimize the damage to Rhineland mental patients. He opted for the second of the two alternatives. Creutz's decision, the court held, was actuated by a sense of duty to his profession and to the patients entrusted to him. Reprising the findings of the Koblenz court in the Scheuern trial, the Düsseldorf court believed that Creutz's resignation would have sounded the death knell for numerous Rhineland patients, because a zealous advocate of euthanasia no doubt would have succeeded him. Intent on curbing the effects of the euthanasia planned for the Rhine province, Creutz attended a meeting sponsored by the KdF in Berlin, where, in the presence of 50 to 60 health-care professionals, Viktor Brack discussed Hitler's order to set euthanasia in motion, alluding to the secret draft of a law that would one day place the program on firm legal standing. At this meeting, Werner Heyde outlined the categories of patients exempt from the program. These categories included patients capable of work, patients whose mental illness was war- or age-related, foreigners, and patients incapable of transportation.[12]

After this meeting in Berlin, according to the court's findings of fact, Creutz organized his own conference of directors from public mental hospitals and nursing homes within his administrative district of Düsseldorf-Grafenberg, scheduled for March 29, 1941. At this conference, he tried to marshal resistance to the euthanasia program. Acknowledging that open rebellion against the measures would be futile, he urged his audience to remain at their posts and save as many patients from transport that they could. This could be accomplished by broadly interpreting the criteria for exemption as outlined by the Berlin authorities, particularly in the home institutions of the patients and in the transit centers. Creutz recounted the categories of patients exempt from transport, then added that the range of those exempted could be enlarged by identifying patients injured in accidents as suffering from war-related disabilities. Furthermore, Creutz suggested that diagnoses of schizophrenia among elderly patients be changed to age-related pathology. The participants in this conference agreed with Creutz that it was more advisable to remain at their posts and save whoever they could than to resign and leave their patients vulnerable to a potentially less sympathetic replacement.[13]

On the same day that this conference of directors convened in Düsseldorf, a commission from Berlin consisting of five doctors under the leadership of Professor Paul Nitsche appeared at the Andernach mental hospital. Nitsche, like Heyde, was a T-4 chief medical expert and (beginning in December 1941) the head of T-4's Medical Office; later on, he would develop the scheme to kill mentally handicapped patients surreptitiously with overdoses of luminal. After examining some of the Andernach patients, Nitsche and his colleagues prepared a list of patients selected for liquidation to be given to Andernach's director upon his return from the Düsseldorf meeting. The patients on this list numbered 225 men and 245 women. They would not be transported from Andernach to Hadamar until June 7, 1941, but when the operation was set in motion, it unfolded with lethal thoroughness: with only a handful of exceptions, all transferred patients were gassed after arrival at Hadamar. A similar procedure took shape at the new transit center Galkhausen, where three of the five doctors from the Nitsche commission prepared lists of patients (255 men and 154 women) for transportation. A number of these selectees were later withheld, so that a total of 232 men and 141 women were transferred from Galkhausen in late May 1941 to Hadamar for killing.[14]

Typically, Creutz received the transport lists from Berlin, and he forwarded them to the home institutions along with an order to have the patients noted on the lists prepared for transfer to the transit centers of Andernach or Galkhausen. After the patients were transported, the home institution returned the lists to Düsseldorf, indicating in the "Remarks" column the names of patients exempted from transport. From Düsseldorf the lists were re-routed to Berlin. The transferred patients were received in special subdepartments within the transit centers; at Galkhausen, the men were accommodated in a subdepartment headed by a Dr. We., the women in one headed by a Dr. R. Creutz had assigned Dr. We. to the post of departmental doctor in Galkhausen in March 1941 from the Grafenberg institution. The director of Grafenberg, a Dr. Sioli, informed him prior to his departure of the euthanasia program now underway in the Rhineland. Sioli also told him he had been assigned to Galkhausen "as an especially reliable doctor" who could be entrusted with the order to sabotage the operation to the best of his abilities. Shortly after he assumed his duties, Creutz briefed him on the tasks and goals that lay ahead of him as part of the plan to work at cross-purposes with the Berlin authorities. Dr. R., on the other hand, was at Galkhausen at the time it was transformed into a transit center, serving there as head doctor in the women's department since 1938. Beyond rumors, Dr. R. knew little about the euthanasia program until relatives of patients killed at Hadamar contacted him with news of their deaths. His suspicions then grew that the patients had been the victims of foul play. Later, the director of Galkhausen, Dr. Winkel, apprised him of the program, emphasizing the broad latitude he and other doctors could exercise in withholding patients from transportation.[15]

The Düsseldorf court found that both We. and R. did everything in their power to undermine the government's campaign against the disabled. They embellished their assessments of their patients' capacity for work even in especially severe cases, sometimes discharging their patients from the hospital in order to remove them from transport. The court was satisfied that We. had practiced this deception in thirty-four cases and R. in forty cases. Both had regularly approached the relatives of patients to submit requests for release, coaching them on the proper method for submitting such petitions. In one case cited by the court, R. was involved in an abortive attempt to "abduct" a patient vulnerable to transport. After this abduction was foiled by a staff nurse, R. demonstrated his willingness to give it a second try, in the event the danger of transportation was imminent.

We. and R.'s efforts received the unwavering support of Creutz back in Düsseldorf. Creutz approved all petitions for release submitted to him from Galkhausen. Their collective efforts to subvert the operation provoked numerous warnings from the T-4 offices in Berlin, which admonished Creutz over the phone to implement the measures more rapidly and with greater efficiency. In March 1941, Gekrat proposed to Governor Haake the immediate removal of patients from four Nassau institutions as a way to erase the backlog caused by the retarded pace of transfer from the Rhineland institutions. Catching wind of this communiqué, Creutz persuaded Haake to reject Gekrat's proposal. At a directors' conference in Düsseldorf in July 1941, Creutz again underscored the importance of restricting the operation as much as possible. Two months later, in September 1941, he was notified in a letter signed by Werner Heyde that the euthanasia program had been terminated "for technical reasons."[16]

The court had little documentary evidence on which to make a finding about the success of Creutz and his fellow conspirators in their attempts to oppose the program. Instead, it was largely confined to witness testimony (including that of Creutz, We., and R., all witnesses with a motive to lie). The best it could determine was that, of the 5,046 patients identified for transport by the Berlin authorities, approximately 946 were ultimately transferred to Hadamar for liquidation.

Several months before the official stop of the program, Creutz received a visit from Hans Hefelmann and Richard von Hegener of Berlin's Reich Committee. They confided in Creutz that the committee had launched a new program to euthanize mentally ill children in specially created "children's wards." Rhineland facilities were to play a part in this expansion of the killing project. Creutz was ordered to establish in Galkhausen and in another institution yet to be determined two such wards. He expressed his misgivings about this operation, but the committee representatives were unmoved. Thereafter, Creutz remonstrated with the Berlin offices until in July 1941 he received a letter from Viktor Brack accusing him of intentionally obstructing installation of the wards in the Rhineland. Brack warned Creutz that if he did not change his view on the matter, he would face dismissal from his job as well as a complete overhaul of the Rhineland's institutional system. Creutz gave Brack's letter to Haake, who resented the charges of misfeasance against one of his officials. Haake contacted *Reichsleiter* Philipp Bouhler about the dispute. Haake and Bouhler arrived at an agreement that a children's ward would be established at the Waldniel mental hospital. Haake overcame Creutz's hesitancy about participating in the operation of the ward by assuring him it would be wholly subordinate to the Reich Committee and that he would need only to worry about installing and assigning a nursing staff to it.[17]

As with the adult operation, Creutz resolved to cooperate with the children's program only to the degree necessary, all the while pursuing a plan of subversion and sabotage. Choosing a house in Waldniel as the site for the proposed children's ward, Creutz temporized by having it thoroughly renovated, a project that lasted several months, and by insisting on outfitting it with a hard-to-obtain X-ray machine (although no such equipment was needed in the ward). Not until October 1941 was the ward ready to receive its new director. Creutz's report to the Berlin Reich Committee that he was unable to find anyone willing to serve as the ward's director became the occasion for Berlin to appoint its own man, a doctor from Saxony named Georg Renno.

Renno was no stranger to killing mental patients: he had served for a time as a gassing technician at the Hartheim killing center before taking up duties as director of the Waldniel children's ward in October 1941. Before Renno could begin his work at Waldniel, he suffered a hemorrhage that rendered him unable to fulfill his responsibilities. Renno proposed Dr. Hermann Wesse as his replacement. During Wesse's prior visits to see his wife, who was a staff doctor in Waldniel's adult section, Wesse had declared his support for euthanasia to Dr. Renno. These declarations no doubt commended him to Renno as his possible successor. The Reich Committee's Hefelmann and von Hegener vetted him at a meeting in the waiting room of the Düsseldorf train station. Afterward, they adjourned to the offices of the provincial government, where they informed Creutz that Wesse would succeed Renno in the Waldniel children's clinic. Creutz invited Wesse to wait outside, then complained to Hefelmann and von Hegener that Wesse was not properly trained to undertake the work. Surprisingly, Hefelmann and von Hegener did not override his criticism but suggested that Wesse be sent to the children's ward in Görden for advanced training with Dr. Hans Heinze, the director of the ward and a T-4 expert.

Wesse remained at Görden until February 1942, at which time, primarily at the instance of Creutz, he was sent for further psychiatric training at the Rhine State Clinic for Juvenile Psychiatry in Bonn, where he lingered another seven months. In the meantime, Creutz contacted the Waldniel hospital and demanded that its chief medical advisor, a Dr. Sc., be assigned to monitor Wesse's activities in the children's ward. Creutz personally instructed Dr. Sc. to stop any excessive or careless action by Wesse. With this spy in place, Creutz ordered Wesse's transfer to Waldniel on September 26, 1942. By October, Wesse was active as the director of Waldniel's children's ward, filling out reports on the patients that noted the severity of mental disability (e.g., "idiocy," "feeble-mindedness," "mild, medium, or severe degree") and his evaluation of the child's educational capability. These reports were forwarded to the Reich Committee in Berlin. Weeks later he received a decision from the committee: educable children were to be discharged and children considered incapable of education were to be "put to sleep." The authorization was also euphemistically worded: "The child X is to be brought to therapy." After a final exam, Wesse had two of his nurses, W. and M., administer between three and five tablets of luminal to the child in the evening. Afterward the victim typically fell into a deep sleep before dying one or two days later. Wesse himself informed the relatives that their child had died of an "acute illness." He then falsified the cause of death in the victim's death certificate. In this way, Wesse and his accomplices caused the deaths of "at least" thirty children with lethal overdoses of luminal.[18]

In addition to his involvement in the transports of Rhineland patients during phase one of the euthanasia program and in Wesse's infanticide at the

Waldniel children's ward, Creutz was charged with complicity in the transfers of patients to the Hadamar killing center from 1942 to 1945. The immediate cause of this second wave of transports was the increasingly urgent demand for hospital space because of Allied bombing of German cities. The Rhineland was particularly afflicted with a shortage of available beds. To cure the problem, the Reich Ministry of the Interior suggested that 370 patients be transferred from the monastery of Hoven (which was to be used as a hospital for the bombed-out residents of an old age home in Cologne) to Hadamar. Creutz objected to the suggestion, but his fears were allayed with reassurances that Hadamar would resume its functioning as a normal mental hospital. Nonetheless, Creutz continued to be apprehensive that something would go wrong at this notorious killing center. Wishing to consult directly with the medical staff at Hadamar, he traveled to the institution to inspect it for himself. While there, he encountered former patients from the Rhineland who had been transferred to Hadamar now working on the institution's grounds. He saw no evidence that patients were being put to death within Hadamar's walls. Encouraged by his visit, Creutz returned to Düsseldorf with the belief that transports to Hadamar could move forward without danger to the patients. This trust seemed to have been abused when death notices about the Hoven patients transported to Hadamar poured into Creutz's office. Creutz asked Haake to inquire about the reasons for the deaths. The latter's inquiry disclosed that predominately infirm patients had been transported and that the high incidence of such patients accounted for the mortality rate.

The transportation of patients from Rhineland facilities accelerated from 1943 until the end of the war. With the proliferation of death notices it became clear to Creutz that transferred patients were being killed in the collection centers. In April 1943 Creutz submitted a petition to Josef Goebbels, State Secretary Stuckart of the Reich Interior Ministry, and Karl Brandt, requesting an investigation of why so many patients were dying after transfer. His concerns were dismissed with the reply that the high mortality rates resulted from food rationing required by the war emergency and from transporting severely ill patients. In the meantime, Creutz continued to send patients within the Rhine province to mental hospitals throughout Germany, including the killing centers at the Pomeranian mental hospital, Meseritz-Obrawalde, and Gross-Schweidnitz in Saxony. Some were dispatched to the General Government in Poland (that part of occupied Poland not formally annexed to the German Reich). Interested in establishing his own collection center for mentally disabled transferees from the Rhineland staffed with Rhineland medical personnel, Creutz sent one of his physicians to the General Government to investigate the feasibility of such a plan. His representative negotiated with local authorities to make the institution of Kulparkow near Lemberg available for this purpose. Between August 1943 and May 1944, Dr. R. and several nurses from the Rhineland were transferred to the Kulparkow institution.[19]

This period of deportations between 1942 and the end of the war coincided with the wild euthanasia characteristic of phase two of the killing program. For the Rhineland as for much of the German Reich, the selection of patients in this phase was made not on the basis of forms but by the home institutions themselves. Although the Berlin authorities stood behind the program from beginning to end, their presence was now less conspicuous, their role restricted to identifying hospital space made available by the transports and to providing transportation.

The Düsseldorf state court found that Creutz fulfilled all of the elements of aiding and abetting murder as well as crimes against humanity under Law #10. Creutz was not, however, a perpetrator but an accomplice, because he "by no means desired the result as his own." The court next turned to consider whether Creutz's acts were objectively illegal. We will recall that the court in the Scheuern case deemed Todt's and Thiel's actions illegal but acquitted them based on a "collision of duties" (that is, the duty to remain aloof from criminal wrongdoing and the medical duty to save as many patients as they could). In the Rhineland case, by contrast, the court held that the doctrine of "extra-statutory necessity" (*Übergesetzlicher Notstand*) justified Creutz's involvement in the transportation of patients to their deaths. The lay assessors on the court found that Creutz was an unswerving opponent of the operation, sparing no pains to restrict the numbers of patients removed for killing. In order to subvert the aims of the program, Creutz had to project an image to his superiors in Berlin of cooperation with their designs. Wherever he could, Creutz worked at cross-purposes with Berlin: his orchestration of a program of sabotage, his consistent resistance to a children's ward at Waldniel, his opposition to euthanasia enthusiast Dr. Renno, and his planting of Dr. Sc. in the ward to oversee and restrain the actions of Dr. Wesse all attested to Creutz's commitment to impede euthanasia in the Rhineland. The state court was further impressed with the numbers of patients Creutz's sabotage plan had saved: of the 5,000 patients Berlin had earmarked for destruction, only 946 were finally dispatched to the killing centers. Individual cases supported these figures. For example, the court cited the transport lists of September 4 and 13, 1941, which had sent ninety-seven patients to the transit centers of Galkhausen and Andernach for ultimate transfer to Hadamar for killing. Of these patients, sixty-seven were withheld or discharged—a significant accomplishment ascribed to Creutz's rescue plan.[20]

None of these achievements would have been possible without Creutz's limited participation in the killing program, the court stated. Invoking an argument familiar from the Scheuern case, the Düsseldorf court pointed out that resigning from his post would have opened a vacuum quickly filled by Berlin with a zealous euthanasia proponent. In this regard, the court found meaningful the example of the mental health system in Vienna during the war. Informed by Brack of the planned euthanasia program in early 1940, the advisor (*Referent*) for Vienna's health-care system, a Prof. Dr. Gu., resigned his position in protest. The result was that Berlin appointed an ideological Nazi to the post, who implemented euthanasia killing in Vienna's mental hospitals remorselessly and in full compliance with Berlin's wishes. Consequently, 50 percent of Vienna's mental patients were destroyed—a figure that dwarfed the mortality rate of 7.5 percent in the Rhine province. Had Creutz followed Gu.'s example and resigned his post, the Rhineland likely would have experienced a death rate similar to Vienna's.[21]

Creutz's difficult but conscientious choice to remain in his job inevitably ensnared him in criminality. His situation, the court analogized, was like that of a man who encounters three mountain climbers hanging from a rope over a sheer precipice. The only means of saving any of the climbers is to cut the rope they are clinging to, with the aim of at least saving one of them; a failure to act would consign all of them to certain death. By cutting the rope and rescuing one of the climbers, the man's action was justified by the extraordinary circumstances of the predicament in which he found himself. The court considered the metaphor of the three mountain climbers applicable to the Rhine province case. In each case, the actor must decide either to renounce any involvement, thereby ensuring destruction of the patients, or to participate in a criminal enterprise in order to save as many as possible. Creutz, a confirmed enemy of euthanasia, elected to rescue patients in the only manner available to him and did a creditable job of it. His actions relating to the 946 adult patients transported to their deaths in 1941 and the 30 children killed in the Waldniel children's ward from 1942 to 1943 were justified under the legal doctrine of extrastatutory necessity. Thus, he was acquitted of both aiding and abetting murder and crimes against humanity in these two instances of mass killing.[22]

Regarding the transportations of patients between 1942 and 1945 for the purpose of freeing up hospital space, the court likewise found Creutz innocent of wrongdoing. Although some patients were murdered in facilities like Meseritz-Obrawalde, there was no evidence that Creutz was aware they were being transported to their deaths. With this final acquittal, Walter Creutz walked out of the Düsseldorf courtroom on November 24, 1948, a free man.[23]

The Galkhausen staff physicians, Drs. We. and R., raised the same extrastatutory necessity argument to defend their participation in the euthanasia program. Although they, like Creutz, fulfilled the objective elements of the offense of aiding and abetting murder, they too were acquitted as saboteurs of euthanasia. Dr. We. exploited every opportunity to foreground his patients' status as war heroes or foreign nationals to secure their exemption; in other cases, he exaggerated a patient's fitness for work or deliberately misrepresented a patient's psychopathy as being war-related. Several witnesses vouched for Dr. R.'s vocal opposition to the euthanasia program. One witness, a Protestant minister, related that R. had confided in him that he had remained at his post only to save patients. Other witnesses described how R. had subverted the program by exempting certain patients from deportation to Hadamar. The two doctors, like Creutz, faced a dire "conflict of duties" that forced them to choose between abandoning their patients to almost certain doom or collaborating minimally in the euthanasia program so as to rescue whoever they could. The court held that this "collision of duties" operated as a "justifying ground" to acquit both We. and R. of all charges.[24]

The last group of defendants in the Rhine province case to be acquitted on the basis of a collision of duties was two University of Bonn professors, Kurt Pohlisch and Friedrich Panse. Pohlisch enjoyed a triple appointment as a professor of psychiatry and neurology at the University of Bonn, head doctor of the university's mental clinic, and director of Bonn's provincial mental hospital. Panse, who had befriended Pohlisch during their studies together at the University of Berlin, used his connections with Pohlisch in 1936 to obtain an appointment as chief doctor at the Provincial Institute for Psychiatric and Neurological Genetic Research in Bonn. In 1937 Panse became a lecturer at the University of Bonn, where he taught courses on racial hygiene. Both men joined the National Socialist party that same year.

Although witnesses at the trials of Pohlisch and Panse lionized them for their commitment to pure science, the professors' research on eugenics during the 1930s suggests anything but disinterested science. Under the auspices of the Central Office for the Hereditary Biological Inventory, they worked on developing a national genetic data bank to record the racial-hygienic background of the German population. Pohlisch and Panse's contribution was a prodigious archive containing eugenic information on 300,000 residents in the Rhine province. Their work on this project brought them into contact with a rogues' gallery of future euthanasia killers, including Herbert Linden, future T-4 chief medical expert and Reich Commissioner for Mental Hospitals.[25]

In April 1940, Pohlisch and Panse attended a recruitment meeting of mental health professionals in Berlin presided over by Viktor Brack. During this meeting, it was generally agreed that all schizophrenics hospitalized without improvement in their condition for a period of five years, as well as all "feeble-minded" patients not regarded as essential workers, were to be killed after inspection of their registration forms by government experts. In the aftermath of the meeting, both men served for a time as T-4 medical experts reviewing these registration forms until summer 1940. The court determined that in 10 of the 300 to 400 cases Pohlisch examined, he had affirmed a basis for proceeding with euthanasia; the figure for Panse was 15 of 600 cases. These actions, the court found, furthered the goals of the Berlin authorities to annihilate disabled patients deemed "unworthy of life," thus fulfilling the elements of the offense of aiding and abetting murder and crimes against humanity. (The professors were accomplices rather than perpetrators because they did not embrace the killings "as their own," but participated in euthanasia solely on behalf of the T-4 leadership.)

Pohlisch and Panse claimed that their engagements with the T-4 program were all actuated by a desire to subvert it from within. One witness at trial testified that the two professors had objected to the killing program at the April meeting. They had characterized the meeting as a success in terms of restricting the categories of patients subject to euthanasia. The Düsseldorf court found evidence to support this testimony, such as proof that the two men had proposed revising the registration forms to include additional categories of exemption from transport. Panse had persuaded the Berlin authorities to exempt some patients from transfer in order to use them as specimens in high school instruction; Pohlisch convinced them that a determination could not be made based only on the registration forms but also required a personal examination. Furthermore, the court found that the agreement to exempt patients capable of work from transport was the result of the professors' lobbying efforts. Summing up their role at the April conference, the court concluded: "It must be said that in the conference considerable restrictions were achieved and both defendants contributed to it through their suggestions."[26]

With respect to their roles in completing the registration forms, the court accepted Pohlisch and Panse's assertion that they so rarely identified a patient for transport that Berlin eventually cancelled shipment of the forms to them. The court was also receptive to their argument that they selected for transport only patients whom they believed were terminal cases likely to die before removal could occur, or who were so ill that they would be exempted under Berlin's guidelines on patients incapable of transport. Not one of the patients they had selected, the professors declared, were killed as a result of their selection. The court tended to agree with them, noting that the mortality rates in the Andernach and Galkhausen facilities (serviced by the Bonn professors) were lower than other institutions in the Rhine province from May to July 1941. Based on this evidence, the state court held that it was "not only possible, but highly probable" that the defendants' arguments were correct and that their work on the registration forms never resulted in the deaths of any patients.[27]

The Düsseldorf court had no difficulty in justifying the Bonn professors' actions on the ground of a "collision of duties." On the basis of "proven innocence," Pohlisch and Panse were, like Walter Creutz, acquitted of all charges.

The court's tribute to the Bonn professors is oddly discordant with what we know of their research in racial-hygiene during the 1930s. To suggest that such research, conducted under the aegis of the Nazi state, was not overtly political disregards the historical record. Further, in his 1961 judicial testimony before his death by suicide, T-4 Obergutachter Werner Heyde dismissed Pohlisch's self-exculpatory portrayal of himself as a saboteur of euthanasia, countering that Pohlisch was "uninterruptedly active as an expert" for Berlin, and that at the April 1941 conference he enthusiastically supported the euthanasia plans outlined by Viktor Brack. These facts, coupled with Pohlisch's energetic exertions to prepare a draft of a euthanasia law (later vetoed by Hitler out of fear of foreign propaganda), cast the defendants' moral "dilemma" in a different and unflattering light.

In the court's defense, much of this information was unknown to it in 1948 when it proclaimed that the defendants had "pursue[d] the higher duty to save at least a part of the patients who would otherwise be lost." Both men resumed their psychiatric careers after their acquittal. In this way, the three defendants acquitted in the Rhine province case were beneficiaries of West Germany's peculiar "policy toward the past" that emerged in the later years of the 1940s—a policy that included the reintegration into professional life of former Nazi officials. Before Creutz, Pohlisch, and Panse could move on with their lives, however, they faced yet another round of judicial proceedings.

In German criminal law, by contrast with its Anglo-American counterpart, both the defendant and the government are entitled to appeal a decision that either believes is legally deficient. (In U.S. and English law, the principle of double jeopardy interposes an absolute barrier to any such appeal by the government of an acquittal.) In the Rhine province case, the state prosecutor appealed the Düsseldorf state court's decision directly to the Supreme Court for the British Zone, arguing on appeal that the court had misapplied the doctrine of "extrastatutory necessity." The Supreme Court agreed and reversed the lower court's verdict regarding Creutz, Pohlisch, and Panse because it was based on a misinterpretation of extrastatutory necessity. According to the higher court, this doctrine was inapplicable in cases where two groups of *people* were involved—that is, one group to be saved and another to be sacrificed. Only when two legal *duties* were in conflict and the actor performed the higher of the two duties at the expense of the lower could the defense be successfully invoked to justify violating the law. Clearly, the Supreme Court for the British Zone felt that the Düsseldorf court had endorsed the defendants' sacrifice of "hopeless" patients in the interests of saving other patients.* This was a grave legal error, the Supreme Court held, because you could not compare the two groups and proclaim one worthier of being saved than the other. Implicit in the Supreme Court's opinion is a subtle rebuke directed at the lower court for assigning the lives of "incurable" patients to a less valuable class of "legal goods" than the lives of healthier patients.[28]

In January 1950 the case was retried in the Düsseldorf state court on re-mand from the Supreme Court for the British Zone. The authors of the sec-ond opinion were unfazed by the higher court's criticism. They continued to laud Creutz for hazarding his own life and career on behalf of his patients, describing him as a man who had pushed himself "to the very brink of the concentration camp" in his efforts to save lives. In minimal deference to the Supreme Court's ruling, the state court declined applying extrastatutory ne-cessity a second time; instead, it found that Creutz was "exempt from punish-ment" because he had acted blamelessly. For the Düsseldorf court, even this lenient outcome insufficiently recognized Creutz's valor. By the time of Creutz's second acquittal, the Supreme Court for the British Zone was no longer avail-able to chasten the state court: in 1950 it had been replaced by West Germany's Federal Supreme Court, which exhibited a less critical attitude toward the findings of the lower courts in these cases.[29]

The Rhine province was not the first case to acquit euthanasia accom-plices of criminal wrongdoing; that distinction belongs to the Scheuern trial. The cases of Creutz, Pohlisch, and Panse, however, were the first euthanasia trials to portray these accomplices as moral superheroes, dedicated to saving human lives on peril of being thrown into a concentration camp. By the time of Creutz's retrial in October 1950, the reservations expressed by the Koblenz court in the Scheuern trial ("whether the defendants are able inwardly to feel themselves free of any guilt is a matter for their personal conscience") had dissipated. Increasingly, courts were using triumphalist moral language to de-scribe the participation of euthanasia defendants in the mass destruction of the mentally disabled. For German critic of postwar German justice Jörg Friedrich the Rhine province case was a judicial and moral outrage. "Only this judiciary, itself well-schooled in murder, could extol to his patients a nine-

---

* The Supreme Court for the British Zone (OGHBZ) was frequently at odds with regional courts in West Germany in the postwar years. The antagonism may have resulted from the OGHBZ's role in ensuring that Allied Control Council Law #10 was properly observed in trials conducted by regional courts. As Dick De Mildt has observed, the perception by some German jurists that Law #10 violated the ban on ex post facto laws within German jurisprudence may have sparked their resentment of it. See De Mildt, *In the Name of the People*, 358n39.

hundred-fold murder accomplice as an idol of morality," Friedrich corrosively remarked.[30] The Düsseldorf court's example did not fall on flinty soil. It flourished in the verdicts of subsequent courts, transforming men into virtuous paragons who, in a different era, would have earned the label of murderers.

The Württemberg Case

One of the more bizarre of the "collision of duties" euthanasia cases involved four doctors in the Württemberg mental health administration. Their twelve-day trial is remarkable for the range of verdicts it issued for these euthanasia killers: two acquittals on a theory of collision of duties, one acquittal for lack of evidence, and a conviction of the primary defendant, albeit with a mitigated sentence that reflected the court's unwillingness to condemn his murderous complicity on moral grounds.

The leading defendant in this case, Dr. Otto Mauthe, was the former chief medical officer for the mental health system in Württemberg's Ministry of the Interior. Mauthe was commissioned to implement the euthanasia program in the state of Württemberg. Acting on this commission, he ensured that registration forms were distributed and properly completed in the forty-eight institutions within his jurisdiction. In late November 1939, he informed these mental institutions via a decree from the state Ministry of the Interior that war conditions required that certain patients be transferred, as ordered by the Reich Defense Ministry. The institutions receiving transports were to provide notice to the patients' relatives. After this decree was disseminated, lists with names of patients to be transported were sent to the home institutions, which were expected to ready the patients for transfer. These patients were later transported to the killing center of Grafeneck (and, after its closure, to Hadamar), where with few exceptions they were murdered. In order to prevent discharge of patients before they could be transported to their deaths, the Ministry of the Interior issued a decree in September 1940 prohibiting discharges without the ministry's approval.

The killing center Grafeneck came into existence in October 1939 when, on orders from Berlin, a former castle belonging to the Samaritan Foundation Association was converted into a euthanasia center for mentally handicapped patients. The rooms within the Grafeneck facility were used as office space for the T-4 staff. The actual extermination room was located in a shack formerly used for farming. This inauspicious structure was converted into a gas chamber. Adjacent to it, three crematoria were installed to dispose of the murdered patients' bodies. A large wooden barracks and doctor's office stood nearby. When the mentally disabled arrived at Grafeneck, usually in busloads of approximately seventy-five people, they were brought into the receiving barracks, disrobed by nursing personnel, and led to the examining doctor. A minute-long physical exam ensued. Occasionally, the exams resulted in an exemption of the patient from killing. The vast majority, however, were conducted into the gas chamber, which, in an eerie prefiguration of the gas chambers at Auschwitz, was disguised to resemble a shower room, complete with mock water faucets. Once all patients were in the chamber, the door was shut and locked, and the chamber filled with carbon monoxide gas. Within minutes the patients were dead. Their bodies were removed and immediately cremated. The presiding doctor recorded false causes, dates, and places of death on the victims' death certificates. The Registry Office of Grafeneck officially registered them as suffering death from "natural causes." In an effort to obstruct public knowledge of the killings, the Grafeneck staff monitored the hometowns of the victims with colored pins stuck into a map of Germany. In this way, they could ensure that suspicion would not be aroused by issuing too many death notices for patients from any one location.

The Grafeneck killing center took a frightful toll of lives during its short-lived existence from October 1939 until mid-December 1940. Some 10,654 disabled patients were killed there during this fourteen-month period. After its doors were closed in December 1940, the Hadamar institution took up where Grafeneck had left off. Evidence admitted at Mauthe's trial indicated that 267 patients from Württemberg institutions were killed at Hadamar. In addition to these killings, at least 93 children were transported to children's wards outside Württemberg, chiefly Eichberg, where they were murdered.

Otto Mauthe typified a new species of criminal that appears for the first time in history during the era of Nazi genocide, the "desk murderer" (*Schreibtischtäter*). Although never harming anyone directly, he consigned thousands of patients to their deaths with the stroke of his pen. Based on the evidence before it, the state court of Tübingen was convinced that Mauthe played a central role in the administrative measures essential to the successful implementation of the killing program—primarily in the form of preparing and sometimes personally signing decrees issued by the Württemberg Ministry of the Interior. The court enumerated a list of incriminating decrees authored by Mauthe, each of which promoted euthanasia in some material respect. The decree of June 10, 1940, for example, required mental health officials in Stuttgart to prepare lists of patients for transport to Grafeneck. Another one (August 9, 1940) prohibited the Liebenau institution from informing relatives of transportees of their removal. He issued the decree of June 5, 1941, to the Weinsberg mental hospital, ordering the transport of patients to the Hadamar killing center. It was further proven that Mauthe himself had visited institutions in Württemberg in order to complete registration forms that had been improperly filled out. Patients identified by Mauthe on these forms were later transported and allegedly killed. The record teemed with other evidence adverse to Mauthe, including situations in which he overruled exemptions made by other doctors and ordered their transport to Grafeneck. It was also shown that he had pacified the victims' families with false assurances about their fates.

In its deliberations about Mauthe and his codefendants, the state court of Tübingen departed from the custom established in earlier euthanasia trials and elected to apply Control Council Law #10's crimes against humanity (Article II, 1c) rather than German law to the defendants' crimes. German law, the court held, was ill-suited to deal with the "mass criminality" perpetrated by the Nazi state. For the court, the German Penal Code did not anticipate participation in mass murder, "but rather a multiple participation in a single murder"; and because the code had no category for mass murder, mass killings under the code that numbered in the hundreds and thousands were "impossible." German law, in the presence of Nazi genocide, curled back upon itself. Therefore, Law #10's crimes against humanity was the appropriate theory of criminal liability to be applied in this case.[31]

Mauthe (or his attorney) must have taken note of the Scheuern and Rhine province cases, for he raised the collision of duties as a defense at trial, arguing that he had participated in the euthanasia program only to hamstring its aims from the inside. The Tübingen court acknowledged the legal validity of extrastatutory necessity and collision of duties, but insisted that they could be applied only when "strict requirements" were met in a given case. Turning to Mauthe, the court had little problem concluding that he did not satisfy these requirements. Mauthe, it held, did not collaborate in euthanasia in order to save lives, but out of fear for personal disadvantages he might otherwise face, especially to his professional advancement. Further, he did not exploit all opportunities for saving patients, using his freedom of discretion; rather, he expressly avoided saving patients because of his "exaggerated anxiety and bureaucratic indifference." (In one example, he refused to support an exemption lest the SS investigate or his superior should disapprove.) The court described ten separate instances in which Mauthe failed to authorize discharge for a patient when there was abundant opportunity to do so. These examples belied his claim that he sought every opportunity to rescue patients from transportation to the killing centers.[32]

Similarly, Mauthe neglected opportunities to extricate children from transport to the children's ward at Eichberg, despite his awareness that patients were being killed there. These examples decisively proved that Mauthe, even if he inwardly disapproved of euthanasia, nonetheless colluded in it—not out of a desire to save his patients, but out of fear for his position. For this reason, the court rejected his collision of duties defense.

In sentencing Mauthe, the Tübingen court counted as factors in mitigation his "weakness," which rendered him vulnerable to "general political pressure and the much stronger personality of his superior, Dr. Stähle." The court even conceded that Mauthe may have been inwardly willing to save patients, but his "anxiety and bureaucratic inhibition" paralyzed his ability to act. For his role in facilitating the killings of 4,000 people, he was given a five-year jail term. Mauthe did not even serve this mild punishment; not long after the trial, his sentence was suspended and Mauthe was released from prison.[33]

A second physician convicted by the Tübingen court was the acting director of the Zwiefalten mental institution, Dr. Alfons Stegmann, charged with delivering his patients for transportation and killing. Stegmann claimed he had known nothing about the purpose of the transports until after the transports' departure—an assertion refuted by witness testimony that Dr. Stähle had enlightened him on the reason for the transports in February 1940. Moreover, his behavior during the period of his directorship at Zwiefalten contradicted his "sabotage" argument. He not only maintained regular contact with euthanasia specialist Dr. Ernst Baumhardt, but made regular voluntary visits to the killing center at Grafeneck. On one occasion, he caught a lift in a Gekrat bus to go cherry picking in Winnenden. At one point on this outing, a cigarette pasted to his lip, he commented to a bystander as a mentally ill woman was loaded onto the bus: "There goes my bride!" The court described such detachment from the plight of these doomed human beings as "cool" and "cynical," belying his claim that he had always resisted the T-4 killing program. Nor did Stegmann's documented exemptions of patients capable of work weigh in his favor, because they were fully within the scope of permissible action as defined by the Berlin authorities. Far more damning was his gratuitous act of selecting 75 patients for transport from 120 photocopies given him by Dr. Baumhardt. This act, in concert with others, sufficiently proved he was more inclined to promote than to resist the killing program.

Despite his clear support of Nazi euthanasia and his proven contribution to the deaths of hundreds of patients, Stegmann received a trifling jail term of two years. The court considered several factors in mitigation of his punishment: his collaboration was "relatively small"; he did not himself design the killing program; and he was a young doctor at the time, installed during the war as director of a large mental hospital, and thus merely responded to decisions made by his superiors. These considerations, as we have seen in other cases (such as the trial of Mathilde Weber), were typical of sentencing under German criminal law: real responsibility for institutional criminality was securely lodged at the top of a bureaucratic hierarchy. The farther down the hierarchy a defendant was, the greater the probability the defendant would qualify for extenuated punishment.[34]

The third and final physician convicted by the court, Stegmann's successor as director of the Zwiefalten institution, a Dr. F., also enjoyed a significant reduction of her sentence. She was charged with committing a crime against humanity for her role in preparing transports of patients from Zwiefalten based on the transport list. The Tübingen court acquitted her in nearly every case, finding no evidence to contradict her claim that she had exempted patients from transfer on her own initiative. In the cases of three specific patients, however, the court declined an outright acquittal. These cases involved patients killed with lethal injections of scopolamine and trional ordered by Dr. F. At trial, she tried to portray the injections as designed to alleviate the suffering of terminally ill patients, not to induce their deaths. Her self-exculpatory declaration, however, was inconsistent with an earlier confession she had made during an interrogation in Freiburg, in which she had admitted to injecting the moribund patients with lethal overdoses in order to abbreviate their lives. Because she had not caused their deaths "cruelly," "maliciously," or out of "base motives" but "solely out of pity," and because these three killings were unrelated to the Nazis' brutal campaign to destroy "life unworthy of life," they were neither a crime against humanity nor murder under German law. Instead, her acts constituted manslaughter under section 212 of the German Penal Code.[35] Clearly sympathetic to Dr. F., the court sentenced her to a prison term of one-and-a-half years (the minimal legal punishment for each case of manslaughter, or six months per death).

Although the collision of duties defense found no application in the convictions of Mauthe, a Dr. S., and Dr. F., one defendant in the Württemberg trial did successfully invoke it to secure his acquittal. This defendant was a medical specialist in psychiatry, a Dr. E., indicted for accompanying Mauthe on his trips to various mental institutions in Württemberg for the purpose of completing registration forms on their patients. Dr. E. argued at trial that he and Mauthe made these trips only to strike from the transport lists the names of patients capable of work, and thus, far from promoting euthanasia, they had actually restricted it. Finding Dr. E.'s defense unrefuted by the evidentiary record, the Tübingen court acquitted him on the basis of a collision of duties.[36]

The Württemberg trial in 1949 encapsulates in miniature the tolerant spirit of the post-1947 euthanasia trials. When it did not acquit a euthanasia doctor outright, as it did Dr. E., the Tübingen court meted out comparatively trivial sentences for egregious violations of the law of nations. A mathematical computation, for example, throws into disturbing bas-relief the court's lenient attitude toward Mauthe: if we divide the total number of hours in a five-year prison sentence such as Mauthe received (and ultimately did not serve) by the total number of his victims (4,000), we arrive at a figure of approximately ten hours of jail time per killing. Willfully or not, such a sentence conveys a message to the rest of society that this type of killing is of a different order of wrongdoing than conventional homicide—an order of wrongdoing that society may condone, because it lacks the reprehensibility of conventional murder.

In the 1960s, polls of West German citizens indicated that many wished for the prosecution of National Socialist crimes to come to an end, in part because many Germans regarded the crimes committed during the era of National Socialism as something other than true criminality. A German expert on the prosecution of Nazi crimes, Herbert Jäger, once commented that the "good citizen" did not object to state-sponsored mass murder, but to "nonconformist" murder outside the boundaries of the well-ordered state. Nor was this prejudice restricted to German laypeople. In the twenty years after the war, German courts typically reserved their harshest punishment for the *Exzesstäter* (excess perpetrators), those killers who committed crimes of violence beyond the scope of what was ordered (*auf eigene Faust tut*, literally "acting on one's own fist"). The psychopathic killer received the scorching reprobation of the German courts, while the "small wheels" within the machinery of destruction often escaped condign punishment. For Jäger, one of the foremost goals of prosecuting Nazi crimes was to cultivate an awareness in the German population that violence performed on the orders of the highest state leadership *is* criminal. Under this standard, the trial of the Württemberg doctors can only be regarded as a spectacular failure.[37]

The Baden Case

As we saw in the Württemberg trial, the T-4 functionaries in Berlin sometimes worked through local state authorities to accomplish their aims of implementing euthanasia. In other cases, they worked directly with mental institutions themselves. For this reason, officials in the provincial government sector—especially the health departments within local ministries of the interior—could become essential partners in the destruction of "unworthy" life. The example of State Councillor Fritz Bernotat of Hessen-Nassau comes readily to mind; without his sedulous efforts on behalf of euthanasia, the killing program in Hessen-Nassau would never have functioned with the same harrowing efficiency that it achieved under his guidance. The work of local officials like Bernotat was fraught with potential for appalling destruction. Otto Mauthe's hands were dripping with the blood of 4,000 disabled patients; Bernotat's victims can be numbered in the tens of thousands.

On May 1, 1950, the state court of Freiburg im Breisgau convened to retry Otto Mauthe's counterpart in the Baden Interior Ministry, Dr. Ludwig Sprauer, and the former director of the Illenau and Wiesloch psychiatric hospitals, Dr. Josef Artur Schreck. Accused of involvement in the euthanasia program, both defendants had been convicted in an earlier proceeding in November 1948 of crimes against humanity and aiding and abetting murder; both were given lifelong prison terms. Their conviction was duly appealed and the verdict partially reversed by the Freiburg Court of Appeals on technical legal grounds. The case thereafter was remanded to the lower court for retrial in May 1950.

Dr. Ludwig Sprauer was the director of the Health Department (Department IIIb) of the Baden Interior Ministry. As director he controlled twelve mental hospitals in Baden, including state, district, and religiously affiliated institutions. In October 1939 Sprauer was summoned to the Reich Ministry of the Interior in Berlin, where Herbert Linden informed him that war conditions required reserve hospitals. Linden then swore Sprauer to secrecy and told him about plans to euthanize incurable mental patients "in the sense of the Binding-Hoche proposals." By "granting" these patients a "mercy death," the necessary beds would be made available for use as reserve hospitals. Linden assured Sprauer that a "legal foundation" for the killing program existed, but that a euthanasia law had not yet been enacted. Until its formal legalization, the program was backed by a September 1939 authorization by Hitler. Sprauer's role was to facilitate registration and transportation of incurable patients in Baden institutions.[38]

Despite Sprauer's willingness to collaborate in the killing program, medical personnel throughout Baden resisted its implementation. The court was aware of only two directors of Baden mental hospitals who failed to oppose the operation: Sprauer's codefendant Josef Artur Schreck and a Dr. Gercke. The rest engaged in a relatively successful plan of sabotage. On one occasion, in early December 1940, a Gekrat transport leader left the institution of Jestetten with an empty bus because the staff doctor and chief nurse had refused to surrender their patients to him. The director of the Fussbach institution went so far as to don his SS uniform when the Gekrat busses arrived and launch into a heated argument with the transport leader, the result of which was that only thirty of the ninety patients designated were finally transported. These and other incidents of resistance, however, did not spur Sprauer into opposing the euthanasia program; on the contrary, he scotched resistance wherever it appeared. His tactics of quashing opposition ran the gamut from threats of imprisonment to "collegial" invitations to take extended vacations. On another occasion, he transferred a Dr. L., a staff physician at the Illenau institution who had protested the killing program, to the health office in Karlsruhe.

As in the Rhine province, a sabotage "conspiracy" embracing all of Baden's directors except Schreck and Gercke developed. These doctor-saboteurs resolved to subvert the killing program by discharging patients, transferring them to work positions, or removing them to private institutions where they would be out of harm's way. They also exempted patients from transport by characterizing them as capable of work. Opportunities arose during this sabotage initiative for Sprauer to cooperate with it. The director of the Emmendingen facility, a Dr. Ma., asked Sprauer to authorize exemption of twelve children who were capable of working independently of supervision. Sprauer refused, and the children were transported from Emmendingen to Grafeneck. Sprauer's obduracy persuaded Dr. Ma. to withhold patients without first obtaining his permission. When Sprauer learned of this, he reprimanded Ma. for his act of sabotage, and warned him that if he continued he would face dismissal, or possibly even his own personal transport to Grafeneck.

The court accepted Sprauer's representation that the euthanasia program profoundly disturbed him. "A false bureaucratic ambition and submissiveness to authority," however, impelled his collaboration with the program. Fears that a critical attitude toward it would prejudice his career haunted him, causing an almost knee-jerk submission to orders issued "from above." (In the words of one witness, "what came from Berlin was Gospel for [Sprauer].") "He did not want to lose his job in the ministry," the court held, "where after a few years he hoped to rise to the position of a ministerial councillor." The court had no doubt that Sprauer perceived the wrongfulness of the program, and that he even suffered grievous mental stress over it; but his "loyalty to duty" overrode his moral compunction. Periodically, in response to the pleadings of institutional directors, Sprauer reluctantly approved exemptions; but in these cases he usually required that other patients incapable of work be substituted. The court attributed his submissive attitude toward authority to a "character weakness." Notwithstanding this infirmity in his personality, he was always conscious that the killing program and his actions in connection with it were wrongful.[39]

In its assessment of Sprauer's conduct, the Freiburg court adopted the by now familiar taxonomy of perpetrators of and accomplices to National Socialist euthanasia. The perpetrators were "Hitler and his henchmen"—Himmler, Bouhler, Brandt, Linden, and Brack. These were the men at the top of the Nazi power structure who "initiated" and "guided" the euthanasia program from its inception—men who acted out of "base motives" and "maliciously" to destroy patients they considered "superfluous eaters." Sprauer's work as the director of the Baden Interior Ministry's health department, on the other hand, classified him as a "typical accomplice" to the mass murders committed by the Nazi leadership corps. By consigning patients to transports that he knew would result in their deaths, Sprauer fulfilled the objective elements of the offense (both a crime against humanity and aiding and abetting murder). His argument that his actions were justified by an extrastatutory necessity, inasmuch as any refusal to collaborate would have meant dismissal from his job and certain "professional disadvantages" harmful to both himself and his family, was dismissed by the court. According to the court, prejudice to one's career was not a compelling legal interest under the doctrine of extrastatutory necessity—certainly not one that would justify sacrificing the lives of patients.[40] Any duress Sprauer experienced was legally negligible; under German law, only an "immediate threat to life and limb" rose to a level sufficient to justify or excuse a criminal act. He had no reason to fear for his personal safety, or for the safety of his family, in the event of a refusal to cooperate with the euthanasia program. On May 2, 1950, after a two-day trial, the Freiburg court found him guilty of aiding and abetting numerous murders and of crimes against humanity.

Because the death penalty had been abolished in Germany in 1949, the court meted out to Sprauer an eleven-year jail term. Within months after he was sentenced for his role in helping to murder 3,000 persons, the Freiburg prosecutor's office suspended Sprauer's punishment and released him from prison. Simultaneously, the government of Baden-Württemberg awarded him a pension of DM 450 per month. The effort beginning in 1945 to purge the German civil service of former officials of the Nazi government was unraveling as the decade wound down; of the party members dismissed from their jobs in 1945, increasing numbers of them were reintegrated into the German civil service by the early 1950s. Sprauer was one, but by no means the only, example of this trend.

One of the decisive proofs against Sprauer's argument that he had always sought to undermine the euthanasia program was his nomination of Dr. Josef Artur Schreck to serve as a medical expert for the operation. Sprauer must have known of Schreck's supportive attitude toward euthanasia; his work on behalf of T-4 would not disappoint Sprauer's trust in him. Schreck had not always been an adherent of destroying "life unworthy of life." Not until the work of Binding and Hoche was published in 1920 did he embrace euthanasia as a "humane" method for ending the lives of severely mentally handicapped patients. He believed euthanasia should be restricted to two groups of patients: "full idiots" and those who had become feebleminded as a result of accident or illness. Administering a "mercy death" to the latter group, he felt, was particularly humane, because it would spare them the indignities of an institutionalized existence—a deliverance he himself would desire if he were in such a condition. The court noted that Schreck continued to adhere to these ideas until the day of his trial.

Schreck's contributions to the killing program occurred in two official capacities: as an institutional director and as a T-4 expert. He served at various times as director of three Baden mental hospitals, as well as the temporary director of the children's ward in another institution. As director at the Rastatt hospital, he received registration forms for 580 of his patients in late 1939. Although he, like his colleagues at other Baden institutions, had not been informed of their purpose, he nevertheless intuited what was afoot, suspecting that a "program along the lines of Binding/Hoche might be involved." Evidence indicated that between 15 and 20 percent of his patients were capable of work and enjoyed a cognitive life in which they were responsive to their environment. This notwithstanding, when Rastatt was dissolved in June 1940 a contingent of registered patients was brought in seven transports to Grafeneck and gassed. Schreck, who had meanwhile been informed of the purposes of the transport, did nothing to impede it. He tried to console a distraught nurse by referring to the exigencies of the war, assuring her that it was a "completely humane" proceeding.[41]

At one of the Baden institutions under his direction, moreover, Schreck proved himself a devoted adherent of the killing program. In one case cited by the court, Schreck provided a diagnosis of a patient on the registration form that almost guaranteed his transportation, describing him as a schizophrenic "with considerable disintegration of the psychological personality." A physician familiar with the patient challenged Schreck's assessment at trial, calling the patient a "mild case with no disintegration of the personality." Schreck's summary of the patient's length of time in the institution was likewise inaccurate: in contrast with Schreck's assertion that he had been institutionalized "with brief interruptions" since June 1917, the court found that from 1917 to 1940 the patient had spent as many as eighteen years outside hospitals—hardly the continuous institutionalization punctuated by "brief interruptions" alleged by Schreck. Miraculously, this patient survived the killing program and was at the time of the trial alive and doing productive work.

Schreck's brief stint as director of the children's ward at the Wiesloch institution also incriminated him in the killing program. At the suggestion of Sprauer, Herbert Linden appointed Schreck to this directorship, communicating to him that the children in the ward were to be euthanized. Until its dissolution in June 1941, twelve children were killed there, the last one in May. They ranged in ages from three to five and were characterized as "full idiots" beyond treatment. The children were killed with two or three injections of luminal, which induced terminal pneumonia in the victims. The first three killings were performed by Schreck himself, as were the autopsies on their corpses. Defending his actions, Schreck claimed they were motivated by purely humanitarian concerns, because it was "inhumane" to prolong the life of a child who lacked a complete brain or suffered hydrocephaly.

The gravamen of the charges against Schreck, however, was his work as a T-4 expert. After Sprauer had recommended Schreck as ideologically reliable, he was ordered to report to Herbert Linden in Berlin in February 1940. In

Berlin he and fifteen other doctors attended a meeting chaired by Viktor Brack, who related that because of unspecified "war conditions" the "ancient problem of euthanasia had again become acute." Brack told his audience that the Reich Chancellery had already prepared a law on the subject, but it could not be published during the war, and thus had to be treated as a "secret Reich matter." The victims were to include all patients under institutional care for longer than five years, excepting war veterans, foreigners, and patients capable of useful work. Photocopies of the registration forms were then exhibited to the participants, along with an explanation of how the medical experts were to evaluate them. At the end, all participants were asked if they were willing to work as medical experts for the euthanasia program. Schreck told the court he had freely accepted the offer, because the program coincided with his own philosophy on euthanasia. He added, however, that he fully believed in the legality of the program when he agreed to collaborate with it.[42]

From March until December 1940, Schreck assessed some 15,000 registration forms sent him by the T-4 front office, the Reich Cooperative for State Hospitals and Nursing Homes. The first shipment contained 350 to 400 forms from three Baden institutions, among them forms on patients he knew personally. Thereafter he requested that he be sent forms only from non-Baden institutions, in order to ensure his ability to judge them objectively. Notwithstanding his claims that he evaluated each form assiduously, the court rejected any suggestion that an accurate portrait of a patient could be gleaned from the modest information contained on the registration forms—least of all an adequate basis for determining whether a patient was incurable. The court considered Schreck intelligent enough to understand this inadequacy and thus accountable for making life-and-death decisions based on them.

The Freiburg state court's legal analysis of Schreck's crimes closely paralleled its assessment of Sprauer. Schreck, like Sprauer, was deemed an accomplice to murders committed by the real perpetrators, the "Berlin planning and leadership circle." Although the court refused to treat him as a perpetrator, it did consider Schreck's contributions to the murder of mental patients substantial. These contributions, moreover, were neither justified by Schreck's alleged belief in a wartime emergency that excused his actions, nor his claim that he had assumed Nazi euthanasia was a rational and humane extension of the Binding/Hoche thesis regarding "life not worth living." Declining to pass on the legality of a program faithfully modeled on the Binding/Hoche guidelines, the court stated that the government's war on the disabled had nothing in common with the arguments of Binding/Hoche—a patent discontinuity of which Schreck must have been aware. Because Schreck must have seen the startling lack of congruence between the two, it followed that he may have been a true believer in the "crass utilitarian consideration" that underpinned the whole operation, "namely, the exclusion of superfluous eaters in the interest of securing nourishment and the need for hospital space." And yet, despite his willingness to participate in the destruction of "superfluous eaters," the court did not find that he was fully aware of the illegality of his actions. Rather, he suffered from "legal blindness," a failure to grasp the criminality of his role in the program that did not rise to the level of an exculpatory "lack of awareness of illegality" (which would have acquitted Schreck on the basis of a mistake of law), but was less morally reprehensible than a conscious flouting of the law.

The court's reasoning here becomes murky. It seems to be saying that Schreck did not fully appreciate the illegality of his actions, but this lack of awareness did not rise to the level of a mistake of law sufficient to acquit him of the charges. The court compared the motivational complexes of both Sprauer and Schreck:

> While in Sprauer's case an exaggerated need for authority led to his legal blindness, Schreck succumbed to an inward development, at the beginning of which—and this makes the participation of highly esteemed men and psychiatrists in the operation especially tragic—stood an actual pity for the sickest of the patients. . . . The same man reputed to have a paternal and benevolent attitude toward his patients clearly expressed the view, when filling out forms on his Illenau patients . . . , that valuing a human life was no longer for him a precise procedure. These failures cannot be regarded as accidental, but are the symptoms for the destruction of the professional ethic, which every doctor had to suffer who involved himself in the extermination program.[43]

In this way, the court blurred the contours of Schreck's personal responsibility for his actions, locating their origins in the depraving influences exerted by the killing program and its economistic philosophy on all its accomplices.

The court convicted Schreck, as it had Sprauer, of aiding and abetting murder under German law and crimes against humanity under Law #10 on May 2, 1950. These convictions related to his work as an expert evaluator and to his actions as director of the three Baden hospitals under his direction. He was acquitted of the homicide charge for his personal involvement in killing the three children in the Wiesloch children's ward, because he was motivated in these three cases by the desire "to deliver them from their incurability and incapacity." Unlike the Berlin authorities, who routinely lied to the victims' families, Schreck had informed the children's families that euthanasia was the best means of ending their child's suffering; thus, his conduct could not be regarded as deceptive. Because these killings were not prompted by any of the motives required by the German law of murder, they were instances of manslaughter under section 212. For the same reason, the children's deaths were not crimes against humanity, insofar as Schreck did not commit them with a sense of "damaging human dignity through the cruelty and pitilessness of his actions." The court sentenced him to a jail term of eleven years. Like Sprauer, he was soon released from jail, serving only a year of his sentence.

The Baden case represents both a deviation from and a continuance of the post-1947 trend toward leniency in German euthanasia trials. On the one hand, the Freiburg court refused to accept the defendants' claim of extrastatutory necessity; on the other, it treated both defendants as accomplices rather than perpetrators, ascribing their motives to an obsequious careerism (Sprauer) and the "tragic" perversion of a once high-minded concern for human life (Schreck). In Schreck's case the court's dismissal of the charges for murder and crimes against humanity as applied to the deaths of the three Wiesloch children even implied that he had acted compassionately to end human suffering.

The trials of euthanasia defendants in the aftermath of the Baden case are notable for their renewed willingness to acquit on the basis of extrastatutory emergency. Beginning in the early 1950s, moreover, a novel theory won acceptance in West German courts as a defense to the charge of euthanasia-related homicide. That theory—the "exertion of conscience" defense—and its endorsement by West German jurists reveals the extent to which the yearning for an end to the prosecution of Nazi-era crimes had infiltrated the judiciary's attitudes about euthanasia criminality. To a significant degree, this yearning was impelled by a desire for restored national power after the catastrophe of Germany's defeat in 1945. We turn to this new series of verdicts and the rationale invoked to support them in the next chapter.

> Political language . . . is designed to make lies sound truthful
> and murder respectable, and to give an appearance of solidity
> to pure wind.
>
> —GEORGE ORWELL, "POLITICS AND THE
> ENGLISH LANGUAGE" (1950)

Chapter 5 | LAW AND POWER

THE WEST GERMAN EUTHANASIA TRIALS, 1948–1953

THE RENEWAL OF THE COLLISION OF DUTIES DEFENSE

The West German euthanasia trials between 1948 and the mid-1950s occurred during a tumultuous era in German and international history. The U.S. goal of integrating into the Western alliance a democratic and pro-U.S. Germany became a pillar of European foreign policy in both the Truman and Eisenhower administrations. As early as 1949, the Pentagon and State Department realized the military inadequacy of NATO troop strength as compared with the Soviets: its undersupplied twelve divisions were dwarfed by the USSR's twenty-seven. A solution to this mismatch, in the minds of Secretary of State Dean Acheson and Pentagon policymakers, was to rearm West Germany and shore up NATO's ground forces with German soldiers. Opinion about German rearmament was divided within the State Department; some officials feared French and Soviet responses to any plan to revive the German military. The reservations of these critics, however, were dealt a severe blow with the outbreak of the Korean War. Acheson saw Soviet fingerprints all over the North Korean invasion and inferred that the USSR might also be willing to launch a surprise invasion in Europe. In September 1950 Acheson proposed at a meeting of French and British foreign ministers the establishment of a transnational European army that would include German troops. Although the U.S. plan for a European Defense Community would ultimately founder in 1954 when the French rejected it, the aim of German rearmament was achieved with the incorporation of a new West German military into NATO in May 1955.[1]

The idea that West Germany must have sound democratic credentials if it were to enjoy the most visible badge of sovereignty, rearmament, influenced the German state's policy on war crimes trials. Obviously, contemporary Germans burdened with allegations of committing Nazi war crimes could not shore up the Free World's bulwark against Soviet Communism. As scholars of postwar Germany have demonstrated, the Federal Republic of Germany employed various strategies to advertise its reinvention as a democracy protective of human rights and freedoms. Philosemitism was one such strategy: through public avowals of exaggeratedly positive attitudes toward Jews, the Germans served notice on the world community of their readiness to regain the status of a sovereign country. Another bona fide display of Germany's rebirth as a democratic state was anti-Communism. Given the penchant after the war to classify both National Socialism and Communism under a common "totalitarianism," the Cold War rhetoric and policies of the fledgling state were outward symbols of West Germany's transformation from authoritarianism to a militant democracy—broadminded, tolerant of diversity, yet prepared to defend the West from a Communist despotism likened in postwar years to Nazi tyranny. As a whole, philosemitism and anti-Communism confirmed West German claims to moral, political, and social legitimacy, and buttressed German assertions of national power at a time when the Federal Republic was in its infancy.[2]

The prosecution of Nazi criminals was enmeshed in this complex skein of geopolitics and the quest for revived national power. Like philosemitism and anti-Communism, the abolition of trials of Nazi-era perpetrators became part of a strategy to regain German sovereignty. One gambit in this strategy was the *Bundestag*'s Christmas Amnesty of 1949, which freed Nazi defendants sentenced to jail terms of six months or less—a decree that affected nearly 700,000 West Germans. On January 1, 1951, it was the Americans' turn: the U.S. occupation authorities amnestied Nazi defendants convicted at Nuremberg with sentences of less than fifteen years. This decree released convicted industrialists like Alfried Krupp and Fritz ter Meer, co-founder of the I. G. Farben slave labor concern at Auschwitz. By February 1951 every industrialist war criminal had been released.

In that same year, the *Bundestag* promulgated the "131 Law," deriving its name from Article 131 of the 1949 German Constitution. Article 131 had assumed responsibility for regulating the "legal condition" of former Nazi bureaucrats, many of whom had fled eastern Germany with the collapse of the Third Reich and were now unemployed in the western part. Others had been expelled from the civil service by denazification procedures for their proven Nazi past; at least one-third (100,000) of the bureaucrats covered by Article 131 had been classified as "compromised" by denazification courts. The 1951 law based on Article 131 was a coup for this group of erstwhile Nazi functionaries. It required federal, state, and local governments to allocate at least 20 percent of revenue paid for salaries to employ the 131 beneficiaries. Although the law excluded former officials classified as "major offenders," in reality few of the "131'ers" (only 1,227) were affected by the restriction. In this fashion, former *Gauleiters* and Security Service commanders who had successfully concealed their past and received mild classifications were able to reenter the West German civil service.[3]

These developments in the early 1950s were both symptoms and causes of a nationwide amnesia that crept over West Germany about its recent genocidal past. In the years that followed, ex-Nazi officials were reabsorbed into German society, many of them into state and local government. At the same time, in those trials of Nazi criminals that did take place, German courts acquitted euthanasia defendants with reference to extrastatutory necessity and a new theory to justify acquittal: the defendant's inability to "exert his conscience" sufficiently to recognize the illegality of his actions. This new defense became another implement in the West German judiciary's toolbox to exonerate euthanasia killers and liquidate the era of Nazi war crimes trials.

Theologians for Acquittal: The Hannover Province Case

The doctrine of extrastatutory necessity, used as a means of acquitting euthanasia doctors, was in temporary eclipse in the Württemberg and Baden cases. In July 1950 the eclipse came to a dramatic end in a series of cases that acquitted entire slates of defendants, many of them deeply involved in murdering disabled patients during the war. In retrospect, it is clear that these trials signify the high-water mark in the history of euthanasia acquittals by German courts.

The verdict in the first of these trials was published in late July 1950 by the state court of Hannover. The defendants were three officials in the provincial government of Hannover: Dr. Ludwig Gessner, former governor of the Hannover province, and two of his departmental chiefs within the public health department, Dr. Georg Andreae and Dr. F. This trio distributed decrees of the Reich government for the province of Hannover, by means of which patients were transported to transit centers before being transferred to killing institutions.

For their roles in this apparatus of destruction, the defendants were charged with aiding and abetting murder and crimes against humanity.

Euthanasia came somewhat late to the former Hannover province. When the Berlin authorities decided during summer 1940 to include the province in the killing program, it had already been implemented for some time in Pomerania, Vienna, Freiburg, Tübingen, Württemberg, Hessen, Saxony, and the Rhine province. Responsibility for inaugurating the program that summer in the Hannover province fell to the three defendants. At the time the provincial government administered the mental institutions at Göttingen (700 patients), Lüneburg (1,100 patients), Osnabrück (700 patients), Wunstorf (500 patients), and Hildesheim (1,200 patients). In addition to these public hospitals, the Hannover province contained religiously affiliated institutions, including one on whose board of directors Dr. Andreae served. In some of these hospitals the provincial government accommodated disabled patients from the Hannover province. Hannover patients were also to be found in institutions outside the borders of the province: forty patients were lodged in the Wittekindshof institution near Oeynhausen, seventy at Tillbeck, fifty at Dorsten, and a handful at Sandhorst near Aurich. The grand total of patients entrusted to the provincial government for care amounted to 7,000; of this number, approximately 4,000 were within the province's own institutions, while 3,000 were housed in contracted institutions. All of these hospitals, provincial, religious, and contracted, would be swept up in the T-4 euthanasia plan.[4]

In July 1940 the first registration forms poured into the Hannover province from Berlin. An accompanying instruction sheet ordered the provincial administrators to have the forms completed and returned to Berlin by August 1, 1940. In February 1941 the first transport lists arrived for the institutions of Göttingen, Lüneburg, and Hildesheim, containing the names of 200 patients. Each of the three institutions had to select 120 patients from the lists of 200 and prepare them for transfer. Transports based upon these lists occurred on March 7 (Lüneburg and Hildesheim) and March 11 (Göttingen). The first transports of 121 patients from Göttingen on March 11, 1941, went to the killing centers of Sonnenstein and Hadamar. The patients dispatched to Sonnenstein were gassed in April 1941, those to Hadamar in June 1941. Other institutions were obliged to transport their hand-chosen patients on April 22 and 24 (Osnabrück) and April 23 and 24 (Wunstorf). A third wave began in July and August 1941. By the end of the first phase in the euthanasia program, 1,669 patients had been transported from provincial and contracted institutions within the Hannover province from a total patient population of 7,000. All transports were conducted, at least in part, by T-4's Gekrat. Even after Hitler had officially ended euthanasia in August 1941, more than twelve transports from Hannover province institutions occurred. As late as February 16,

1943, twenty-five patients were transported from Osnabrück to the Pomeranian institution of Meseritz-Obrawalde. Although the defendants were originally charged with these later transports, as well as a transfer on September 21, 1940, of 185 mentally ill Jews from the Wunstorf institution to an "unknown destination" in Poland, the court refused to consider them in its assessment, thus restricting their liability to the transports between March 1941 and August 1941.[5]

The governor of the Hannover province, defendant Ludwig Gessner, first learned about the euthanasia planned for the region in early summer 1940, shortly before Berlin sent registration forms to the province's mental hospitals. Even prior to this time, he had heard rumors that patients were being destroyed in other parts of the German Reich. In response to his inquiries to Berlin, he received a visit in June 1940 from two members of the Reich Chancellery. These men informed Gessner of plans to implement "humane" euthanasia in the Hannover province. When Gessner inquired about the legal basis for such a measure, he also was told a law had not yet been decreed because Hitler feared its impact on foreign propaganda. Nevertheless, Hitler's full authority stood behind the program. At this point, according to the Hannover state court, Gessner resolved to do everything in his power to thwart the extension of euthanasia to his own province. He contacted his subordinate within the provincial administration for mental hospitals, Dr. Georg Andreae, about compiling a list of reasons describing why euthanasia was impracticable in the Hannover province. Gessner then sent a memorandum to the Reich Minister of the Interior, Dr. Wilhelm Frick, setting forth his objections to the program. In the memo—drafts of which were unavailable to the court, as they were allegedly destroyed in a fire that gutted the state office buildings in 1943[*]— Gessner expounded six reasons for his principled opposition to the killing program:

1. Killing mental patients did not promote the philosophy of the Nazi Party. This occurred much more through hindering the congenitally ill from reproducing by sterilization.

2. The financial burden of caring for the mentally disabled in the Hannover province was bearable, in part because of subsidies from private payors. Thus, the euthanasia measures were not needed from an economic standpoint.

3. Neither diagnoses nor prognoses with respect to mental illness were certain enough to justify the extreme measure of killing patients.

---

[*] Several witnesses at trial vouched for the existence of the memorandum, including Dr. Walter Creutz, already acquitted because of an analogous sabotage plan in the Rhine province.

4. The euthanasia measures could produce internal political problems, especially because the Church and a significant percentage of the population clearly condemned euthanasia.

5. It is unclear how these ideas, once set in motion, might ramify further, and to which group of patients the exterminatory philosophy of euthanasia might next be applied.

6. The euthanasia program would bring large numbers of health-care professionals into a crisis of conscience.

Conspicuously absent from the memo, as the court noted, were ethical and religious reasons for staying the hand of euthanasia. At trial, Gessner explained this absence with reference to the ideological disposition of his audience: only practical considerations would have had any chance of swaying the true believers within the Berlin government.

Quite apart from the ethical issues involved, Gessner's six objections were eminently sensible, but they did not influence the decisions of the Berlin authorities. Although Frick was sympathetic to Gessner's argument, Hitler, who had apparently been informed of the memo's contents, dismissed Gessner's misgivings and insisted on proceeding with euthanasia. Gessner contacted the president of the Hannover province, a man who had boasted he had the ear of Hitler, about persuading the Führer to reconsider the killing program for the province. Neither he nor his successor agreed to approach Hitler about the subject. Gessner's remonstrance with Linden was likewise unsuccessful. In December 1940 and January 1941, the head of the Rhine province system for mental hospitals, Walter Creutz, visited Gessner and Andreae in Hannover. The purpose of the visit was to discuss common strategies they could pursue to minimize the destructive effects of euthanasia. They came to the conclusion that the three governors of the provinces of Hannover, the Rhineland, and Westphalia had to be persuaded to oppose the killing program. This proved to be a pipedream, as we saw, when the governor of the Rhine province, Haake, declined to support the resistance after learning that the Führer backed the operation.[6]

The court accepted the defendants' representations that their efforts to curb the euthanasia program were thwarted at every turn. Departmental chiefs within the Reich Ministry of the Interior reacted with horror when Gessner discussed with them the possibility of sabotage. Gessner sent Andreae to Berlin to inquire further about the legal basis for the operation, where he met with Werner Heyde. Andreae communicated to Heyde his and Gessner's qualms about euthanasia, to which Heyde replied that the system of transit centers would reduce the risk of error. As for the legality of the program, Heyde showed Andreae Hitler's euthanasia decree of September 1, 1939, but reminded him of the confidentiality of the matter. Andreae later relayed these details of his interview with Heyde to Gessner. Together, they agreed there was nothing further they could do to deter the implementation of the program in the Hannover province, because it had the unqualified support of Hitler.

When the first transport lists arrived in Gessner's office in February 1941, Gessner ordered Andreae to summon the directors of the three affected institutions (Göttingen, Lüneburg, and Hildesheim) to Hannover to discuss the situation. Andreae was to impress upon the directors Gessner's oppositional attitude toward the euthanasia plan. At trial, the directors in attendance at this meeting testified that Andreae made such a "depressed impression" on them that they immediately discerned his opposition to the killing program. From the beginning of their discussion, Andreae made clear to them Gessner's critical attitude. One of the directors, a Dr. Gr., expressed his belief that "such a thing could not be desired by the Führer." Andreae thereupon revealed to him the existence of the Hitler decree that Heyde had shown him. He then gave each director a list with the names of 200 patients, from which they were to select 120 for transfer.[7]

In the months after this February 1941 colloquy, Andreae consulted with Dr. Heyde to obtain exemptions from transport for certain patients. He then reduced to writing the categories of patients to be exempted and attached them to a decree signed by Gessner, which was forwarded to Hannover mental institutions along with the second series of transport lists on March 25, 1941. The patients to be exempted were those suffering from war-related injuries, age-related senility, dementia, or infectious illness; patients incapable of train transportation; and, finally, workers essential to the operation of the institution. According to the court, Andreae strove to expand the range of exemptions from transport. In an April 1941 letter to the directors of the province's mental hospitals, he related that not only patients suffering war injuries were to be withheld, but also all army veterans whose frontline military service could be verified (e.g., through possession of the Front Warrior's Cross or evidence of war wounds). When the Berlin authorities caught wind of this new exemption, the T-4 transport office objected, claiming that in the transport lists for the Göttingen institution three patients were deemed front veterans and withheld from transport. The same occurred with other transport lists in the province. In a May 1941 letter to the provincial government, Gekrat asserted that exemptions could not be conducted solely because a patient served at the front; exemption extended only to patients whose mental illness was caused by injuries suffered in the war. The state court of Hannover cited Gekrat's letter as evidence of the thoroughness with which the Berlin offices scrutinized the province's exemptions—proof of the considerable limitations on the defendants' freedom of action.[8]

In response to Gekrat's criticism, Andreae negotiated with Dr. Heyde a new set of criteria for exemption that would be acceptable to Berlin. Andreae set forth the new standards in a letter to the directors of Hannover's mental hospitals:

> The following may be withheld from transport:
>
> 1. War-injured. Under this category fall not only pensioners, but also those who can be proven to suffer from a [war-related] wound. . . .
>
> 2. Participants in the war who have received war decorations, e.g., the Iron Cross 2nd Class, Decoration of the Wounded. This does not include the War-service Cross or the Front Warrior Decoration. Participants in the war who have acquired special decorations or recognition in the field, without being in possession of decorations. The decision I retain personally for myself [Andreae]. . . .
>
> 9. Patients with a sound capacity for work.
>
> 10. Other patients who enjoy special grounds, like capacity for imminent discharge, significant retention of personality, a heartfelt relationship with their relatives or an exceptional hardship for them. I will make the decision about these groups.[9]

By the end of the euthanasia program in the Hannover province in August 1941, the court found that only 231 deaths attributable to euthanasia killing could be proven "with certainty" (3.3 percent of all institutionalized patients in the province). The court, however, believed the actual number of victims was much higher. Its opinion was based on statements made by the Hadamar T-4 doctor, Hans-Bodo Gorgass, who testified that approximately 90 percent of the 1,669 patients transported to killing centers during the first phase were destroyed. If Gorgass's estimate was accurate—and the court believed it was—then the figure had to be adjusted to 1,500 victims, or 21 percent of the province's institutionalized population.[10]

The indictment charged Gessner with crimes relating to his role in signing the order that implemented the killing program in Hannover province (decree of March 25, 1941) and otherwise promoting the transport of patients to their deaths. Similarly, Andreae was charged with relaying the transport order to the directors of the Göttingen, Lüneburg, and Hildesheim institutions and distributing transport lists. He was also accused of issuing a series of orders, which he either drafted or signed himself, that promoted the implementation of transports in the province. (The prosecutor withdrew additional charges for Andreae's participation in the transport of Jewish patients in September 1941 and twenty-five patients from Osnabrück to Meseritz-Obrawalde.) A Dr. F., the medical departmental chief in the provincial government, was charged with overriding the reluctance of one institutional director at the directors' meeting in February 1941, admonishing him that he had no choice but to transport his patients. He was also charged with promoting the killing program by signing transport orders and refusing to agree to exemptions proposed by some of the Hannover institutions.

In its deliberations on the evidence, the state court of Hannover was visibly sympathetic to the defendants. Although it conceded the defendants' role "as intermediate authorities" in transmitting the Berlin decrees to the provincial hospitals, the court insisted the defendants acted independently "only in the cases of exemptions, which, far from advancing the killing program, actually constricted it." The defendants' guiding principle throughout was "to defend the most vulnerable of the patients from transfer to the killing centers." In this respect, the court held, "they succeeded to a large degree." The court sketched the familiar dilemma facing the defendants in 1941: they could either resign their posts and thereby abandon their patients to certain disaster, or they could remain at their posts and rescue as many as possible. Through no fault of their own, the defendants were caught in a "tragic situation," in which either alternative they chose would result in the "severest consequences." In a remarkable passage, the court confessed to the inability of the law to deal adequately with this "conflict of conscience." Nothing in the German Penal Code afforded a solution to this dilemma.[*] The excuse of necessity was inapplicable, because the defendants feared no danger to themselves in the event of their resignation. Berlin would not only have accepted Gessner's withdrawal, but would have encouraged it, because it would have vacated his position for a more ideologically suitable replacement.

Finding the German Penal Code unhelpful on the issue, the court turned to the literature of German jurists like Eberhard Schmidt and Helmut von Weber, who believed an "extrastatutory justificatory ground" existed in such cases. The court quoted Schmidt's statement in a 1949 article: "The state may not charge the commission of an illegal act against a person in a situation of moral distress, who without moral fault is forced to commit an illegal act, the noncommission of which would burden his moral conscience."[11] The opinion notes that the *Schwurgericht* adopted Schmidt's position. Complementary with Schmidt's statement, the court invoked the mystical language of Helmut von Weber, cited two years previously by the state court of Koblenz in the Scheuern case:

> The solution of such conflicts can be found only in the conscience; the individual must come to terms with his God about it. The legal order

---

[*] The doctrine of extrastatutory necessity was not codified in the German Penal Code until 1975.

provides no standard for its solution. On account of this deficit in competence, however, the decision made by someone after earnest examination of his conscience should not be criminalized.

The Hannover court expressed its agreement with this mystagogic interpretation, holding that "whoever therefore decides in such a conflict to remain at his post, at the price of participating in a criminal operation in order to rescue whoever can be rescued, should be excused from criminal wrongdoing."[12]

The prominence of theology in the court's verdict was accentuated by the testimony of Protestant ministers during the trial. Asked about the church's view of the defendants' actions, a Pastor D. of the Inner Mission replied, "[I]t was solely a matter for the individual person . . . to make a decision that he would be able to defend before his conscience and before his God." Pastor D. related the example of the Württemberg monks who, refusing to be a party to euthanasia, quit their posts in protest. The price, however, was a higher mortality rate among the patients of their hospital. In his view, the higher duty was to remain with one's patients and to do everything possible to shield them from harm—a view that Pastor D. claimed the deceased Pastor von Bodelschwingh of the Bethel institution had shared. Such testimony further convinced the *Schwurgericht* "that the actions of the defendants are morally justified." The defendants were therefore acquitted by reason of an "extrastatutory collision of duties that excludes fault."

Much of the court's rationale in the Hannover province case derived from the alleged moral probity of the defendants and the (relatively) low mortality rate among provincial hospitals, for which the defendants were given partial credit. As Dick de Mildt rightly observes, because the documentary record was largely destroyed during the war, much of the evidence favorable to the defendants was obtained from the defendants themselves or from their medical colleagues, some of whom (like Creutz) had faced similar indictments for their participation in the killing program. Each of the defendants had longstanding affiliations with the Nazi Party, to which he owed his professional advancement in the provincial ministry. All three of them were members of the bastion of ideological Nazism, the SS. Despite these allegiances, the court accepted witness accolades about the defendants' decency and professionalism on their face. In de Mildt's words, "such an approach made the exoneration of the former 'euthanasia' accomplices an almost foregone conclusion."[13]

Quite apart from its questionable assessment of the defendants' professional record, the court's treatment of the "collision of duties" defense is conceptually fuzzy. Typically, a collision of duties involves a situation in which an actor confronts two mutually irreconcilable legal duties; by performing one, the actor necessarily violates the other. In its verdict the court does not specify the conflicting duties. The defendants assuredly had a legal duty not to collude in the destruction of their patients; but in what sense did they have a legal duty to rescue as many patients as possible? The example of the Württemberg religious order cited by Pastor D. is illustrative here: the monks refused to collaborate in the killing, but their "distancing" of themselves from the crime violated no law. Although Pastor D. opined that the brothers were derelict in satisfying the demands of the *moral* law—an opinion the court apparently shared—they cannot be accused of violating a *legal* duty, which is precisely what the collision of duties requires. This conceptual obscurity in the court's position may have propelled it into the arms of theology for a solution: where the law afforded no relief, God would.

Expendible Life Revisited: The Andernach Case

The spectacle of euthanasia accomplices leaving German courtrooms as free and morally rehabilitated men reached its peak in the July 1950 retrial of the director and staff doctor of the Andernach mental hospital. The director was Dr. Recktenwald, who had occupied that position at Andernach in the Rhine province since 1934; his subordinate, Dr. Kreitsch, had worked as chief doctor of the Andernach men's ward since 1932. In July 1948, they were both charged and prosecuted for aiding and abetting murder and crimes against humanity for their contributions to Nazi euthanasia. Both were convicted. A year later their appeal finally made it to the appellate court of Koblenz, which reversed their conviction and remanded the case to the state court of Koblenz for retrial. Their acquittal in the second state court proceeding firmly cemented the case within the strain of euthanasia verdicts that not only exonerated their defendants, but transformed them into champions of higher virtue. Further, the case is without peer for its keen interest in the defendants' state of mind during their participation in the Nazi euthanasia program.

Rhineland mental hospitals received their first registration forms from the Reich Ministry of the Interior in June 1940. The secrecy draped over the killing program concealed its true purpose from the institutional directors. As previously noted, many of them assumed the forms were being compiled for statistical reasons; others believed they were designed to register workers for the armaments industry. Recktenwald thought the forms were part of a planned division of mental institutions into nursing homes for more advanced cases and mental hospitals for less severe patients. Kreitsch assumed the forms related to a Reich card index maintained on mental patients. Guided by these erroneous assumptions, doctors throughout the Rhine province, including the defendants, filled out the forms and returned them to Berlin. When the provincial ministry discovered the actual reason for the forms, Walter Creutz took affirmative steps to hinder the extension of euthanasia to the Rhineland.

His efforts, however, miscarried when state governor Haake refused to oppose a measure supported by Hitler. The Berlin authorities demanded that the Andernach and Galkhausen institutions be converted into transit centers for assembling the patients designated for euthanasia. The two facilities were chosen because of their proximity to arteries of transportation: with ready access to the autobahn and the German rail system, T-4 could more easily transfer the doomed patients from the transit centers to the killing institutions. Only the directors of Galkhausen and Andernach were to be initiated into the killing program; all other staff members were to be kept in the dark.[14]

When Creutz informed Recktenwald of the operation, Recktenwald allegedly threatened to quit. Creutz pleaded with him to remain in his job and save as many patients as he could. He then told Recktenwald about Werner Heyde's promise that a subsequent exam could be performed in the transit centers, on the basis of which patients might be exempted from transport. Such exams would afford an opportunity to save patients who would otherwise be killed. Creutz's suasion was effective, in part because he told Recktenwald that Dr. Kreitsch and another doctor had been designated to perform the subsequent exams at Andernach. According to the court, after his conversation with Creutz, Recktenwald spoke with other physicians about his "crisis of conscience." All told him he ought to remain in his job and collaborate with Creutz's sabotage plan. An attorney friend from Wuppertal explained to him that mere participation in the operation to oppose it from within did not fulfill the elements of homicide. These inputs apparently tipped the scales even further in favor of his participation. He agreed to remain director of Andernach in order to work at cross-purposes with the euthanasia program.

On March 29, 1941, Recktenwald attended a meeting of the directors of Rhineland mental hospitals in Grafenberg held by Walter Creutz. At this meeting Creutz unveiled his plan to mount a concerted sabotage of the euthanasia program. After securing the assent of all the participants to his plan, Creutz described how they could minimize the number of transportees by consciously bringing as many patients as possible within the exemptions Berlin had allowed. This could best be accomplished by exploiting the vagueness of Berlin's directives in subsequent examinations conducted in both the home institutions and the transit centers. Creutz urged his listeners to practice chicanery as needed in order to save patients' lives: thus, where appropriate, they were to characterize the condition of patients injured in accidents as being combat-related. Throughout his presentation Creutz emphasized the need for caution, because the Berlin authorities, he warned, would analyze their exemptions and might require Creutz personally to justify them. In the sabotage plan Creutz outlined, Recktenwald and Kreitsch confronted the most "thankless task": they were to devise some way of exempting patients transferred to the Andernach transit center who had been deemed "hopeless" by their home institutions.[15]

For intensity of interest in a defendant's psychological makeup, none of the postwar trials of euthanasia defendants matched the Koblenz court in the Recktenwald case. The court was impressed with Recktenwald's "humanistic education," which supposedly inoculated him against the "realistic utilitarian thinking" of Nazi euthanasia. The court also stressed Recktenwald's pioneering work in modern psychiatric therapy. He was the first director of an institution in the Rhine province to apply "the most modern methods of healing to 'hopeless' cases," including work, insulin, and shock therapy. "It would have been foreign to his life's work," the court maintained, "if he who had dedicated his life to the mentally ill and observed a strict professional ethos, should now violate all his sacred principles and his life's work by killing the very patients so dear to him." Recktenwald had never flinched from expressing his critical attitude toward the euthanasia program, an attitude he shared not only with his friends and most intimate colleagues, but with T-4 potentates like Hefelmann, von Hegener, Heyde, and Paul Nitsche. These Nazi worthies were aware of Recktenwald's position and complained about it. Heyde and some of his colleagues met in Düsseldorf to reexamine some of the patients Recktenwald had exempted from transport.

As for Dr. Kreitsch, the court described him as enjoying the "complete faith" of Recktenwald. Creutz regarded him as a staunch opponent of euthanasia, and for this reason appointed him to conduct the subsequent examinations of patients at Andernach. Based on his known antipathy for the killing program, Kreitsch was inserted as a monkey wrench to disrupt the smooth functioning of the operation. His task was to examine the patients earmarked for killing by the Berlin expert evaluators and to propose to Dr. Recktenwald possibilities for their exemption. One witness testified that Kreitsch had confided in him his uncompromising rejection of euthanasia, referring to it as a "disgrace."[16]

In the eyes of the court, the heart of the prosecution's case against Recktenwald and Kreitsch was their collaboration with the transport of patients from Andernach to Hadamar in 1941. Between May 9 and July 11, 1941, some 517 patients were sent from their home institutions in the Rhine province to the transit center at Andernach. After July 11 until the cessation of euthanasia in August 1941, another 352 transportees arrived there from the same home institutions. Upon arrival at Andernach, Recktenwald examined each patient as well as the accompanying medical records. Although he had been sent the "worst material," he and Kreitsch subjected the patients to work therapy treatment, managing in some cases to enable the patient to perform "productive work," which Recktenwald then used as a ground for exemption.

"This intensive treatment of the transferred patients," the court remarked, "already violated Berlin's orders, because Berlin had permitted only a subsequent exam in the transit center, not treatment of the patients removed there." Of the 517 patients transferred to Andernach before July 11, Recktenwald and Kreitsch exempted 42 of them from transport to Hadamar. The court was convinced that several of these exemptions were patent acts of sabotage. It reconstructed the final lists of the numbers of the disabled later transferred to Hadamar, arriving at a figure of 447 patients ultimately killed in Hadamar after transport from Andernach. Because of Hitler's order in late August 1941 to stop the killing program, the additional 352 patients transferred to Andernach after July 11 were spared killing at Hadamar. The court added this figure to the 42 patients exempted by the defendants (including 26 who had died in the meantime of natural causes) to reach a grand total of 420 patients rescued by them from the euthanasia program, or 50 percent of the patients originally earmarked for killing.[17]

We may question the court's fuzzy math in arriving at this percentage, but there is no disputing the court's admiration for the defendants' achievement—especially as compared with other provincial German health systems during the war. As the Düsseldorf court had done in the Creutz trial, the Koblenz court cited the example of Professor Gu., the head of the Vienna health system, who had refused in 1940 to collaborate in the killing program and was replaced with a more pliable representative. The result was the extermination of one-half of Vienna's disabled patients. One witness, the chief doctor at the Bethel institution, testified that the staffs of two institutions, Stettin and Zwiefalten, had refused to complete the T-4 registration forms. Consequently, teams of SS doctors arrived at the hospitals to perform their own examinations on the patients, resulting in their near total destruction. Comparison with the other Rhine province transit center, Galkhausen, also accrued to Recktenwald's credit. Of the 542 patients transported to Galkhausen, the medical staff exempted 24 and discharged 2—figures that fall short of Andernach, which had exempted 37 of the 517 patients and discharged 5. At trial, witnesses—all of them doctors—declared that to abandon the patients and miss the opportunity to save at least some of them would have been an act of desertion.

In assessing the defendants' culpability in furthering the criminal aims of T-4, the court found no evidence that the defendants promoted the killing program through their actions. They did not select patients for transport to Andernach; this had been done chiefly by the Berlin commission under Professor Paul Nitsche. The subsequent examinations undertaken by the defendants did not facilitate the program, but rather stymied it by exempting some patients who would have been transported to their deaths but for the exams. The critical issue, however, was the defendants' role in transporting patients *not* considered suitable for exemption. These non-exemptions, the court held, did not promote the euthanasia program, because they involved the most "hopeless" cases; their exemption would have aroused the suspicion of the Berlin authorities, who would surely have sent their own commission to Andernach to examine and transfer the patients to Hadamar. Had Recktenwald exempted all the patients transported to Andernach, regardless of their condition, he would have endangered Creutz's sabotage plan and Berlin would have recognized immediately what Creutz and his fellow saboteurs were doing. Far from promoting Berlin's design, Recktenwald made extraordinary contributions to foil it, especially by applying his modern therapeutic measures to improve the conditions of some severely ill patients to the point where he could justify their exemption. This was an important point for the court: Recktenwald managed to rescue patients whom his co-conspirators in the sabotage plan "had not dared to retain." For this reason, Recktenwald and Kreitsch's role in the province-wide sabotage plan was "essential" and "decisive."[18]

Recktenwald and Kreitsch were finally acquitted on the basis of a collision of duties. On the one hand, they had the legal duty "to use their medical arts for the healing of their patients to the best of their ability"; this duty could be satisfied only "if they participated in the operation and accepted the necessity of surrendering the unsavable." On the other hand, they had a legal duty to abstain from participation in the killing of patients. This second duty, in the view of the court's *Schwurgericht*, was subordinate to the overriding duty to save patients. To hold the defendants criminally liable for aiding and abetting murder under these circumstances would violate the "natural sense of justice" (*natürliches Rechtsempfinden*). Insofar as the court restricted its rationale for acquittal to the collision of duties, its decision was defensible. In a strange obiter dictum, however, the court also justified its acquittal of the defendants with reference to preserving the "higher legal good"—that is, the lives of the healthier patients—by sacrificing the lesser good—that is, the lives of the "hopeless" cases. Such a sacrifice, the court stated, "is not illegal"; it is comparable to the case of a doctor aborting the life of a fetus (the lesser legal good) to save the life of the mother (the higher good). By injecting this reflection into its verdict, the court suggested that the value of human lives could be measured against each other, and one group legally proclaimed superior to the other. Such a style of thought, as noted in connection with the Creutz trial, is redolent of the Nazis' own hierarchy of valuable and less valuable groups of human life. It suggests that, however subtle or unconscious, the judges shared an affinity with the Nazi thought world that affected their deliberations on the defendants' complicity in murder.

The diametrical interpretations of the factual record in the Andernach case underscores the power of nonlegal factors to shape and even determine the outcomes of trials. Recktenwald and Kreitsch emerged from the Koblenz courtroom not only assoiled of all wrongdoing, but as moral heroes. That this interpretation was not the only one deducible from the evidence is demonstrated by the defendants' conviction in the first trial. With reference to the same factual record, the Koblenz court in the first proceeding arrived at a dramatically different conclusion:

> [The defendants] consciously let themselves become engaged in the murderous undertaking of the euthanasia program. They willingly, if reluctantly, accepted the role designed for them . . . and by and large performed it as expected of them. By doing so they made an essential contribution to the euthanasia program and were links in the chain which runs from the "Führer Chancellery" and the Reich Ministry of the Interior down to the gas chamber and the crematorium in Hadamar.[19]

In the theoretical discourse of Critical Legal Studies, such a dissonance among interpretations of the same evidentiary record is called "flipability." The term is a playful but incisive critique of the indeterminacy of legal "facts" and doctrines—an idea that challenges at its root the very idea of value-free adjudication.[20] The "flipability" of legal decisions points to the role of non-formalistic factors in legal reasoning, such as social, economic, or political considerations that often function as the de facto motors driving judicial process. The force of these extra-juridical factors may operate consciously or unconsciously within the minds of judges, and in different degrees of intensity at various times. Again, it cannot be stressed enough that the German judges in these cases were steeped in a cultural milieu thirsting for a break with the recent National Socialist past, and yearning for a fresh start at a renewed German nationhood.

Leniency and the True Believer: The Eglfing-Haar Case

In the 1947 U.S. Doctors' Trial, a schoolteacher named Ludwig Lehner testified about his visit to the Eglfing-Haar mental hospital during the war. In the course of his visit, the institution's director, Dr. Hermann Pfannmüller, escorted him to the children's ward. Along the way, Pfannmüller's language was peppered with references to "life unworthy of life." Arriving in the ward, he pulled a child out of his bed and showed him to the onlookers. "While he exhibited the child like a dead rabbit," Lehner testified, "he stated with the air of an expert and a cynical grin: 'With this one it will only be two or three more days.' The image of the fat grinning man, in his pudgy hand the whimpering skeleton, surrounded by the other starving children, I can never forget."[21]

In March 1951 it was Pfannmüller's turn to stand before the bar of justice, charged with murder for his role in transporting patients to killing centers and for the deaths of children in the Eglfing-Haar children's ward. At the time of his trial, Pfannmüller was in his mid-sixties, and thus belonged to the cohort of Nazi doctors subjected to the traumas and privations of World War I. Unlike most of the doctors we have considered, who typically joined the Nazi Party after 1933 for career-related reasons, he was an "old fighter" (*alter Kämpfer*) who had joined the party in the early 1920s. His reputation as a devoted Nazi and medical expert earned him appointment to the Office for Technology, in which he was tasked with medically examining the "talented" children of soldiers killed in action in order to determine whether they were genetically "worthy" of preferential investment by the office. The Nazi Party recognized his skills by using him as an expert lecturer in public meetings. The aim of his lectures was to "instruct" the German population on the contents of the recently promulgated Hereditary Health Law from the perspective of "racial-political" and "hereditary-medical" concerns.[22]

At trial Pfannmüller told the court he had become involved in the euthanasia question after the death of his father. The elder Pfannmüller suffered from a chronic kidney disorder that caused him terrible pain until he received a lethal injection from his attending physician. This experience was seared into the junior Pfannmüller's mind, as were his experiences during the Great War as a doctor in the psychiatric hospital in Homburg, where he witnessed the deaths of patients "like flies" from malnutrition "under the most horrifying conditions." According to Pfannmüller, the highest mortality rate affected the "working patients," while the incurable non-working patients, the "human corpses," survived. After the war, still affected by his experiences, he delved into the literature on euthanasia, especially the work of Alfred Hoche and Karl Binding. This work left a lasting impression on Pfannmüller's thought. He even had occasion to meet Hoche during a congress in Freiburg in 1922. In this fashion, as related in his own words, he became a firm adherent of euthanasia.

The Bavarian government appointed Pfannmüller director of the mental institution of Eglfing-Haar in 1938, a position he held until the end of the war. In November 1939 he submitted a report to the public insurance examining board regarding the maintenance of "life unworthy of life" in state hospitals. He voiced his opinion on the need to "eradicate" such patients with lapidary clarity:

> As a confessionally unattached and fervent National Socialist director of
> a mental hospital, I feel myself obligated to demonstrate an actual
> conservation measure that is suitable to influence favorably the economic
> standing of the institutions. In this position, I believe it appropriate to
> refer clearly to the need for us doctors to grasp the importance of eradicat-
> ing life unworthy of life. Those unfortunate patients who live only a

shadow life of a normal human being, who have become perfectly useless for social membership in the human community by virtue of their illness, whose existence is to themselves, their relatives, and their surroundings a torment and a burden, must be subjected to rigorous eradication.

Pfannmüller continued:

Precisely these days, in which the heaviest sacrifice of blood and life is demanded of our most valuable men, teach us emphatically that it should not be possible on economic grounds to fill institutions with living corpses for the sake of a high principle of medical care that is no longer relevant. For me it is unimaginable that the best, blooming youth die at the front while incorrigible asocials and irresponsible antisocials have a secure existence in our institutions.

The "high principle of medical care" Pfannmüller referred to is the physician's devotion to the well-being of the patient, as enjoined by the Hippocratic oath.

Sometime in summer 1940 he attended a meeting in Berlin to discuss the overcrowding in German mental institutions and ways to provide health care to patients amenable to treatment. In attendance were Philipp Bouhler, Reich Health Leader Leonardo Conti, Viktor Brack, Karl Brandt, and Herbert Linden. At this meeting, according to Pfannmüller, Bouhler revealed that all institutionalized patients were to be medically evaluated in order to separate the incurable patients from those responsive to treatment. The incurables would ultimately be accommodated in facilities specially equipped for their care. For this purpose, registration forms would be distributed to all institutions, which were to be filled out and returned to the Reich Cooperative for State Hospitals and Nursing Homes in Berlin. Here, expert commissions would review the forms to determine whether the patient should be transported to the special facility.

At Eglfing-Haar, Pfannmüller distributed the forms to his staff doctors and explained to them the guidelines for filling them out. He also swore them to the strictest secrecy. After his doctors had completed the forms and returned them to Pfannmüller, he examined the patients himself to guarantee the accuracy of the report. He then sent the forms with his signature to Berlin. In September 1940 Berlin notified him that a certain number of incurable patients were to be transported on orders of the Reich Defense Commissar. He was to prepare the patients whose names appeared on the transport list for a trip lasting several hours. Gekrat in Berlin would contact him with dates for picking up these patients. The court could not determine whether Pfannmüller knew of the true purpose behind the first transport, the patients of which were murdered almost without exception. It was proven, however, that after the first transport had left, Bouhler visited him at Eglfing-Haar and showed him

Hitler's decree of September 1, 1939, explaining that the selected patients were to receive a "mercy death." Despite Bouhler's disclosure, Pfannmüller continued to prepare his patients for transfer to the killing centers at Grafeneck and Hartheim. Nearly all were killed. The last transport before the cessation of the official killing program in August left Eglfing-Haar in June 1941.[23]

According to the court, Pfannmüller was aware that at least 918 of the patients who left Eglfing-Haar were being transported to their deaths. Exact figures regarding how many of these transportees were actually killed were unavailable, because Pfannmüller incinerated the institution's records before the arrival of U.S. troops.

In addition to his complicity in sending patients to the killing centers, Pfannmüller was charged with collaborating in the destruction of handicapped children. In October 1941 he installed a children's ward at Eglfing-Haar to receive the Reich Committee children, that is, children designated for killing by T-4's Reich Committee for the Scientific Registration of Severe Hereditary Ailments. The determination was made by three T-4 evaluators, who conveyed their assessment to the child's home institution. The designated children were either killed on the spot or transferred to a children's ward designed, like Pfannmüller's, for the express purpose of killing them. The ward at Eglfing-Haar accommodated on average between fifty and sixty children. When the "treatment authorization" arrived from Berlin, Pfannmüller examined the affected children; if he was satisfied that the child was incurable, and thus a specimen of "life unworthy of life," he authorized his staff doctor to euthanize the child. From October 1941 until late April 1945 at least 120 children, ranging in ages from a few months to sixteen years, were killed with overdoses of luminal (usually sprinkled in their food) or with injections of morphine and scopolamine. Death typically occurred within three days, although some patients suffered longer death throes, dying of acute pneumonia after three weeks. The advantage of these forms of killing, by Pfannmüller's own admission, resided in their close resemblance to natural causes of death—a charade important to the success of the operation, because it hoodwinked parents who visited their children on a regular basis.

Around the time that the "special treatment" was administered, the parents or relatives were notified that their child was incurably ill. A short time later, a letter arrived informing them their child had died and the burial already concluded. In no cases were bodies returned to the next of kin. The letters often cited pneumonia or tuberculosis as causes of death. On Pfannmüller's orders the corpses of the dead children were dissected and their brains sent to a research center in Berlin, where they were processed into cross sections. In at least two cases involving severely deformed children, Pfannmüller himself gave the lethal injections.

Pfannmüller's defense insisted that euthanasia was justifiable on ethical and moral grounds. Euthanasia might be debated and discussed, as it had been for centuries, but attaching criminal liability to its practitioners was inadmissible. As he had at the U.S. Doctors' Trial, he struck the pose of a humanitarian committed to the welfare of his patients. Although the Munich state court refused to accept these arguments as a basis for acquittal, it treated Pfannmüller with kid gloves he hardly deserved. First, in the face of evidence that showed Pfannmüller's calloused attitude toward the mentally disabled, the court characterized him as an accomplice, not a perpetrator, because he "by no means had the *animus auctoris* [intent to act for one's own purposes]," and "stood outside the actual circle of those who drove forward these mass killings of mental patients."[*] Second, Pfannmüller could be convicted only of aiding and abetting manslaughter, not murder, because he was unaware "of those circumstances of the crime which made the killing of the transported patients either malicious or cruel" as required by the German law of murder. Acknowledging that the overarching euthanasia program was a "malicious and cruel procedure," the court refused to characterize Pfannmüller's role in it with the same language. The court conceded that he had been aware the patients and their relatives were being deceived about the goals of the transports, but held it was unproven that he had been personally aware of "the methods of selection, the fundamentals according to which the selections were made, and the entire tactics of deception outside his own institution." Apparently, in the eyes of this court, such knowledge was essential to finding him guilty of aiding and abetting murder for organizing transports of his own patients to their deaths. All that could be proven was that he aided and abetted a form of killing that fell short of legal murder—namely, manslaughter (*Totschlag*). Third, the court inexplicably denied that the destruction of disabled children in the Eglfing-Haar ward amounted to murder, because none of the conditions for murder specified by section 211 were present: the killings were not base, malicious, or cruel. In fact, the court accepted Pfannmüller's self-portrayal as an advocate of euthanasia for "humane" motives.[24]

Finally, the Munich state court paid Pfannmüller the courtesy of denying any wrongdoing for his role in starving patients to death through a premeditated system of reduced food rations. Because of dislocations caused by the war, the Bavarian Interior Ministry published an order on November 30, 1942, instructing the directors of Bavarian mental hospitals to provide a "special

---

[*] The court's view of Pfannmüller stands in stark contrast with Viktor Brack's testimony at the Doctors' Trial, where Brack identified Pfannmüller as an important cog in the euthanasia machine.

ration" (*Sonderkost*) for their non-working patients. This special ration was to be stripped of fat and meat, and consisted of little more than boiled vegetables and water. The court timidly referred to the special ration as a means of transferring essential nutriment from non-working to working patients. In fact, at the conference of directors that preceded publication of the November decree, Dr. Valentin Faltlhauser, director of the Kaufbeuren mental hospital, declared that after cancellation of the formal euthanasia program in August 1941, eliminating patients could now be done by gradually starving them to death. The *Sonderkost* was Faltlhauser's brainchild, and he left no question that it was intended to cause the patient's death within three months.[25] Not surprisingly, Pfannmüller offered a more benign interpretation of the special ration: it was designed only to guarantee the working patients an extra portion to compensate for their higher expenditure of calories, not to cause the deaths of non-working patients through starvation. He claimed that he had personally instructed his chief cook to supplement the *Sonderkost* with meat and fat, and that he had even sampled it on several occasions. The court accepted Pfannmüller's account without demur, calling the *Sonderkost* "meager fare," but denying that it caused malnourishment, because the addition of fat in the preparation furnished the necessary amount of protein. Because Pfannmüller's aim with the *Sonderkost* was not to starve bedridden patients, the court acquitted him of all deaths associated with it.

Notwithstanding his documented collaboration in the murders of patients, the Munich court convicted Pfannmüller of aiding and abetting manslaughter. In considering his punishment, the court reprised Pfannmüller's self-portrait as a humanitarian—and did so in the cadences of social Darwinism: "On the basis of his experiences within his own family and during his time as a doctor in mental hospitals in the First World War, he became convinced that the killing of incurable patients was a deliverance for them. *It was a measure tantamount to a natural selection process*" (emphasis added). Moreover, the court considered it a factor in mitigation that Pfannmüller, like all Germans under Nazism, was no doubt influenced through war propaganda to assign a reduced moral value to human life, thus transmuting the act of killing into something trivial. In view of these mitigating factors, as well as his grave illness and advanced age, he was sentenced to a five-year prison term. This sentence was further whittled down to two years after crediting him with time already served.

The Pfannmüller case, although not acquitting its defendant outright, was nonetheless a travesty of justice in the postwar era. The case indicated the German judiciary's willingness not only to treat egregious offenders as accomplices (a trend emerging already in the late 1940s), but to deny altogether that their actions were murder under German criminal law. The novelty of the Pfannmüller case, as German expert on Nazi criminality Willi Dressen has asserted, is its denial of the element of "malice" (*Heimtücke*)* in its assessment of euthanasia killing. As we have seen in our analysis of the German cases, courts rarely found that defendants acted out of "base motives." In most of the trials we have examined, however, German courts upheld the existence of malice in order to find defendants guilty of aiding and abetting murder. The Pfannmüller case changed the complexion of this assessment. In the ensuing years covered by our study, no euthanasia doctors would be convicted by West German courts of murder. Pfannmüller's trial was a decisive step down this path toward leniency and acquittal.

THE TURN OF THE SCREW: THE "EXERTION OF CONSCIENCE" CASES

On March 18, 1952, the West German Supreme Court issued a verdict destined to have a profound impact on the adjudication of euthanasia trials thereafter. The High Court held that a defendant could be punished for a criminal act only if he or she was capable of conforming to the law's requirements. When perpetrators, after maximum exertions of their understanding, could not reconcile the demands of the law with their own conscience, no criminal liability attached if they chose to follow their conscience in violation of the law—so long as they acted "conscientiously."[26]

The Supreme Court's holding would offer regional courts fresh opportunities to acquit euthanasia defendants in the years after 1952. A trio of cases decided in December 1953 premised their acquittals on this "exertion of conscience" doctrine. An analysis of the opinions reveals that, as in the extrastatutory necessity/collision of duties cases, the outcomes of these trials were conditioned less by the neutral application of legal theory to the facts than by the court's preexisting will to acquit.

The Conscientious Childkiller: The Sachsenberg Case

Among the first cases to acquit a euthanasia defendant on the basis of an "exertion of conscience" defense was that of Dr. Alfred Leu, a physician at the Sachsenberg psychiatric hospital near Schwerin (in the province of Mecklenburg) where he had worked from 1929 until April 1945. In his first trial in October 1951, Leu was charged with complicity in the murders of adults and

---

* *Malice* under German law means that a defendant has killed or collaborated in killing in a manner that exploits the vulnerability of the victim. Secretly lacing a victim's food with poison, for example, qualified as a "malicious" killing in the earlier cases.

children at the Sachsenberg institution. His defense was the classic sabotage argument: he collaborated in the killings only in order to minimize the damage and save as many people as possible. Had he resigned his post, a more zealous doctor would have replaced him, resulting in the deaths of still more patients. The state court of Cologne accepted this argument, holding that it would be a miscarriage of justice to convict a defendant ensnared like Leu in a "tragic predicament." Leu was acquitted and his case appealed to the German Supreme Court, which reversed and remanded it for retrial.

In its findings of fact on retrial, the Cologne state court found that Leu filled out the first shipments of registration forms without knowledge of their purpose. Not until late 1940 or early 1941 did he learn of the euthanasia program. With the discovery, he realized that open refusal to complete the forms would invite a visit from a commission of SS doctors whose ideological zeal would ensure that two-thirds or more of his patients would be registered for the killing program. He resolved to continue filling out the forms in order to accentuate, where possible, his patients' capacity for work. In this way, he could bend and distort his reports to save patients who otherwise would fall prey to the assessments of an SS physician. He felt obligated by his "medical conscience" to contribute to the destruction of hopeless terminal cases so as to save patients still amenable to therapy. This was the strategy Leu followed henceforth, the court found. On one occasion in early 1941, Leu added the names of three newly arrived patients to a transport list. They, along with a collection of patients from Leu's nursing station, were taken to the killing center at Bernburg and gassed.[27]

In summer 1941 the military confiscated the Lewenberg mental institution for use as a military reserve hospital. Lewenberg was the site of a children's ward designed to euthanize handicapped youngsters. With the conversion of Lewenberg into a military hospital, the 280 patients of its children's ward were sent to Sachsenberg, where they were accommodated in Leu's empty nursing station. (His station had been depopulated by the transports to Bernburg.) Sachsenberg's director, Dr. Fischer, appointed Leu head of the new children's ward and reported the appointment to the Reich Ministry of the Interior. In September 1941 the Reich Chancellery summoned Leu to a meeting in Berlin with the directors of the Reich Committee, Drs. Hefelmann and von Hegener. During this meeting the committee's directors told Leu that the new ward in Sachsenberg under his supervision would undertake the destruction of disabled children. Leu claimed at trial that he declined his participation in the planned measures, a refusal that Hefelmann and von Hegener accepted. This notwithstanding, a few weeks later "treatment authorizations" arrived at Sachsenberg from the Reich Committee, identifying 180 patients in Leu's children's ward for euthanasia. The Reich Committee's chief medical experts had chosen these patients based on forms submitted to them by the former head of the ward at Lewenberg.

In a subsequent meeting with Hefelmann and von Hegener, Leu was told he could exempt 5 percent of the children from transport without any further justification. They also permitted him to withhold other children from transfer, so long as he could support the exemption in writing to the Reich Committee in accordance with the applicable guidelines (i.e., the educability of the exempted child). Returning to Schwerin, Leu decided to assume responsibility for the killing program in the ward. Leu claimed he knew the killing program was wrong, even if it was sanctioned by a valid law; on the other hand, cooperating with it was the only way to rescue some of the children from death. The court sketched Leu's dilemma as a prototypical collision of duties: "The defendant stood before a choice: either to distance himself from the killing and refuse the order given by Berlin, thereby abandoning two-thirds of his department to destruction; or to carry out the extermination orders, thereby participating in the deaths of some children in order to rescue a considerable number of other patients who would otherwise be killed." Leu felt compelled by his conscience to "sabotage the goals of the Reich Committee and the euthanasia program it sponsored." He thus believed it was his duty to collude in the destruction of a "limited" number of patients to save others.[28]

Having made his decision, Leu spoke with the Sachsenberg director, Dr. Fischer, about detailing experienced nurses to the operation. Leu chose the four nurses himself, whom he initiated into the plan to kill "incurable" children on orders from Berlin. The children would be dispatched with excessive dosages of veronal and luminal. Afterward, he swore each of the nurses to silence about the program. When the first lists of patients arrived from Berlin, they contained the names of 180 children. The court found that Leu exceeded the Reich Committee's guidelines in exempting 110 children from euthanasia. The remaining 70, described by one witness as being in a "horrible" physical state, were killed in the ward.

In the striking incongruity between the adverse evidence of criminal wrongdoing and the final verdict of acquittal, the Leu case may be unique among German euthanasia trials. Statements by Leu in support of the euthanasia program were abundantly documented. Several witnesses testified that Leu had professed to them his unwavering commitment to euthanasia. Other witnesses stepped forward to incriminate Leu, claiming that they personally witnessed unaccountable deaths in the departments under his supervision. These witnesses attested to their beliefs at the time that Leu had caused the patients' deaths through overdoses of narcotics. Their belief rested on the observed fact that patients who seemed perfectly healthy were dead only days later. A staff doctor at Sachsenberg, a Dr. Br., described events in Leu's stations that convinced him the defendant was murdering his patients with overdoses. Dr. Br. had been so upset by these occurrences that he spoke of the Sachsenberg facility as a "murder institution." He believed Leu continued to kill adult patients after the children's operation had been set in motion. Another witness claimed Leu had killed between 200 and 300 adults at Sachsenberg with overdoses of veronal—a charge the witness had leveled against Leu sometime in 1941. Leu had denied the charge at the time but characterized euthanasia of incurable patients as a "welcome measure." During their meeting with the Berlin authorities, Leu denounced this witness and Dr. Br. to the Reich Committee. Hefelmann and von Hegener responded by praising Leu as a "great guy" who "acted entirely in accordance with the wishes of the Reich Committee."

Leu's defense against these allegations during his trial was predictable: he had projected the appearance of being an adherent of euthanasia in order to avoid suspicion. Had he gone public with his inward opposition to it, his reports to the Reich Committee would have been analyzed with a fine-tooth comb, thus jeopardizing his sabotage scheme. To the charges that adult patients were killed with overdoses of narcotics, Leu countered that the witnesses had misinterpreted their brief glimpse of patients in a drug-induced deep sleep, mistaking them for patients on the verge of death. Leu denied authorizing the killing of adults with excessive dosages of veronal or luminal. The narcotics he administered were all in the medically prescribed doses to alleviate chronic motor restlessness. Finding the witness testimony credible, the lay assessors nonetheless refused to accept it. According to the assessors, the witnesses were not in a position to observe and report accurately on occurrences in Leu's station. They knew nothing about the patients' medical histories or the narcotics prescribed for them; they made no inquiries of the nursing staff nor ascertained the actual cause of death through autopsy. Fatal to the acceptance of their testimony was the witnesses' inability to cite a single verifiable case in which drug overdoses caused by Leu resulted in a patient's death. To the witnesses' adamant claim that healthy patients who entered Leu's station were seen shortly thereafter in a coma-like state followed by reports of their deaths, the court replied that they may not have seen what they thought they saw. The patients' conditions might have been caused by liberal doses of narcotics given to suppress their violently restless motor activity, as Leu had claimed. Their subsequent deaths may have ensued as a result of prolonged sleep that weakened the patients through inactivity and malnutrition, making them more susceptible to illness. The court accepted this improbable scenario as "unrefuted" against Leu.[29]

Acquitting Leu of the charge of killing adults at Sachsenberg, the court next turned to the children's ward killings. Here, the court appeared to accept Leu's representation of sabotage in toto. Leu, the court held, had participated in euthanasia only to save as many patients as possible. He could not, however, have carried off the deception unless he conveyed the impression of being an ardent supporter of euthanasia. This could be accomplished only by characterizing some of the children in the forms as incurable and incapable of work. Although this effectively sealed the fates of these children, any other characterization would have excited Berlin's attention, and his sabotage plan would have been betrayed. He would then have been dismissed from his position and a more ideologically committed doctor appointed to succeed him. He sacrificed children "who were, from a psychological standpoint, completely below the zero line" in order to rescue other patients. Despite numerous witnesses who testified that Leu was a true believer in loyal service to the killing program, the court accepted Leu's claim that he had to transmit this impression to everyone around him lest his opposition plan be foiled. A lack of collegial solidarity in Sachsenberg, moreover, may have deterred Leu from sharing his mind with his colleagues. In sum, the court endorsed Leu's defense that his "actual inner attitude" toward euthanasia was critical and oppositional, not supportive.

With respect to the undisputed killings in the children's ward, the court refused to consider them base or malicious. Respected scholars like Binding and Hoche had debated for decades the permissibility of "delivering from their vegetative existence" severely ill patients. Leu was aware of this debate, and his ideas about euthanasia reflected the academically serious—and non-reprehensible—thoughts of sober men. He was also familiar with the results of the Melzer survey conducted in the early 1920s, indicating that many parents advocated the "mercy killing" of their severely handicapped children on humanitarian grounds. Leu's attitude toward the deaths of these incurable patients was thus not "base" as defined under the German law of murder. Neither was it malicious, because Leu did not exploit the victims' vulnerability in a reprehensible manner. Because Leu's involvement in the killings did not constitute murder, the only charge he faced was the lesser included offense of manslaughter.[30]

At this point in its verdict, the court could have simply acquitted Leu on the basis of a collision of duties. It had already set forth, albeit implausibly, a fact pattern that led to such an interpretation. Instead, the court introduced a new exculpatory rationale into euthanasia adjudication—the "exertion of conscience" defense. The court began by citing the "landmark" decision of the German Supreme Court from March 1952, in which the High Court held a criminal action punishable only if the defendant was able to conform to the demands of the law. At the same time, the defendant had the duty to "exert his conscience" in a degree commensurate with his life experience and professional training in determining whether a contemplated action was legal. Conversely, if an actor faced with a conflict between the demands of the law and the demands of his conscience chose to follow his conscience, then he could not be held criminally liable. His immunity to criminal guilt, however, assumed that "he has exerted the intellectual and moral powers of his conscience in order to recognize what is right or wrong, and acts in accordance with this insight." This exertion of conscience defense became the crux of Leu's acquittal. The law required Leu to refrain from killing; yet, his conscience commanded him to participate outwardly in it for the purpose of rescuing patients. Leu had "exerted his conscience" to its utmost extent and felt that he had to follow its insistent voice. On this ground, Leu was exonerated of all criminal charges related to the deaths of children in the Sachsenberg ward.[31]

From both a legal and a moral perspective, the Leu verdict may be the most extraordinary of the postwar euthanasia trials. In contrast with some of the other defendants acquitted after 1947 (such as Creutz and Recktenwald), Leu had not only transferred patients to their deaths in the killing centers but had organized and administered euthanasia *with his own hands*. Yet, the Leu decision provided West German courts with yet another rationale for acquitting medical killers.

Doing Away With the Monsters: The Uchtspringe Case

At roughly the same time as the Cologne court freed Alfred Leu, the state court of Göttingen applied a similar rationale to the cases of two doctors implicated in euthanasia killings, Gerhard Wenzel and Hildegard Wesse. Wenzel was accused of either personally administering or authorizing nursing staff to poison 130 children during his tenure from June 1941 to August 1943 as director of the children's ward at the Uchtspringe mental hospital (near Magdeburg). His codefendant was his successor in the directorship of the children's ward, Dr. Hildegard Wesse (wife of the ill-starred T-4 doctor Hermann Wesse), charged like Wenzel with killing approximately sixty disabled children with overdoses of morphine, but also with giving lethal injections to thirty female patients.

In May 1941, Wenzel was serving as head doctor on a Luftwaffe field air base in France, when he was summoned to the KdF in Berlin. On arrival he was received by Hefelmann, von Hegener, and the director of the Uchtspringe mental hospital, a Dr. B. During their discussion, Wenzel was asked about his attitude toward the euthanasia of "fully idiotic children." He replied that these "life forms" were an "onerous psychological burden" for their doctors, nursing personnel, and their families. As a doctor at Uchtspringe, Wenzel was often approached by parents requesting that he "deliver" their children from suffering. Based on these experiences, he considered euthanasia an ethically defensible solution to incurable suffering, provided that it was regulated by a legal procedure. Hefelmann replied that a legal basis for euthanasia had been established, at which point he read the Hitler order and the draft of a euthanasia law to Wenzel. For "war-related reasons" the law was unpublished, although, Hefelmann assured him, it was known within the state service. Hefelmann outlined the work of the Reich Committee, then informed Wenzel he was being declared "indispensable" and reassigned to the children's ward in Uchtspringe. As the ward's director, he would receive transports of mentally handicapped children whom he was to observe and later report on to the Reich Committee. The report would summarize the patient's condition with special attention to their responsiveness to treatment. The incurable children were to be killed, and doubtful cases would be reserved for further observation or discharged. Wenzel accepted the job offered him and returned to his unit in France.[32]

A few weeks later, he reported to Uchtspringe's children's ward, which housed between 350 and 400 children in four separate buildings. He remained there (with one interruption in his service) until August 1943, when he tendered his resignation. During his time as director of the ward, the court estimated he had prepared 1,000 to 2,000 reports, characterizing eighty children as incurable. The euphemistically worded "authorizations for treatment" arrived from Berlin for these children. Wenzel understood the word "treatment" in the Berlin authorizations to mean "killing." He passed on the authorization to the station nurse, who gave the children overdoses of luminal in their soup or milk in accordance with Wenzel's instructions. These overdoses caused the patients' death within a few hours. Sometimes Wenzel ordered the ward nurse to inject the children with morphine; on occasion he injected them himself. He concocted false causes of death in the notices sent to the children's parents, partly because euthanasia was top-secret, partly to spare their feelings.

Wenzel's defense at trial was that he had believed at the time in the ethical permissibility of euthanasia. Eminent cognoscenti had discussed it for decades, and it had won not a few respected proponents. He had accepted the expertise of the Reich Committee, the leaders of which were represented to him as the leading experts in the field. Procedurally, every safeguard against abuse had been observed. His involvement in killing was purely scientific and humane. For these reasons, he argued, he should be acquitted on the basis of a mistake of law (Verbotsirrtum).

Previous euthanasia defendants had, of course, raised similar arguments. Typically, however, West German courts until the Uchtspringe trial had rejected this defense, claiming that no matter how much support for euthanasia was marshaled by the Nazi authorities, a reasonable person could plainly see that the mass murder of defenseless patients violated the "natural moral law," which was superior to the positive law of the Third Reich. Because natural law was accessible to all rational beings, all were bound by its prescriptions and prohibitions, no matter what the law of a particular government commanded.

The Göttingen state court did not deny the existence or obligatory quality of the natural law; instead, it adopted a highly subjective analysis of the actor's ability to discern whether his conduct violated the law or not. An actor's duty to "exert his conscience" hinged on "the circumstances of the case and the life and professional background of the individual." This meant that the actor had to "mobilize all his intellectual powers of recognition and all his conceptions of value . . . to develop a judgment about the legality or illegality of a certain action. If, notwithstanding [such exertion], he is unable to perceive the illegality of his action, his error is unavoidable, and he cannot be held criminally liable for it."[33]

The court found that Wenzel fell into this category of actors whose exertions of conscience were incapable of grasping the wrongfulness of their actions. During his meeting in Berlin with Hefelmann and von Hegener, it was explained to him that a euthanasia law existed and was known throughout the civil service, although it remained unpublished. The court accepted his claim that he had trusted in the representations by the leading men of the KdF. These considerations were the prelude to an extraordinary disquisition by the court on "life unworthy of life," the destruction of which, the court noted, could not be regarded "a priori" as "immoral." In the pre-Christian era, authorities as various as Plato and Seneca had expressed support for destroying "monsters" (*Monstra*). Under the influence of the Catholic Church, which branded euthanasia a hubristic intervention in affairs better left to God, the destruction of unworthy life entered a period of eclipse. Nevertheless, there was evidence of its resurgence in the late medieval era in Thomas More's *Utopia* (1516), which "discusses the putting to sleep of incurable patients . . . in a way that reveals the social thought [of the time]." In his *Table Talks*, Martin Luther had advocated drowning a twelve-year-old child believed to be a changeling, because it was legal to kill a mere "piece of flesh" that had "no inner soul." The court admitted that German law in the modern period had criminalized such killing, but added that "permitting [it] is not entirely strange to [German law]." The court cited nineteenth-century authorities like the Pandects and the Prussian General State Law, which had given special dispensation for "doing away with the monsters." Even the Braunschweig Penal Code of 1840 had punished a mother convicted of killing her baby "lacking human form" with only a minor fine and a jail term of six weeks.

The court cited Binding and Hoche to show how earnestly the subject had been taken up in the interwar years. It quoted from *The Permission to Destroy Life Unworthy of Life* that "it can be forbidden from neither a legal, social, ethical, nor a religious viewpoint to destroy these individuals, who form the horrid counterpicture of authentic humanity, and who in almost every case arouse the horror of those they meet." On the contrary, "it strains the concept of humanity to want to preserve life unworthy of life unconditionally." According to the court, these ideas were endorsed by many other authorities, including German, Swiss, and Danish politicians during the 1920s, as well as theologians like Dr. Thrändorf, who chided a culture that would "let capable people go to rack and ruin in favor of incapable members of the society, for whom new palaces were built and who lived a carefree life at the expense of the healthy taxpayer." The opinions of learned jurists, doctors, politicians, and theologians confirmed the intuitive feelings of the German people. The Göttingen court referred to the high percentage (73 percent) of parental support for covert euthanasia expressed in the 1920 Melzer survey. One father quoted by the court wrote: "Certainly there are many who deplore the barbarity and heartlessness [of euthanasia], but that is of course the outpouring of a false humanity; the outsider cannot in such cases pass judgment." For the court, the overwhelming support for euthanasia "cannot simply be shrugged off."

These ruminations led the court to conclude that euthanasia "cannot be called . . . a measure that contradicts the general moral law, or the fundamental ideas of justice and humanity." Wenzel was aware that "leading minds" had approved the "release" of "life unworthy of life." In view of this broad, centuries-old support for the idea among distinguished thinkers and the public at large, how could Wenzel be charged with knowingly violating the natural law when he put these ideas into practice? Nor could Wenzel have "exerted his conscience" sufficiently to grasp the illegality of the Reich Committee's program: it had all the outward indicia of "orderliness," including panels of expert evaluators who enjoyed reputations for working "carefully and conscientiously." Although the procedures may not have conformed perfectly to those prescribed by Binding and Hoche, Wenzel could not be charged with knowledge of these minor deviations. Insofar as Wenzel's experience with the bureaucratic guidelines that structured euthanasia was concerned, "the procedure offered . . . security against abuses and gross errors." Because Wenzel "could not have arrived at a different result by a more conscientious examination [of the matter]," he had to be acquitted of the killings in the Uchtspringe children's ward.[34]

Wenzel's replacement as director of the children's ward, Dr. Hildegard Wesse, came to Uchtspringe from the University Clinic for Children in Leipzig. Prior to this appointment, she had been the director of the men's department in the Waldniel institution. In August 1943 she arrived at Uchtspringe as Wenzel's successor. She did not immediately assume the directorship of the children's ward, however; this position was held by her husband, Hermann Wesse, until he was inducted into the German army in December 1943. At this time, and with alleged reluctance, she became director of the children's ward, a position she held until July 1945. She had first become aware of the euthanasia program during her work at the Waldniel institution, when her husband became director of the Waldniel children's ward in October 1942. Around this same time, on orders from the Reich Committee, he had introduced the euthanasia of "fully idiotic" children into the ward. At trial she claimed her husband only acquainted her with his work in broad strokes, because he wanted to spare her, as a woman, so grave a "psychological burden." A lesser gentleman, Dr. Werner Catel (a member of the planning committee for the children's euthanasia and one of its three expert evaluators), provided her with more detailed information during her stint at the Leipzig Clinic. He told her that three experts had been charged with overseeing the program. He reassured her that only "full idiots" were being targeted, and that killing could go forward only when all three experts had agreed the case was hopeless.

When she was appointed to replace her husband in the children's ward, Hildegard Wesse claimed she had misgivings—not because she disapproved of euthanasia, which she affirmed in theory, but because she did not know if she was equal to the task of carrying it out herself. She eventually accepted the appointment, however, and thereafter carried out the same type of killing that Wenzel had done before her. From January 1944 to January 1945 she prepared 400 to 500 reports on the ward's children for review by the Reich Committee. Like Wenzel, she offered her prognosis on the children, characterizing them either as incurable or as capable of improvement. Because the Berlin authorities generally followed her recommendations, she assumed the committee's experts were carefully examining each case she submitted. When Berlin sent "treatment authorizations" to her for sixty children, she instructed the floor nurse to give the children doses of luminal or trional tablets in their food. The children lost consciousness and died after a couple of days. For hardier children she ordered morphine injections, which were administered by the nurse or Wesse herself. After their deaths, Wesse sent notices to the children's families listing fabricated causes of death. She had no compunction about this deception, because she felt it was "right" to spare their feelings.[35]

Wesse, like her predecessor Wenzel, was acquitted of wrongdoing in connection with the killings in the Uchtspringe children's ward. The rationale for acquittal of the charge was the same in both cases: like Wenzel, Wesse could not have exerted her conscience any further to understand the wrongfulness of her actions. She reasonably assumed the procedure was "well-organized and reliable from an ethical-medical standpoint." The cautious attitudes exhibited by the experts in the Reich Committee reassured her that the program was being administered conscientiously and with scientific precision. She had, in short, no good reason to doubt the ethical or legal timbre of the killing procedure. According to the court's interpretation, it was ethically and legally defensible for a lower-level functionary to accept a "conscientious" and "scientifically precise" procedure ordered by the top of the institutional chain.

If Wesse's activities had been restricted to the children's ward, she would have walked out of the Göttingen courtroom a free woman. Her murderous work at Waldniel, however, also involved thirty disabled women, and for these killings the court refused to accept a mistake of law. At the end of 1944, Wesse was informed of Berlin's decision to order the killing of mentally ill adults in the Waldniel men's and women's departments. By contrast with the procedure in the children's ward, no prior observation and expert review would be observed with these killings, because this would unduly delay the process. Wesse was assigned responsibility for euthanizing incurable patients in the women's department. She accepted the assignment, reasoning to herself that the pressures of the war had forced Berlin to deviate from the cautious procedures that governed euthanasia in the children's ward. Another doctor segregated the severest cases among the female patients and removed them to Wesse's children's ward. She reviewed the patient records of these handicapped women and decided to "put to sleep" thirty of them. Wesse carried out the killings of these women herself with morphine injections. At her trial, she raised the defense that she was motivated by pity to destroy these patients, and that she never doubted their killing was in harmony with the wishes of the Berlin authorities.

Apparently, the Göttingen court's magnanimity toward the killers of disabled patients was not unlimited, because it rejected Wesse's argument and held her criminally liable for the deaths of the thirty women. The critical factor in distinguishing these killings from the euthanasia of the children was their unregulated character. The killings were done on a summary basis, without procedural safeguards in place to convey the appearance of ethical and legal legitimacy. Had Wesse roused her conscience sufficiently—as was her legal duty—she would have recognized the glaring illegality of these makeshift orders. "If she had [exerted her conscience]," the court held, "then, with her exceptional intelligence, she would have seen that something was not in order—that entrusting a young assistant doctor [like herself] with deciding alone about the euthanasia of mental patients is simply indefensible." In other words, she would have understood that any "law" that permitted such a haphazard procedure "must have exceeded the limits of what is legally permissible." Wesse could have acted differently than she did; she could have expressed to the Reich Committee, with whom she was on good terms, her refusal to participate in the anarchic destruction of patients. Because she failed to "exert her conscience according to the measure of her intellectual powers to recognize what is right and wrong," she was criminally liable for these deaths.[36]

Despite this finding, the court refused to characterize her killings of these women as murder under German law, inasmuch as the killings lacked the characteristics of reprehensibility (base motives, maliciousness, and so forth). For this reason, she was convicted of manslaughter. In the sentencing phase of the trial, the court considered mitigation appropriate because Wesse had been medically trained in an era when "utilitarian considerations" undermined the doctor-patient relationship. She was given a remarkably lenient jail term of six months per patient killed, a sentence the court deemed "appropriate and sufficient." But even this disproportionate punishment was never carried out, because on December 27, 1954, the Göttingen court decreed the sentence null and void.*

The Uchtspringe case represents with the verdict in Leu the floodtide in the coddling of euthanasia defendants by West German courts. Leu, Wenzel, and Wesse had all killed scores of patients, often with their own hands. If, as Ulrich Herbert argues,[37] the Christmas Amnesty of 1949 had sent a message to the German population that the era of punishing Nazi crimes had ended, then the wave of acquittals in the early 1950s culminating in the exoneration of the child-murderers Leu, Wenzel, and Wesse must have been seen for what it was—a sign of the refusal of West German courts to convict the murderers in their midst.

The Cruel Month: The Warstein Case

T. S. Eliot may have thought April was the "cruelest month," but from the perspective of postwar justice that title better describes the month of December 1953, when three separate courts in three trials acquitted euthanasia defendants. We have already discussed two of these cases. The third and final case involved two doctors, a Dr. P. and a Dr. S., employed during the war in the largest of the Westphalian mental hospitals, Warstein. Dr. P. became director of Warstein in July 1934; Dr. S. served as assistant doctor there beginning in January 1931, rising to chief doctor in March of that year. In 1937, S. also assumed the directorship of a ward created at Warstein by P. to accommodate mentally ill patients with tuberculosis. During the war, both men split their professional lives between military service and work at Warstein.

Warstein was swept up into the killing operation in summer 1941, along with the other Westphalian mental hospitals. From June 1941 to August 1941, some 2,720 patients from these institutions were transferred to transit centers in Hesse. Of this number, the Dortmund state court found that 1,227 patients

---

* Nullification of the sentence was carried out pursuant to the "Law for Exemption from Punishment" (*Straffreiheitsgesetz*) of 1954, which exempted from punishment cases of manslaughter punishable with a prison term of three years or less. The law covered crimes committed between October 1, 1944, and July 31, 1945. See de Mildt, *In the Name of the People*, 354n151.

were subsequently sent to killing centers and gassed. Only 125 of the 2,720 transferees survived the transfer. The fate of the remaining 1,368 patients, however, was unknown. Ten transports with 902 patients were transferred from Warstein to the transit centers. It was proven that, from 1941 to 1944, 401 of these patients died and 36 survived. What became of the other 465 could not be ascertained at the time of the trial.

The transports from Warstein followed the same pattern that prevailed in other home institutions throughout Germany. Registration forms were sent to Dr. P. for distribution to his staff doctors, who filled them out on their patients and returned them to Berlin. Months later, transport lists from Berlin arrived in P.'s office. The court was satisfied that both defendants were aware of the purpose of the transports when they assembled their patients for transfer. The indictment charged them with aiding and abetting murder and crimes against humanity for their knowing participation in furthering these transports of patients designated for killing.[38]

The defendants' odyssey through the German judicial system was one of the most sinuous among the euthanasia cases. The trial in December 1953 was the end of a long, snaking road of indictment, acquittal, appeal, and retrial, involving not fewer than three separate trials (the first in October 1948) and two appellate reviews and reversals. The number of conflicting verdicts and counter-verdicts offers a poignant example of the "flipability" in post-1947 euthanasia judgments. The will to exonerate the defendants was present already in the 1948 trial, when the Schwurgericht of Münster acquitted P. and S. on the ground of an extrastatutory necessity. By December 1953, thanks to the German Supreme Court's verdict of March 18, 1952,[39] a new rationale had emerged to support the defendants' acquittal: the exertion of conscience doctrine. Although the Dortmund state court found that both men had knowingly promoted the crime of murder, it also found that neither was aware that his actions were illegal. The court's holding was grounded in an acceptance of the defendants' argument that they had participated in euthanasia only to save as many of their patients as possible. By remaining in their posts and sabotaging the program where they could, the defendants had rescued as many as 30 percent of their patients by striking their names from the transport lists, discharging them from the hospital, or arranging their transfer to Catholic hospitals not yet imperiled by the killing operation. Both defendants moreover were devout Catholics without ideological ties to the Nazi Party. Clearly, they had fully "exerted" their consciences and decided to "remotely collaborate" with the euthanasia program in order to undermine it. Despite their conscientious reflection, they had no awareness that their minimal promotion of the killing program was illegal—quite to the contrary, they believed that outward compliance with the program in order to save patients was legally required.

The Dortmund court, unlike the earlier state courts that had acquitted P. and S., did not hold that it was legal to sacrifice some patients in order to save others. Rather, it held that the defendants were justified in believing their contributions to the sacrifice of some patients were legally permitted. This was because of the "moral turbulence" of German society under the Third Reich, a time "when normal values had been overturned." Legal authorities had disagreed on the wrongfulness of sacrificing some in order to save others; thus, a defendant could not be held accountable for conscientiously "arriving at an erroneous decision," about which even distinguished jurists could not agree. This applied a fortiori to P. and S., who were "insufficiently prepared and armed for the decision of such an extraordinarily difficult question of law and conscience." The court went on:

> The measure of the required exertion of conscience depends on . . . the life and professional background of the individual. The entire educational and professional training of the defendants—in their specializations one-sidedly medical—were not oriented to communicate to a young person sufficiently clear and unambiguous. . . . The defendants were therefore, through no fault of their own, intellectually and spiritually unequipped for an extraordinarily complicated situation. They lacked the casuistic, ethical, and legal education for the correct solution. Insofar they cannot be held criminally responsible for their erroneous decision.[40]

P. and S., in brief, had "exerted their conscience" to the maximum degree. Nothing further could have been required of them.

The Sachsenberg, Uchtspringe, and Warstein cases—all decided in December 1953—inaugurated a subtle shift in the acquittal of euthanasia doctors. The prior tendency to acquit them with recourse to a collision of duties or extrastatutory necessity gave way by 1953 to acquittals based on "exertion of conscience" (a form of mistake of law). The new emphasis on a defendant's capacity for moral reflection held sway in West German courts for the next two decades.

Flipability and the Case of Dr. Sch.

One defendant who did not appear in the Warstein case of December 1953 was a doctor of law and Westphalian civil servant, Dr. Sch. He had been indicted along with P. and S. in 1948 for aiding and abetting murder and crimes against humanity, based on his participation with them in organizing the Nazis' euthanasia program in Westphalia. At the first trial in October 1948, he claimed he had no knowledge of the killing ordered by the authorities and had therefore only unwittingly promoted the euthanasia program by forwarding Berlin's registration forms and transport lists to Westphalian mental institutions. The *Schwurgericht* in Münster agreed that no evidence existed to prove his knowledge of the goals of the transports. At this same trial, Sch.'s codefendants P. and S. had admitted to knowing of the lethal purpose behind the transports but argued they had collaborated only to avoid greater harm to their patients. Both were acquitted on the basis of an extrastatutory necessity. In March 1949, the Supreme Court for the British Zone reversed the verdict of the Münster *Schwurgericht* and remanded the case for retrial, noting the contradictions in the findings of fact regarding Dr. Sch. On remand, in August 1949 the Münster court convicted Dr. Sch. of aiding and abetting murder. The German Supreme Court rejected his appeal of this verdict in November 1952. He thereafter filed a petition for amnesty, which effectively stayed execution of the sentence against him.

In November 1954 he applied for a new trial, now arguing that, contrary to his claims in earlier trials, he really had known all along about the euthanasia program but decided quietly to join the sabotage operation of other provincial doctors. No doubt emboldened by the exertion of conscience cases, he added that he had searched his conscience at the time and decided it was not wrongful to sacrifice some patients in order to save others. His applications were rejected in May 1955. He appealed this determination to the appellate court in Hamm, which overturned the lower court's rejection in May 1956, thereby permitting a new trial. The case went forward on January 28, 1959.[41]

Ample evidence was available to rebut Dr. Sch.'s defense that he had acted only in the best of faith to minimize the damage of the killing program. Unlike his earlier codefendants, Dr. Sch. had failed to raise this defense until six years after his first trial in 1948. Second, his political affiliations suggested that Nazi functionaries had considered him a reliable party member to whom sensitive party offices could be entrusted. Two witnesses testified during his trial that he had always impressed them as a devout National Socialist. Despite the shadow this evidence cast on Sch.'s defense, the Münster state court acquitted him of aiding and abetting murder. (Crimes against humanity under Control Council Law #10 ceased to be chargeable against defendants tried in West German courts for Nazi crimes after August 31, 1951.) The court clearly felt that he had "exerted his conscience" to the best of his ability, qualifying his actions as the product of a mistake of law. Complicating Sch.'s ability to discern the wrongfulness of his conduct was the novelty of the situation he found himself in—a situation for which his legal studies could not have prepared him. "The situation here was completely new," the court held. "Never before in history had a state ordered the mass killings of innocent patients. . . . Accordingly, the defendant could find no solution to the problem in his studies of legal literature." The court found it meaningful in this context that Sch. was "only of mediocre talent as a jurist."[42]

With his acquittal in 1959, Dr. Sch. could join the ranks of other Nazi defendants scrubbed clean of moral and legal blemish for their willing participation in the Third Reich's assault on humanity.

DEVELOPMENTS IN THE PROSECUTION OF NAZI EUTHANASIA POST-1953

German physicians and civil servants were not the only beneficiaries of the judiciary's lenient attitude toward euthanasia crimes. Since the late 1940s, German courts had declared nursing staff involved in killing patients innocent of criminal wrongdoing. Even before the "exertion of conscience" cases, German courts had acquitted nurses with reference to the mistake of law doctrine, on the grounds that their lack of education rendered them incapable of recognizing the illegality of their actions, or that the Führer order backing it up had no legal effect.[43] The same rationale was employed to acquit the nursing staff of the Meseritz-Obrawalde institution, prosecuted in the Munich state court in 1965. The court iterated the familiar language about the defendants' intellectual and moral incapacity to understand that killing patients was illegal. By virtue of this defect, they could not "exert their conscience" sufficiently to adjudge the euthanasia program wrongful, especially because their supervisor-doctors ordered it, a law was alleged to support it, and neither the police nor the local prosecutors had intervened to stop it. The "fog of doubt" enveloping their actions prevented any morally autonomous action.[44]

The trend toward acquitting euthanasia defendants based on an exertion of conscience/mistake of law rationale would continue after 1965. In 1967, T-4 gassing technicians Heinrich Bunke, Aquilin Ulrich, and Klaus Endruweit were acquitted because an "unavoidable mistake of law" clouded their "awareness of the illegality of their actions." Although the German Supreme Court reversed their acquittal in 1970, the case on remand eventuated in yet another miscarriage of justice: Bunke, Ulrich, and Endruweit were declared "unfit for trial" on medical grounds, and a fourth T-4 doctor prosecuted with them, Kurt Borm, was acquitted in 1972 by the Munich state court on a mistake of law theory—a verdict upheld by the Supreme Court on appeal in 1974. As Willi Dressen has observed, the decision in the Borm case contradicted the holdings of earlier courts that no defendant could invoke his or her reliance on a law repugnant to the "natural law."[45] Dressen's statement is partially correct: the Munich court's verdict *did* clash with the holdings of earlier courts. That turn, however, had occurred much earlier than 1972, as the exertion of conscience cases of the early 1950s prove.

The German euthanasia trials demonstrate that the law can be a fragile refuge for justice. A defining feature of criminal law is its role in reducing interpersonal violence between members of a social order. Rather than entrust justice to private individuals and personal blood feuds, society vests the determination of guilt or innocence in a court system charged with applying the law with fairness and impartiality. Legal "science," not extrajuridical forces, is supposed to govern a court's deliberations. During the Third Reich, the homicide laws had failed to arrest Germany's descent into genocide and mass murder. In the postwar era, law revealed itself again to be at the mercy of geopolitical, ideological, and psychological forces. Whether using the language of extra-statutory necessity, collision of duties, or exertion of conscience, West German courtrooms after 1947 became a force field in which these vectors were given free play. The upshot, as we have seen, was the acquittal or lenient treatment of hundred- and thousandfold murderers.

Even the U.S. euthanasia trials were not immune to such forces. From the beginning of their plans to try Nazi war criminals, the United States had committed itself to the position that the crimes of euthanasia doctors (like those of Nazi perpetrators generally) were bound up with the Nazis' plot to wage aggressive war. By killing patients, resources could be freed up to supply the army in its campaign to Germanize the European continent. The United States hewed to this interpretation for political reasons: if the euthanasia program was disconnected from Nazi military aggression, a precedent would be set for intervening in the domestic affairs of sovereign nations. The principle of sovereignty was at the center of U.S. concern. Commitment to a war-centered theory of genocide led the United States to construe Nazi euthanasia as an outgrowth of Hitler's boundless imperialism—a conception that relegated the ideology of destroying "life unworthy of life" to a secondary role. By the late 1940s, as the horizon of the Cold War lowered over Europe, acquittals in both U.S. and West German courts became more common. Although the law demanded the prosecution and punishment of war criminals, the will to acquit won out. Once more, as it had during the war, the law had proven to be deficient as a firewall against criminality and injustice.

Examination of the U.S. and West German euthanasia trials opens a window on the role of extralegal factors in criminal adjudication. The trials show us how easily the law becomes the servant of power, and that power, rather than exerting its influence from a position external to legal process, is in reality deeply interfused with it. What legal positivists have for decades ascribed to a realm extrinsic to law is, on the contrary, intrinsic to it. In the U.S. and West German euthanasia cases, the ability of power to affect legal adjudication was so pronounced that it inverted burdens of proof. For the United States, the principle of assuming innocence until guilt is proven was overturned during the Hadamar and medical trials. For U.S. officials, to sever the euthanasia program from the conduct of the war had portentous longterm implications for U.S. sovereignty. Concerns with preserving national power induced U.S. jurists to assume the guilt of euthanasia defendants as co-perpetrators with Hitler of the crime of waging aggressive war. For the Germans, their presumption of guilt with formal indictment was similarly inverted: they tended to assume the innocence of euthanasia defendants (especially after 1947) and sought ways to vindicate this presumption. With respect to the West Germans, too, power considerations played a central role in this transposition. Seeking to recoup a national sovereignty that had seemed irrecoverable in May 1945, by the late 1940s West German authorities felt the need to close the book on their criminal past. Psychological, political, and geopolitical needs made such closure possible. Democratic, philosemitic, capitalist, and anti-Communist, the new Federal Republic turned a fresh, unblemished countenance to the Western allies, prepared to defend the West against the Soviet menace. Behind that carefully rouged face lay the rot of a past that would prove in coming years—and in defiance of all efforts to deal with it—to be unmasterable.

In the end it is the mystery that lasts and not the explanation.
—SACHEVERELL SITWELL, "FOR WANT OF THE GOLDEN CITY"

CONCLUSION

In November 1954 Dietrich Allers, a German jurist who had served as the manager of T-4's Central Office, sent a letter to his former colleague and fellow jurist Reinhold Vorberg, the one-time director of Office IIc of the KdF. Sanguine about the changed fortunes of T-4 perpetrators in the years since the end of the war, Allers wrote:

> Take a look around and think back to the time around 1947.
> At that time, all of us envisioned a miserable personal future
> for ourselves. Today most of us have again become something,
> and it is my opinion that we should not demand too much.
> Certainly quite a few people who held totally different
> positions [before] have landed well on their feet.[1]

Allers may have spoken too soon: in December 1968 he and Vorberg were convicted of complicity in the deaths of 70,273 mentally ill patients during the war. Vorberg was sentenced to a ten-year jail term, Allers to eight years. (They were credited with time already served during preventive detention and freed without spending a day in jail.) Their subsequent conviction notwithstanding, Allers's rosy assessment of the improved situation of euthanasia killers after

1947 was an accurate one. Our study of the verdicts from the U.S. and West German euthanasia trials confirms his perspective on postwar justice in the Federal Republic. It suggests the following periodization: a brief two-year interval between 1945 and 1947 characterized by convictions of euthanasia defendants as perpetrators of murder or crimes against humanity, and an extended period after 1947 characterized by the lenient treatment of these defendants, including mild sentences, acquittals, and, in the event of conviction, their portrayal as accomplices rather than perpetrators.

In the German trials, the precedent of the Bathtub Case was applied with greater frequency after 1947 to reduce the defendants' wrongdoing from perpetration to complicity. Relatively new defenses, such as extrastatutory necessity and collision of duties, were adopted to acquit participants in the euthanasia program. By the early 1950s, in the wake of a German Supreme Court decision on the mistake of law doctrine, German courts employed a different theory to exculpate euthanasia defendants—the exertion of conscience defense. None of the facts in the cases we examined compelled West German courts to accept any these defenses. Just as easily, the courts could have rejected the proffered defenses as insufficient to justify participation in a program to kill the mentally disabled. Not value-free legal science but political, social, and cultural forces were at work in these trials, shaping, forming, and often distorting the courts' verdicts.

The adjudication of euthanasia criminality in the postwar years was a subset of a larger confrontation with the manifold crimes of National Socialism. Like Nazi criminal trials generally, the euthanasia cases were instrumentalized after 1947 to enable the West German state to achieve full sovereignty. In short, they became an important fourth pillar of what Norbert Frei has termed West Germany's "policy toward the past," which Frei described as consisting of (1) amnestying Nazi perpetrators, (2) integrating them into the new Federal Republic, and (3) "normatively demarcating" West Germany from anti-democratic movements on the right and the left. To this trinity of factors can be added judicial lenience toward German professionals like the doctors, nurses, and bureaucrats examined in this study. Many of the individuals we have discussed returned after their trials to a medical practice or the civil service where they became unobjectionable professionals of the Federal Republic. Whether through liquidating trials, acquitting the defendants, or mitigating their punishment, the West German judiciary contributed to the Federal Republic's quest for national power by facilitating the reintegration of compromised elites into postwar German society.

The Cold War was a boon to this quest for German sovereignty. The defense of Western Europe required a democratic West Germany securely moored to the United States as a counterweight to the Soviet bloc. With the proclamation of the Truman Doctrine in 1947, the United States made clear its intention to oppose with "counterforce" the USSR throughout the world—an intention that signified U.S. commitment to establishing West Germany as a member in good standing of the Atlantic alliance. By 1950 the United States was seeking support in Europe for a European Defense Community, to which a rearmed West Germany would contribute troops. The West Germans were in a position to bargain, and they did not hesitate to use it to their advantage. As we have seen, the nascent Cold War created the opportunity for the Federal Republic's leaders to offer the West a quid pro quo: recovery of sovereignty, which included quashing legal proceedings against Nazi war criminals, in exchange for West Germany's participation in the anti-Soviet alliance. In the *Bundestag* debates about German rearmament preceding the General Treaty of May 1952, the sentiments of a majority of the delegates were forcefully expressed in a resolution, setting forth demands "that those Germans charged with war crimes and either already convicted by Allied courts or still held without a verdict be released, so long as what is at issue is not a crime as the word is ordinarily understood, that is, for which a single individual is responsible. An objective examination of the individual cases must follow without delay."[2] Such demands were in keeping with the German chancellor's view that only the "real criminals" of the Nazi regime should be punished, while soldiers and others who merely discharged their duty—those who did not commit "a crime as the word is ordinarily understood," to quote the *Bundestag* resolution—would suffer no legal prejudice. In this manner, the geopolitical realities of the Cold War became the occasion for an internal repression of Germany's recent past, an act of forgetting driven by the desire to rekindle national power.

The quest for renewed sovereignty, anchored in a policy of amnesty, integration, normative demarcation, and liquidation of continued trials of Nazi perpetrators, serviced profound psychological needs in the immediate postwar era. It both palliated the sting of a calamitous military defeat and nurtured a tottering sense of hope for Germany's survival as a sovereign country. Perhaps for this reason, the course charted by the Federal Republic received broad support within the German population, from lawyers like the Heidelberg Circle, journalists, church leaders, fugitives from the East, and small parties in the Bundestag (e.g., the Free Democratic Party [FDP] and the German Party) to representatives of major political parties like the CDU and Social Democrats, who felt growing popular pressure to bring to an end the era of Nazi war crimes trials. Such an end would not only certify the Federal Republic of Germany to the world as a nation ready to assume its role in the coalition against "totalitarianism"; it would also deflect the gaze of social control from the crimes of German elites in a society still characterized by the paradigm of a shame culture.[3]

National self-esteem was at stake should the trials continue and German elites be punished. The euthanasia trials were deeply entangled in this political, geopolitical, and psychological maelstrom.

If power lay at the root of West Germany's suppression of further trials, considerations of national sovereignty also affected the prosecution of Nazi euthanasia defendants in U.S. military courts. Even before the end of the war, the United States discussed the possibility of making conspiracy the center-piece of postwar trials of Nazi war criminals. Faithful to the originators of the conspiracy theory, the U.S. drafters of the London Charter regarded all crimes leveled against the major war criminals—crimes against peace, war crimes, and crimes against humanity—as outgrowths of the Nazis' conspiracy to wage ag-gressive war against the countries of Europe. On this theory, Nazi criminality was a byproduct of the plan to bring Europe under the heel of German domin-ion. Euthanasia emerged as a scheme to transfer resources from "useless eaters" to German soldiers in order to fortify them in their conquests. The theory of conspiracy enabled U.S. prosecutors to charge their defendants as perpetrators rather than as accomplices. By contrast, West German courts did not regard euthanasia as driven by the engine of a conspiracy to wage aggressive war. Instead, particularly from 1945 until 1947, they focused on their defendants' actual contributions to the euthanasia program, guided by the principle of individual culpability. At no time did German triers of fact impute criminal liability vicariously to an accused. This was a considerable advantage for the defendants, one that, when reinforced by the society-wide aspiration to free Germany from the incubus of its Nazi past, tended toward mild punishments and acquittals.

Differences in approach to euthanasia criminality—the United States guided by conspiracy, the Germans by individual culpability—did not stop here. The U.S. view of its jurisdictional rights over Nazi defendants also differed from the German conception. For the United States, the Third Reich's violation of the traditional Laws of War created the jurisdictional basis for both the IMT and the U.S. NMT. I have repeatedly emphasized that the Anglo-American jurists were not particularly concerned with the ex post facto question. In response to objections about the retroactive effect of prosecuting Nazi war criminals, the Anglo-Americans replied either that no ex post facto problem existed, because the defendants were charged with violating internationally recognized principles of law; or, in the alternative, that the need to punish these terrible crimes outweighed the principles of legality (e.g., the ban on retroactive punishment). By contrast, German courts were more sensitive to the principles of legality, chiefly because they formed the backbone of the continental tradition of law. From the end of the war until the early 1950s, German courts neutralized the ex post facto problem by insisting on their defendants' ability to grasp the wrongfulness of Nazi euthanasia based on an intuitive perception of natural law. The principle of abstaining from the murder of innocents might have been suspended by the criminal orders of the Nazi state, but it was still codified in the universal law of nature, to which all rational beings had access. By 1953, this revival of natural law was tacitly overruled as West German courts began to express doubts about the ability of euthanasia defendants to comprehend the wrongfulness of their actions. Henceforth, all that would matter was whether defendants had in good faith roused their consciences in an effort to understand the moral quality of their contemplated acts.

The changes in the administration of justice described above were far from a mechanical application of neutral legal principles. Rather, they were to a significant degree the products of extralegal factors, chief among them the craving for restored sovereignty. The potency of extra-juridical forces was such that it inverted burden of proof standards in both sets of national trials. The geopolitical need to link euthanasia with the plan to wage aggressive war led the United States to presume the euthanasia defendants guilty; the West Germans' need to recover their sovereignty and forget their traumatic past led them to presume their defendants innocent.

The conclusions yielded in this study contradict Robert Jackson's optimistic assertion at Nuremberg that the IMT would be "an independent agency responsible only to the law." Jackson's hopeful statement sums up the aspirational core of Anglo-American principles of due process and the rule of law. In reality, the law in the trials we have examined was captive to the political needs (real or perceived) of the United States and West Germany in the postwar era. We should hardly be shocked by the degree to which power politics affected Nazi trials beginning in 1945. The United States has long been allergic to international organizations that might, however remotely, erode its sovereignty: subversion of Turkish war crimes trial proposals after World War I, the refusal of the U.S. Senate to join the League of Nations in 1919, refusal to ratify the 1948 U.N. Convention on Genocide until 1986, and recent opposition to the International Criminal Court are all examples of U.S. historical distrust of international bodies. In view of this history, we should not puzzle over U.S. insistence on knitting together all aspects of Nazi criminality (especially euthanasia) under a grand theory of conspiracy to wage aggressive war—even if such a theory obscured the actual misdeeds of Nazi doctors or distorted history on behalf of realpolitik. As for West Germany's judicial confrontation with its criminal past, it is hardly surprising that a nation accused of participating in the murder of millions would flinch when examining its recent forays into genocide with the probing eye of the criminal law—particularly when the recollection of these events was still painfully fresh. To expect a disinterested pursuit of justice in such circumstances may be to expect too much.

It is of course tempting to blame the West Germans for failing to impose punishment on the likes of Leu, Recktenwald, and Wenzel commensurate with their abhorrent crimes. In any moral analysis, however, condemnation is justified only if the actor could have acted differently but consciously chose an unethical path. Norbert Frei makes a powerful case that a more searching confrontation with perpetrators of Nazi crimes after the war might have jeopardized West Germany's reinvention as a democratic, pro-Western state. Continued engagement with war crimes investigations was unpopular among the German populace. Facing popular pressure, and harried by far-right extremists who waved the bloody shirt of war crimes trials in a bid to win votes, the CDU-CSU and SPD had little room for maneuver. The Federal Republic's "policy toward the past" was an expedient strategy to placate the West German people, secure votes for the mainstream parties, and fend off the threat posed by extremists within the FDP and the German Party. Any other approach may have driven the German electorate to turn to authoritarian "alternatives."[4]

In a review of Frei's book, Jeffrey Herf takes issue with his defense of West Germany's policy toward the past. For Herf, Frei's evidence does not support the claim "that democratization had to arrive in precisely this way." Rather, a more intensive judicial investigation of the crimes of National Socialism may have not only strengthened democracy within the Federal Republic, but would have tapped the vibrant memories of eyewitnesses to ensure maximum prosecution and punishment of Nazi offenders. In the end, Herf concludes, "a different path to democracy . . . was conceivable"—a path that, far from skirting war crimes trials, would have plunged the Germans into their very heart.[5] Herf's critique proceeds from the aspirational core of war crimes trial theory, the notion articulated by Robert Jackson that the pure pursuit of justice should guide society's treatment of heinous criminality. Given the actual constraints facing political leaders like Konrad Adenauer in postwar West Germany, however, the liquidation of war crimes trials may have seemed the only tenable solution at the time to stabilize German democracy, particularly with radicals in the wings poised to exploit the war criminal issue for their electoral advantage.

The behavior of other actors in Germany's war crimes drama, on the other hand, is more culpable. Members of the amnesty lobby—churchmen, lawyers within the Heidelberg Circle, ex-soldiers, journalists, and many others—were less concerned with placing the new German democracy on secure footing than in avoiding the evocation of a painful and incriminating national disgrace. Yet, even with respect to these groups, our moral condemnation should be tempered by the awareness that resistance to publicizing atrocities committed in the name of the nation-state is not a peculiarly German phenomenon. The "imagined communities" conjured by the nationalist imagination breed an imaginary self-esteem that rises or falls with the fortunes of the state. The glorious deeds of the nation infuse the citizens with pride; the infamous crimes of the nation diminish that self-esteem, provoking demoralization or denial of terrible truths. When the most visible source of national pride, full sovereignty, is involved, and when recovery of sovereign power intersects with the yearning of millions to repress the memory of past crimes in which many had participated, an honest confrontation with the nation's history is, at best, unlikely. This is true for any country, be it capitalist or communist, a dictatorship or democracy.

"That four great nations, flushed with victory and stung with injury, stay the hand of vengeance and voluntarily submit their captive enemies to the judgment of the law is one of the most significant tributes that Power has ever paid to Reason," Robert Jackson famously averred in his opening statement before the Nuremberg IMT. To a degree, Jackson was assuredly correct. Contrary to Soviet (and even British) proposals to shoot Nazi war criminals in a massive auto-da-fé after the war, the Big Four subjected the major war criminals to a legitimate, litigated trial, complete with defense counsel and the opportunity to call and cross-examine witnesses. What Jackson did not see when he uttered these words was that Power would have its revenge on Reason in the years between 1945 and 1953. Ultimately, our expectations that prosecution of human rights offenders can be, in Jackson's words, "responsible only to the law" may be excessive, as the history recounted in this study shows.

A considerable amount of history has been covered in these pages. We have traced the rise of negative eugenics in Germany during the scarifying years of the Weimar Republic, culminating in the rise to power of a political party that located negative eugenics at the center of its ideology. We have seen how negative eugenics led to the Nazi euthanasia program in 1939, and we have witnessed the process whereby euthanasia became both precedent and training ground for the extermination of entire ethnic groups, particularly the European Jews. We have studied U.S. and West German judicial responses to euthanasia criminality—responses that were conditioned by both the need to punish appalling forms of criminality and to preserve (United States) or recover (West Germany) national sovereignty.

In closing, I would like to consider briefly some additional conclusions that might be gleaned from the trial records we have considered. Because of the traumatic character of Nazi genocide and the complexity of judicial encounters with it, the crime and its punishment naturally invite a broad summing up—an effort to find some nugget of wisdom in an event so terrible and a suffering so vast. What remains of this woeful history for us today? How might we appropriate the significance of Nazi crimes and their punishment in our contemporary world? I would like to ponder two important lessons suggested by the trial materials: the first related to the nature of prosecuting state-sponsored crimes, the second to the nature of the crimes themselves.

First, in examining the historical prologue to the IMT and U.S. NMT, we saw that legal niceties like the ban on ex post facto prosecutions evaporated in the face of Nazi crimes. Questions of jurisdiction and retroactivity were subordinated to the need to punish these enormities. Although the Martens Clause had opened the door to criminalizing acts not specifically condemned by the 1907 Hague convention ("until a more complete code . . . has been issued, . . . belligerents remain under the . . . law of nations"), no international instrument had proscribed crimes against humanity until the London Charter in 1945. In the years since the Nuremberg trials, international law has condemned with exquisite particularity the kinds of excesses perpetrated by the Nazis: the U.N. Convention for the Prevention and Punishment of the Crime of Genocide (1948), the four Geneva conventions for the Protection of War Victims (1949), the Helsinki Accords (1975), and the Protocol Additional to the Geneva Conventions Relating to the Protection of Victims of International Armed Conflicts (1977) all seek to criminalize Nazi-style assaults on civilian populations. Enhanced linguistic specificity, however, does not mean that current international statutes will cover all future acts of global violence, given the human imagination's endless fecundity in devising new methods of torture and mass death. If we someday face a situation similar to that confronting the Allies in 1945, the will to punish can be expected to outweigh formalistic concerns about retroactivity and due process.

Second, a crucial factor in a criminal regime's ability to transvalue the morality of a civil population is time laden with intense experience. Most of the perpetrators in this study retained their awareness that killing innocent people was wrongful at some level, be it legal or moral. In some cases (regrettably few in number), doctors approached about collaborating in the euthanasia program refused to participate. When Ludwig Sprauer informed the director of the Illenau institution, a Dr. R., about the program in December 1939, R. flatly rejected Sprauer's invitation to collaborate with it. Thereafter, Dr. R. vainly tried to organize a resistance among other Baden directors against Sprauer before taking a three-month "vacation." On his return, he continued to joust with Sprauer over exempting Illenau from the euthanasia program. Sprauer not only refused to grant this exemption, but demanded that R. prepare a list of sixty patients for transport to the transit center of Reichenau. His efforts to oppose the program thwarted, R. retired a few months later.[6] Other directors of Baden institutions opposed attempts to transport patients from their facilities to the killing center at Grafeneck. The examples of Dr. R. and the Baden directors prove that not all German physicians had abandoned devotion to the welfare of their patients.

Why was this so? The Nazi Party was only in power twelve years—long enough to affect the moral landscape in Germany, but not long enough to effect a complete "transvaluation" of German mores. Yet, the Nazis were remarkably efficient in investing this brief window of opportunity for indoctrination with maximum propaganda effect. The time available to them, in other words, was laden with the experience of the National Socialist thought world. Despite the brevity of the regime's existence, evidence of an incipient transvaluation does exist, particularly within the indoctrinated party cells of the SS, Gestapo, and Security Services. Hans-Heinrich Jescheck, during the war a *Wehrmacht* officer serving in eastern Europe, had occasion to observe the combat units of the SS. He was struck by the fact that these SS soldiers neglected the recovery and care of their wounded comrades, an attitude that contradicted the duty to care for the war-wounded within the German army. The stormtroopers had internalized the Nazi Party's ethic of the total expendibility of the individual—a transvaluation of values the Nazis had effected in less than a decade. In the field of Nazi medicine, German bioethicist Eckhard Herych relates the story of his now deceased godmother, who was educated at the chief medical training center for SS doctors, the Würzburg College of Medicine. Throughout most of her postwar career, she was able to dissemble her attitudes toward the mentally disabled. At the end of her life, however, the onset of senile dementia made it increasingly difficult to hide her feelings. On one occasion, as she was walking with Herych through the crowded streets of a German city, she encountered a handicapped person in a wheelchair, about whom she quipped: "We would know what to do with him back then."[7] The menace in this remark is unmistakable: she was clearly referring to the Nazi euthanasia program. If the Nazis could transform the moral consciousness of the party's ideological vanguards within twelve years, what might they have achieved with more time?

The baneful genius of National Socialism was to mobilize tens of thousands of ordinary citizens to engage in acts of almost inconceivable violence. Its success was partly the result of the insinuation of National Socialist values into the moral resources of common people. By exploiting negative attitudes toward minority groups like the mentally disabled, Jews, and others, the Nazis "miked" the internal auditoria of their accomplices, making them receptive to the criminal messages of party ideology. The voices of conventional morality, however, were never entirely silenced; many of the perpetrators retained a clear understanding that Nazi violence was both illegal and immoral.

These aspects of Nazi criminality—the mundaneness of the killers and their unremarkable vulnerability to the commands and enticements of a genocidal system of authority—suggest that the evil done by the National Socialists was not interred with their bones. The words of the late Fritz Bauer, a judicial activist in the prosecution of Nazi criminals in West Germany until his death in 1969, reach us over the ruin of decades with a disturbing hint of prophecy: "It appears certain to me that nothing belongs to the past, everything is still present and can become future."

NOTES

INTRODUCTION

1. Michael H. Kater, *Doctors under Hitler* (Chapel Hill: The University of North Carolina Press, 1989), 54–74.

2. Alexander Mitscherlich and Fred Mielke, *Das Diktat der Menschenverachtung* (Heidelberg: Lambert Schneider, 1947).

3. Alfred Möhrle, "Der Arzt im Nationalsozialismus: Der Weg zum Nürnberger Ärzteprozess und die Folgerungen daraus," *Deutsches Ärzteblatt* 93: 43 (25 October 1996), C-1952. The actual number of German doctors involved, directly or tangentially, in Nazi criminality has never, to the best of my knowledge, been ascertained with a reasonable degree of certainty. Based on the work of Ernst Klee, a ballpark figure of a few thousand seems appropriate.

4. Dick de Mildt, *In the Name of the People: Perpetrators of Genocide in the Reflection of their Post-War Prosecution in West Germany* (The Hague: Martinus Nijhoff Publishers, 1996), 20ff. The statistics quoted pertain only to West German convictions, not to the total number of Nazi defendants tried and convicted by the Allies in both the IMT and their own national trials. A Federal Justice Ministry investigation in 1965 disclosed that 5,000 Nazi defendants were convicted in the three western occupation zones, more than 12,000 in the southern occupation zone, more than

24,000 in the USSR, more than 16,000 in Poland, and another 1,000 in other foreign trials. The sum total was in excess of 80,000 Germans prosecuted and convicted between 1945 and 1965 for Nazi crimes. Report of the Federal Justice Ministry (1965), cited in "Die Zentrale Stelle der Landesjustizverwaltungen zur Aufklärung von NS-Verbrechen," unpublished article issued by the Central Office of the State Judicial Administrations for the Clarification of Nazi Crimes, Ludwigsburg, Germany.

5. De Mildt, *In the Name of the People*, 27–28.

6. Norbert Frei, *Adenauer's Germany and the Nazi Past: The Politics of Amnesty and Integration*, trans. Joel Golb (New York: Columbia University Press, 2002), chapters 6, 8, and conclusion passim; Jeffrey Herf, *Divided Memory: The Nazi Past in the Two Germanys* (Cambridge: Harvard University Press, 1997), 217–218; Ulrich Herbert, *Best: Biographische Studien über Radikalismus, Weltanschauung und Vernunft, 1903–1989* (Bonn: Dietz Verlag, 1996), 455–460; Wolfgang Benz, "Nachkriegsgesellschaft und National Sozialismus: Erinnerung, Amnestie, Abwehr," in *Erinnern oder Verweigern*, Dachauer Hefte 6 (Dachau: Verlag Dachauer Hefte, 1990), 13–21. A typical example of this style of (specious) argument presents itself in the agitation for a general amnesty of the "so-called war criminals" (as the critics of continued trials derisively called them). Critics charged that the "war criminals" were ordinary Wehrmacht soldiers being tried for carrying out purely military functions. The reality was different: of the 603 prisoners in Allied custody in spring 1952, only 88 were soldiers, and the remainder were Gestapo, euthanasia, and concentration camp personnel.

7. On the common charge that prosecution of crimes against humanity violated the non crimen principle, see Adalbert Rückerl, *The Investigation of Nazi Crimes 1945–1978*, trans. Derek Rutter (Hamden, CT: Archon Books, 1980), 35–39. Regarding German perceptions of denazification, see Norbert Frei, *Adenauer's Germany and the Nazi Past*, 27–39; Frank Stern, *The Whitewashing of the Yellow Badge: Antisemitism and Philosemitism in Postwar Germany*, trans. William Templer (Oxford: Pergamon Press, 1992), 145–149.

8. Alexander and Margarete Mitscherlich, *The Inability to Mourn: Principles of Collective Behavior* (New York: Grove Press, 1975). See also the discussion of the Mitscherlichs' thesis by de Mildt, *In the Name of the People*, 23–25.

9. Aleida Assmann and Ute Frevert, *Geschichtsvergessenheit/Geschichtsversessenheit: Vom Umgang mit deutschen Vergangenheiten nach 1945* (Stuttgart: Deutsche Verlags-Anstalt, 1999), 88–96, 143–144.

10. Jörg Friedrich, *Die kalte Amnestie: NS-Täter in der Bundesrepublik* (Munich: Piper Verlag, 1994), 202, 206; Telford Taylor, *Final Report to the Secretary of the Army*, CD-Rom (Seattle, WA: Aristarchus Knowledge Industries, 1995), 280, 298; Norbert Frei, *Adenauer's Germany*, chapters 6 and 7, passim; Ulrich Herbert, *Best*, 437–461.

11. The conception of a "policy toward the past" (*Vergangenheitspolitik*) embracing amnesty, integration, and normative demarcation is taken from Frei, *Adenauer's Germany*. Other scholars have made arguments reminiscent of Frei's: see, for example, J. Friedrich, *Die kalte Amnestie*; Ulrich Herbert, *Best*; Frank Stern, *The Whitewashing of the Yellow Badge*; Aleida Assmann and Ute Frevert, *Geschichtsvergessenheit/Geschichtsversessenheit*; Clemens Vollnhalls, "Zwischen Verdrängung und Aufklärung. Die Auseinandersetzung mit dem Holocaust in der frühen Bundesrepublik," in *Die Deutschen*

und die Judenverfolgung im Dritten Reich, ed. Ursula Büttner (Hamburg: Hans Christians Verlag, 1992), 357–392; Jeffrey Herf, *Divided Memory.*

12. Frank Stern, *The Whitewashing of the Yellow Badge,* 351–352. Adenauer would continue to link the quashing of war crimes trials with the recovery of national sovereignty. In August 1951, he and his advisors developed a plan for a "security treaty" with the West, which connected the "war criminal problem" with restoration of German sovereignty through termination of the occupation statute. See Norbert Frei, *Adenauer's Germany,* 179–180.

13. Willi Dressen, "NS-'Euthanasie'-Prozesse in der Bundesrepublik Deutschland im Wandel der Zeit," in *NS-"Euthanasie" vor Gericht: Fritz Bauer und die Grenzen juristischer Bewältigung,* eds. Hanno Loewy and Bettina Winter (Frankfurt: Campus Verlag, 1996), 55.

14. See, for example, Frank M. Buscher, *The U.S. War Crimes Trial Program in Germany, 1946–1955* (New York: Greenwood Press, 1989); Norbert Frei, *Adenauer's Germany;* Ernst Klee, *Was sie taten—Was sie wurden: Ärzte, Juristen und andere Beteiligte am Kranken- oder Judenmord* (Frankfurt am Main: Fischer Taschenbuch Verlag, 1998); Ulrich Herbert, *Best;* Frank Stern, *The Whitewashing of the Yellow Badge;* Assmann and Frevert, *Geschichtsvergessenheit;* Vollnhalls, "Zwischen Verdrängung"; Jeffrey Herf, *Divided Memory;* Hanna Schissler, ed., *The Miracle Years: A Cultural History of West Germany, 1949–1968* (Princeton: Princeton University Press, 2001); Friedrich, *Die kalte Amnestie.*

15. E. H. Carr, *What Is History?* (London: Penguin Books, 1976), 98.

16. On the methodology of contingency in historical study, see Michel Foucault, "Nietzsche, Genealogy, History," in *The Foucault Reader,* ed. Paul Rabinow (New York: Pantheon, 1984), 76–100; Gavin Kendall and Gary Wickham, *Using Foucault's Methods* (London: Sage Publications, 1999), 5–9; Gilles Deleuze and Félix Guattari, "Rhizome," in *A Thousand Plateaus: Capitalism and Schizophrenia* (London: Athlone, 1988).

17. "Charter of the International Military Tribunal," Article 6(c), United States, Office of Chief of Counsel for War Crimes, Trials of War Criminals before the Nürnberg Military Tribunals, vol. 1 (Washington, D.C.: Government Printing Office, 1949–1953), xii.

18. *Report of Robert H. Jackson, U.S. Representative to the International Conference on Military Trials, London 1945* (Washington, D.C.: Department of State, 1949), 47.

19. Adelheid L. Rüter, C. F. Rüter, H. H. Fuchs, and Irene Sagel-Grande, eds., *Justiz und NS-Verbrechen: Sammlung deutscher Strafurteile wegen nationalsozialistischer Tötungsverbrechen 1945–1966* (Amsterdam: Amsterdam University Press, 1968–1981).

20. These include *Süddeutsche Juristische Zeitung, Neue Juristische Wochenschrift, Monatschrift für Deutsches Recht,* and *Juristische Schulung.*

21. Ernst Klee, *Dokumente zur "Euthanasie"* (Frankfurt am Main: Fischer Taschenbuch, 1997); Michael R. Marrus, *The Nuremberg War Crimes Trial, 1945–46: A Documentary History* (Boston: Bedford Books, 1997).

22. Henry Friedlander, *The Origins of Nazi Genocide: From Euthanasia to the Final Solution* (Chapel Hill: The University of North Carolina Press, 1995); Ernst Klee, *"Euthanasie" im NS-Staat: Die Vernichtung "lebensunwerten Lebens"* (Frankfurt am Main: Fischer Taschenbuch, 1986).

23. De Mildt, *In the Name of the People*.

24. On the differences between U.S. and German criminal procedure, see Dünnebier, "Der amerikanische Strafprozess im Spiegel der Rechtsprechung des Court of Appeals," *Neue Juristische Wochenschrift* (hereafter *NJW*) 27 (1952): 1040, 1042; Schmidt-Leichner, "Deutscher und anglo-amerikanischer Strafprozess," *NJW* 1 (1951): 7.

I. THE EMPEROR OF ICE-CREAM:
NATIONALIST SOCIALIST EUTHANASIA, 1933–1945

1. *U.S. v. Karl Brandt et al.* (The Doctors' Trial), National Archives and Records Administration (hereafter NARA), RG 238, M887, 2545.

2. See Klee, *"Euthanasie,"* 18; Friedlander, *Origins*, 12; Ulrich Herbert, "Wissenschaft und Weltanschanung. Der Rassismus als die Biologisierung des Gesellschaftlichen" (Geschichte der Medizin Freiburg, Freiburg, Germany, photocopy), 3; Michael Burleigh, *The Racial State: Germany 1933–1945* (Cambridge: Cambridge University Press, 1991), 34; Burleigh, *Death and Deliverance: "Euthanasia" in Germany 1900–1945* (Cambridge: Cambridge University Press, 1994), 11; Paul Weindling, *Health, Race, and German Politics Between National Unification and Nazism, 1870–1945* (Cambridge: Cambridge University Press, 1989), 394; Robert N. Proctor, *Racial Hygiene: Medicine under the Nazis* (Cambridge: Harvard University Press, 1988), 178; Jörg Michael Fegert, "Der Weg zum Nürnberger Ärzteprozess und die Folgerungen daraus," *Deutsches Ärzteblatt* 93:43 (October 25, 1996), C-1953.

3. Burleigh, *Death and Deliverance*, 11.

4. Ibid., 15–17.

5. Friedlander, *Origins*, 15.

6. Quoted in ibid.; Weindling, *Health, Race, and German Politics*, 395.

7. Karl Binding and Alfred Hoche, *Die Freigabe der Vernichtung lebensunwerten Lebens: Ihr Mass und Ihre Form* (Leipzig: Verlag von Felix Meiner, 1920), 39–40.

8. Burleigh, *Death and Deliverance*, 20.

9. Quoted in ibid., 22–23.

10. A. E. Hoche, *Krieg und Seelenleben* (Freiburg-im-Breisgau and Leipzig: Speyer & Kaerner, 1915); Friedlander, *Origins*, 9–10.

11. Quoted in Robert Wistrich, *Who's Who in Nazi Germany* (London: Routledge, 1995), 213; Weindling, *Health, Race, and German Politics*, 454.

12. Friedlander, *Origins*, 26; Proctor, *Racial Hygiene*, 361n33.

13. Weindling, *Health, Race, and German Politics*, 533; Friedlander, *Origins*, 28–29; Gisela Bock, *Zwangssterilization im Nationalsozialismus* (Opladen: Westdeutscher Verlag, 1986), 324–325.

14. Götz Aly, "Medicine Against the Useless," in *Cleansing the Fatherland: Nazi Medicine and Racial Hygiene*, eds. Götz Aly, Peter Chroust, and Christian Pross (Baltimore: Johns Hopkins University Press, 1994), 59.

15. Quoted in Klee, *"Euthanasie,"* 37.

16. Testimony of Karl Brandt, *U.S. v. Karl Brandt et al.* (The Doctors' Trial), NARA, RG 238, M887, 2401.

17. Statement of Albert Hartl in the public session of the Schwurgericht III/70, Frankfurt a.M., 24 February 1970.

18. Statement of A. Hartl; see also Gitta Sereny, *Into that Darkness: An Examination of Conscience* (New York: Vintage Books, 1983), 66–68.

19. Friedlander, *Origins*, 39. As the manuscript of this book was being prepared for publication, German government archivists announced their discovery of the Knauer child's true name, Gerhard Kretschmar, the disabled infant son of a German farmhand from a town in Saxony, Pomssen. The child's identity was found in records from the Nazi era maintained by the Stasi, the East German secret police. Irene Zoech, "Named: The baby boy who was the Nazis' first euthanasia victim—Germany 'confronts the truth' with memorial list headed by blind and deformed five-month-old," *Sunday (London) Telegraph*, 15 October 2003, 29.

20. Klee, *Dokumente*, 67; Burleigh, *Death and Deliverance*, 93; Friedlander, *Origins*, 40; Ian Kershaw, *Hitler 1936–1945: Nemesis* (New York: W. W. Norton, 2000), 257.

21. Friedlander, *Origins*, 40.

22. Ibid., 43; Wistrich, *Who's Who in Nazi Germany*, 31.

23. Klee, *Dokumente*, 68; Friedlander, *Origins*, 44.

24. Ibid.

25. Ibid.

26. Excerpted in Klee, "*Euthanasie*," 80; Friedlander, *Origins*, 45.

27. Ibid.

28. Much of my narrative closely follows Friedlander's account of the Kinderaktion, *Origins*, 45ff.

29. Friedlander, *Origins*, 48–49; Burleigh, *Death and Deliverance*, 101.

30. Friedlander, *Origins*, 54.

31. JuNSV, Lfd. Nr. 155b; JuNSV, Lfd. Nrs. 117a, 155a, 211; Letter of the Reich Committee for Scientific Registration of Severe Hereditary Ailments to Ministerial Councillor Stähle, Ministry of the Interior, Stuttgart, 11 September 1942, excerpted in Klee, *Dokumente*, 238.

32. Statement by W. Heyde, 25 October 1961 (V1), excerpted in Klee, "*Euthanasie*," 84. On this crucial meeting of euthanasia doctors in Berlin, see Klee, "*Euthanasie*," 83–84; Klee, *Dokumente*, 68; Burleigh, *Death and Deliverance*, 113; Friedlander, *Origins*, 64–65. A former student of Alfred Hoche, Heyde was one of the central figures in the planning and implementation of euthanasia. In addition to his duties as an SS doctor and a chaired professor in Würzburg, Heyde was the head of T-4's Medical Department until late 1941 and a T-4 expert evaluator in the adult euthanasia program. On Heyde's postwar career, which ended with his suicide in pretrial custody in 1964, see Klaus-Detlev Godau-Schüttke, *Die Heyde/Sawade Affäre: Wie Juristen und Mediziner den NS-Euthanasieprofessor Heyde nach 1945 deckten und straflos blieben* (Baden-Baden: Nomos Verlagsgesellschaft, 1998).

33. Urteil des LG Stuttg. vom 15.9.67 (Ks 19/62), quoted in Klee, "*Euthanasie*," 84.

34. Interrogation of Hans Heinrich Lammers, 25 October 1945, NARA, M1270, Roll 11, 876–877.

35. Nuremberg Document NO-824, excerpted in Klee, *Dokumente*, 85.

36. Friedlander, *Origins*, 68.

37. On the erection of the camouflage organizations, see Friedlander, *Origins*, 73–74; Klee, *Dokumente*, 93; Klee, *"Euthanasie,"* 102–103, 166–167; Aly, "Medicine Against the Useless," 38.

38. Friedlander, *Origins*, 75–76; Klee, *"Euthanasie,"* 87–88.

39. For a facsimile copy of the Merkblatt, see Klee, *Dokumente*, 96.

40. Friedlander, *Origins*, 77.

41. Aussage Fritz R. vom 10. March 1967 (Heyde Verfahren), excerpted in Klee, *Dokumente*, 97–98; Friedlander, *Origins*, 83.

42. Friedlander, *Origins*, 83–84; Klee, *"Euthanasie,"* 124–130.

43. Friedlander, *Origins*, 85.

44. Ibid., 84.

45. *JuNSV*, Lfd. Nr. 225, 13.

46. StA Düsseldorf, Verfahren Widmann, 8 Ks 1/61 (8 Js 7212): interrogation Albert Widmann, 11 January 1960.

47. Aussage Gerhard Bohne in der U-Haft in Tübingen, am 14. 10. 59 (V5), quoted in Klee, *"Euthanasie,"* 110, 111; Friedlander, *Origins*, 87; Klee, *Dokumente*, 20–21, 26; Wistrich, *Who's Who*, 278–279.

48. Friedlander, *Origins*, 93.

49. Aussage der Schwester Isabella W. vom 13 February 1946 (4aJs3/46 StA Ffm.), excerpted in Klee, *Dokumente*, 115–116.

50. Vernehmung Vinzenz Nohel durch die Kriminalpolizei in Linz vom 4 September 1945 (Vg 10Vr2407/46 LG Linz), excerpted in Klee, *Dokumente*, 124; Friedlander, *Origins*, 97–98.

51. Friedlander, *Origins*, 98–102; Klee, *Dokumente*, 139–140; Klee, *"Euthanasie,"* 149–153.

52. Aussage des als "Standesbeamter" in Grafeneck eingesetzten Kriminalbeamten Hermann H. vom 15 October 1947 vor dem AG Münsingen (Grafeneck-Verfahren), excerpted in Klee, *Dokumente*, 138.

53. Friedlander, *Origins*, 107–108; Klee, *"Euthanasie,"* 292–293.

54. Friedlander, *Origins*, 108; Klee, *"Euthanasie,"* 267–268.

55. Friedlander, *Origins*, 110. See also Klee, *"Euthanasie,"* 340–341.

56. Predigt von Clemens August Graf von Galen, Bischof von Münster, am 3 August 1941 in der Lambertikirche, in Klee, *Dokumente*, 193–198; Klee, *"Euthanasie,"* 336.

57. Aly, "Medicine Against the Useless," 39, 46.

58. Klee, *Dokumente*, 283.

59. Friedlander, *Origins*, 152.

60. Testimony of Karl Brandt, NARA, RG 238, M887, 2532.

61. On the theme of T-4's continued involvement in killing after the alleged stoppage, see Klee, *"Euthanasie,"* 441; Friedlander, *Origins*, 155.

62. On the topic of Allied bombing of German cities, see Martin Middlebrook, *The Battle of Hamburg: Allied Bomber Forces Against a German City in 1943* (New York: Charles Scribner's Sons, 1981), 328; Eric Markusen and David Kopf, *The Holocaust*

and Strategic Bombing: Genocide and Total War in the Twentieth Century (San Francisco: Westview Press, 1995), 156–168. For a recent account of Allied bombing from the German civilian perspective, see Jörg Friedrich, *Der Brand: Deutschland im Bombenkrieg 1940–1945* (Munich: Propyläen Verlag, 2002).

63. Interrogation of Karl Brandt, NARA, M 1270, Roll 2, 0285–0286. See also Direct Examination of Karl Brandt, NARA, RG 238, M 887, Roll 4, 2315–2316.

64. Letter from Dietrich Allers to the Mental Institution Lüneburg, dated 17 June 1943, quoted in Klee, *Dokumente,* 284.

65. Aly, "Medicine Against the Useless," 84–87.

66. Aus "Informationsdienst Rassenpolitisches Amt der NSDAP-Reichsleitung" vom 20 June 1942, Nr. 126, excerpted in Klee, *"Euthanasie,"* 357; H. W. Kranz, "Weg und Ziel bei der Lösung des Problems der Gemeinschaftsunfähigen," in *Nationalsozialistischer Volksdienst,* November 1942, quoted in Klee, *"Euthanasie,"* 356.

67. Klee, *"Euthanasie,"* 362–363.

68. Ibid., 365–366; Friedlander, *Origins,* 161. On the Germans' use of forced eastern workers during the war, see Ulrich Herbert, "Racism and Rational Calculation: The Role of 'Utilitarian' Strategies of Legitimation in the National Socialist 'Weltanschauung,'" *Yad Vashem Studies* 24 (1994): 131–195.

69. Raul Hilberg, *The Destruction of the European Jews,* vol. III (New York: Holmes & Meier, 1985), 873; Klee, *"Euthanasie,"* 371; Friedlander, *Origins,* 284.

70. Friedlander, *Origins,* 143–144.

71. Ibid., 146–148.

72. Ibid., 150. The gassings of concentration camp prisoners under Operation 14f13 resumed in 1944. At the Hartheim killing center, they continued until November of the same year. Zentrale Stelle Ludwigsburg (518 AR-Z 235/1960), excerpted in Klee, *Dokumente,* 271–272.

73. Zentrale Stelle Ludwigsburg (518 AR-Z 235/1960), excerpted in Klee, *Dokumente,* 271–272.

74. Götz Aly, *"Final Solution": Nazi Population Policy and the Murder of the European Jews,* trans. Belinda Cooper and Allison Brown (London: Arnold, 1999), 223–224.

75. Klee, *Dokumente,* 272; Aly, *"Final Solution,"* 223–224; Klee, *"Euthanasie,"* 371–372; Friedlander, *Origins,* 286–287.

76. Friedlander, *Origins,* 286–287; U.S. Holocaust Memorial Museum, *Historical Atlas of the Holocaust* (New York: MacMillan, 1996), 76.

77. Friedlander, *Origins,* 286–287; Klee, *Dokumente,* 260.

78. Sereny, *Into That Darkness: An Examination of Conscience* (New York: Vintage Books, 1983), 109; Klee, *"Euthanasie,"* 376–377.

79. The data are from Ino Arndt and Wolfgang Scheffler, "Organisierter Massenmord an Juden in nationalsozialistischen Vernichtungslagern," *Vierteljahrshefte für Zeitgeschichte* 24 (1976): 105–135; LG Düsseldorf, Urteil Hermann Hackmann, 8 Ks 1/75, 30 June 1981, 89–90; Franciszek Piper, *Die Zahl der Opfer von Auschwitz,* trans. Jochen August (Oswiecim: Verlag Staatliches Museum, 1993). See also Gerald Reitlinger, *The Final Solution* (New York: A. S. Barnes & Company, 1961), 500–501.

2. CONSTRUCTING MASS MURDER:
THE UNITED STATES EUTHANASIA TRIALS, 1945–1947

1. M. Cherif Bassiouni, *Crimes Against Humanity in International Law* (The Hague: Kluwer Law International, 1999), 61–62; see also the 1907 Hague convention at sections 6–8 of the Preamble.

2. Marrus, *The Nuremberg War Crimes Trial*, 19.

3. Moscow Declaration, 1 November 1943, excerpted in Marrus, *The Nuremberg War Crimes Trial*, 20–21.

4. Martin Gilbert, *Winston S. Churchill, 1941–1945: Road to Victory* (London: William Heinemann, 1986), 1201–1202; Winston S. Churchill, *The Second World War*, vol. 5: *Closing the Ring* (New York: Bantam Books, 1962), 319–320.

5. Henry Morgenthau Jr., *Memorandum for President Roosevelt*, 5 September 1944, excerpted in Marrus, *The Nuremberg War Crimes Trial*, 24–25; Bradley F. Smith, *Reaching Judgment at Nuremberg: The Untold Story of How the Nazi War Criminals Were Judged* (New York: Basic Books, 1977), 22–25.

6. Henry L. Stimson, *Memorandum Opposing the Morgenthau Plan*, 9 September 1944, excerpted in Marrus, *The Nuremberg War Crimes Trial*, 26–27. See also Smith, *Reaching Judgment*, 24–25.

7. Marrus, *The Nuremberg War Crimes Trial*, 27–28; Smith, *Reaching Judgment*, 26–27.

8. Smith, *Reaching Judgment*, 28.

9. Henry L. Stimson, Edward R. Stettinius Jr., and Francis Biddle, *Memorandum for the President*, 22 January 1945, excerpted in Marrus, *The Nuremberg War Crimes Trial*, 31.

10. *Memorandum of Conversation of Edward R. Stettinius Jr. and Samuel Rosenman with Vyacheslav Molotov and Anthony Eden, in San Francisco*, 3 May 1945, excerpted in Marrus, *The Nuremberg War Crimes Trial*, 35–36; Telford Taylor, *Final Report to the Secretary of the Army*.

11. See "Charter of the International Military Tribunal," Articles 6, 9, and 10, in *Trials of War Criminals before the Nuremberg Military Tribunals* (The "Green Series") (Washington, DC: Government Printing Office, 1949–1953), xi–xii.

12. Robert H. Jackson, *Report to the President*, 6 June 1945, excerpted in Marrus, *The Nuremberg War Crimes Trial*, 42.

13. Marrus, *The Nuremberg War Crimes Trial*, 186.

14. Hersh Lauterpacht, "The Law of Nations and the Punishment of War Crimes," *British Year Book of International Law* 21 (1944): 58–95; Marrus, *The Nuremberg War Crimes Trial*, 187.

15. Charter of the IMT, Article 6, xii.

16. In the continental tradition of jurisprudence, the requirement that criminal laws be specific, clear, and non-retroactive is part of the "principles of legality." According to Bassiouni, "the drafters of the Charter found it necessary to establish a link between 'war crimes' and 'crimes against humanity' in order to meet the minimum threshold of the 'principles of legality.'" Bassiouni, *Crimes*, 49. Smith makes a similar observation about the linkage of crimes against humanity with war crimes, as

does Douglas. See Smith, *Reaching Judgment*, 14; Lawrence Douglas, *The Memory of Judgment: Making Law and History in the Trials of the Holocaust* (New Haven: Yale University Press, 2001), 50–53.

17. IMT 19:470–472, excerpted in Marrus, *The Nuremberg War Crimes Trial*, 188.

18. R. H. Graveson, "Der Grundsatz 'nulla poena sine lege' und Kontrollratsgesetz Nr. 10," *Monatschrift für deutsches Recht* (1947): 279. In support of his claim, Graveson cited the comments of the U.S. law professor Jerome Hall: "And why should a person who has committed an obviously immoral crime not be punished on the basis of a law decreed after the fact? . . . Does not substantive justice demand that this question be answered in the affirmative?"

19. Report of Robert H. Jackson, 46, excerpted in Marrus, *The Nuremberg War Crimes Trial*, 41; IMT 2:98, excerpted in Marrus, *The Nuremberg War Crimes Trial*, 79.

20. Telford Taylor, *Final Report to the Secretary of the Army*.

21. Ibid. See also Control Council Law #10, excerpted in *Trials of War Criminals Before the Nürnberg Military Tribunal under Control Council Law No. 10* (The Green Series), 1: xvi–xviii.

22. Charter of the International Military Tribunal, *Trials of War Criminals*, 1: xii.

23. Control Council Law #10, *Trials of War Criminals*, 1: XVII.

24. The *Einsatzgruppen* case prosecuted Otto Ohlendorf and twenty-three other commanders of mobile killing units; the Krupp case tried the munitions magnate Alfred Krupp and eleven of his directors for plunder and using Jewish slave labor.

25. *JuNSV*, Lfd. Nr. 017.

26. In addition to the common law of war, military commissions in 1945 derived their legal jurisdiction from two statutory sources: the U.S. Constitution, Article I, paragraph 8 (delineating the "Powers of Congress"), and the Articles of War. Their competency and form may also be affected by non-statutory sources like Supreme Court and Attorney General opinions and treaties. See A. Wigfall Green, "The Military Commission," *The American Journal of International Law* 42:4 (October 1948): 832–848.

27. National Archives Microfilm Publications Pamphlet Describing M 1078, *United States of America v. Alfons Klein et al.* (Case Files 12-449 and 000-12-31), 8–15 October 1945, 2; Letter from Col H. H. Newman, Acting Adjutant General, to Commanding Generals of the Eastern and Western Military Districts, dated 25 August 1945, RG 338, M 1078, Roll 1, 23–26. Military Government Courts were established as early as September 1944 by Ordinance No. 2 and received jurisdiction inter alia over offenses in the U.S. zone against "the laws and usages of war." See Military Government—Germany, Supreme Commander's Area of Control, Ordinance No. 2, "Military Government Courts," MGR 23–215; Eli E. Nobleman, "The Administration of Justice in the United States Zone of Germany," *Federal Bar Journal* 8 (1946): 70–97.

28. NARA, RG 338, M 1078, Roll 1, 572.

29. Ibid., 652. See also Gerhard L. Weinberg, *A World at Arms: A Global History of World War II* (Cambridge: Cambridge University Press, 1994), 766–767.

30. NARA, RG 338, M 1078, Roll 1, 665. The legalist objection to my contention that a paramount concern with its sovereignty determined U.S. interpretations of Nazi euthanasia is that, under international law prior to 1945, a war crimes tribunal

could prosecute an act as a war crime only when the act was related to waging war. In his Report of the Deputy Judge Advocate for War Crimes—European Command, Lt. Col. C. E. Straight defended U.S. Army jurisdiction over Nazi war crimes because they met the following criteria: "(1) the act must be a crime in violation of international law, (2) there must be disparity of nationality between the perpetrator and the victim, and (3) the criminal act must have been committed as an incident of war." On a legalist theory, then, the United States had little choice but to connect euthanasia (as well as other Nazi atrocities) to Hitler's war of aggression if the United States wanted to abide by the principles and traditions of international law. My thesis in Chapter 2, by contrast, holds that the sovereignty issue, rather than strict adherence to international law and conventions, was uppermost in the minds of the U.S. authorities. See Report of the Deputy Judge Advocate for War Crimes—European Command, June 1944 to July 1948, NARA, RG 549, 59 (citing U.S. v. Lehmann, et al., opinion DJAW, March 1948, Case No. 000-50-06).

31. NARA, RG 338, M 1078, Roll 2, 35.

32. Ibid., 51.

33. Ibid., 54.

34. See, for example, *Bouie v. Columbia*, 378 U.S. 347 (1964); Model Penal Code section 2.04(3)(b); Wayne R. Lafave and Austin W. Scott Jr., *Criminal Law* (St. Paul: West Publishing, 1972), 366.

35. See the direct and cross-examinations of witnesses Judith Thomas, Margaret Borkowski, and Emmy Bellin, NARA, RG 338, M 1078, Roll 2, 58–120.

36. See the testimony of Alfons Klein, NARA, RG 338, M 1078, Roll 2, 175–227; testimony of Heinrich Ruoff and Karl Willig, ibid., 344–368.

37. Testimony of Alfons Klein, NARA, RG 338, M 1078, Roll 2, 215, 261–268.

38. NARA, RG 338, M 1078, Roll 2, 393–394.

39. Ibid.

40. Ibid., 180ff., 319ff., 334.

41. Testimony of Major Herman Bolker, pathologist for the War Crimes Investigating Team No. 682, NARA, RG 338, M 1078, Roll 1.

42. NARA, RG 338, M 1078, Roll 2, 209ff. (Statement of Alfons Klein); 341ff.; 647 (Statement of Heinrich Ruoff).

43. Ibid., Roll 1, 53 (Statement of Adolf Wahlmann).

44. Ibid., 523–526 (Interrogation of Karl Willig).

45. Ibid., 391–405, 429–430.

46. Report of Robert H. Jackson, 299, quoted in Marrus, *The Nuremberg War Crimes Trial*, 122.

47. Telford Taylor, *Anatomy of the Nuremberg Trials: A Personal Memoir* (Boston: Little, Brown, 1992), 80.

48. *Trial of the Major War Criminals before the IMT*, 2:242ff., excerpted in Marrus, *The Nuremberg War Crimes Trial*, 123–124.

49. Marrus, *The Nuremberg War Crimes Trial*, 124.

50. Smith, *Reaching Judgment*, 72. Woodward wrote: "There was indeed no plot . . . the other Great Powers knew in 1937 that German military preparations were on a scale to make Germany stronger. . . . It is therefore unreal—and it will seem unreal to

historians—to speak of a German 'plot' or 'conspiracy' [merely because the Powers were ready] to condone all German breaches of faith and to make agreements with the German Government." The IMT judges struck a compromise in their verdicts on the conspiracy count: they affirmed the existence of a conspiracy dating back to the time of the Hossbach memorandum in November 1937 but restricted the conspiracy solely to the plan to wage aggressive war, not to the commission of war crimes or crimes against humanity.

51. Memorandum from Telford Taylor to Robert Jackson on Further Trials, 30 January 1946, NARA, RG 260, box 2.

52. Memo from Jackson to Taylor, 5 February 1946, NARA, RG 238; Taylor's letter to Howard Petersen, 22 May 1946, NARA, RG 238; Memo from Taylor to Secretary of War, 29 July 1946, NARA, RG 153/84-1, box 1, folder 2.

53. Udo Benzenhöfer, "Die Auswahl der Angeklagten," *Deutsches Ärzteblatt* 93:45 (November 8, 1996): 8. November 1996 (21), C-2057; Paul Weindling, "From International to Zonal Trials: The Origins of the Nuremberg Medical Trial," *Holocaust and Genocide Studies* 14:3 (Winter 2000): 370–371; Taylor's letter to Petersen, 30 September 1946, NARA, RG 153/84-1, box 1, folder 2.

54. Telford Taylor, *Final Report to the Secretary of the Army*, 155.

55. Weindling, "From International to Zonal Trials," 379–380.

56. Ibid., 380–381.

57. *Trials of War Criminals before the Nuremberg Military Tribunals under Control Council Law #10*, I: 8–17.

58. See Peter H. Merkl, *Political Violence Under the Swastika* (Princeton, N.J.: Princeton University Press, 1975); Michael Mann, "Were the Perpetrators of Genocide 'Ordinary Men' or 'Real Nazis?' Results from Fifteen Hundred Biographies," *Holocaust and Genocide Studies* 14:3 (Winter 2000): 335, 343–347.

59. On the details of Brandt's life, see Interrogation of Karl Friedrich Brandt, 26 November 1946, NARA, RG 238, M 1091, Roll 9, 18–20; Interrogation of Karl Friedrich Brandt, 1 March 1947, NARA, RG 238, M 1091, Roll 9, 6–12.

60. NARA, RG 238, M 887, Roll 4, 2439–2440.

61. Ibid., Roll 1, 61, 11508.

62. Interrogation of Viktor Brack, 4 December 1946, NARA, RG 238, M 1091, Roll 8, 7–8. Like many other young Germans attracted to Nazism, including Karl Brandt, Brack came from an ethnic German background.

63. This information is gleaned from the following interrogations of Viktor Brack: 4 September 1946, NARA, RG 238, M 1091, Roll 8, 1–3; 4 December 1946, NARA, RG 238, M 1091, Roll 8, 2–5; 19 June 1947, NARA, RG 238, M 1091, Roll 8, 4.

64. Interrogation of Viktor Brack, 4 September 1946, NARA, RG 238, M 1091, Roll 8, 8, 14–17, 22.

65. Interrogation of Viktor Brack, 19 June 1947, NARA, RG 238, M 1091, Roll 8, 16–17.

66. NARA, RG 238, M 1091, Roll 8, 17–19. On the Himmler speech, see Herbert Jäger, *Verbrechen unter Totalitärer Herrschaft* (Freiburg i.B.: Walter-Verlag, 1967), 278–279.

67. Quoted in Jörg Friedrich, *Die kalte Amnestie*, 58.

68. NARA, RG 238, M 887, Roll 8, 7485. Raul Hilberg assesses Brack's humanitarian pose with acerbic succinctness: "Brack was deeply implicated in the euthanasia program, of course, and in March 1941 he proposed mass sterilizations of Jews. Furthermore, by early fall 1941, he offered to send his chemical expert, Dr. Kallmeyer, to Riga, which at that moment was a place considered for the establishment of gas chambers. Some humanitarian." Letter to the author from Raul Hilberg, 28 September 2000 (author's private collection).

69. NARA, RG 238, M 887, Roll 8, 7520.

70. Ibid., 7524.

71. Ibid., 7531.

72. See ibid., Roll 11, 11393ff.

73. Jäger, *Verbrechen unter Totalitärer Herrschaft*, 353.

74. See Jaspers's interviews in *Der Monat* 152 (1961): 15ff., and *Der Spiegel*, 11 (1965): 57; Hannah Arendt, *Eichmann in Jerusalem: A Report on the Banality of Evil* (New York: Penguin Books, 1977), 268–269. For Jaspers, crimes against humanity were also crimes against humankind. On this ground he objected to the Israeli Supreme Court's jurisdiction to punish Adolf Eichmann, arguing that because the Final Solution, as a crime against humanity, was a crime against the human race, only an international tribunal could mete out punishment to him. Arendt articulated a similar distinction between war crimes and crimes against humanity.

3. FIRST RECKONINGS: THE GERMAN EUTHANASIA TRIALS, 1946–1947

1. See Rückerl, *The Investigation of Nazi Crimes*, 34. Dick de Mildt notes that Law #10's prohibition of German prosecution of crimes committed by Germans on non-Germans was not always obeyed, inasmuch as in the period from May 1945 to January 1950, 61 of the 260 Nazi murder trials in West German courts involved the killing of non-Germans. De Mildt, *In the Name of the People*, 22.

2. For a discussion of some of the differences between Law #10 and section 211, see the State Court of Koblenz's discussion in *JuNSV*, Lfd. Nr. 225, 52–53; Henry Friedlander, "The Judiciary and Nazi Crimes in Postwar Germany," *The Simon Wiesenthal Center Annual*, 1 (1982): 31–32; Friedrich, *Die kalte Amnestie*, 152–153.

3. *Jacobs v. State*, 85 S. 837 (Ala. App 1918). In traditional Anglo-American criminal jurisprudence, as Albert Lévitt summarized in 1922, "an intent is not an essential ingredient of a statutory crime; . . . A crime does not consist of an act and an intent, but simply an act." Albert Lévitt, "Extent and Function of the Doctrine of Mens Rea," *Illinois L. Review* 17 (1922): 586.

4. RGSt. 74: 84. See also Friedlander, "The Judiciary and Nazi Crimes in Postwar Germany," 36; Friedrich, *Die kalte Amnestie*, 360. On the distinction between perpetration (*Täterschaft*) and complicity (*Teilnahme*) in German criminal law, see Albin Eser, "Strafrecht," in *Staatslexikon*, ed. Görres-Gesellschaft, 7th ed. (Freiburg: Verlag Herder, 1989), 338–339; Hans-Joachim Korn, "Täterschaft oder Teilnahme bei staatlich organisierten Verbrechen," *NJW* 27 (1965): 1206–1210; Hans-Heinrich Jescheck, *Lehrbuch des Strafrechts: Allgemeiner Teil* (Berlin: Duncker & Humblot, 1988), 580–633.

5. Gustav Radbruch, *Rechtsphilosophie* (Stuttgart: Koehler, 1973), 182; Radbruch, *Rhein-Neckar Zeitung* vom 12 September. 1945, reprinted under the title "Fünf Minuten Rechtsphilosophie," in Rainer Schröder, *Rechtsgeschichte* (Munster: Alpmann & Schmidt, 1992), 327.

6. Manfred Walther, "Hat der juristische Positivismus die deutschen Juristen wehrlos gemacht?" *Kritische Justiz* (1988): 275; Schröder, *Rechtsphilosophie*, 163. On the postwar crisis in German jurisprudence, see Eberhard Schmidt, *Gesetz und Richter: Wert und Unwert des Positivismus* (Karlsruhe: Verlag C. F. Müller, 1952), 12–14. Schmidt points out that uncertainty about legal interpretation caused German courts at all levels to waver between natural law and positivism. See also Gustav Radbruch, "Gesetzliches Unrecht und übergesetzliches Recht," *SJZ*, 5 (August 1946): 105.

7. Radbruch, "Gesetzliches Unrecht," 105; "Wiedergutmachungsrecht," *SJZ* (1946): 36.

8. Radbruch, "Gesetzliches Unrecht," 105ff.

9. See Gustav Radbruch, "Erneuerung des Rechts," in *Der Mensch im Recht* (Göttingen: Vandenhoek und Ruprecht, 1961), 107ff.; Fritz Bauer, "Im Kampf um des Menschen Rechte," ([1955] 1998) in *Die Humanität der Rechtsordnung: Ausgewählte Schriften* (Frankfurt: Campus Verlag, 1998), 41; E. Schmidt, *Gesetz und Richter*, 14. Helmut Coing attempted to amplify the kind of natural law Radbruch had merely gestured toward; see Coing, "Die obersten Grundsätze des Rechts. Ein Versuch zur Neugründung des Naturrechts," in *Schriften der Süddeutschen Juristenzeitung*, 4 (1947). For a view critical of these efforts, see Hans Welzel, *Naturrecht und materiale Gerechtigkeit. Prolegomena zu einer Rechtsphilosopie* (Gottingen: Vandenhoeck & Ruprecht, 1962).

10. See Hans-Ulrich Evers, "Zum Unkritischen Naturrechtsbewusstsein in der Rechtsprechung der Gegenwart," *Juristenzeitung* 21 (April 1961): 241; *Entscheidungen des Reichsgerichts in Zivilsachen*, 118, 325, 327; *Entscheidungen des Bundesgerichtshofs in Zivilsachen* (hereafter BGHZ), 3, 106; *Entscheidungen des Bundesgerichtshofs in Strafsachen* (hereafter BGHSt), 6, 46; BGHSt, 4, 385, 390; BGHZ, 11, 34. For other Supreme Court cases expressing similar views, see BGHSt, 2, 238; BGHSt, 2, 177. Radbruch's formula was also taken up by the Federal Constitutional Court (*Bundesverfassungsgericht*, or BVerfG). On the influence of Radbruch on the Supreme Court and Constitutional Court, see Björn Schumacher, "Rezeption und Kritik der Radbruchschen Formel," Ph.D. dissertation (Göttingen University, 1985), 31–103. For differences between the Supreme Court's interpretation of natural law and that of the Constitutional Court, see Evers, "Zum unkritischen Naturrechtsbewusstsein," 241.

11. *NJW* (1949): 473ff.; *Deutsche Richterzeitung* (hereafter DRZ) (1950), 302; *Deutsche Rechtsprechung* 1; DRZ (1947), 343.

12. *JuNSV*, Lfd. Nr. 011, 156, 175; *Anmerkung*, *SJZ* (1947), 633–635.

13. Ibid., Lfd. Nr. 017, 350–352. For other euthanasia verdicts employing the same natural law discourse (including verdicts resulting in acquittal), see *JuNSV*, Lfd. Nrs. 014 (the Kalmenhof case), 102 (the Rhine province case, especially the part of the verdict pertaining to Hermann Wesse), 211 (the Baden case), 271 (the Eglfing-Haar case), 380 (the Westphalian case), 381 (the Uchtspringe case), and 383 (the Sachsenberg case).

14. The new issue for German courts was formulated by the Göttingen state court in 1953: "whether the defendants were able to become aware of [the wrongfulness of Nazi euthanasia] through a proper exertion of their conscience." *JuNSV*, Lfd. Nr. 381.

15. *JuNSV*, Lfd. Nr. 003, 33–35.

16. W. von Henle und Franz Schierlinger, eds., *Strafgesetzbuch für das Deutsche Reich* (Munich: C. H. Beck'sche Verlagsbuchhandlung, 1912), 227.

17. Lothar Dombrowski, ed., *Strafgesetzbuch: Textausgabe mit den wichtigsten Nebengesetzen und Kontrollratsgesetzen* (Stuttgart: W. Kohlhammer Verlag, 1948), 83.

18. Quoted by Roland Freisler, "Gedanken über das Gesetz zur Änderung des Reichstrafgesetzbuches," *Deutsche Justiz, Rechtsplege und Rechtspolitik* (26 September 1941), 934.

19. Postwar German jurists defended the revised version of section 211 as a law untainted by National Socialist ideology, claiming it was modeled on Article 99 of the outline for the Swiss Penal Code of 1918. See Dombrowski, *Strafgesetzbuch*, 83; Schönke, *Deutsche Juristische Zeitung* (1947), 77; OLG Köln in DRZ (1946), 94.

20. *JuNSV*, Lfd. Nr. 003, 36–38.

21. Ibid., Lfd. Nr. 011, 142.

22. Ibid., 143–144.

23. Ibid., 145.

24. Ibid., 147.

25. Ibid., 147, 160.

26. Ibid., 147–148.

27. Ibid., 149.

28. Ibid., 150.

29. Ibid., 150, 161.

30. Ibid., 151.

31. Ibid. Two other station nurses, identified in the verdict only as K. and F., were charged in the Eichberg killings, but they were acquitted for lack of evidence.

32. *JuNSV*, Lfd. Nr. 011, 164–165.

33. Ibid., Lfd. Nr. 017, 326–327.

34. Ibid., 359–360.

35. Ibid., 325.

36. Ibid.

37. Ibid., 325–326.

38. Ibid., 317.

39. Ibid., 357–358.

40. Ibid., 358–360.

41. Quoted in Friedrich, *Die kalte Amnestie*, 191.

42. *JuNSV*, Lfd. Nr. 017, 345.

43. Ibid., 372. In German criminal law, unlike its Anglo-American counterpart, the government can appeal a verdict unfavorable to it. Under Anglo-American law, appeal can only be made by the defendant; issues of guilt or innocence resolved in the defendants' favor are considered res judicata (matters adjudicated) that are not subject to appeal.

44. *JuNSV*, Lfd. Nr. 014, 230; Klee, *Dokumente*, 62–63.

45. *JuNSV*, Lfd. Nr. 014, 230–231.

46. Ibid., 233.

47. Ibid., 232–233.

48. Ibid.

49. Ibid., 235–236.

50. Ibid., 236.

51. Ibid.

52. Ibid., 236–237.

53. Ibid., 250–251.

54. Ibid., 251.

55. Ibid., 237–238.

56. Ibid., 238.

57. Ibid., 238–239.

58. Ibid., 239–240.

59. Ibid., 259–260.

60. Ibid., 274–275.

61. Koppel S. Pinson, *Modern Germany: Its History and Civilization* (Prospect Heights, IL: Waveland Press, Inc., 1989), 554; Holger Herwig, *Hammer or Anvil? Modern Germany 1648–Present* (Lexington, MA: D. C. Heath & Company, 1994), 368–369; Mary Fulbrook, *The Divided Nation: A History of Germany, 1918–1990* (New York: Oxford University Press, 1991), 162–163.

62. *JuNSV*, Lfd. Nr. 117, 59.

4. LUCIFER ON THE RUINS OF THE WORLD: THE GERMAN EUTHANASIA TRIALS, 1948–1950

1. Taylor, *Final Report to the Secretary of the Army*, 261.

2. Frei, *Adenauer's Germany*, 179–183; Thomas Allen Schwartz, "Die Begnadigung deutscher Kriegsverbrecher: John J. McCloy und die Häftlinge von Landsberg," VfZ, 38 (1990): 382–383.

3. Frei, *Adenauer's Germany*, 94, 191–201; Herbert, *Best*, 455–456.

4. 61 RGSt. 242 (1927).

5. *JuNSV*, Lfd. Nr. 088, 255.

6. Ibid., 255–256.

7. *JuNSV*, Lfd. Nr. 088, 261. The "collision of duties" defense, a species of the doctrine of necessity, is conceptually distinct from extrastatutory necessity. The latter contemplates the sacrifice of one "legal interest" (*Rechtsgut*) in order to preserve another legal interest deemed superior to it. A person would be justified, for example, in taking someone else's car without his permission in order to drive a gravely ill child to the hospital. A collision of duties, on the other hand, exists where an actor faces two mutually irreconcilable duties and elects to avoid the greater injustice by violating one of them. To have applied the theory of extrastatutory necessity in the Scheuern case would have meant branding the lives of one group of patients as more valuable than those of the group sacrificed—a style of thought reminiscent of

National Socialism. This point was not lost on the Koblenz court; regrettably, its subtlety eluded later courts.

8. *JuNSV*, Lfd. Nr. 088, 261–264.

9. Ibid., 262, 267.

10. Ibid., Lfd. Nr. 102, 476–477.

11. Ibid., 477.

12. Ibid., 478.

13. Ibid., 479.

14. Ibid., 479–480.

15. Ibid., 480–481.

16. Ibid., 482.

17. Ibid., 483.

18. Ibid., 484–485.

19. Ibid., 486–487.

20. Ibid., 492–497.

21. Ibid., 499.

22. Ibid., 500–501.

23. Ibid., 502–504.

24. Ibid., 504–512.

25. Ibid., 513; de Mildt, *In the Name of the People*, 157–158.

26. *JuNSV*, Lfd. Nr. 102, 514–517.

27. Ibid., 518.

28. Ibid., 535. Since its inception in the 1920s, "extrastatutory necessity" has pertained to things protected by the law, or "legal interests" or "goods" (such as bodily integrity, freedom, honor, or property), which come into conflict in a situation not of the actor's own making. The classic example is dynamiting a house to prevent fire from engulfing the entire neighborhood. The two legal interests in such a case— preserving the house to be dynamited versus preserving the neighborhood—are in conflict with each other. German law in this scenario would justify destroying the one house to save the others, because the "legal interest" of many houses is superior to that of a single house. In such a case of extrastatutory necessity, the doctrine operates to justify the actor's conduct. In reversing the lower court's verdict, the Supreme Court for the British Zone was sending an unequivocal message that the doctrine of extrastatutory necessity could not be used to justify the sacrifice of one group of people for another, because human lives were not "legal interests" that could be measured against one another.

29. De Mildt, *In the Name of the People*, 156. On the origins and purpose of the Supreme Court for the British Zone within the postwar administration of justice in Germany, see de Mildt, *In the Name of the People*, 358n39; Martin Broszat, "Siegerjustiz oder strafrechtliche Selbstreinigung: Vergangenheitsbewältigung der Justiz 1945– 1949," in *VfZ*, 4 (1981); Wolfgang Benz, "Die Entnazifizierung der Richter," in *Justizalltag im Dritten Reich*, eds. Diestelkamp and Stolleis (Frankfurt am Main: Fischer, 1988), 112–130. The Supreme Court for the British Zone also reversed the lower court's verdicts regarding We., R., Pohlisch, and Panse, but on different legal grounds that do not concern us in this chapter. See *JuNSV*, Lfd. Nr. 102, 538–544.

30. Friedrich, *Die kalte Amnestie*, 228.

31. *JuNSV*, Lfd. Nr. 155a.

32. Ibid.

33. De Mildt, *In the Name of the People*, 107.

34. *JuNSV*, Lfd. Nr. 155a.

35. Section 212 defines "manslaughter" simply as a killing that does not qualify as murder under section 211.

36. *JuNSV*, Lfd. Nr. 155a.

37. See Regina Schmidt and Egon Becker, "Reaktionen auf politische Vorgänge," in *Frankfurter Beiträge zur Soziologien*, Bd. 19 (Frankfurt am Main: Europäische Verlagsanstalt, 1967), 117ff. See also the following trials: the Treblinka trial (especially the court's differential treatment of Kurt Franz and Gustav Münzberger), *JuNSV*, Lfd. Nr. 596 (1965); the trial of Josef ("Sepp") Hirtreiter, *JuNSV*, Lfd. Nr. 270 (1951); the Auschwitz trial, *JuNSV*, Lfd. 595 (1965); and the *Einsatzgruppen* trial, *JuNSV*, Lfd. 555 (1963). Jörg Friedrich's discussion of these trials is particularly trenchant in *Die kalte Amnestie*, 350–378. For Herbert Jäger's comments on the goals of prosecuting Nazi crimes, see Jäger, "Strafrecht und nationalsozialistische Gewaltverbrechen," *Kritische Justiz* 1 (1968), 148–149.

38. *JuNSV*, Lfd. Nr. 211.

39. Ibid.

40. The insensitivity of Sprauer's defense here is noteworthy: it amounted to the assertion that his professional career was a higher legal good than the lives of Baden mental patients.

41. *JuNSV*, Lfd. Nr. 211.

42. Ibid.

43. Ibid.

5. LAW AND POWER: THE WEST GERMAN EUTHANASIA TRIALS, 1948–1953

1. On the convoluted history of the furor over the proposed European Defense Community (EDC), see Walter LaFeber, *The American Age: U.S. Foreign Policy at Home and Abroad Since 1896*, vol. 2 (New York: W. W. Norton & Company, 1994).

2. Frank Stern, *The Whitewashing of the Yellow Badge*, 300; Eleonore Sterling, "Judenfreunde. Fragwürdiger Philosemitismus in der Bundesrepublik," *Die Zeit* (October 12, 1965). Sterling's appraisal of the function of philosemitism in postwar Germany also applies to the suppression of continued trials of Nazi defendants; for Sterling, philosemitism "has less to do with Jews, and more with reasons of state and foreign policy," insofar as it certified "as already completed a process and product as yet only in the state of emergence; namely, a true democracy and a positive attitude toward the Jewish minority." On the "normative demarcation" of the Federal Republic from Nazism and Soviet Communism and its instrumentalization to promote the restoration of German sovereignty, see Norbert Frei, *Adenauer's Germany*, chapters 10–12.

3. Ulrich Herbert, *Best*, 483–484; Friedrich, *Die kalte Amnestie*, 282–291.

4. *JuNSV*, Lfd. Nr. 226, 94–95.

5. Ibid., 95.

6. Ibid., 99.

7. Ibid., 99–100.

8. Ibid., 100–101.

9. Ibid., 102.

10. Ibid., 113.

11. The quote is from Schmidt, *Süddeutsche Juristische Zeitung* (1949), 569.

12. *JuNSV*, Lfd. Nr. 226, 131.

13. De Mildt, *In the Name of the People*, 168.

14. *JuNSV*, Lfd. Nr. 225, 14–15.

15. Ibid., 18–19.

16. Ibid., 20.

17. Ibid., 28–44.

18. Ibid., 56–59.

19. Quoted in de Mildt, *In the Name of the People*, 164.

20. The neologism "flipability" was coined by Critical Legal Studies theoretician Duncan Kennedy, but its roots go back to Wesley Hohfeld's idea that legal propositions can be "flipped," that is, interpreted in more than one way (and often in contradictory ways). See Wesley Hohfeld, "Some Fundamental Legal Conceptions as Applied in Judicial Reasoning," *Yale Law Journal* 23 (1913), 16.

21. Lehner's testimony from the Doctors' Trial appears in Friedrich, *Die kalte Amnestie*, 75–76.

22. *JuNSV*, Lfd. Nr. 271, 284.

23. Ibid., 285–287.

24. Ibid., 292–295.

25. Faltlhauser's sponsorship of the *Sonderkost* was reported by the director of the Regensburg mental hospital, Dr. Paul Reiss, who was present at the conference of directors in the Bavarian Interior Ministry in November 1942. Reiss offered his testimony before the same Munich court in 1948 that later presided over the Pfannmüller case. The court's institutional memory must have been, at best, a dim one. See 1 KLs 154/48 StA München, excerpted in Klee, *Dokumente*, 286. Faltlhauser was himself indicted for murder in July 1949 for his contributions to the killing of well over a thousand patients at Kaufbeuren. The Augsburg *Landgericht* acquitted him of the murder charge but found him guilty of manslaughter for the deaths of 300 patients. He was sentenced to a prison term of three years by a court that praised him for his "compassion," "one of the noblest motives in human conduct." See *JuNSV*, Lfd. Nr. 162, 180.

26. *BGHSt*, 2, 191.

27. *JuNSV*, Lfd. Nr. 383, 8–9.

28. Ibid., 10–11.

29. Ibid., 14–27.

30. Ibid., 48–53.

31. Ibid., 54–56. The "exertion of conscience" defense appears to be a form of "mistake of law" (*Verbotsirrtum*), that is, the defense that the actor believed in good

faith—and had sufficient reason to believe—that his actions were legally justified. On *Verbotsirrtum* under German law, see Hans-Heinrich Jescheck, *Lehrbuch des Strafrechts*, 405–421.

32. *JuNSV*, Lfd. Nr. 381, 744–745.

33. Ibid., 756–757.

34. Ibid., 758–765.

35. Ibid., 747–748.

36. Ibid., 763–767.

37. Herbert, *Best*, 439.

38. *JuNSV*, Lfd. Nr. 380, 664–674.

39. BGHSt, 2, 194.

40. *JuNSV*, Lfd. Nr. 380, 703–704.

41. *JuNSV*, Lfd. Nr. 380; Lfd. Nr. 480, 3–4.

42. *JuNSV*, Lfd. Nr. 380, 19–21.

43. See, for example, the trials of the Waldniel nurses, *JuNSV*, Lfd. Nrs. 282 (1951) and 339 (1953).

44. *JuNSV*, Lfd. Nr. 587.

45. Dressen, "NS-'Euthanasie' Prozesse," 47. On the convoluted trial history of the four gassing doctors, see de Mildt, *In the Name of the People*, 115–126; Klee, *Was sie taten*, 113–128. Bunke and Ulrich would eventually be re-indicted in the mid-1980s and convicted of aiding and abetting murder.

CONCLUSION

1. Letter from Allers to Vorberg, 20 November 1954, excerpted in Klee, *Was sie taten*, 65.

2. Quoted in Frei, *Adenauer's Germany*, 189.

3. See Assmann and Frevert, *Geschichtsvergessenheit*, 88–96.

4. Frei, *Adenauer's Germany*, 304–307.

5. Jeffrey Herf, "Amnesty and Amnesia," *New Republic* (10 March 2003), 37.

6. *JuNSV*, Lfd. Nr. 211.

7. Interviews with Hans-Heinrich Jescheck (7 March 2000) and Eckhard Herych (3 February 2000), both from the author's private notes.

Amtsgericht	municipal (or district) court
Basic Law	the German Constitution of 1949
Beihilfe zum Mord	aiding and abetting murder
BGHSt	Decisions of the West German Supreme Court in Criminal Matters
BGHZ	Decisions of the West German Supreme Court in Civil Matters
Bundesgerichtshof	West German Supreme Court (post-1949)
BVerfG	West German Constitutional Court
CDU	Christian Democratic Union
DRZ	*German Judges' Newspaper*
Einsatzgruppen	operational units; involved in the mass murder of Jews, the mentally ill, and others in the East
14f13	operation to reduce concentration camp populations through mass killing; made use of T-4 personnel

FRG	Federal Republic of Germany
geheime Reichssache	secret state matter
Gehilfe	accomplice
Gekrat	The Charitable Foundation for the Transport of Patients, Inc.
Gutachter	T-4 medical expert
Heimtücke	element of malice in the German law of murder
ICC	International Criminal Court
IMT	International Military Tribunal
JuNSV	*The Judiciary and Nazi Crimes*
KdF	personal chancellery of Adolf Hitler
Kinderaktion	children's euthanasia operation
Kinderfachabteilung	children's ward
Kripo	criminal police
KTI	criminal technical institute
Landgericht (LG)	state (or regional) court
lebensunwertes Leben	life unworthy of life
Lfd. Nr.	serial number
MDR	*Monthly Journal for German Law*
MGR	Military Government Regulations
Meldebogen	euthanasia program registration forms
NARA	National Archives Records Administration, College Park
niedrige Beweggründe	element of base motives in the German law of murder, section 211
NJW	*New Legal Weekly*
NMT	National Military Tribunal
Notstand	the defense of necessity
NSDAP	National Socialist German Workers Party
Obergutachter	chief T-4 medical expert
Oberlandesgericht	state (or regional) appellate court
OCCWC	Office of Chief of Counsel for War Crimes
OGHBC	Supreme Court for the British Zone of Occupation
Operation Reinhard	the extermination of Polish Jewry
Ostarbeiter	eastern workers

Pflichtenkollision	conflict of duties (as criminal defense)
RAG	Reich Cooperative for State Hospitals and Nursing Homes
Rechtsgut	legal interest
RG	record group
Reichsgericht	German Supreme Court (pre-1945)
RSHA	Reich Security Main Office
schwachsinnig	feeble-minded
Schwurgericht	panel of lay assessors
SJZ	South German Jurists' Newspaper
Sonderbehandlung	Nazi code word for killing
StA	public prosecutor
StGB	German Penal Code
Täter	perpetrator
Teilnahme	complicity
T-4	the adult euthanasia operation, administered by the KdF, Main Office II
Totschlag	manslaughter
übergesetzlicher Notstand	the defense of extrastatutory necessity
uk (*unabkömmlich*)	designation of "indispensable"
Verbotsirrtum	mistake of law
VfZ	*Quarterly Journal for Contemporary History*
"wild" euthanasia	decentralized killing of mentally ill persons after August 24, 1941
Zwischenanstalt	transit center in the T-4 program

BIBLIOGRAPHY

Aly, Götz. *"Final Solution": Nazi Population Policy and the Murder of the European Jews*. Trans. Belinda Cooper and Allison Brown. London: Arnold, 1999.

———. "'Jewish Resettlement:' Reflections on the Political Prehistory of the Holocaust." In *National Socialist Extermination Policies: Contemporary German Perspectives and Controversies*, ed. Ulrich Herbert, 53–82. New York: Berghahn Books, 2000.

———, Peter Chroust, and Christian Pross, eds. *Cleansing the Fatherland: Nazi Medicine and Racial Hygiene*. Baltimore: Johns Hopkins University Press, 1994.

American Tobacco Co. v. U.S., 328 U.S. 781 (1946).

Arendt, Hannah. *Eichmann in Jerusalem: A Report on the Banality of Evil*. New York: Penguin Books, 1977.

Arndt, Ino, and Wolfgang Scheffler. "Organisierter Massenmord an Juden in nationalsozialistischen Vernichtungslagern." *Vierteljahrshefte für Zeitgeschichte* 24 (1976): 105–135.

Assmann, Aleida, and Ute Frevert. *Geschichtsvergessenheit/Geschichtsversessenheit: Vom Umgang mit deutschen Vergangenheiten nach 1945*. Stuttgart: Deutsche Verlags-Anstalt, 1999.

Bass, Gary J. *Stay the Hand of Vengeance: The Politics of War Crimes Tribunals*. Princeton, NJ: Princeton University Press, 2000.

Bassiouni, M. Cherif. *Crimes Against Humanity in International Law*. The Hague: Kluwer Law International, 1999.

Bauer, Fritz. *Die Humanität der Rechtsordnung: Ausgewählte Schriften*. Frankfurt: Campus Verlag, 1998.

Benz, Wolfgang. "Die Entnazifizierung der Richter." In *Justizalltag im Dritten Reich*, eds. Diestelkamp and Stolleis, 112–130. Frankfurt am Main: Fischer, 1988.

———. "Nachkriegsgesellschaft und Nationalsozialismus: Erinnerung, Amnestie, Abwehr." In *Erinnern oder Verweigern*, Dachauer Hefte 6, 13–21. Dachau: Verlag Dachauer Hefte, 1990.

Benzenhöfer, Udo. "Die Auswahl der Angeklagten." *Deutsches Ärzteblatt* 93:45 (8 November 1996): C-2057.

Beyerchen, Alan. "Rational Means and Irrational Ends: Thoughts on the Technology of Racism in the Third Reich." *Central European History* 30 (1997): 386–402.

Biddle, Francis. *In Brief Authority*. Garden City, NY: Doubleday, 1962.

Binding, Karl, and Alfred Hoche. *Die Freigabe der Vernichtung lebensunwerten Lebens: Ihr Mass und Ihre Form*. Leipzig: Verlag von Felix Meiner, 1920.

Bock, Gisela. *Zwangssterilisation im Nationalsozialismus: Studien zur Rassenpolitik und Frauenpolitik*. Opladen: Westdeutscher Verlag, 1986.

Broszat, Martin. "Siegerjustiz oder strafrechtliche Selbstreinigung: Vergangenheitsbewältigung der Justiz 1945–1949." *Vierteljahrshefte für Zeitgeschichte*, 4 (1981).

Buck v. Bell. 274 U.S. 200 (1927).

Burleigh, Michael. *The Racial State: Germany 1933–1945*. Cambridge: Cambridge University Press, 1991.

———. *Death and Deliverance: "Euthanasia" in Germany 1900–1945*. Cambridge: Cambridge University Press, 1994.

Buscher, Frank M. *The U.S. War Crimes Trial Program in Germany, 1946–1955*. New York: Greenwood Press, 1989.

Carr, E. H. *What Is History?* London: Penguin Books, 1976.

Churchill, Winston S. *The Second World War*, Vol. 5, *Closing the Ring*. New York: Bantam Books, 1962.

Coing, Helmut. "Die obersten Grundsätze des Rechts. Ein Versuch zur Neugründung des Naturrechts." In *Schriften der Süddeutschen Juristenzeitung*, 4 (1947).

Deleuze, Gilles, and Félix Guattari. "Rhizome." In *A Thousand Plateaus: Capitalism and Schizophrenia*. London: Athlone, 1988.

de Mildt, Dick. *In the Name of the People: Perpetrators of Genocide in the Reflection of their Post-War Prosecution in West Germany*. The Hague: Martinus Nijhoff Publishers, 1996.

———, and C. F. Rüter. *Die Westdeutschen Strafverfahren Wegen Nationalsozialistischer Tötungsverbrechen 1945–1997: Eine Systematische Verfahrensbeschreibung mit Karten und Registern*. Amsterdam and Munich: APA-Holland University Press/K.G. Sauer Verlag, 1998.

Domarus, Max, ed. *Hitler. Reden und Proklamationen 1932–1945*. Wiesbaden: R. Löwit, 1973.

Dombrowski, Lothar, ed. *Strafgesetzbuch: Textausgabe mit den wichtigsten Nebengesetzen und Kontrollratsgesetzen*. Stuttgart: W. Kohlhammer Verlag, 1948.

Douglas, Lawrence. *The Memory of Judgment: Making Law and History in the Trials of the Holocaust*. New Haven: Yale University Press, 2001.

Dressen, Willi. "NS-'Euthanasie'-Prozesse in der Bundesrepublik Deutschland im Wandel der Zeit." In *NS-"Euthanasie" vor Gericht: Fritz Bauer und die Grenzen juristischer Bewältigung*, eds. Hanno Loewy and Bettina Winter, 35–58. Frankfurt: Campus Verlag, 1996.

Dünnebier. "Der amerikanische Strafprozess im Spiegel der Rechtsprechung des Court of Appeals." *Neue Juristische Wochenschrift*, 27 (1952): 1040–1043.

Entscheidungen des Bundesgerichtshofs in Strafsachen, 4, 6, 11, 46, 385, 390.

Entscheidungen des Bundesgerichtshofs in Zivilsachen, 3, 106.

Entscheidungen des Reichsgerichts in Zivilsachen, 118, 325, 327.

Eser, Albin. "Strafrecht." In *Staatslexikon*, ed. Görres-Gesellschaft, 331–343. Freiburg: Verlag Herder, 1989.

Evers, Hans-Ulrich. "Zum unkritischen Naturrechtsbewusstsein in der Rechtsprechung der Gegenwart." *Süddeutsche Juristische Zeitung* (21 April 1961): 241–248.

Fegert, Jörg Michael. "Der Weg zum Nürnberger Ärzteprozess und die Folgerungen daraus." *Deutsches Ärzteblatt* 93:43 (25 October 1996): C-1953.

Fletcher, George P. *Basic Concepts of Criminal Law*. New York: Oxford University Press, 1998.

———. "Two Modes of Legal Thought." *Yale Law Journal* 90 (1981): 970, 980–982.

Foucault, Michel. "Nietzsche, Genealogy, History." In *The Foucault Reader*, ed. Paul Rabinow, 76–100. New York: Pantheon, 1984.

Frei, Norbert. *Adenauer's Germany and the Nazi Past: The Politics of Amnesty and Integration*. Trans. Joel Golb. New York: Columbia University Press, 2002.

Freisler, Roland. "Gedanken über das Gesetz zur Änderung des Reichstrafgesetzbuches." *Deutsche Justiz, Rechtsplege und Rechtspolitik* (26 September 1941): 929–938.

Friedlander, Henry. "The Judiciary and Nazi Crimes in Postwar Germany." *The Simon Wiesenthal Center Annual*, 1 (1982): 27–44.

———. *The Origins of Nazi Genocide: From Euthanasia to the Final Solution*. Chapel Hill: University of North Carolina Press, 1995.

Friedrich, Jörg. *Die kalte Amnestie: NS-Täter in der Bundesrepublik*. Munich: Piper Verlag, 1994.

———. *Der Brand: Deutschland im Bombenkrieg, 1940–1945*. Munich: Propyläen Verlag, 2002.

Galton, Francis. *Inquiries into Human Faculty and its Development*. London: Macmillan & Company, 1883.

———. "A Theory of Heredity." *The Contemporary Review*, 10 (1875): 80–95.

Gilbert, Martin. *Winston S. Churchill, 1941–1945: Road to Victory*. London: William Heinemann, 1986.

Godau-Schüttke, Klaus-Detlev. *Die Heyde/Sawade Affäre: Wie Juristen und Mediziner den NS-Euthanasieprofessor Heyde nach 1945 deckten und straflos blieben*. Baden-Baden: Nomos Verlagsgesellschaft, 1998.

Gould, Stephen Jay. *The Mismeasure of Man*. New York: W. W. Norton & Company, 1996.

Grabbe, Hans-Jürgen. "Konrad Adenauer, John Foster Dulles, and West German-American Relations." In *John Foster Dulles and the Diplomacy of the Cold War*, ed. Richard H. Immerman, 109–132. Princeton, NJ: Princeton University Press, 1990.

Graveson, R. H. "Der Grundsatz 'nulla poena sine lege' und Kontrollratsgesetz Nr. 10." *Monatschrift für deutsches Recht* (1947): 278–281.

Green, A. Wigfall. "The Military Commission." *The American Journal of International Law*, 42:4 (October 1948): 832–848.

Harris, Sir Arthur. *Bomber Offensive*. London: Greenhill Books, 1947.

Henle, W. von, and Franz Schierlinger, eds. *Strafgesetzbuch für das Deutsche Reich*. Munich: C. H. Beck'sche Verlagsbuchhandlung, 1912.

Herbert, Ulrich. *Best: Biographische Studien über Radikalismus, Weltanschauung und Vernunft 1903–1989*. Bonn: Dietz Verlag, 1996.

———. "New Answers and Questions." In *National Socialist Extermination Policies: Contemporary German Perspectives and Controversies*, ed. Ulrich Herbert, 1–44. New York: Berghahn Books, 2000.

———. "Racism and Rational Calculation: The Role of 'Utilitarian' Strategies of Legitimation in the National Socialist 'Weltanschauung.'" *Yad Vashem Studies* 24 (1994): 131–195.

Herf, Jeffrey. "Amnesty and Amnesia." *New Republic* (10 March 2003): 33–47.

———. *Divided Memory: The Nazi Past in the Two Germanys*. Cambridge, MA: Harvard University Press, 1997.

Herwig, Holger. *Hammer or Anvil? Modern Germany 1648–Present*. Lexington, MA: D. C. Heath & Company, 1994.

Hilberg, Raul. *The Destruction of the European Jews*. New York: Holmes & Meier, 1985.

Hoche, A. E. *Krieg und Seelenleben*. Freiburg-im-Breisgau and Leipzig: Speyer & Kaerner, 1915.

Hohfeld, Wesley. "Some Fundamental Legal Conceptions as Applied in Judicial Reasoning." *Yale Law Journal*, 23 (1913).

Interrogation of Hans Heinrich Lammers, 25 October 1945, NARA, M1270, Roll 11.

Interrogation of Karl Brandt, NARA, M 1270, Roll 2.

Jackson, Robert. *Report of Robert H. Jackson, United States Representative to the International Conference on Military Trials, London 1945*. Washington, DC: Department of State, 1949.

Jäger, Herbert. "Strafrecht und nationalsozialistische Gewaltverbrechen." *Kritische Justiz*, 1 (1968): 143–157.

———. *Verbrechen unter totalitärer Herrschaft: Studien zur nationalsozialistischen Gewaltverbrechen*. Freiburg-im-Breisgau: Walter-Verlag, 1967.

Jaspers, Karl. "Interview." *Der Monat* 152 (1961): 15.

———. "Für Völkermord gibt es keine Verjährung." *Der Spiegel*, 21 (1966): 49.

Jescheck, Hans-Heinrich. *Lehrbuch des Strafrechts: Allgemeiner Teil*. Berlin: Duncker & Humblot, 1988.

Kater, Michael H. *Doctors under Hitler*. Chapel Hill: University of North Carolina Press, 1989.

Kendall, Gavin, and Gary Wickham. *Using Foucault's Methods*. London: Sage Publications, 1999.

Kershaw, Ian. *Hitler: 1889–1936, Hubris*. New York: W. W. Norton & Company, 1998.

———. *Hitler: 1936–1945, Nemesis*. New York: W. W. Norton & Company, 2000.

Kevles, Daniel J. *In the Name of Eugenics: Genetics and the Uses of Human Heredity*. Cambridge: Harvard University Press, 1995.

Klee, Ernst. *Auschwitz, die NS-Medizin und ihre Opfer*. Frankfurt a.M.: Fischer, 2001.

———. *Dokumente zur "Euthanasie."* Frankfurt a.M.: Fischer, 1997.

———. *"Euthanasie" im NS-Staat: Die Vernichtung "lebensunwerten Lebens."* Frankfurt a.M.: Fischer, 1986.

———. *Was sie taten, Was sie wurden: Ärzte, Juristen, und andere Beteiligte am Kranken- oder Judenmord*. Frankfurt a.M.: Fischer, 1998.

———, Willi Dressen, and Volker Riess, eds. *"The Good Old Days": The Holocaust as Seen by Its Perpetrators and Bystanders*. New York: The Free Press, 1991.

Korn, Hans-Joachim. "Täterschaft oder Teilnahme bei staatlich organisierten Verbrechen." *Neu Juristische Wochenschrift*, 27 (1965): 1206–1210.

Krausnick, Helmut, and Hans-Heinrich Wilhelm. *Die Truppe des Weltanschauungskrieges: die Einsatzgruppen der Sicherheitspolizei und des SD, 1938–1942*. Stuttgart: Deutsche Verlags-Anstalt, 1981.

Kühl, Stefan. *The Nazi Connection: Eugenics, American Racism, and German National Socialism*. New York: Oxford University Press, 1994.

LaFeber, Walter. *America, Russia, and the Cold War, 1945–1992*. New York: McGraw-Hill, 1993.

———. *The American Age: U.S. Foreign Policy at Home and Abroad Since 1896*, vol. 2. New York: W. W. Norton & Company, 1994.

Lauterpacht, Hersh. "The Law of Nations and the Punishment of War Crimes." *British Year Book of International Law*, 21 (1944): 58–95

Leffler, Melvyn P. *The Specter of Communism: The United States and the Origins of the Cold War, 1917–1953*. New York: Hill and Wang, 1994.

Lévitt, Albert. "Extent and Function of the Doctrine of Mens Rea." *Illinois Law Review*, 17 (1922): 578–590.

Lewald, Manfred. "Das Dritte Reich—Rechtsstaat oder Unrechtsstaat?" *Neue Juristische Wochenschrift*, 36 (1964): 1658–1661.

Mann, Michael. "Were the Perpetrators of Genocide 'Ordinary Men' or 'Real Nazis'? Results from Fifteen Hundred Biographies." *Holocaust and Genocide Studies*, 14:3 (Winter 2000): 331–366.

Markusen, Eric, and David Kopf. *The Holocaust and Strategic Bombing: Genocide and Total War in the Twentieth Century*. San Francisco: Westview Press, 1995.

Marrus, Michael R. *The Nuremberg War Crimes Trial, 1945–46: A Documentary History*. Boston: Bedford Books, 1997.

Mayer, Joseph. *Gesetzliche Unfruchtbarmachung Geisteskranker*. Freiburg: Herder & Company, 1927.

Merkl, Peter H. *Political Violence Under the Swastika*. Princeton, NJ: Princeton University Press, 1975.

Middlebrook, Martin. *The Battle of Hamburg: Allied Bomber Forces Against a German City in 1943*. New York: Charles Scribner's Sons, 1981.

Mitscherlich, Alexander, and Fred Mielke. *Das Diktat der Menschenverachtung*. Heidelberg: Lambert Schneider, 1947.

———, and Margarete Mitscherlich. *The Inability to Mourn: Principles of Collective Behavior*. New York: Grove Press, 1975.

Möhrle, Alfred. "Der Arzt im Nationalsozialismus: Der Weg zum Nürnberger Ärzteprozess und die Folgerungen daraus." *Deutsches Ärzteblatt* 93:43 (25 October 1996): C-1952.

Müller, Ingo. *Furchtbare Juristen: Die unbewältigte Vergangenheit unserer Justiz*. Munich: Kindler Verlags GmbH, 1987.

National Archives Microfilm Publications Pamphlet Describing M 1078, *United States of America v. Alfons Klein et al.* (Case Files 12-449 and 000-12-31).

Pearson, Karl. *The Life, Letters, and Labours of Francis Galton*, 3 vols. Cambridge: Cambridge University Press, 1914–1930.

Pinson, Koppel S. *Modern Germany: Its History and Civilization*. Prospect Heights, Illinois: Waveland Press 1989.

Piper, Franciszek. *Die Zahl der Opfer von Auschwitz*. Trans. Jochen August. Oswiecim: Verlag Staatliches Museum, 1993.

Proctor, Robert N. *Racial Hygiene: Medicine under the Nazis*. Cambridge: Harvard University Press, 1988.

Radbruch, Gustav. "Erneuerung des Rechts." In *Der Mensch im Recht*. Göttingen: Vandenhoek und Ruprecht, 1961.

———. *Der Geist des englischen Rechts*. Göttingen: Vandenhoeck & Rupprecht, 1956.

———. "Gesetzliches Unrecht und übergesetzliches Recht." *SJZ*, 5 (August 1946): 105–108.

———. *Rechtsphilosophie*. Stuttgart: Koehler, 1973.

———. "Wiedergutmachungsrecht." *SJZ* (1946): 36.

Reitlinger, Gerald. *The Final Solution: The Attempt to Exterminate the Jews of Europe, 1939–1945*. New York: A. S. Barnes & Company, 1961.

Rückerl, Adalbert. *The Investigation of Nazi Crimes 1945–1978*. Hamden, CT: Archon Books, 1980.

———, ed. *NS-Vernichtungslager im Spiegel deutscher Strafprozesse*. Munich: Deutscher Taschenbuch Verlag, 1979.

Rüter, Adelheid L., C. F. Rüter, H. H. Fuchs, and Irene Sagel-Grande, eds. *Justiz und NS-Verbrechen: Sammlung deutscher Strafurteile wegen nationalsozialistischer Tötungsverbrechen 1945–1966*. Amsterdam: Amsterdam University Press, 1968–1981.

Schissler, Hanna, ed. *The Miracle Years: A Cultural History of West Germany, 1949–1968*. Princeton, NJ: Princeton University Press, 2001.

Schmidt, Eberhard. *Gesetz und Richter: Wert und Unwert des Positivismus*. Karlsruhe: Verlag C. F. Müller, 1952.

Schmidt, Regina, and Egon Becker. "Reaktionen auf politische Vorgänge." In *Frankfurter Beiträge zur Soziologien*, Bd. 19. Frankfurt am Main: Europäische Verlagsanstalt, 1967.

Schmidt-Leichner. "Deutscher und anglo-amerikanischer Strafprozess." *Neue Juristische Wochenschrift*, 1 (1951): 7–10.

Schmuhl, Hans-Walter. *Rassenhygiene, Nationalsozialismus, Euthanasie: von der Verhütung zur Vernichtung "lebensunwerten Lebens," 1890–1945*. Göttingen: Vandenhoeck & Ruprecht, 1987.

Schröder, Rainer. *Rechtsgeschichte*. Munster: Alpmann & Schmidt, 1992.

Schüle, Erwin. "Die Zentrale Stelle der Landesjustizverwaltungen zur Aufklärung nationalsozialistischer Gewaltverbrechen in Ludwigsburg." *Juristenzeitung* (1962): 241.

Schumacher, Björn. "Rezeption und Kritik der Radbruchschen Formel." Ph.D. dissertation, Göttingen University, 1985.

Schwartz, Thomas Allen. "Die Begnadigung Deutscher Kriegsverbrecher: John J. McCloy und die Häftlinge von Landsberg." *Vierteljahrshefte für Zeitgeschichte*, 38 (1990): 375–414.

Sereny, Gitta. *Into that Darkness: An Examination of Conscience*. New York: Vintage Books, 1983.

Smith, Bradley F. *Reaching Judgment at Nuremberg: The Untold Story of How the Nazi War Criminals Were Judged*. New York: Basic Books, 1977.

Steinbach, Peter. *Nationalsozialistische Gewaltverbrechen. Die Diskussion in der deutschen Öffentlichkeit*. Berlin: Colloquium Verlag, 1981.

Steininger, Rolf. "John Foster Dulles, the European Defense Community, and the German Question." In *John Foster Dulles and the Diplomacy of the Cold War*, ed. Richard H. Immerman, 79–108. Princeton, NJ: Princeton University Press, 1990.

Sterling, Eleanore. "Judenfreunde. Fragwürdiger Philosemitismus in der Bundesrepublik." *Die Zeit*, 12 (December 1965).

Stern, Frank. *Im Anfang war Auschwitz: Antisemitismus und Philosemitismus im deutschen Nachkrieg*. Gerlingen: Bleicher Verlag, 1991.

———. *The Whitewashing of the Yellow Badge: Antisemitism and Philosemitism in Postwar Germany*. Trans. William Templer. Oxford: Pergamon Press, 1992.

Strafgesetzbuch mit Einführungsgesetz, Wehrstrafgesetz, Wirtschaftsstrafgesetz, usw. 33. Auflage. Munich: C. H. Beck, 1999.

Streit, Christian. *Keine Kameraden: Die Wehrmacht und die sowjetischen Kriegsgefangenen 1941 bis 1945*. Stuttgart: Deutsche Verlagsanstalt, 1978.

Taylor, Telford. *Final Report to the Secretary of the Army*. CD-Rom. Seattle, WA: Aristarchus Knowledge Industries, 1995.

———. *Anatomy of the Nuremberg Trials: A Personal Memoir*. Boston: Little, Brown, 1992.

United States Holocaust Memorial Museum. *Historical Atlas of the Holocaust*. New York: MacMillan, 1996.

United States Military Tribunal. Official Transcript of the Proceedings in Case 1, *United States v. Karl Brandt et al.* (Medical Case).

United States of America v. Alfons Klein et al., NARA, RG 338, M 1078.

United States Office of Chief of Counsel for War Crimes. *Trials of War Criminals before the Nuernberg Military Tribunals*, vol. 1. Washington, DC: Government Printing Office, 1949–1953.

Vollnhalls, Clement. *Entnazifizierung: Politische Säuberung und Rehabilitierung in den vier Besatzungszonen, 1945–1949*. Munich: Deutscher Taschenbuch Verlag, 1991.

———. "Zwischen Verdrängung und Aufklärung. Die Auseinandersetzung mit dem Holocaust in der frühen Bundesrepublik." In *Die Deutschen und die Judenverfolgung im Dritten Reich*, ed. Ursula Büttner, 357–392. Hamburg: Hans Christians Verlag, 1992.

Walther, Manfred. "Hat der juristische Positivismus die deutschen Juristen wehrlos gemacht?" *Kritische Justiz* (1988): 263–279.

Weinberg, Gerhard L., ed. *Hitlers Zweites Buch*. Stuttgart: Deutsche Verlagsanstalt, 1961.

———. *A World at Arms: A Global History of World War II*. Cambridge: Cambridge University Press, 1994.

Weindling, Paul. "From International to Zonal Trials: The Origins of the Nuremberg Medical Trial." *Holocaust and Genocide Studies*, 14:3 (Winter 2000): 367–389.

———. *Health, Race and German Politics Between National Unification and Nazism, 1870–1945*. Cambridge: Cambridge University Press, 1989.

Welzel, Hans. "Die deutsche strafrechtliche Dogmatik der letzten 100 Jahre und die finale Handlungslehre." *Juristische Schulung: Zeitschrift für Studium und Ausbildung*, 11 (November 1966): 421–425.

Wetzell, Richard. *Inventing the Criminal: A History of German Criminology 1880–1945*. Chapel Hill: The University of North Carolina Press, 2000.

———. *Naturrecht und materiale Gerechtigkeit. Prolegomena zu einer Rechtsphilosopie*. Göttingen: Vandenhoeck & Ruprecht, 1962.

Whitfield, Stephen J. *The Culture of the Cold War*. Baltimore: Johns Hopkins University Press, 1996.

Winfield, Percy H. *History of Conspiracy and Abuse of Legal Procedure*. Cambridge: Cambridge University Press, 1921.

INDEX

Hippke, Erich, 13
Hitler, Adolf, *29*, 60, 75, 82, 97, 114, 116, 118, 152, 170, 171, 188, 195, 204, 215; and children's euthanasia, 30; "exclusive" guilt of, 9; medical crimes under, 5; and misgivings about a formal euthanasia law, 37–38, 111; and the order to end phase one of adult euthanasia, 48–49, 56, 98, 180–182; and the order to begin the Final Solution, 99; and secrecy of the euthanasia program, 32; and statement of intent to implement euthanasia under the cover of war, 27; and sterilization of mentally handicapped persons, 25–26; and the text of order of September-October 1939 authorizing euthanasia, 38, 39. *See also Kanzlei des Führers*
Hoche, Alfred, 170; cited in the trial of Alfred Leu, 202; cited in the trial of Gerhard Wenzel, 205–206; and Freiburg state court's legal analysis of Artur Schreck's crimes, 174; and *The Permission to Destroy Life Unworthy of Life*, 21–24; and the utilitarian argument for destroying "life unworthy of life," 40. *See also* Binding, Karl; "Life unworthy of life"
Hohenlychen Group, 93
Holocaust, 55–60. *See also* Auschwitz; Belzec death camp; Brack, Viktor: and complicity in the Final Solution; Chelmno death camp; Final Solution; Hitler, Adolf: and the order to begin the Final Solution; Majdanek death camp; Sobibor death camp; Treblinka death camp
Hoven, Waldemar, 5, 94, 104. *See also* U.S. Doctors' Trial
Huber, Irmgard, 86, 87, 89; trial, conviction, and sentencing of by German court, 133
Hungerkost. See Sonderkost
Huxley, Thomas, 25

Inter-Allied Conference on War Crimes, 65
International Criminal Court (ICC), 16, 221
International Military Tribunal (IMT), 5, 14, 64, 93; charter of, 71, 74, 91; charter of contrasted with Control Council Law #10, 75; and defense of Ernst Kaltenbrunner, 101, 150; and the ex post question, 224; independence of asserted by Robert Jackson, 221, 223; and the Law of Armed Conflict, 220; and trial of the major war criminals, 90; and U.S. plan presented at the San Francisco conference, 68–69. *See also* U.S. Doctors' Trial; United States: National Military Tribunal

Jackson, Robert, 69; appointed U.S. chief of counsel for the prosecution of Axis criminality, 68; charges against the major war criminals set forth by, 75; concerns about a second IMT expressed by, 92; independence of the IMT asserted by, 221, 223; and the London Charter, 71; and the "master plan" theory of Nazi criminality, 70, 90; and need to document history of Nazi crimes, 17; and need to punish Nazi war criminals, 72; succeeded by Telford Taylor as U.S. Chief of Counsel for War Crimes, 91. *See also* International Military Tribunal (IMT)
Jäger, Herbert, 105, 169
Jaspers, Karl, 105
JCS Directive #1023/10, 74, 75; as legal basis for the U.S. Hadamar trial, 78
Jescheck, Hans-Heinrich, 225

Kallmeyer, Helmut, 57
Kalmenhof mental hospital, 51; trial of medical staff members of, 135–144, 149. *See also* Weber, Mathilde; Wesse, Hermann
Kaltenbrunner, Ernst, 101, 150
Kant, Immanuel, 110
Kanzlei des Führers (KdF), 27, 130, 133, 152, 192, 203, 205, 217; and the beginning of children's euthanasia, 28–31; concealment of euthanasia from victims' family members by, 47; and creation of the Reich Committee for the Scientific Registration of Severe Hereditary Ailments, 32; designation of Eichberg mental hospital as a transit center by, 121; established by Philipp Bouhler, 99; and the Hitler euthanasia order of September-October 1939, 38, 78; and release of *Ich klage an*, 49; system of review of registration forms (*Meldebogen*) in, 34–35, 50, 149. *See also* Bouhler, Philipp; Brack, Viktor
Kater, Michael, 4
Kaufbeuren mental hospital, 54, 97, 197, 244n25. *See also* Falthauser, Valentin
Kellogg-Briand Pact, 75
Kihn, Berthold, 37
Klee, Ernst, 18, 47, 49, 55, 227n3

National Military Tribunal (NMT). *See* United
States: National Military Tribunal (NMT)
National Socialist criminality: types of, 5–6
National Socialist German Workers Party
(NSDAP), 25
Natural Law, 8, 16, 108; and prosecution of
Nazi crimes by German courts, 111–118,
204–205, 213, 221. *See also* Radbruch,
Gustav
Necessity (*Notstand*) defense. *See* German
law: necessity (*Notstand*) defense
Nitsche, Paul, 41, 124, 153, 189, 190
North Atlantic Treaty Organization (NATO),
177–178
Nuremberg. *See* International Military
Tribunal (IMT)

Operation Brandt. *See* Brandt, Karl:
Operation Brandt
Operation Gomorrah, 51
Operation Reinhard, 59–60. *See also* Brack,
Viktor: and complicity in the Final
Solution; Final Solution; Heydrich,
Reinhard; Holocaust
Orwell, George, 177

Panse, Friedrich: reversal of acquittal of by
Supreme Court for the British Zone, 162–
163; trial and acquittal of, 151, 164. *See
also* Pohlisch, Kurt; Rhine Province case
Pearson, Karl, 25
Pell, Herbert, 70
Pfannmüller, Hermann: trial, conviction, and
sentencing of, 192–198. *See also* Eglfing-
Haar mental hospital; Euthanasia:
children's euthanasia
Plato, 205
Pohlisch, Kurt: reversal of acquittal by
Supreme Court for the British Zone, 162–
163; trial and acquittal of, 154–164. *See
also* Panse, Friedrich; Rhine Province Case
Potsdam Conference, 142
Principles of legality. *See* Ex post facto laws

Radbruch, Gustav, 112–117. *See also* Natural
Law
Rataczak, Amanda, 119. *See also* Meseritz-
Obrawalde mental hospital; Wernike,
Hilde; Wieczorek, Helene
Reckenwald (no first name given), 222; trial
and acquittal of, 187–192. *See also*
Andernach mental hospital; Kreitsch

Registration forms (*Meldebogen* 1 and 2), 39–
40; as basis for transportation of patients
from Kalmenhof to Hadamar, 135–136; as
basis for transportation of patients from
Scheuern, 148–149; completion of by
Friedrich Mennecke at the Eichberg mental
hospital, 121–123; Pohlisch and Panse
charged with filling out, 160–161; and the
Hannover Province Case, 180; and the
trial of Alfred Leu, 199; and the trial of
Artur Schreck, 173, 174; and the trial of
Dr. Recktenwald, 187, 190; and the trial of
Hermann Pfannmüller, 194; and the trial of
Otto Mauthe et al., 164, 165, 168; and the
Warstein Case, 210. *See also* Euthanasia:
the adult program
Reich Committee for the Scientific Registration of Severe Hereditary Ailments, 136,
143, 155, 204, 206, 208; and the children's
euthanasia, 34–35; comparison of with the
front organizations of adult euthanasia, 39;
correspondence of with Friedrich
Mennecke, 123–124; Hermann Wesse's
report to concerning Jewish patient, 141;
and initiation of Hermann Wesse into
children's euthanasia, 139, 207; and
issuance of "treatment authorizations" to
the Sachsenberg mental hospital, 199–200;
payment of bonuses to Mathilde Weber by,
137; role in vetting Hermann Wesse as
Georg Renno's successor, 156; as screen to
conceal the KdF's role in euthanasia, 32.
See also Euthanasia: children's euthanasia;
Hefelmann, Hans; Hegener, Richard von
Reich Cooperative for State Hospitals and
Nursing Homes (RAG), 39, 40–41, 135,
174, 194. *See also* Euthanasia: and the
adult program; T-4
Reichleitner, Franz, 60
Reich Ministry of the Interior, 157, 170, 181,
182, 192, 199; and creation of T-4 killing
centers, 43; and decree requiring registration of handicapped newborns, 33; and
dispatch of registration forms to Rhineland
mental hospitals, 187; involvement in Nazi
euthanasia, 31; and recruitment of medical
personnel to staff children's wards, 34; and
registration of state hospitals and nursing
homes, 39. *See also* Conti, Leonardo; Frick,
Wilhelm; Linden, Herbert
Reich Security Main Office (RSHA), 35, 42,
101. *See also* Heydrich, Reinhard

Uchtspringe mental hospital, 139; trial of staff physicians of, 203–209. *See also* Wenzel, Gerhard; Wesse, Hermann; Wesse, Hildegard

Ulrich, Aquilin, 213, 245n45

Unger, Hellmuth, 31

Union of Soviet Socialist Republics (USSR), 65, 69, 71, 91, 128, 177–178, 215, 218–219, 223; and the Berlin blockade, 142; and confrontation with the West: *See* Cold War; number of Nazi defendants convicted in after the war, 228n4. *See also* Stalin, Joseph

U.N. Convention on Genocide, 106, 221, 224

United States: conceptions of National Socialist criminality in the courts of, 2–3, 15, 73–74, 76, 78–79, 89–90, 97–98, 100–101, 104, 106, 108, 214; 220; 221; concern for the principle of sovereignty, 16, 62, 63–64, 72, 84–86, 98, 105, 106, 214–215; distrust of international bodies, 221; eugenics in, 3; and ex post facto laws, 72–73, 220; and German rearmament, 177–178, 218–219; National Military Tribunal (NMT), 14, 27, 94, 220, 224; and plan for trying Nazi war criminals before an international tribunal, 68–69. *See also* Cold War; Hadamar trials; U.S. Doctors' Trial

U.S. Doctors' Trial (the Medical Case), 17, 51, 64, 74, 90–104, 145, 192. *See also* Brack, Viktor; Brandt, Karl

Veronal: as T-4 killing agent, 200–201

Vorberg, Reinhold, 217

Wagner, Gerhard, 27

Wahlmann, Adolf, 82, 83, 86–87, 88, 89, 128–129, 133, 134; trial, conviction, and sentencing of by German court, 133, 144; trial, conviction, and sentencing of by U.S. military commission, 82–89. *See also* Hadamar trials

Waldniel mental hospital, 139, 151, 156, 158, 159, 206–207, 208. *See also* Wesse, Hermann

Walther, Manfred, 115

War Crimes, 13–14, 63–65, 69, 72, 75, 105, 146, 220; distinguished from crimes against humanity, 105–106, 238n73; prerequisites of prosecuting by a military tribunal, 235n29. *See also* Crimes against Humanity; Crimes against Peace; Law of Armed Conflict

Warstein mental hospital: trial of staff physicians of, 209–211

Weber, Helmut von, 150, 185

Weber, Mathilde: trial and conviction of, 135–139; retrial, conviction, and sentencing of, 142–144, 167. *See also* Kalmenhof mental hospital; Wesse, Hermann

Weilmünster mental hospital, 149

Weimar Constitution of 1919, 112

Weimar Republic, 24, 223

Wentzler, Ernst, 31, 34

Wenzel, Gerhard: trial and acquittal of, 203–206, 222. *See also* Uchtspringe mental hospital; Wesse, Hildegard

Wernicke, Hilda, 1; trial, conviction, and execution of, 118–120, 144. *See also* Meseritz-Obrawalde mental hospital

Wesse, Hermann, 34, 206; trial of, 135, 139–141, 144, 151, 155–156; conviction and punishment of, 143, 144. *See also* Kalmenhof mental hospital; Weber, Mathilde

Wesse, Hildegard, 203; trial, conviction, and sentencing of, 206–209. *See also* Wenzel, Gerhard; Wesse, Hermann; Uchtspringe mental hospital; Waldniel mental hospital

West Germany: anticommunism in, 178; and Article 131 Law, 10, 178–179; and Basic Law (West German constitution), 142, 178; as bulwark against Soviet communism, 10, 127–128, 144, 146, 177–178, 218–219;and Christmas amnesty of December 1949, 144, 178, 209; demands for amnesty of Nazi war criminals in, 3, 219, 222; denazification in, 3, 8, 178; establishment of, 142; incorporation of into NATO, 178; Law for Exemption from Punishment of 1954 enacted in, 209; percentage of Nazi crimes prosecuted in, 5; philosemitism in, 178; "policy toward the past" (*Vergangenheitspolitik*) in, 218–222; and preoccupation with recouping sovereignty, 3, 108, 178–179, 215, 218–219, 221, 223; rearmament of, 177–178, 218–219; reasons for decline in numbers of convictions of Nazi defendants in, 6–11. *See also* German law

Wetzel, Ernst, 56